American society as a social problem

Robert Gliner

American society as a social problem

THE FREE PRESS   NEW YORK
COLLIER–MACMILLAN PUBLISHERS   LONDON

The Free Press
A Division of The Macmillan Company
866 Third Avenue, New York, New York 10022

Collier–Macmillan Canada Ltd., Toronto, Ontario

Library of Congress Catalog Card Number: 72–87781

printing number
1   2   3   4   5   6   7   8   9   10

copyright acknowledgments

Grateful acnowledgment is made to the following for use of material reprinted herein:

Mulford Sibley, "The Case for Unilateral Disarmament," in Robert A. Goldwin (Ed.), AMERICA ARMED, © 1961 by The Public Affairs Conference, Gambier, Ohio, pp. 112–13, 121. *See pages 302–303.*

From THE ARROGANCE OF POWER, by J. William Fulbright. Copyright © 1967 by Random House, Inc. and Jonathan Cape Ltd. *See pages 125-126, 130.*

From THE CHALLENGE OF MAN'S FUTURE by Harrison Brown. Copyright 1954 by Harrison Brown. Reprinted by permission of The Viking Press, Inc. and McIntosh and Otis, Inc. *See page 164.*

Reprinted with permission of The Macmillan Company from CONTAINMENT AND CHANGE by Carl Oglesby and Richard Shaull. Copyright © 1967 by Carl Oglesby and Richard Shaull. *See pages 117, 127–128, 293–294, 297.*

To Cindy

When they came for the communists, I did not
speak up for I was not a communist. When they came
for the Jews, I did not speak up because I was not
Jewish. When they came for the Trade Unionists, I did
not speak up, because I was not a Trade Union
member. When they came for the Catholics, I did not
speak up, because I was a Protestant. When they
came for me, there was no one left to speak up.

—Martin Niemoeller

contents

two

where can we go?: American society
reconstructed   193

three

how are we going to get there?:
the tactics of reconstruction   271

acknowledgments

I wish to thank Irving Naiburg and Clarice Stoll for their conscientious efforts in critically evaluating this manuscript. I would also like to thank Naomi Katz, Win Salisbury, and Gene Bernedini, for their help on specific chapters. Special thanks goes to my wife Cindy for her critical suggestions and encouragements, without which much of this manuscript would not have been possible. I would like finally to thank the many people who helped type this work: Janice Campisi, Sandra Lindsey, Lynn E. Mayfield, Linda Schwind, Karen Sweetland, and Ann Tsuchiya.

—R. G.

introduction

Everyone knows there are problems in American society: The war in Indochina still rages; racism is rampant; poverty crushes millions of people and the environment is steadily being destroyed; yet, on college and university campuses across the country, many faculty members and students are apathetic and cynical. A college education is seen to be largely irrelevant; there aren't any jobs worth having, even for the graduate. If most young people are alienated by the educational process and from the social system in which they find themselves, why do they then not actively involve themselves in the creation of an alternative society?

A common answer is that the forces which have created these problems are too powerful for us to change—the more we work at such change, the more powerless we feel. *They*—the military, industrial, and political elites—are the problem; there is little we can do right now to counter their influence. At best, we can only react to the decisions they make for us. Why? If "everyone" knows *they* are the root cause of America's social ills, then why do *they* still maintain control? If "everyone" knows that Vietnam, poverty, racism, and pollution are problems, then why do these problems still exist? Why isn't "everyone" working to alleviate them? Why has social change been piecemeal and haphazard, rather then the conscious effort of all Americans?

The knowledge of the existence of social problems has not served to eradicate them. Knowing who the "enemy" is presupposes a correct analysis of social forces—and a willingness to act on it. The question: "What can I do?" is only posed by those who have not adequately conceptualized the problem, and this is, unfortunately, what has happened in the rhetoric of most would-be activists. Given our knowledge of social problems, why hasn't America been transformed?

American society itself has become a social problem, not only for its inhabitants, but for millions of other human beings who share this planet. Nearly all discussions of social problems treat American society as given—its problems are merely forms of deviant behavior: alcoholism, delinquency, mental illness, racism. This approach considers these problems as separate units, and solutions to them become isolated, piecemeal efforts—each problem to be solved without reference to any of the others. But the major problems within this society are interdependent; in order to begin to solve one, you must begin to solve them all; in order to understand any problem, you must consider its relationship to others. If American society is the problem, then you and I are part of the problem, victims of it, responsible for it, and potential agents for doing something about it. In this sense, we are also the "enemy," for it is only through us that America can be changed. To say "it's not my problem" and to refuse to act is to occupy a position which supports the status quo, no matter how much we may rationalize to the contrary. Similarly, while machines were originally created to make production more efficient and to maximize profits, they now dominate our lives, increasingly creating their own imperatives. It does us little good to place the blame on those who initiated the technological revolution or hope that they will alter the system which rewards them. We all profit from this system and suffer from its excesses. Technology controls the lives of managers and workers alike. If we do not like the result, no one is going to change it for us.

Social scientists are also part of this problem; the facts they analyze are not "value-free";[1] but grow out of the context of the society being studied. The very act of choosing one area of study over another connotes a value judgment. Social scientists not only study a given society, they are part of it. Understanding and acknowledging this relationship is binding on all social scientists. While greater validity and accuracy often result when we remove ourselves from the society

we study, our responsibility for that society is in no way diminished. The act of studying American society and its inherent problems requires the student to relate his own life to the problems he is dealing with. It is not enough to describe what *is;* social scientists have to deal with what might be, exploring the implications of their research and making specific proposals for incorporating the results of this research in social policy decisions. Further, such research presupposes a readiness to engage in social action which will bring about change. From this point of view, social action is a valid sociological enterprise. On the other hand, to refuse to spell out what the results of a given study imply in the context of American society is also to make a value judgment; it is to accept the status quo. If the work of the social scientist, by implication, is critical of the workings of American society —and the implications of this are not spelled out—then the social scientist becomes largely irrelevant to the society he would seek to understand. He becomes an elitist, unwilling to accept responsibility for the logic of his own specialty. The public ceases to respect him, because he is unnecessary. What would happen, we might ask, if a medical doctor were to discover evidence which could lead to a cure of cancer, but fail to show how such evidence could be applied in cancer research and treatment? Perhaps, the question each social scientist must ask is whether his discipline is a means of contributing to the understanding of human society, or an end in itself. We know only too well the breed of "pure" scientist who builds atom bombs and when they go off claims that it is "not my problem."

American Society as a Social Problem

Many social problems which are endemic in American society are not defined as such because they question certain basic assumptions of that society. To define work, leisure, and material consumption as problems in themselves would be to question much of the basis for our lives. So we tend to see the problem of work as unemployment rather than alienation, to see problems of material consumption as inflation rather than wastefulness, and to view leisure as number of hours available rather than what can be done during these hours. Moreover, social scientists have had a difficult time conceptualizing certain problems because their subjective elements do not translate into simple terms. This may be one reason why some social scientists are unwilling to accept that the entire society may be at fault. The solution as they see it is a simplistic one; if, for example, the war in Indochina is ended, then alienation from American society will end with it. Most social scientists seem to offer solutions by rearranging the words rather than by examining the context in which the words are employed.

Another way of stating this issue is to say that we may be caught in an "ideological lag": The words which we use to describe the world may no longer have meaning in the situation in which we find ourselves. Therefore, the problems we analyze and the solutions we propose are largely irrelevant. Consider the tendency to define issues in quantifiable terms. For example, to solve the problem of discrimination we register more minority voters and give them an equal chance to buy a house and choose a job among those houses and jobs available. In reality, however, the vote may mean very little if there is no one to vote for and these very houses and jobs may no longer be adequate. These issues are difficult to grapple with because they cannot be readily quantified, just as the causes of dissatisfaction with one's personal relationships may be difficult to measure.

Problems which do not accommodate themselves to our image of the world, on our expectations of how the world is supposed to be,[2] are often regarded as illusions, for they do not fit the "way things are." They are accidents. In the morning it will be better. Peter Berger and Thomas Luckmann put it this way:

> The validity of my knowledge of everyday life is taken for granted by myself and by others until further notice, that is, until a problem arises that cannot be solved in terms of it. As long as my knowledge works satisfactorily, I am generally ready to suspend doubts about it. In certain attitudes detached from everyday reality—telling a joke at the theater or in church, or engaging in philosophical speculation—I may perhaps doubt elements of it. But these doubts are "not to be taken seriously." For instance, as a businessman I know that it pays to be inconsiderate of others. I may laugh at a joke in which this maxim leads to failure, I may be moved by an actor or a preacher extolling the virtues of consideration, and I may concede in a philosophical mood that all social relations should be governed by the Golden Rule. Having laughed, having been moved and having philosophized, I return to the "serious" world of business, once more recognize the logic of its maxims, and act accordingly. Only when my maxims fail "to deliver the goods" in the world in which they are intended to apply are they likely to become problematic to me "in earnest."[3]

American society, however much we would like to believe in it, has become a social problem because it no longer works. A society that allows its assumptions to be questioned risks losing its legitimacy. This is why most of us are often unwilling to recognize that our thinking about America is outmoded. In fact, the more others question, the more we seek to defend, because our very identities are at stake. To say that the American Society which we have come to believe in no longer works, then, is to say that our lives are meaningless and our investments worthless. Yet, a society's self-image, however powerful we may feel ours to be, is socially constructed, and when social conditions change, so too does the image.

Many of our traditional assumptions no longer have value: the Protestant Work Ethic; capitalism; material consumption as a visible sign of success; the idea that man can live apart from and at the same time exploit his natural environment; a laissez-faire attitude towards others (do your own thing, mind your own business); the world as America's playground; our political system as the most democratic; the relevance of the past. Yet, the roles which these values legitimated continue to be performed. We go to work in factories and corporations at jobs which yield little satisfaction and even less responsibility. We purchase a quantity of useless commodities which may help us keep our jobs, but which do not make our lives any more meaningful or our identities any more secure. In the process we drain the land of valuable and irreplaceable raw materials, assuming we will never have to pay for the destruction we render. Since our identities are threatened, we go to great lengths to justify and defend them by imposing ourselves on the world; hence our involvement in Vietnam. Those who question our "right" to do this are put to death, and their country is laid waste, all in the name of values which most Americans do not practice, such as "freedom" and "democracy." And our inability to find satisfaction has bred a pervasive insecurity; we locate the cause of our problems in the lives of others. Through fear of losing even more of their sense of social reality, most people are reluctant to become involved in dealing with social issues or in the lives of other persons, beyond the point of ensuring that these others do them no harm.

Since traditional roles can no longer be justified, we act out of habit, instead of meaningful commitment. The image of American society which we continue to hold onto does not permit us to adopt new roles. But why not give this image up? Why not refuse to perform these roles? The answer, quite simply, is that we are afraid of the consequences. Instead, we look to other people to tell us what we should believe in, what we should buy, whom we should vote for. At the same time we don't want this to be the case; we daydream about another society in which we can play a more meaningful part. We are caught between where we are and where we would like to be; we want to eliminate social problems, but without relinquishing the image of America that causes them. We want to create a new America without giving up anything of the old. It is my contention that only by divesting ourselves of this outmoded image, by having our reality shattered, that American society can be positively transformed.

The consequences of such reality-busting and the means of bringing it about will be examined in the second half of this book. Briefly, reality-busting will lead to a situation where each individual must create his own values and rules to live by. No longer will he be able to rely on tradition or on power elites to make decisions or live his life for him. At the same time, change will become the norm rather than the exception, and society will be seen as process rather than equilibrium. Given our polluted environment, our depleted resources, and our need for technological development, as well as individual autonomy, a planned economy could be created which guaranteed basic food, clothing, and shelter needs, but otherwise left individuals to their own pursuits. The tactics of reality-busting include communal living, experimental education, encounter groups, and various forms of political action.

Our discussion of American society will have a social emphasis. While there may be many structural reasons for American society becoming a social problem—e.g. the capitalist system of production which leads to alienating and exploitative work and interpersonal relationships—such an explanation does little to alleviate the problem, because there is no ready leap from analysis to solution. Though the Marxist may answer that solving the problem means seizing control of the means of production, we would ask, who is going to seize control, and why haven't they already? Racism may be a product of hundreds of years of economic exploitation, but knowing this does not make us any less racist *unless* we are willing to do something about it. Here rests the problem, regardless of the historical antecedents involved. By analyzing our inaction, we may discover an explanation and image of America far different and more complex than we might have expected.

Do the Facts Make a Difference?

You pick up the newspaper. You read reports of chronic flareups in the Middle East, and of continuing starvation in Pakistan. You see that Americans, in one military action or another, still are losing their lives in Southeast Asia. You discover that another riot occurred in Toledo, Ohio. You put the paper down. The next day you go to class and the teacher begins rapping about some of these issues. You think "What's the use—there's nothing I can do." Do the facts make a difference? The class discussion begins. Students give their testimony: "What a terrible problem!" Everyone's concerned about the terrible loss of life. One girl even begins to cry. You hand her a Kleenex. The bell rings. It's a warm day and you follow the other students out onto the mall where you lie down on the grass and look up at the trees and the clouds passing by overhead. The professor's voice goes away. The girl is no longer crying. Everything seems distant. You think about the evening, being with friends. In a month or so, around mid-term time, you'll have to go back and memorize some facts for the multiple-choice test you'll need to pass.

The facts do not make a difference, because they are often not *our* facts. Yet they must be memorized. The social problem of American society does not make a difference for the most part because the people who are involved in the more problematic aspects of this society are not the people *we* know, and the problems they address are not *our* problems. The professor talks about what *one* does in a particular situation—what *everyman* does—not what you do. But then, you are not in that particular situation. The students around the room wait for somebody else to act, to start a movement, to do somehing about the problem, to burn their draft or credit cards.

In this context, who is responsible for the problem of American society? How can we be held responsible for a situation we did not create and did not even know about until our professor and textbook told us? Moreover, what are and have been the consequences of our lack of participation? Some argue, for example, that the person who until recently watched an all-white television cast was just as responsible for racist attitudes as was the member of the Klu Klux Klan who openly attacked the notion of black and white equality. From a broader perspective, can we be held morally responsible for a societal image and value system largely irrelevant to our needs? Traditionally, we are held responsible for the roles we play, but as we no longer take these roles seriously, we are no longer responsible for their consequences. It is within such a context that individuals come to be seen as both victims of American society as well as the enemy of those who would try and change it. They are victims because they are powerless to act on their own and they are the enemy because their very lack of action, commitment, and responsibility ensures that this society will continue functioning in the same problematic manner.

Experience, however, does not necessarily make us more sympathetic to change. Although millions of men fought during World War II, within a five-year period many of these same men who thought they would never have to experience a war again were advocating the *same* tactics for dealing with another international crisis. Had the loss of friends in war faded from their memories so quickly that they could not consider alternative solutions? Similarly, many affluent people who grew up under conditions of poverty forget their relatives who still reside in the ghetto and support political candidates who do litle about the problems of poverty. There must be something more than experience per se which makes us view the facts as important to us, which motivates us to act to eliminate conditions which we and those around us find distasteful. If first-hand experience does not tell us what the problem is, then how can remote lectures and irrelevant textbooks? It is only when the rationalizations which the society offers can no longer justify our poverty experience or the war in faraway Asian jungles which we have fought that we come to view such experiences as social problems which require solutions, and which we must do something about.

This book is divided into three sections: Where Are We?: American Society as a Social Problem; Where Can We Go?: American Society Reconstructed; and How Are We Going to Get There?: The Tactics of Reconstruction. The first section consists of a discussion of the problems an outmoded reality structure or image of American society has created, why this is a social problem, and why we are all responsible for it—not in terms of who initially created it, but in the sense of living within the image it fosters and consequently legitimating its existence. The second section will focus on breaking out of this image —reality-busting—and on creating a new society. The third section presents tactics for the creation of an alternative America. This book is not meant to be an exhaustive account of specific strategies for changing American society; rather, it is designed to provide a rationale and analysis for motivating individuals toward initiating such change.

—Robert Gliner
California State University, San José

Notes

1 Robert W. Friedrichs, *A Sociology of Sociology* (New York: The Free Press, 1970).
2 Kenneth Boulding, *The Image* (Ann Arbor: University of Michigan Press, 1956).
See also Kenneth Boulding, *The Meaning of the Twentieth Century* (New York: Harper Colophon, 1965).
3 Peter Berger and Thomas Luckmann, *The Social Construction of Reality* (Garden City, N. Y.: Doubleday & Company, Inc., 1966), p. 44.

one

where are we?: American society as a social problem

1

work: the mental dropouts

Why does the thought of finishing college make us uneasy? The answer is because we know we'll have to go to work, only we don't know what we'll work at, and we're not particularly interested in finding out. What is the reason for this lack of interest? Why don't we already know what we're going to be when we grow up?

A short time ago these questions were considered irrelevant at best, for most high school and college students knew where they were going and most looked forward to getting there. Though this may have been a state of false-consciousness induced in us by the "system," most people didn't question it. There was always the chance the myth was true—Charles Percy was president of Bell and Howell at the age of twenty-eight and a United States Senator shortly thereafter. Some of us still look forward to working (assuming we can find a job), but before getting too excited about what we'll find when we get there, we should examine our expectations. This chapter pinpoints certain problematic aspects of work in contemporary America. Work has alienated Americans because most of the time it seems to be without meaning. Yet we continue to pay lip-service to the value of work—we kneel daily before the altar in a church whose God has ceased to visit.

Services are conducted five days a week, but the worshipers' minds are elsewhere—prayers are said, but only the lips move. Priests hear confessions repeated each day out of habit, yet no one repents. It matters only that we attend regularly. Only the most ardent worshipers go to heaven, but no one knows who they are. Meanwhile, outside, chanting "sinners," adorned with beads and beards, sniff flowers and burn incense in praise of a different god.

Man Did Not Always Live by Work Alone

Living in American society, where work is still the ordering force for much of adult life, we might be forgiven for supposing all civilizations throughout history have been devoted to work. This is not the case. The early Greeks and Christians repudiated work, the former for a world of leisure and philosophic debate, the latter for contemplation and religious devotion. While Greek society was able to achieve this life style on the basis of slave labor, it did not follow that for the "citizen" work was of much value: work was not of value in itself, though most people did work. In fact, work did not take on central ideological importance for most people until the Renaissance. It was during this period that Western man's conception of work and its place in society began to change. Before this period, Western societies were feudal: the aristocracy concentrated most of their lives on the art of ruling and the pursuit of leisure; a small craft-oriented middle class painstakingly produced commodities or engaged in trade or commerce; and a large class of peasants worked the land and were watched over by the aristocracy.[1] The rich assumed that the poor were incapable of taking care of themselves. The aristocracy viewed itself as benevolent and used its power to structure the morality and religious values of the poor, as well as to keep them in their place. The relationship between the rich and the poor was self-justifying, for since the rich were obviously successful, they deserved to dominate and control the poor: whereas the poor were obviously unsuccessful and, therefore, could not take care of themselves. This relationship was further enhanced by an ideology which considered poverty to be the result of vice and laziness, the only cure for which was hard work. The Catholic Ethic stressing satisfaction with one's station in life or with one's calling tied in with this conception—salvation could only be expected if one accepted and worked diligently at his occupation.[2] However, not all peasants or nobles were Catholics—most work did not connote great religious or ideological importance. People worked because they needed to eat, and for no other reason. With the advent of the industrial revolution, the Catholic ideology began to break down.

The new middle class of entrepreneurs did not inherit responsibility for the poor from the aristocracy.[3] Their conceptions of the meaning of work were different, as were their views of the place and importance of work in society. As science developed, progress became an important byword of the industrial revolution. Progress in the industrial sphere depended on maximizing efficiency of production for maximum profit. To assume responsibility for the poor detracted from these goals. The new capitalism alienated men from the products of their labor, and separated them from their homes and families. Work conditions became geared toward mass production; workers became objects to be manipulated. Salvation, for the new rich, no longer lay in tending large feudal estates; rather, immortality was based on power and profit in the marketplace. In theory, the poor would be taken care of, for once they consented to work in the industrial plants of the middle class, they had to be kept healthy in order to maximize production. In practice this consideration was often ignored because most workers accepted the conditions of their labor regardless, largely because of the promises held out, because there was no longer anything else ideologically legitimate or otherwise which they could do to sustain themselves, and because there were always others who would be willing to take their place if they did not accept these conditions. In essence, the poor could no longer physically or psychologically rely on the rich for sustenance or protection: they had to rely on themselves. A new doctrine of self-help developed, called the Protestant Ethic by future social commentators.[4] This Ethic succeeded in showing that it was the worker's religious duty to strive to work hard so that he too might enjoy the same fruits from his labor as did those who employed him, and in so doing, achieve salvation. However, even in this early period there was little chance for the worker to rise above his position, for employees were told to emphasize the quality of submissiveness as their ideal on-the-job work conduct, a quality hardly designed to enable them to rise above their brethren in the factory to a position of management and responsibility.

Sometime after the discovery of America, the Protestant Ethic crossed the Atlantic on the back of what Herbert Spencer was to call Social Darwinism. The idea of the survival of the fittest reinforced the workers' desire for the salvation already achieved by the rich.[5] The early open-market capitalist American economy flourished under this ideology. All the worker needed to do was imitate those attributes of his superiors which made them rich, and he too could claim the banner of success. Horatio Alger was born.

There were other aspects of American society which helped shape the importance given to work. Great individual effort was required to tame the lands of the expanding frontier. Farms had to be hewn out of the wilderness, beaver and buffalo hunted down, killed, and skinned. The frontier demanded many of the same motivational characteristics as the Protestant Ethic: hard work, self-reliance, efficiency, and—above all else—a desire to compete. The free-wheeling nature of the frontier matched that of early American capitalism. Men came to be known by what they had done—how many Indians they had killed; how far they had risen in the factory; how much they owned; how much they made. Success became a quantitative attribute,[6] as did salvation, for the size of the factory a man owned defined whether or not he had been saved. Science had defined progress as material advancement over nature; technology dealt with numbers. If a problem could be quantified, it could be solved—all that could not be quantified was irrelevant, all that could not be seen did not matter. Mysticism and metaphysics were inefficient; they could not produce; they were dead. American society thrived on quantification, and it was such quantification that came to define achievement, for this appeared to be the only way achievement could be measured.[7]

The importance of self-help ideologies to industry began to change, however, after the turn of the century, and particularly after World War I. Many workers had already suffered greatly at the hands of the capitalist ideology—overcrowded work conditions, long hours, poor pay, little chance for advancement, repetitive, boring occupational tasks—all in the name of efficiency and the maximization of profit (salvation). Such exploitation made the Protestant Ethic a sham, and the new merging of factories into corporations spelled the demise of the applicability of this ideology for one's day-to-day life. Yet though the myth was no longer relevant, it continued to exist in the minds of most workers, for work was still necessary for survival, no matter how alienating and worthless it might be. The new corporate complexity demanded different types of occupational skills. Superficial cooperation, and manipulation, rather than competition, came to be emphasized on the managerial level. Skills that the worker had learned on the assembly line were no longer relevant to getting ahead. Moreover, the worker could no longer rely on himself for mobility up the factory or corporate hierarchy. Only certain attributes were needed at the higher levels, and management devised tests to ascertain whether or not a given worker had such attributes. These tests were designed to ferret out psychological character traits such as the ability to get along with, manage and use other men. This "scientific management" bred dependency rather than individual initiative, and clashed with earlier conceptions of individual ability and self-motivation.[8] A new common basis developed between management and workers: both were to be measured by certain psychological characteristics; the former had superior psychic traits while the latter lived with inferior capacities. The worker could hope to get ahead, but, as in the earlier Catholic Ethic, there was nothing he could do to further this hope except do the job set down for him by the men he wanted to replace.

Not only did the worker become dependent upon management, but with increasing bureaucratization and technological specificity, he found himself fitting the prescriptions of his job. He became dependent on an assembly line which ordered his time and told him how much he had to produce in order to keep his position. He lost control over his work situation and the meaning given that situation. The problem of getting ahead had been quantified through machines and tests, yet in the process, the worker too became a number, he no longer mattered, he could be too easily replaced, as he had in the minds of most managers by the profit system. In the face of this situation, informal work groups developed which employed norms and sanctions to keep their members in line and to insure job security.[9] But even these work groups had to fit into the pattern established by the technological conventions under which they dwelled. The discovery of these informal groups prompted management to consider a "human relations" approach to job satisfaction, which considered how a worker's relations with others on the job were an important source of morale. For the most part, however, the job itself was not changed or made more challenging, rather "fringe benefits" were increased to make the boredom and repetitive nature of the job itself more bearable.

After World War II, specialization increased still further with the development of new consumer and clerical industries, as well as an enlarged civil service. As the number of available tasks increased, satisfaction with these tasks appeared to decrease, for there was little self-worth to be gained by screwing nuts and bolts on automobile chassis all day long, just as there was little individual value and meaning to be gained in filling out mountains of paper work associated with middle-management, white-collar positions. Speaking of the workers, Daniel Bell points out:

Their behavior itself is a judgment. It appears in the constant evasion of thought about work, the obsessive reveries while on the job and the substitution of the glamour of leisure for the drudgery of work. Yet the harsher aspects are present as well. These take the form of crazy racings against the clock to vary the deadly monotony, of slowdowns—the silent war against production standards—and most spectacularly in the violent eruptions of wildcat strikes against "speed up" i.e., changes in the time required to complete a job.[10]

And for their counterpart, the white-collar employee, the middle-management man:

While new conditions brought many new opportunities based mainly upon the expanding specialization of labor, such opportunities existed in a different context which demanded new personal skills and discipline. Ironically, instead of bringing contentment, new opportunities often encouraged insecurity. A vague dissatisfaction persisted as men became afraid that the job they had was not as good as the one available. With one eye focused on the main chance, the individual tended to lose the intrinsic satisfaction of work as work tended to become a mere means to other ends. . . . The size and impersonality of organizations may also encourage anxiety. Feelings of helplessness and of frustration occur as organizational power and demands checkmate the individual's claims for autonomy.[11]

Changing Meanings and Conceptions of Work: Ends Become Means

We have seen that the meaning derived from and associated with work has changed over the past two hundred years. Most work is still ultimately related to maximizing profit, and workers are used accordingly by management. In day-to-day work tasks man no longer determines the final products of his labor—even if he happens to know what that final product is. In earlier craft-oriented societies, usually it was man who shaped what he made; he could see his contribution to society. This is no longer the case. At best, a team of workers turns out a given product, while the corporation takes credit for this production. Consequently, a worker identifies with his place of work, rather than with his labor per se [12] or with the profits stockholders may reap. When asked what he does for a living, many workers reply that they work at GE, GM, or FMC. The worker's specific position within one of these large corporations remains ambiguous. The individual employee no longer has a future; rather it is the corporation which employs him that has the future. Consequently, the worker

Courtesy of Gyula Szabo

identifies progress as synonymous with the growth of the corporation or factory, rather than with his individual achievement or movement up the organization ladder. As the worker can no longer take credit for what the organization makes, he is also no longer responsible for its end products. But then, neither is the corporation or factory, for jobs are delegated and run by authorless manuals, and stockholders may be vacationing in Europe. The worker only gets out of the job what he puts into it; however, he never knows when he has put in enough. Since there is *no one* to blame for lack of challenge and meaning to be gained from a specific occupational task, he can only blame himself. It is his fault that the rewards he has come to expect never materialize.

There is another aspect to this situation. By accepting company definitions of what must be done at work and what types of rewards can be expected, the worker conditions himself to accept the definitions of other large-scale political and social institutions in American society. Since he can no longer be the judge of his own worth or destiny, he becomes dependent on impersonal authorities, machines, and rules to regulate and give meaning to his existence. Values which grew out of a period of rapid entrepreneurial development emphasizing individual achievement and competition become outmoded in the face of contemporary economic realities. As Presthus points out, at mid-century only 15 percent of the work force was self-employed; the rest were employed by others.[13] It is, therefore, not only a matter of receiving one's salary from someone else, it is the psychological character of this relationship which is important. The relationship is one-way: workers receive decisions, definitions, and money, just as they receive definitions from the reality framework as to what is a legitimate contribution to society.

The Protestant Ethic required that an individual work in order to feel useful and to achieve salvation or legitimacy in the context of American society. But how can a worker feel useful if he is mass producing commodities which are not really necessary for survival? How can a worker feel useful if the only motivation he gets from his job is a weekly paycheck? How can a worker feel he is making a contribution if he is not even doing the work; if instead, he acts as an appendage to a machine which doles out a finished product?

Marx held that such alienation existed because workers did not own or reap the profits of their labors. Yet, given large scale industrialization and bureaucratization—both in the East and in the West—distinctions between what we have come to know as "socialism" in practice and what we label as "capitalism" break down.

Most of us have acknowledged that work has become a means to another end. It enables us to buy material goods, to find security in the face of economic wants, to make friendships, to fill up empty time, and as relief from boredom. Many of these rationalizations develop after a given occupational task loses whatever intrinsic worth it once held. Nonetheless, many workers are so reluctant to accept any of these justifications that they still act *as if* there were something left to make, a new can opener perhaps, or an advanced dishwasher which does not need soap.[14] Indeed, Galbraith has observed in another context [15] that as consumers now need to be told what they need to buy, so too, the worker must be told what he needs to produce for the health and welfare of his corporation and American society. This becomes, according to Paul Goodman, "make-work"—commodities are designed for early obsolescence, such as cars that need to be replaced every two years so that workers can continue making new ones.[16] Advertising is used as much to keep workers on the job, as to get them to buy what they produce. As the cycle continues, few seem to be able to get off the treadmill.

There are persons who do enjoy working in corporations and factories. These individuals are concentrated in higher management positions where there is a degree of control, challenge, and decision-making. Others enjoy such work, not necessarily for the job itself, but rather because one might as well "like" what he has to do, since there are no other options available. Consequently, many studies of job satisfaction find that workers have a positive attitude toward factory or corporation work—aside from the fringe benefits—because to admit otherwise would be to say they are wasting their time. We must appear positive to protect our investment.[17] It should be reiterated that work, per se, is not dissatisfying, rather the type of work most persons in America have to do is.

Professionals also enjoy a degree of responsibility and self-worth. But even here increasing specialization in technique is taking more and more initiative and responsibility away from individuals. This is also the case in hospitals and universities.[18] At the same time we are witnessing a relatively new trend toward professionalism. Consider how custodians and maintenance men are now called sanitary engineers. It is felt that by taking on a professional label and the higher status commonly associated with it, the jobs and tasks performed will somehow shed their tedious nature, become more glamorous and useful. This often proves to be self-deluding. No matter what you call it, sweeping floors and cleaning toilets is still sweeping floors and cleaning toilets.

One other fundamental change has occurred in the worker's outlook. We have assumed that the worker wants a responsible position, that he earnestly desires more challenge and decision-making capability. In *The Organization Man,* William Whyte pointed out that this is not necessarily the case, particularly among white-collar, middle-management personnel.[19] What is desired among this group is security, not the risks of responsibility. Getting along in order to get ahead often means just getting along. The indications are that the rewards held out by the work ethic are no longer enough—there are home, family, health (ulcers and heart attacks), and consumer goods to think about as well. Even when it can be found, responsible and challenging employment does not have the meaning it once did. Success is no longer defined solely in terms of occupation.

This is particularly reflected in the culture heroes of our society. Children rarely play electrician or insurance executive, nor do folk tales idolize these occupational roles. Bennett Berger comments:

Consider the strain on our moral vocabulary if it were asked to produce heroic myths of accountants, computer programmers, and personnel executives. We prefer cowboys, detectives, bull fighters, and sports-car racers, because these types embody the virtues which our moral vocabulary is equipped to celebrate: individual achievement, exploits, and prowess. Again, I should make clear that this is not a criticism of what we have become and certainly not a celebration of the harmony between Soviet society and culture; it is, rather, an analysis of why we are uneasy about what we have become. A culture which has not learned to honor what it is actually committed to produce creates an uneasy population.[20]

Horatio Alger is replaced by *The Man in the Gray Flannel Suit*, who rejects the chance of executive responsibility in favor of home and family. There are no heroes of work-culture because a computer programmer is no hero. But there is more to it than that—since nothing really *happens* at work, we wish to forget about it entirely. Often, only those who make fun of our occupations are admired, for they help us relieve some of the tensions of our split existence.

Other studies also demonstrate that work is no longer our "central life interest." Robert Dubin, in a study of industrial workers concluded:

> Considering the pattern of responses to all questions, we found that only 24 percent of all the workers studied could be labeled job-oriented in their life interests. Thus, three out of four of this group of industrial workers did not see their jobs and work places as central life interests for themselves. They found their preferred human associations and preferred areas of behavior outside of employment.[21]

Another study conducted by N. C. Morse and R. S. Weiss asked both white- and blue-collar workers whether or not they would continue in the same kind of work if "they inherited enough money to live comfortably." Below are the results of their inquiry: [22]

Occupational Group	Affirmative Replies
Professional	68%
Sales	59
Managers	55
Skilled Manuals	40
Service	33
Semi-skilled Operatives	32
Unskilled	16

The impact of automation has not reversed this trend; it has accentuated it. While some workers may like to play with knobs on complex machinery, watching this machinery stamp out milk bottles and soup cans, the resulting "independence" has also made for increased isolation from other workers:

[A] sample of workers from an automated plant were asked whether they would prefer a shorter work week, increased wages, or longer vacations if any of these alternatives were made possible by automation. Almost three-fourths indicated a preference for a shorter work week over either more pay or longer vacations. One apparent reason for this preference is the very nature of production line work. Jobs of this kind have characteristically required little exercise of skill, responsibility, or initiative and have offered little variety in the types of tasks performed. Automation does not appear to have significantly altered these characteristics of production line work. Machine operators in the automated plant, while having somewhat more responsibility in that there is a larger machinery investment per worker, do not need appreciably greater skill and many feel they have an even less important part in the total work process than had been the case in plants using conventional machining techiques. Neither does the change from actually operating a machine to pushing a button or watching a panel of lights or guages offer much more relief from the monotony of repetitive operations on the job. In short, automation has not altered the fact that most production line jobs do not produce the kind of occupational involvement or identification necessary to make work a satisfying experience.[23]

In our society work is still sacred, yet there are many who, for one reason or another, cannot work, and in the future the number of jobs available may be severely reduced. Automation increasingly limits the number of skilled, semi-skilled, and unskilled workers needed by industry. Ph.D.'s and engineers are finding difficulty securing employment. This is in large part due to our priorities, but many existing occupations will be eliminated, and unless our society is radically transformed, few new occupations will be created. Goodman has stated that youth are often kept in schools longer while many workers are forced to retire earlier, if for no other reason than that they must be kept off the work force. If this is the case, then individuals will have to start thinking about what they will do if they cannot work at all. What can the salesman say to justify his being fired because he cannot keep up with his younger colleagues, or the coal miner who cannot be retrained for another job, or the farmer whose acreage is no longer large enough to be economically profitable? If we do not work, there is nothing for us to do, we are not considered *men*. Moreover, work is what our lives revolve around; if our jobs are taken away, we will have to find a substitute locus of identity formation and maintenance. Yet, our economy is a productive one. Is there any reason why we should all work, why we should all live up to the Protestant Ethic, why we should not have a right to a share of the national wealth without working in corporations, factories, or social service agencies?

Man as Machine: The Technological Imperative

It is not only work per se which orients most of our lives, but also the technological environment which surrounds the work process and which has come to color most aspects of life in our society. In fact, technology creates its own value framework, its own image of the world. As Jacques Ellul points out:

> Technical progress . . . is no longer conditioned by anything other than its own calculus of efficiency. The search is no longer personal, experimental, workmanlike; it is abstract, mathematical, and industrial. This does not mean that the individual no longer participates. On the contrary, progress is made only after innumerable individual experiments. But the individual participates only to the degree that he is subordinate to the search for efficiency, to the degree that he resists all the currents today considered secondary, such as aesthetics, ethics, fantasy. Insofar as the individual represents this abstract tendency, he is permitted to participate in technical creation, which is increasingly independent of him and increasingly linked to its own mathematical law.[24]

While technology makes industrial labor and production more efficient and profitable, workers come to view their lives as part of the image that machine technology creates, and this image must be maintained at all costs. If we are subordinate to a machine and the dictates of technology on the job, then we often come to view our lives in the same subordinate position, and according to the same technological values. And, "only technique can sit in judgment of itself."[25] If something goes wrong on the job, it is the machine's fault. No one is personally responsible. This has led Paul Goodman to say:

> Trapped in a system, people carry on functions often fraught with colossal or catastrophic consequences without being personally engaged in the functions at all. They are personnel.[26]

Only technique can sit in judgment of itself, because it lies within a closed system or reality framework, it creates its own imperatives. It takes technical concepts and inventions to correct its faults. The consequences of technique can only be examined in the light of what other technical options are possible. As Ellul states:

> Technique, in its development, poses primarily technical problems which consequently can be resolved only by technique. The present level of technique brings on new advances, and these in turn add to existing

technical difficulties and technical problems, which demand further advances still. . . . For example, to make housework easier, garbage disposal units have been put into use which allow the garbage to run off through the kitchen sinks. The result is enormous pollution of the rivers. It is then necessary to find some new means of purifying the rivers so that water can be used for drinking. A great quantity of oxygen is required for bacteria to destroy these organic materials. And how shall we oxygenate rivers? This is an example of the way in which technique engenders itself.[27]

Corporate Capitalism

We have shown how the rise of large corporations and technological change have disadvantaged the average worker. At the same time, the marketplace values of capitalism have undergone change: the free enterprise of the individual businessman in competition with others has been modified by the monopolistic tendencies of several hundred large corporations and their subsidiaries. Besides making it impossible for the average worker or organization man ever to own such a business enterprise, we may ask what other effects capitalism has had on the workers. Thus far we have dealt with workers immersed in organizational and manual tasks from which they found little reward beyond their paycheck. What are the imperatives of American business enterprises?

Oligopolistic capitalism creates a situation in which a few large firms in a given economic specialty come to dominate the field, regulating prices, and in some cases agreeing on how the market will be divided.[28] Oligopoly developed because of corporate Darwinism (capitalism) which meant that only those corporations survived that could expand their markets and grow in size while driving out the competition. This often meant gobbling up smaller companies. Today this works in the following way: First, most corporations are too large from a purely organizational point of view to be able to bring about immediate changes in their "line." The production of given commodities requires long term planning. Many huge corporations do not engage in taking risks. They don't need to. Rather, they let smaller entrepreneurs develop innovations and then buy them out. This way, they can wait until the product is developed without risking large sums and taking the chance of failure, both technologically and in creating a demand for the product. Second, price cuts initiated by one corporation are immediately followed by price cuts from other firms in the field, making such a measure economically unsound. Rather, profits are made by: (a) cutting production costs; (b) increasing the size of the domestic and overseas market (the number of people willing to purchase the product) through advertising; (c) increasing the number of products sold; and, (d) selling to the government (weapons for defense, for example).[29] Other economists would point out, however, that effective advertising and the lowering of prices can, at least in the short run, increase a firm's percentage of the existing market.

Large corporations must forever be acquiring new markets to increase profits in order to keep up with the field. In this sense, the corporation has become the new capitalist.[30] The creation of new products means constantly exploiting underdeveloped nations for raw materials at cheap prices, which results often in both scarce national resources and ultimately in ecological disaster. It follows that in an expanding economy workers must constantly be urged to buy more goods, both to maintain the health of the economy, and to keep their job (producing the very commodities they are urged to consume). The psycho-social need of the worker to consume superfluous commodities as a way of achieving identity exactly matches the need for corporations to sell him such commodities.

Exploitation by corporations of those who either work for them or consume their products results in alienation and what one writer has termed as scarcity in the land of plenty.[31] We are never satisfied with what we have; there is always something we must buy. Although overt signs of ruthless competition and ensuing interpersonal alienation within the factory and organizational complex may have disappeared, there are still those of us—the majority—who are powerless to control the organizations which, essentially, dictate the terms on which we live our lives.

NOTES

[1] Rinehard Bendix, *Work and Authority in Industry* (New York: Harper Torchbooks, 1963), p. 47.

[2] *Ibid.*, p. 48.

[3] *Ibid.*, pp. 89–111.

[4] For a discussion of the impact of religion on technology and vice versa, see Max Weber, *The Protestant Ethic and the Spirit of Capitalism;* also the Bendix work cited above.

[5] Bendix, *op. cit.*, p. 259.

[6] For a discussion of the particular "quantitative" nature of Americans, see

Geoffrey Gorer, *The American People* (New York: W. W. Norton & Company, Inc., 1964), pp. 131–171.

[7] Robin Williams, *American Society* (New York: Alfred A. Knopf, Inc., 1966), p. 418.

[8] Bendix, *op. cit.,* p. 308.

[9] Elton Mayo, *The Human Problems of an Industrial Civilization* (New York: The Macmillan Company, 1933).

[10] Daniel Bell, *The End of Ideology* (New York: The Free Press, 1962), p. 239. See also Robert Dubin, "Industrial Worker's Worlds," in A. Rose, *Human Behavior and Social Processes* (Boston: Houghton Mifflin Company, 1962), pp. 147–266; Ely Chinoy, *Automobile Workers and the American Dream* (Garden City: Doubleday & Company, Inc., 1955); Charles R. Walker and Robert H. Guest, *The Man on the Assembly Line* (Cambridge: Harvard University Press, 1962); parts of Robert Blauner's *Alienation and Freedom* (Chicago: University of Chicago Press, 1964); Paul Goodman, *Growing Up Absurd* (New York: Random House, Inc., 1956); and David Riesman, *Abundance for What?* (Garden City: Doubleday & Company, Inc., 1965), particularly p. 163.

[11] Robert Presthus, *The Organizational Society* (New York: Random House, Inc., 1965), pp. 16–17. See also, David Riesman, *Abundance for What?* and Ernest Van Den Haag, *Passion and Social Constraint* (New York: Delta, 1965), pp. 289–298.

[12] Bennett Berger, "The Sociology of Leisure: Some Suggestions," in Erwin O. Smigel, *Work and Leisure* (College and University Presses, 1963), p. 35.

[13] Presthus, *op. cit.,* p. 79.

[14] Sebastian de Grazia, *Of Time, Work and Leisure* (Garden City: Doubleday & Company, Inc. 1964), p. 3.

[15] John Kenneth Galbraith, *The Affluent Society* (New York: Mentor Books, 1958), pp. 124–130.

[16] Goodman, *op. cit.*

[17] Robert Blauner, "Work Satisfaction in Modern Society," in Price, *Social Facts* (New York: The Macmillan Company, 1969), p. 123.

[18] See, for example, Paul Goodman, *Community of Scholars* (New York: Vintage Books, 1962).

[19] William Whyte, *The Organization Man* (Garden City: Doubleday & Company, Inc., 1956).

[20] Berger, *op. cit.,* p. 32.

[21] Robert Dubin, "Industrial Workers' Worlds: A Study of the 'Central Life Interests' of Industrial Workers," in Smigel, *op. cit.,* p. 60.

[22] Cited in Presthus, from N. C. Morse and R. S. Weiss, "The Function and Meaning of Work and the Job," *American Sociological Review,* vol. 20, p. 197. See also Chinoy, *op. cit.;* and Walker and Guest, *op. cit.;* C. Wright Mills, *White Collar* (New York: Oxford University Press, 1956). The work of the other authors mentioned has been cited above. See also Georges Friedmann, *The Anatomy of Work* (New York: The Free Press, 1964);

Simon Marcson, *Automation, Alienation, and Anomie* (New York: Harper & Row, Publishers, 1970).

[23] William Faunce, *"Automation and Leisure,"* in Smigel, *op. cit.,* p. 89.

[24] Jacques Ellul, *The Technological Society* (New York: Random House, Inc., 1967), p. 68.

[25] *Ibid.,* p. 134.

[26] Paul Goodman, *People or Personnel* (New York: Random House, Inc., 1963), p. 76.

[27] Ellul, *op. cit.,* p. 92.

[28] Paul A. Baran and Paul M. Sweezy, *Monopoly Capital* (New York: Modern Reader, 1966), pp. 56–58. See also Morton Mintz and Jerry S. Cohen, *America, Inc.* (New York: Dell, 1972).

[29] *Ibid.,* pp. 117, 150.

[30] *Ibid.,* p. 42.

[31] Philip Slater, *The Pursuit of Loneliness* (Boston: Beacon Press, 1970).

2

consumption for what?: the new survival

If our occupational task is not worthwhile, there is always the paycheck at the end of the week. We work in order to consume. Yet, most consumption—outside of basic food, clothing, and shelter needs —like work, cannot be said to confer meaning or a worthwhile identity. Do scads of consumer goods really satisfy? Are consumption and other leisure pursuits an adequate compensation for the hours spent at work? Are these activities an acceptable substitute for purposeful work? And, is consumption merely a technological and therefore, in human terms, wholly inadequate response to a moral or philosophical problem?

The value attached to work, as we have seen, has changed over the centuries. In the societies of ancient Greece and Rome, which held work to be full of drudgery and pain fit only for slaves to perform, leisure was cultivated. On the other hand, in contemporary industrial societies, leisure is disdained, and work is regarded as of the highest importance.[1] In contemporary American society, as the number of work hours decreases, consumption has gained in importance. However, there appears to be a conflict or cultural lag in "official" conceptions of the place of leisure and consumption in the value structure of

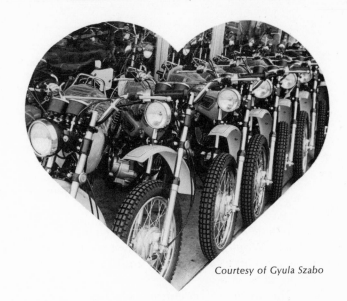

Courtesy of General Motors

Courtesy of Gyula Szabo

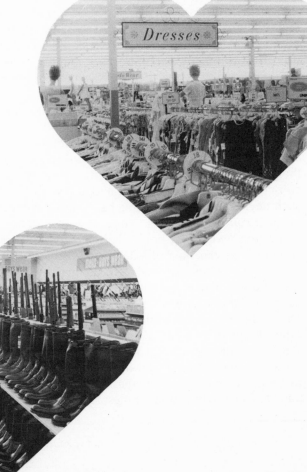

Courtesy of Gyula Szabo

American society, for work is still held in a place of high regard. This lag, however, might be only a surface phenomenon. Berger has commented

> That one finds it emotionally more difficult to beg off (for phony reasons) from a previously accepted invitation to a party given by a friend, than to call the boss to say one's sick and not coming to work, suggests that leisure obligations are *more* thoroughly internalized than obligations to work? [2]

Wouldn't we rather go sailing for an afternoon, than "work" at the library? Wouldn't we rather buy a car than work making the fender of one, hour after hour in a factory? Which do we prefer: going shopping or going to work?

The meaning of consumption has taken on added importance. People have always had to consume basic commodities in order to survive; yet it is only in this century that individuals have had to be told what these basic needs and commodities are.[3] Today advertising serves this function. In the past, consumption and leisure prepared the individual for work. You went to the market and bought enough food to eat in order to be able to work the following day. Little thought was given to buying per se because identity could supposedly be derived from work. As this identity was lost, consumption became important in its own right. When we go to the department store, we are not only buying what is necessary for physical survival, we are buying an identity. What we purchase tells us who we are. This identity is seen in quantitative, rather than in qualitative terms. Americans have always had a particular propensity for solving problems by quantifying them, by developing some sort of technical device to cope with their consequences. The production and stockpiling of commodities is one such device. You may no longer say "I'm a computer gauge watcher," but you *can* certainly say, "I'm a new car, a new house, a new dress, and a new swimming pool." People can see these things, and these commodities can be "added on to" you. The problem is quantified, for as our identity was formerly defined by the question: "What do we produce at work?" and subsequently, "What do we do there?" it has now come to mean, "What do we buy with the salary we make?" The problem of what to do at work is not dealt with, because among other things it is largely a *qualitative* problem. Rather, the solution is sought in what *can be* quantified: consumption.

After World War II, and into the 1950s, as consumer goods began to be produced in ever increasing numbers and varieties, status and identity came to be based on these commodities. David Riesman coined the phrase "keeping up with the Joneses." Vance Packard wrote *The Status Seekers*. Both of these authors dealt with the cultivating of consumer tastes as a "full-time" occupation, since work had ceased to be self-involving. If we could outdo our neighbors at the shopping center then we were somehow better than they were. Moreover, this meant that we were more useful and were making a more significant contribution than they were to American society. If Mr. Jones bought a new car or put in a swimming pool, then we would have to follow suit, or suffer the consequences. These consequences were often quite serious—for example, being ostracized by neighbors who would comment about our property as they would walk past:

"Simon still has that old car." (It is three years old.)

"Yeah, guess he must be having trouble, never thought he was right for this block."

"And that old coat he wears to the club . . . that style went out years ago."

"If he doesn't put that pool in, property values in the neighborhood are going to suffer. . . ."

"Hey, there he is now . . . he looks so sad, look at those lines under his eyes."

No one could stay ahead for long, if for no other reason than that it became virtually impossible to get ahead, to be a frontiersman in the supermarket. Industry, resting on the cornerstones of profit and efficiency, needed mass production of consumer goods. To insure rapid turnover, commodities were only designed to last a short period of time, both in terms of the psychological need for these commodities, but also in terms of their ability to function. It became common for a car to break down after two years and for its style to look old-fashioned and ill-equipped for contemporary living. Progress became "our most important product," as signified by booming sales and brightly lighted supermarket counters. Retailers introduced credit-buying so that no one would have to save his pennies: buy now, pay later. The influx of new products signified the scientific advancement American society was undergoing. All one had to do was go into the supermarket and he knew that things were okay, the economy was booming, even if his particular job was boring and lacked meaning, even if he could not get ahead of the Joneses.

When it came down to it, however, no one wanted to be too far ahead, because no one wanted to be *that* different. Being too far ahead can often be worse than being behind, unless one has been raised in a social class where being ahead is a way of life. We buy something, and no one follows suit, so we begin to question our own

judgment—perhaps we have made a mistake. Maybe there's something
the matter with owning the item we recently purchased. Others begin
to look at us strangely—what a *weird* coat! Who would paint a house
that color? Doesn't he have any respect for his neighbors?

And, as on the job, satisfaction is guaranteed, not in what you
purchase, but in identifying with the larger entity—with the shelves
of cleverly packaged do-dads. In each case a sense of security is obtained, a feeling that everything is all right after all. For could so much
be produced and consumed if it weren't? As Packard has commented:

> How much should we rejoice when General Electric introduces a toaster
> with nine buttons, which makes it possible to obtain a piece of toast
> in any of nine shades? How much should we rejoice when another com-
> pany introduces a mechanical martini-stirring spoon, which relieves the
> person stirring from the labor of twisting his wrist? And what American
> housewife is dreaming of the day when she can prepare breakfast by
> simply flicking a bedside switch, which will turn on an electronic recipe
> maker coded on punch cards? [4]

This is "progress"?

The attitude we adopt towards consumption and leisure becomes
the same as that which we adopt towards our occupation. Time devoted to consumption and leisure must be spent profitably with no
minutes wasted. If they are, one gets the feeling that he has not been
useful, and therefore, his actions cannot readily be justified. As Walter
Kerr points out:

> We are all of us compelled to read for profit, party for contacts, lunch
> for contracts, bowl for unity, drive for mileage, gamble for charity, go out
> for the evening for the greater glory of the municipality, and stay home
> for the weekend to rebuild the house. Minutes, hours, and days have been
> spared us. The prospect of filling them with the pleasures for which they
> were spared us has somehow come to seem meaningless, meaningless
> enough to drive some of us to drink and some of us to doctors and all of
> us to the satisfaction of an insatiate industry. In a contrary and perhaps
> rather cruel way the twentieth century has relieved us of labor without
> at the same time relieving us of the conviction that only labor is mean-
> ingful.[5]

Our wives, girl friends, sisters, brothers, husbands, boy friends show
us what they got *on sale*—it matters very little whether or not they
actually need what they purchased. If work no longer provides a justification for one's life, the tasks once played there are played for keeps
during leisure and in the calculation of how much time is to be spent.

Involvement has changed—the supermarket and department store have become the substitute, for some of us, for the meaning which work once provided. This is equally true for many women whose alienating work is at home.

Advertising: Tell Us What We Need

Advertising has come to play a vital role in the American economy for two main reasons: the commodities produced need to be sold for the economy to continue to function, and consumers must have their "wants" justified. Unless commodities are purchased in ever-increasing numbers, the economy will collapse, for it rests on an over-supply of goods. The "free-enterprise" system responds not to demands of the market, but to markets created through the use of advertising.[6] As Potter comments:

> Advertising is not badly needed in an economy of scarcity, because total demand is usually equal to or in excess of total supply, and every producer can normally sell as much as he produces. It is when potential supply outstrips demand—that is, when abundance prevails—that advertising begins to fulfill a really essential economic function. In this situation the producer knows that the limitation upon his operations and upon his growth no longer lies, as it lay historically, in his productive capacity, for he can always produce as much as the market will absorb; the limitation has shifted to the market, and it is selling capacity which controls his growth. Moreover, every other producer of the same kind of article is also in position to expand output indefinitely, and this means that the advertiser must distinguish his product, if not on essential grounds, then on trivial ones. . . .[7]

And, as we explained above, advertising serves the indirect function of keeping people employed. If no one buys, there is nothing to produce, and thus, no jobs.

Consumers must also have their "wants" justified. As we have seen, individual needs to consume have changed considerably since the turn of the century, and perhaps even more so in the last twenty-five years. Today we "need" a new car every two years; we "need" a new dress every month or two—not because the old ones are worn out but because fashions change. There is always the chance we will be "them" (and not "us") and it is this hope that keeps us standing in line waiting to purchase happiness.

Commodities flow as directives in the corporation, from the top down.[8] We have the choice of whether or not to purchase a specific item, but there is little chance for us to create our own consumer products. The problem conditions the solution. As in the technological revolution, the rhetoric has created the rules of the game, and though the name may change, the rules never do, for such "deviant" images do not exist in the universe of discourse supplied through the mass media.

The individual consumer never knows when he has consumed enough, for he is responding to impersonal guidelines rather than to specific individuals and directives or personal needs. He is a spectator who must buy his ticket as the price of admission into society where he may watch others play. But everyone is watching everyone else. The only professional teams are those the corporations furnish to sell their products, to keep the spectators identified with the action. The teams compete to make the game interesting, though the score is often fixed in advance. Though most of us are only spectators, involvement is kept high by the expectations that we may get a chance to play. But as with all spectator sports, the game is soon over and we must return home, filled with expectations of the next day's game. We gradually take off our mementos one by one and hang them in the closet. Soon we slip beneath the sheets, tired and nagged by the growing feeling that perhaps we did not purchase enough—there is something that we must yet buy.

We feel secure when we are buying and wearing what others are buying and wearing and when we see ourselves reflected on billboards and television sets. In fact, some corporations are quite candid in their ads: "—Buy a Buick . . . something to believe in." Our security is based upon belief in these commodities. But the rhetoric and expectations which flow from it do not match our world—those quiet moments when we stand naked and alone, knowing that we are not free to choose, that we do not need or want what we have purchased, that we have been manipulated, and that we are helpless in this assault upon our senses.

Of course not everyone will accept this admittedly pessimistic picture. Some see the problem only in terms of protecting the consumer from price fixing and false advertising. What constitutes false advertising is the misrepresentation of commodities, not the relationships resulting from the purchase of commodities. A window cleaning preparation takes off waterpaint rather than oil paint, but the advertisement says that it is taking off oil paint. This is false advertising. Nothing is said however of a couple embracing after *he* used Right Guard, or of the portrayal of a marriage ceremony after the use of a new mouth wash. No one asks why we need so many commodities. Many critics of the consumer economy find themselves caught in the rhetoric of the very process which they are attempting to criticize. If we can only rid ourselves of all this "junk," they say, the problem will be solved.[8] Only by "junk" they are referring to the purchase of a Chevrolet, rather than a Cadillac, or a pair of pants from Penny's rather than Magnin's. Reformists address themselves to quality, but the basic problem remains: There is no reason to suppose that a Cadillac will bring any more happiness than a Chevrolet, or that the purchase of one model will preclude the need to buy another one from the same manufacturer when the style is changed or the ashtrays get dirty. Dependence on commodities per se still exists. Nor is there any more "free choice." It's just that much more expensive.[9]

Such criticism as this is permitted within the system. The old adage —caveat emptor—let the buyer beware, should, perhaps, be rendered: Let the buyer beware that he is buying.

The buyer should also beware that his consumption is destroying the environment, for all of these materials must someday be discarded —but where and how? The factories turning out more and more consumer goods are poisoning the air and water with chemicals; cars lie rusted and broken on hillsides; freeways become ever more congested. Ecological problems are a direct concomitant of our increasing desire to consume. The prevailing idea is that we buy more; what we do with the item once we have purchased it or how we dispose of it, is rarely considered. Since many items are designed for early obsolescence, this problem is an acute one. It's not enough to pick up a few scraps of paper lying in the street and feel we've solved the ecology problem. In Chapter 7 this issue will be further elaborated, but the ideology of consumership has much to do with the existence of the problem in the first place, and can only be solved when the issue of consumption is dealt with.

Women as Commodities

Advertising reflects and capitalizes in particular on the role women play in American society. Women in advertisements are forever scrubbing floors, dying their hair, applying feminine deodorant spray so that they may catch a man or hold the one they have. They are treated as weak, timid creatures—at the beck and call of men who want them to massage their egos by darning their socks, or making love. And most women until recently have readily accepted this image because there was no other option open to them. From early childhood, girls are taught the roles society expects them to play, carrying dolls, helping their mothers with the dishes or the preparation of supper. As men dominate and control positions of power and influence in America, women are forced to accept the secondary status allotted them, regardless of their own unique attributes as human beings. What is the product of a particular socialization process, an image, becomes defined as "natural"—all women do this, all men do that.[10] In American society it has been useful for women to be placed in a certain position, to fit a certain image much as it was useful for black men and women to be transplanted from Africa to work as slaves on Southern plantations. While men are out making "crucial" decisions and exploring new frontiers in the office, women act as their personal slaves by safeguarding and cleaning their "castles," or adorning fold-outs in their magazines as sex objects. Indeed, as men have become more and more powerless in their occupations, women pose a greater and greater threat to the already fragile security and identities men seek to maintain.

This situation is particularly reflected in terms of occupational possibilities and salaries. It is still considered "unusual" and difficult for women to become professionals, though almost half of all women work outside the home. This is primarily because women are not expected to have work as their primary area of interest and because granting equal occupational status with men would eliminate the only role a man can supposedly perform (he cannot have children, and in our society, cannot raise children). Moreover, women receive lower average salaries than men.[11] But there is little evidence that women cannot perform most occupational tasks their male counterparts perform.

The result of this socialization process, which is furthered and enhanced by advertising, is to make women feel uncomfortable when they are not washing dishes, diapering babies, or buying clothes whose chief appeal is to the male ego.[12] Males too are exploited by the same types of advertising, forced to live up to a "male chauvinist" image, as well as to work at alienating and de-humanizing occupations. Discrimination is perpetuated through consumership, as each sex attempts to maintain the self-image they have been socialized into.

The Pill People: The Medicine of Mass Society

One example of how consumption has become a way of life centers around the advertising and purchasing of pills. Medicine has become a new form of consumption.

When faced with boring jobs, empty relationships, and other "existential" problems, often the easiest way out seems to pop a pill. One has only to look at television, or listen to the radio, to find out how popular such a "cure" is. A short time ago you could take Excedrin (a form of aspirin) for any one of several hundred types of headaches. The advertisement on TV would read: Your wife didn't make your favorite breakfast; therefore, you have Excedrin headache number 271. Other companies advertise pills for the "blahs" when you feel down and want a picker-upper. Still other companies have pills for states of mind when you don't feel you need anything at all. Many college students rely on No-Doz or some other stimulant to keep them awake through final examinations.

The drug companies (whose aim is, after all, profit) [13] tell the consumer what he needs to improve the quality of his life. There is always something new for a headache or cold, even if it's merely a re-packaging of what has been on the market for years.

Like other commodities, drugs are packaged and marketed and, for many persons they serve the same functions; their consumption can be justified by the same kinds of rhetoric. The more drugs that are produced, and consumed, the better we assume our health to be. The assumption is that the day will come when we shall live in a world from which conflict, discomfort, and pain have been banished; presently, these things are considered as forms of deviant behavior which must be relieved by a mental or physical doctor. But since so many suffer from these maladies, we should ask ourselves whether ill health is not perhaps the norm, and good health a deviation. As René Dubos has pointed out:

> Is it not a delusion to proclaim the present state of health as the best in the history of the world, at a time when increasing numbers of persons in our society depend on drugs and on doctors for meeting the ordinary problems of everyday life?[14]

Are those human beings who consume large amounts of drugs, who live in crowded, smog-infested cities, the same persons they were before such consumption and habituation? Aren't these drugs changing man's biological as well as mental character? Yet, if we build up immunity to diseases by taking shots or consuming pills, the environment which we face will not necessarily change. Perpetual euphoria leads to a boredom that provokes a use of ever more drugs in a seemingly never-ending cycle. Man must adapt to his environment, and if that environment is only perceptually altered through the use of chemicals, then it is only in a drugged state of mind that human beings will be able to survive.

Another serious problem—caused by the proliferation of drugs— is that they can only treat the symptoms of a disease, they do little about the causes. George Johnson reminds us that:

> The point that you and I need to remember about the mood-changing and mind-changing drugs is that they can only treat *symptoms*.
>
> They can *modify* our reaction to our environment, and help us function more "normally" in our thinking and emotional behavior, but they cannot *change* us.
>
> They can do nothing to alter our heredity—and neither can we.
>
> They can do nothing about our home, business, or social conditions— but we probably can.
>
> They can't change our social or economic position—but we can.[15]

Drug-taking itself is only an indication of the plight of many Americans who are desperately looking for a cure to relieve them of the emptiness and boredom they feel when confronted with irrelevant role options. The individual is presumed to be the problem rather than the society.

Leisure: The Protestant Ethic Revisited

Leisure may be defined as that period of time during which we are free to do what we want—when we don't have to do anything.[16] What is significant about most concepts of leisure is that they have negative connotations.

> Margaret Benning calls it a kind of non-living, with the accent on the *negative* rather than the positive. Now you can take a vacation which needs no planning, travel in a car that needs no lubrication, wear shirts which require no ironing, and take pictures with a camera that needs no focusing. You can play golf with no walking, reduce with no dieting, exercise with no moving, and garden with no planting.[17]

The idea of a holiday as not having to do something—"I didn't have to go to work today," or "I don't have to go to class today"—is also common. With the supposed increase in free time (due to shorter work weeks, forced unemployment, or no work week at all), what has happened to leisure? Can we really relax during this free time? Are we supposed to?

Leisure in American society traditionally served the function of providing time to recuperate from work. It served the same function as R and R (Rest and Recreation) for troops in the army. The period of relaxation was designed to make individuals work better on the job by providing them with time off to rid themselves of tensions and anxieties which the job created. As the job lost much of its meaning, and as the number of hours worked per week began to decline, workers were faced with the prospect of spending long hours off the job. What were they to do with this free time? Besides buying commodities, they also began to do other things—take vacations, fix up the house, and watch television. They applied the same attitudes toward leisure as they had applied toward work and consumption. In effect, they were and are working at their leisure; and *consuming* their leisure time. Such consumption is guided by the same principles which guide material consumption and work: profit, efficiency, are you being useful, are you making a contribution, and progress. No time is to be wasted; every moment must be justified. Why?

The answer seems to lie in the idea that since work is longer involving, we feel a sense of emptiness from time spent on the job. Thus, we redouble our efforts during leisure hours so that our lives may be justified. The Protestant Ethic has been ingrained in most of us since childbirth, and since it now makes little sense when applied to work, it is used instead as a motivating force in leisure. As in work and consumption, such leisure is quantified so that it can be measured and an accurate summation of the day's activities calculated. I spent an hour practicing the piano; we spend an hour in the park; she spent the night with me; we necked for fifteen minutes. So too, the numbers game is played: I went to ten concerts last year; I read 150 pages today. Such measurement helps place us in a status ratio with our peers. The implication of going to ten concerts is that we are becoming cultured: our time is well spent. It makes little difference if we slept through the concert, or spent our time daydreaming, or even "hustling." Our visit has been counted and others know of our activity— where we were. Perhaps because it is difficult to measure, the quality of the experience is ignored. For the "head," the attitude is much the same, only the words are different. Someone says to you: "Ever dropped any acid (LSD)?" You say: "I took 500 mics (micrograms) last night." He says: "That's nothin', you don't feel anything unless you've tried a thousand." Of course the ante goes up—soon it's 2000, then 2500.

Is this type of leisure really involving? Is it an effective substitute for work? How can leisure be involving when so much time is spent calculating whether or not what you are doing can be shown to be worthwhile? Does this attitude cause more anxiety than it alleviates? Perhaps this is not leisure we have been describing, but another form of work. If leisure is defined as doing nothing, or as letting oneself go without regard to how much the experience will be worth, then probably little leisure exists. Walter Kerr points out that even when such moments occur, they bring discomfort rather than satisfaction:

> I am not alone . . . in feeling guilty when I read a book I don't have to read. . . . "Guilt" is a strange word to have become associated with the experience of pleasure. It suggests, to begin with, that we have a deep conviction of time wasted, of life wasted, of worthwhile opportunities missed, whenever we indulge ourselves in a mild firtation with leisure. There are valuable things we might be doing if we were not goldbricking just now; those valuable things might prove enormously useful to society, to our families, to our own souls; in goldbricking itself there is no value. We are either laborers in the vineyard or slackers in the shade.
>
> The conviction goes deeper. When we turn down the chance to turn an idle hour to profit, we are not merely failing in a social obligation but we are failing in a moral one. What we are doing is not only boorish and uncooperative. It is wrong.[18]

Many workers who are either physically incapacitated, or who are forced into early or late retirement due to automation or age requirements, do not welcome "leisure" at all. For them "leisure" means, in effect, freedom to die, for their chief means of ordering their existence and of justifying their lives has been forcibly taken away from them. You see them in the local bar, or rocking back and forth on their porches, thinking about the good old days, sometimes projecting their bitterness and resentment on to children who happen to wander past. They have a difficult time substituting leisure for work as a means of personal involvement in society. Rather, they still view work as the only possible option. There are no other alternatives but "waiting for the end."

As scientific advances in medicine have enabled more people to live longer and the number of years worked has been reduced, a "new" population category has been created: the aged. As the extended family has been reduced, few grandparents are accepted into the homes of their children as permanent residents. For many of these "senior" citizens who are no longer able to fend for themselves, this has meant selling their homes and moving into "retirement" communities or villages situated for the most part in California and Florida. Here, surrounded by modern conveniences, they band together, out

of sight of their youthful relations, waiting to die. For many time becomes a heavy burden. They live in expectation of a visit from their
children or grandchildren, listening for phone calls, waiting for the
mailman with a letter for them. Yet, even if they are in full possession
of their faculties, American culture is youth-oriented and has little
further use for those well past youth. The aged can rarely emulate the
examples they see on TV—the images presented are those of and for
another generation. No longer able to work or to play, many aged
wait, attempting to forget that death is as much a part of a nature as
youth.

Spectators in the Land of Plenty

On the surface Americans are busily engaged in their leisure pursuits—
recreation, the arts, committee work, and home re-modeling. But as
these events are quantified and judged largely by the hands of the
clock (even charity falls under this label—"I gave ten hours to the
Red Cross last week"), they seem to lose much of their significance.
Leisure pursuits are the means to an end; they are rarely pursued in
and for themselves. As rapid occupational mobility from one job to
the next has produced a kind of transiency towards one's place of
residence, so too, credit-buying and constant shifts in what one is
supposed to do with his leisure time have produced the same sort of
attitude toward consumption and leisure. There is no permanency in
any of it—nothing lasts; one is constantly on the move, along gaily
festooned supermarket counters, or on the highway to the latest "un-
discovered" hideway. Vacations are often marathon speed contests.
Individuals drive as fast as they can in their new cars to get to Yellow-
stone or Yosemite, only to discover upon getting to their destination
that thousands of others had the same idea, and that the campgrounds
look like a stadium parking lot on the day of the big game. Upon
arrival, our vacationer doesn't know what to do with himself. He must
pick out a new destination he can hurtle toward, or buy, or consume.
He reads advertisements of Bermuda, flies there, and spends his vacation wondering what he is supposed to be doing in order to have a
good time.

Many Americans have become spectators in their leisure time. We
watch others perform, whether on TV or in stadiums. Or, we go on
vacation and watch nature from our fast-moving cars. We forget that
we, too, are a part of nature; that nature may be watching us. There
is a sense of futility in all this, and it expresses itself in the passivity of
the spectator. For as the individual has lost control over his work

activities, so too has he lost control over his leisure time. Conditioned to be manipulated, he accepts his position. Many consumers even understand the game they are involved in, but there are few other games to play. This has bred a kind of non-involvement or retreatism. Children, for example, watch much TV, but it matters little what is on. Housewives go shopping every Saturday, not because they have something they want to buy, but because they want to make sure that there is something left to buy, that their world is secure, that new commodities are still being produced and are available. Since few persons have to save for anything anymore, items can be purchased almost at will, but the purchasing is automatic and the items often lie in closets for months after they have been brought home from the department store. But if we are only half involved in what we are doing, what are we really involved in? Perhaps we are involved in nothing. We are a summation of the empty images we see advertised on our TV sets, images we can never become, but which we nevertheless watch with fascination as we watch animals in the zoo. But it is difficult to tell who is in the cages. The world becomes a psuedo-event which has been created for us and we are psuedo-events playing out our psuedo-lives.[19] Joy and laughter are generated by applause signs built into the heads of viewers by constant advertisements. One laughs when he is supposed to, only the jokes are no longer funny—the response comes *too* quickly. As leisure tends less and less to recreate us, we hunger for the quiet methodicity of work. Riesman notes:

> In this new perspective, leisure, which was once a residual compensation for the tribulations of work, may become what workers recover from at work (as children recover from vacation at school)! . . . Work may appear as a last remnant of rootedness, of "grounding," in a world of such mobility that goals, including the nature of status itself are being continuously redefined in experiences away from work.[20]

Culture too becomes just another ingredient of mass consumption. We can go out and buy a novel by Kafka and put it on our bookshelves and call ourselves existentialists, but we only know what the word means because of a definition we have had to memorize for our introductory philosophy class, and next week we'll be Zen Buddhists, and the following week. . . . There is so much pie to eat, that we never get to really taste the full flavor of it, and end up having to take an Alka Seltzer or something stronger for relief.

We find ourselves caught adrift between the images we see portrayed for us in the mass media or on the faces of our "happy" neighbors, and the boredom and uselessness we seek to escape from when we are by ourselves, at home, in school, at work, or in the department store. We can never return to the simplicity and "innocence" of the past when we knew what we needed, nor can we quite attain the boundless joy of affluence, the rewards we were promised for dying our hair blond. Nor can we stay where we are, being pushed and pulled this way and that by a reality which seeks to sell us on its significance. Though many of the commercials we seek lack credibility, we continue to watch and to listen, for we want to believe that what we are seeing and hearing is true. If it were not so, how could we otherwise justify the hours spent on these activities? Moreover, if the images presented are not true, then neither is the reality we have come to depend on. If none of it means anything, then we are free to create our own meanings. But that very freedom breeds chronic insecurity, for we have been conditioned to look to others and to things outside of ourselves to tell us what we are supposed to do, and to define what is useful and worthwhile. And no matter how boring and stultifying this present reality may be, it appears that we do not wish to escape its confines.

NOTES

[1] For discussion of this see Sebastian De Grazia, *Of Time, Work, and Leisure* (Garden City: Doubleday & Company, Inc., 1962).

[2] Bennet M. Berger, "The Sociology of Leisure: Some Suggestions," in *Work and Leisure,* ed. by Erwin O. Smigel (College and University Press Services, 1963), p. 39.

[3] John Kenneth Galbraith, *The Affluent Society* (Boston: Houghton Mifflin Company, 1958).

[4] Vance Packard, "The Waste Makers," in Perrucci and Pilisuk, *The Triple Revolution* (Boston: Little, Brown and Company, 1968), p. 315.

[5] Walter Kerr, *The Decline of Pleasure* (New York: Simon & Schuster, Inc., 1965), pp. 39–40.

[6] David M. Potter, *People of Plenty* (Chicago: University of Chicago Press, 1958), pp. 172–173.

[7] *Ibid.*

[8] For discussion of the creation of these images see Vance Packard, *The Hidden Persuaders* (New York: Simon & Schuster, Inc., 1957).

[9] Norman Jacobs, *Culture for the Millions* (Boston: Beacon Press, 1961).

[10] Helen Mazer Hacker, "Women as a Minority Group," in Betty Roszak and

Theodore Roszak, *Masculine/Feminine* (New York: Harper & Row, Publishers, 1970).

[11] Women's Liberation Writing Collective, "The New Feminism," *Ladies Home Journal*, August, 1970. See also Vivian Gormick and Barbara K. Moran, eds., *Woman in Sexist Society* (New York: Basic Books, 1971).

[12] Mirra Komarovsky, "Cultural Contradictions and Sex Roles," *American Journal of Sociology*, 52, 1946.

[13] George Johnson, *The Pill Conspiracy* (New York: Signet, 1967), p. 109.

[14] René Dubos, *Mirage of Health* (Garden City: Doubleday & Company, Inc., 1961), p. 32.

[15] Johnson, *op. cit.*, p. 47.

[16] For example of such definitions see Sebastian De Grazia, *Of Time, Work and Leisure* (Garden City: Doubleday & Company, Inc., 1962); Erwin O. Smigel, ed., *Work and Leisure* (New Haven: College and University Press, 1963); Josef Peiper, *Leisure the Basis of Culture* (New York: Mentor, 1962); and Joffre Dumazedier, *Toward a Leisure Society* (New York: The Free Press, 1967).

[17] Charles Brightbill, *The Challenge of Leisure* (Englewood Cliffs, N.J.: Spectrum), p. 26.

[18] Kerr, *op. cit.*, p. 46.

[19] Daniel Boorstin, *The Image* (New York: Harper & Row, Publishers, 1964).

[20] David Riesman, *Abundance for What?* (Garden City: Doubleday & Company, Inc., 1964), p. 152.

3

if you're not alienated, you don't have any friends

You are walking along the street and someone approaches. You may want to take a closer look at the other person, but as he draws near you avoid his glance. Instead you gaze down at your feet, or up into the trees, until he has passed. You are afraid to make contact.

Many Games, But Few Players

Increasing bureaucratization, industrialization, and material consumption have created more role possibilities and ever more complex role relationships, yet this proliferation of roles has not made for more satisfactory relationships. Rather, as there are more roles, and more people to assume them, a deeply involving relationship becomes more difficult to sustain. We never seem to have the time to sit down and talk. It is as if we were afraid that by staying put it would limit our chances. If we are enjoying ourselves at a party, and someone comes in and says, "Hey, I hear there's a party at Frank's," invariably, we feel that we must go to Frank's or else run the risk of missing something— someone to fall in love with; a fight; sounds of the latest records; the sight of nudity; some hilarious jokes and byplay. Once at Frank's place we keep asking, "What's happening? What's happening?" as if saying these words will make something happen, as if it were necessary for something *to happen* for the party to be a success.

What *has* happened is that we have become dependent on other people to supply us with what is missing from our lives: excitement, satisfaction—meaning. We need other people to tell us when we are having a good time, to tell us what constitutes a good time. It is only when we wake up the morning after the party with a hangover, without anyone else around us, that we glimpse the nature of our dependence. But we don't stay alone for long; rather, we call up a friend to find out whether or not it was a good party, and whether or not we had a good time. We are what is called by David Riesman "other-directed":

> What is common to all other-directed people is that their contemporaries are the source of direction for the individual—either those known to him or those with whom he is indirectly acquainted, through friends and through the mass media. This source is of course "internalized" in the sense that dependence on it for guidance in life is implanted early. The goals towards which the other-directed person strives shift with that guidance: it is only the process of paying close attention to the signals from others that remains unaltered throughout life.[1]

In contrast, there are people who can be identified as either "tradition-directed" or "inner-directed." Tradition-directed people are those who live in small tribal units where values change very little from generation to generation. In these societies, the past is a guide and the basis for the present. Inner-directed people are those who follow the moral and ethical precepts of their childhood or early training. Inner-directedness characterized the age of industrialization—entrepreneurs assumed the values of their parents (hard work, competition, and success) and their lives were an expression of these values. However, as work becomes less meaningful, and consumption less satisfying, many members of the middle as well as some members of the working class are beginning to turn to other people, and look to individuals to provide them with satisfaction and meaning, where, previously, they had turned to advertisers and politicians. These individuals are more often than not of the same generation. Since traditional values of work and consumption are no longer relevant, there is little to be gained from memorizing the values of different generations who had held these values; the problems of a generation can only be tackled by that generation. Thus, only those who face the same "reality" can act as judges of that "reality."

It has been pointed out that since individuals no longer have an adequate conception of what an acceptable and worthwhile identity is, they must turn to others who will in turn define the characteristics of such an identity.[2] They substitute the opinions others have of them for the opinion they have of themselves, as a means of evaluating themselves. Thus the expectations and values of others fill the void made by the loss of meaningful work. By this process of "indirect self-acceptance" we deny our own feelings in deference to those of others.

Why do we do this? The answer is: We dare not risk the disapproval of others. Doing our *own* thing requires an ego strong enough to withstand the pressures of the social group we are in. But how is this strength to be developed? On a diet of television and mass education programmed to tell us what to do and how to think? If an individual cannot create an identity out of his own experimentation, his ego is likely to be fragile. Having little chance to develop a "self-sufficient" ego and to stand against group pressure, he risks social suicide, for there is nothing to replace the images and identities the group supplies. Since isolation is too painful, we prefer interpersonal security at any cost. We keep our antenna out to pick up the signals of others—the fads, the hints, the innuendoes, the subtle suggestions to change our hair style, to bob our nose, to bathe more frequently, to stop being obnoxious, to be polite. If we pick them up, perhaps we can become a member of an "in-crowd." The price we pay for admission is that we are often at the mercy of others' opinions of our actions and thoughts—if they do not like what we say or do, it is we who must change, not they, for it is our behavior which is challenging the norms of the group. We must, therefore, *manipulate* others to our best advantage, to vote for us, to show that we are most popular.

Our problem is that the image we foster for ourselves is not one we have created, but rather one which the group presents to us. What we must do is show the other members of the group that we can wear their image as well as they can. Simultaneously, the other members of the group are manipulating us in the same way, and the group itself is being manipulated by the larger image of American society which *it* is attempting to maintain. After the original formation of an image by a particular group (that is, hippies) the message is transmitted by the mass media to other groups who mimic it. The original process of creating the image out of one's own personal experience is lost; only the image itself remains.

Since we must constantly be on the lookout lest we violate group norms, the security we expect from a group is a false one. We have to conceal "information" which may be used against us, and we are

anxious lest we reveal aspects of ourselves we prefer to hide. In keeping up our guard against the invasions of others, we learn to control ourselves, to laugh on cue when the applause sign goes on. We wish to believe in the truth of the larger reality, that the group's values are worthwhile and meaningful. To believe otherwise would be to risk absurdity—for why play a game no one believes in? Why manipulate others, if there is nothing to manipulate them for? Often the means become the ends—manipulation is all there is.

As in work, consumption, and leisure, such manipulation becomes justified in terms of the utility of relationships. How useful is he to you, what can he do for you, how much will she give you? Though such utility is rarely weighed in monetary terms, the meaning which the rhetoric of the monetary system conveys is nevertheless maintained. Individuals come to be viewed as objects for the enhancement of one's image—but this image is often borrowed from those whom one is trying to purchase. These "consumption goods" become paintings in our living room, we hang them on the wall for show and tell—oh, I know him; I slept with her; he said hello to me today—just as we become adornments for the rooms of others. We count our possessions (friends) to find out who we are, and to gauge how far we have to go. We are rarely secure because there is always someone left to buy, and until we win them they are a threat to the image we wish to maintain. Such purchases are rarely satisfying, for as in most conspicuous consumption, there is nothing to do with the product once we own it, rather, we must go on consuming, for such products rarely live up to their expectations. Means and ends fuse under the bright lights of false advertising—seduction leads not to eternal bliss, but rather to more seduction. Boredom with one's toys often sets in early, and then the batteries run out anyway. Such purchases are viewed quantitatively, rather than qualitatively—it's how many people we know, or their status that counts, not the relationship we have with them. It is only quantitative criteria which can be easily evaluated and judged by others—and the judgment of others determines the success of the relationship.

But do others really care what we do? Are they watching? Raise the shade in the living room, look out, where are they? Behind the bushes in the front yard? In the back seat of the car? In a helicopter hovering nearby? Or are they inside our heads?

As Sidney Jourard put it: "In the ultimate victory of the commissar, each man becomes the unchallenged commissar over himself!" [3]

We thus learn to play different roles in different groups and to change roles on cue, as an actor or actress will change attire between scenes. There is no longer any one stable role to play, just as there is no longer any central identity from which to orient our behavior. Ironically, this may breed more insecurity than going it alone:

In our society, the frequency of role change, the ambiguity of roles, the mutability and diversity of their definition, and our unavoidable lack of preparation breed much confusion and anxiety, a sense of discomfort and alienation. We feel unable to identify the self with any role. Yet when it is not bounded by status and role and firmly related to a system of expectations that gives orchestral support to its solo performance the self is hardly identified. It may never take shape, remaining outside of its many activities, ever ready to play new roles but never fully invested in any. In the end, no self is experienced—only impersonations, psuedo-personalities which do not amount to one identifiable person.[4]

In the face of this transiency and manipulation we become dis-involved from the roles we are playing and from the games which link those roles together. We gradually realize that when we are totally obligated toward others (to make sure we do not offend these others) we end up offending ourselves. We remember (in a brief flash between martinis, or taking the kids to cub scouts or in mowing the lawn) that perhaps we have an obligation to ourselves as well as to others, and in fact we cannot be obligated to others fully unless they know who we are—who it is that is taking the kids to cub scouts and mowing the lawn.

As we become afraid of revealing aspects of ourselves which the group may not be willing to tolerate, so too we become unwilling to trust anyone, for trust implies that we know who it is that we are putting our trust in. On a nickel is the adage, "In God We Trust." Yet if "God" is a pseudopersonality, then how can we place our faith in Him? Who would deposit money with a banker who is unreliable, who may at any moment confiscate our life savings and run off to South America? Information we reveal may be used against us to discredit our performance, the image we are attempting to maintain. The inability to trust others hampers how intimate we can be with them. It also destroys any chance for honest communication. Although many of us are ostensibly involved in the lives of others, we are very lonely, for real involvement does not take place.

For many of us, the playing of traditional roles is only surface behavior—our minds are occupied elsewhere. We are involved neither in what we are doing nor in what we are saying. We are playing back tape recordings we have memorized; the recordings have not changed in years, though the speakers have aged. Though many of us under-stand each other, we have nothing left to say to each other. We are bored. We are tired of faking, of smiling on cue, of laughing at jokes told over and over till the punch line acts as a stimulus to yawn. There is a proliferation of roles and relationships, but the roles and relation-ships seem ever less meaningful. Those significant roles which exist are played out as daydreams beneath ongoing conversations which act as fronts and disguises for what is really taking place. Life is a formality which comes to be lived on two levels; between listening to a lecture, writing notes *and* thinking about seducing the person who sits two rows in front of you, between making tin cans at the factory *and* dreaming about sport fishing, between doing the dishes *and* thinking about all the short stories you packed away somewhere, between talking to someone we've known for years *and* at the same time thinking about someone else we'd rather be with, though we can't think of who.

Overt activity and interaction are cut off from covert day dreams and desires, yet only the overt, the pseudo, is permitted, has prescribed rules, and can be judged by others. It does not matter that our heads are not where they seem to be; what matters is that our bodies are there to be counted, that we bear allegiance to the "flag," though its insignia is constantly changing. No wonder that we often appear apathetic and lethargic, lack motivation to interact with others and cannot get out of the rut for fear of showing who we really are, of getting hurt, of being worse off. Of course this assumes that we know who we really are, and that our private self is different than our public one. Perhaps individuals have incorporated the TV image of themselves to such an extent that this image is who they really are—they are not schizophrenic after all. "We are what we pretend to be." [5]

The games exist, but who is playing? How much are we involved? Does following the rules add significance and meaning to our existence? Are we "better people" for having played along? [6] Who are we playing along with? If there is no well-defined reference group or "significant other" which has a stable identity with which we can empathize, it is difficult to find a stable identity. We can seldom be satisfied with a particular reference group, because reference groups are transient, changing as rapidly as other fads and consumer goods. In fact, as we add more roles, we meet fewer persons who can define who we are, what roles we are supposed to be playing, what these relationships entail, or when we have fulfilled the requirements and done enough. Peer groups cannot provide us with the security and meaning that American society lacks, for even when we have switched our allegiance from vertical to horizontal security (from our relation with those above and below us in status, to those of equal status, age and interests), these relations are still based on treating people as objects and manipulating them. Even our marital partners can become objects. As roles become increasingly transitory, we attempt to grasp our spouses ever tighter lest this one chance for stability vanish. Yet, in so doing, we choke and destroy our relationship.

The desire for possession is the same desire that advertising promotes—I'll have one of those, and one of those, and that one over there—only in this case, it is people we are buying, rather than things, though the distinction is not very clear. Individuals get used to marketing themselves, to see what kind of price they will fetch on the open counter or display. Everyone is always available to be purchased, or to have a new relationship with someone. Marriage is no longer a bind. (At least one in four ends in divorce.) This "permanent availability" has had its effect on raising children:

> The concurrent assumptions of universal, permanent availability and orderly replacement suggest that the socialization of children be aimed at maximizing their market position in permanent availability (to the degree that permanent availability becomes the traditional norm). As a perennially marketable product, the child is required to develop (a) a pleasing personality, (b) competence in interpersonal relations, (c) a pleasant appearance, and (d) occupational career skill regardless of sex (not only to secure a good marriage but also to facilitate disengagement from an "unsatisfactory" marriage). The parents are correspondingly obligated to provide appropriate aid to enhance the market position of their children during childhood and adulthood.[7]

If your wife or husband is just another one of your possessions, and comes to be treated in the same way as other objects you own or control—shined up once in awhile to show your guests, but otherwise stored out of the way—then you soon want to buy more, not necessarily because you need one, but because you are bored with the one you have and the advertisers have a model out this year with a shorter skirt or longer beard.

In marriage, the individual is expected to accept permanency, whereas he has been raised to expect impermanence and a constant change in relationships. For many persons marriage represents the first opportunity to do something on one's own, yet most of us do not accept this chance; rather we look to see what image we are supposed to live up to, how we are supposed to play at man and wife. We fake happiness and repress, at least until the next divorce, what we would really like to do. The TV tells us what we would really like—that blond running down the beach or an Aqua Velva man. But, no matter how many marriages we have, we are still chasing an illusion. Marriage becomes another game not to take seriously, another set of relationships in which we are not really involved. Yet, when asked if we are happy, we reply in the affirmative, for with so much invested, and few other legitimate options available, we would be foolish not to admit to a certain degree of satisfaction.

But Aren't We All Individualists?

The description we have just rendered is perhaps offensive. It assumes that we are afraid to take a step or utter a word without first consulting our friends, TV guide, or our professors. Obviously, most of us are able to navigate the day-to-day circumstances of our lives without such consultation, or at least we believe this is the case. Even though we are dependent on friends for support and reinforcement, there are so many possible reference groups or subcultures for us to belong to, that we are still able to maintain a certain amount of choice: others may define what role options are available, but there are so many such options that this does not limit our individuality. Moreover, man is a social being; it is only through our interactions with others that we find out who we are, learn appropriate forms of communication, and experience existence. People are dependent on each other for both enjoyment and survival. Just as most problems in American society are interdependent, so too, are most Americans: we need other people, and they need us. Our discussion has also implied that the experience of "other-directedness" is a characteristic of only our society. But it has been a characteristic of most industrial societies. The problem, however, is the way Americans interpret and structure their interdependence, not that they are interdependent. The dichotomy between being individualists and being conformists has made us both indiivdualists and conformists. We are individualists in the sense that all Americans are supposed to do their own thing, make up their own minds, smoke their own cigarettes, regardless of what others do. However, we are conformists in accepting the role options open, in letting others define these options for us, in wanting them to tell us how to do our own thing.

It has been observed [8] that while all of us ostensibly want to be identified as individualists, the result has been mass uniformity, rather than the proliferation of differences.[9] We find ourselves in a paradox. On the one hand, we want to resist the demands of the techno-structure and group pressures for unwarranted conformity; on the other hand, we want the security and community that only group techno-structure occupational and consumer roles can provide. We are raised to believe in individualism, but the only options open to us make for acceptance of often outmoded group and societal norms and

values, which create the very insecurity we seek to escape from and
which make real individualism impossible. Though the reaction against
the blatant conformity of the 1950s is ostensibly severe—"doing your
own thing" becoming the catchword of the counterculture—underneath little has changed, for the process itself has not been altered.
The search for individualism, then, often becomes synonymous with
accepting insecurity, alienation, and lack of communication, the very
problems which this search is designed to alleviate. Such contradictions
are soon resolved, or at least temporarily hidden, for there is little
room to break the norms of one's reference group, nor can most
persons live without these norms and the legitimacy and rewards they
imply. We have lost our own ability to accept or reject other's definitions of who we are, and in the process have failed to achieve a
compromise between doing our own thing, and doing what others
want us to do: seeing our freedom as part of our interdependence
with others, rather than as a war of all against all. Our "individualism"
leads us away from confrontations, has us avoid all social conflicts and
problems; our susceptibility to group pressures reinforces our desire to
withdraw, to leave others alone, to mind our own business, lest we
too get hurt.

I Don't Believe in Money: Alienation
for Fun and Profit

The result of this combination of conformity and individualism produces a new and acceptable identity (alienation!) which is in turn
co-opted by the mass media and Madison Avenue to sell more of the
same. Alienation is not new, but rarely has it so dominated the rhetoric
and style of our lives, often to the detriment of solving the very
problem it raises. Alienation is now our national pastime. It has become a product which can be marketed to all sides of the "generation
gap," and to all shades of the political spectrum. Parents are alienated
from their children and take Excedrin and Alka Seltzer for relief or buy
"hippie" clothing so they can become "pals." Writers of the youth
culture meanwhile go on talk shows for the purpose of circulating and
popularizing their wares, gaining status and meaning from the alienation they have analyzed and claim to be suffering from. Alienation has
become a primary means of social mobility as "revolutionaries" become co-opted and manipulated by the mass public as symbols for
emulation, use the profits from their books, speeches, and records to
buy the very homes, cars and material affluence their rhetoric detests.
And the cooptation continues through encounter groups which charge

a hundred dollars a weekend to alleviate the problem. Who wants to become unalienated? Why drop the only identity worth holding? If you're not alienated, you don't have any friends.

Who Is Responsible? Give Me Liberty or Whatever Else You Have

We are born into a society which preaches individualism yet presumes we will yield to structural and other-personal definitions of who we are and what we can become. We cannot be held responsible for our actions; we are "only following orders" (however subtly they maybe transmitted, they *are* orders). So, it is not we who are accountable, it is *they*. And, no one is, finally, responsible, for there are always others. We act with immunity for if we have little understanding of who we are, we also have little idea of what we have done. Our reluctance to become "involved" reinforces our lack of responsibility.

Attuned to, but not involved in, others' activities, the individual has to memorize how he is supposed to behave, rather than go through the experience of discovering how he wants to behave:

The majority of his values are introjected from other individuals or groups significant to him, but are regarded by him as his own.

The source or locus of evaluation on most matters lies outside of himself.

The criterion by which his values are set is the degree to which they will cause him to be loved or accepted.

These conceived preferences are either not related at all, or not clearly related, to his own process of experiencing.

Often there is a wide and unrecognized discrepancy between the evidence supplied by his own experience, and these conceived values.

Because these conceptions are not open to testing in experience, he must hold them in rigid and unchanging fashion. The alternative would be a collapse of his values. Hence his values are right. . . .

Because they are untestable, there is no ready way of solving contradictions. If he has taken in from the community the conception that money is the summum bonum and from the church the conception that love of one's neighbor is the highest value, he has no way of discovering which has more value for *him*. Hence a common aspect of modern life is living with absolutely contradictory values. We calmly discuss the possibility of dropping a hydrogen bomb on Russia, but then find tears in our eyes when we see headlines about the suffering of one small child.

Because he has relinquished the locus of evaluation to others, and has lost touch with his own valuing process, he feels profoundly insecure and easily threatened in his values. If some of these conceptions were destroyed, what would take their place? This threatening possibility makes him hold his value conceptions more rigidly or more confusedly, or both[10]

To paraphrase Ortega y Gasset, we have all of the rights, but none of the obligations—because we do not know our rights.[11] How can we feel any obligation toward or responsibility for what is not ours? How can we feel free, if we do not know what freedom means?

The anxiety which this situation often breeds is in part due to a "cultural lag" in the images we use to present ourselves to the world. The lag is represented along different dimensions: between traditional images of who we are and contemporary images; between who we are and who we would like to be; and between who we are and who we think we are. Our self-conceptions and images are out of touch with the social world in which we find ourselves. We may rarely experience these dichotomies, however, because our language does not see them. We may find ourselves with a static conception of a dynamic social world. We feel boredom, insecurity, and anxiety, yet we do not know where these feelings come from—there is no place for them in our vocabularies. The more these feelings increase, the more we attempt to hold onto outmoded images of ourselves and our world, when we should be letting go.[12] Though our conceptions of the world, of ourselves, and of reality may be outmoded, we continue to believe in them, as though there were no other conceptions, and even though we are often quite uninvolved in their consequences.

For example, we may go to school with the conception that what we are learning is preparing us for a meaningful and worthwhile occupation. When we graduate we discover not only that we were not being trained for the job we will work at, but that there are few worthwhile jobs to be had. We must, therefore, alter our conception of who we are, and what place in the world we will occupy. But, instead of refusing to work, we continue to accept and labor at jobs which do not meet our expectations—because we have memorized our conception of the world and our place in it and because this process does not permit or accept alternatives to what others tell us exists. In a similar sense:

> The man who, through education and training, has learned to find his greatest fulfillment in reading or art or hairstyling or general scholarship rather than in athletic or business competition, must find ways to reconcile his preference with many age-old images regarding "masculinity." The college-educated woman who finds happiness and self-respect in professional achievement has the task of reconciling her learned needs

and preferences with the "feminine" image which continues to define womanliness in terms of domestic and mothering abilities.[13]

Who Is Sick?

Unsatisfactory interpersonal relationships ultimately take their toll in terms of physical and mental health. Most people who experience constant anxiety cannot ascertain the causes. They are unable to cope with their social and physical environment, yet lack words to express what they feel, because our language does not adequately conceptualize contemporary interpersonal problems.[14] Many psychiatrists often confuse the symptoms of an individual's mental illness with its causes, and in treating the former, they do little about the latter. If an individual feels alienated because he is powerless to solve a social problem, regardless of how he feels when he leaves the therapist, does not his being cured depend on something being done about his social situation? In assuming the sanctity of the "system," many psychiatrists who operate within the framework of the social status quo do so with little prospect of ever finding a cure for the patient who seeks their assistance. In fact, much of his "sickness" enables the patient to cope with a bizarre or absurd world. The schizophrenic, for example, is relating in the only way that he can, to a society which is itself experiencing what increasingly appears to be an irretrievable breakdown.

> Sickness is a way of blocking off aspects of the environment so that the patient may then be adequate to the remainder of his world. We cannot assume in the usual oversimplified way that the patient automatically wants to get well; we must assume, rather, that he cannot permit himself to give up his neurosis, to get well, until other conditions in his existence and his relation to his world are changed. This indicates immediately the inadequacy of the concept that neurosis is a failure of adjustment. Neurosis is precisely the opposite; it is a method of adjustment, and the trouble is that it is all too successful; it is a method of adjustment to a curtailed world.[15]

Sickness itself may be the only realistic way of coping with a reality perceived as incurably sick.

As long as we share our neuroses, everything is assumed to be normal. However, when attempts to cope seem to threaten or unduly annoy those around us, we are judged "insane" and we risk incarceration. Once this label of madness is attached, it becomes difficult to discard. In our society when we visit a "head doctor" we are presumed to be mentally ill—it is up to us to prove our sanity. Mechanic has shown this in a recent study:

> In the two mental hospitals studied over a period of three months, the investigator never observed a case where the psychiatrist advised the patient that he did not need treatment. Rather, all persons who appeared at the hospital were absorbed into the patient population regardless of their ability to function adequately outside the hospital. In this regard, it is important to note that mental hospitals care for more than the mentally ill. The unwanted, the aged, the indigent, the lonely, and others often enter public mental hospitals voluntarily.[16]

We may be committed by relatives or friends *without* our consent, for once the matter reaches a court hearing, the judge and court psychiatrist work on the assumption that we are ill, and they have little time in which to decide whether we are not. Attempts on our part to prove sanity are considered proof of incorrigibility or signs of mental derangement.[17] This point is controversial, so let us take a brief look at the following findings resulting from a study done in Cook County (Chicago), Illinois:

> The sharp dichotomy between statutory and actual commitment procedures in Illinois is best illustrated by . . . examples of the Cook County Mental Health Clinic in operation. (1) To satisfy the "formality" of a physician's certification of insanity, the certificates are signed as a matter of course by staff physicians of the Mental Health Clinic after little or no examination and after the alleged mentally-ill has *already* been brought in for confinement. Moreover, the *same* staff doctor is one of those later appointed to handle the examination for the court, eliminating the possibility of one doctor acting as a check on another, which is the very purpose of requiring *two* medical examinations. (2) As might be expected, the examination by the state physicians is given great, if not decisive, weight at the court hearing. The flaw is that the so-called "examinations" are made on an assembly-line basis, *often being completed in two or three minutes, and never taking more than ten minutes.* Although psychiatrists agree that it is practically impossible to determine a person's sanity on the basis of such a short and hurried interview, doctors at the Mental Health Clinic recommend confinement in 77 percent of the cases. It appears that in practice the alleged-mentally-ill is presumed to be insane and bears the burden of proving his sanity in the few minutes allotted him. (3) A person's last opportunity to demonstrate his sanity is at the court hearing, yet doctors at the Mental Health Clinic keep all the "patients" under such heavy sedation that many of them appear stuporous

at their hearings and are unable to intelligently defend themselves for that reason alone. (4) It is apparently the practice of the Clinic not to notify persons threatened with incarceration of their right to counsel or a jury trial, and indeed to reprimand or dismiss workers who do inform the alleged-mentally-ill of their legal rights.[18]

Once committed, we stand little chance of leaving the institution unless we conform to the role of being mentally ill, and accept the personality offered by the staff at the institution.[19] Attempts to "buck the system" only serve to work against us, and are judged as indications that we do not want to cooperate, that we don't want to "get well." Finally, even if we were "sane" upon entering the mental hospital, the chances of our remaining sane in such a situation are remote, for there is no one within the institution to validate it. In no time at all we too begin to think that we are ill, because this is the role we find ourselves expected to play. Of course, not all mental illness can be accounted for in this manner, and many persons do urgently need psychiatric care, though there are many others who treat therapy or visits to a "shrink" as a new consumption good, hoping to buy friendship and meaning. Yet, as long as we lack a viable ideology and our outmoded value system continues to frustrate our search for identity and meaning, those mental illnesses which have an immediate social derivation will continue to affect us.

NOTES

[1] David Riesman, *The Lonely Crowd* (New Haven: Yale University Press, 1958).

[2] Snell Putney and Gail Putney, *The Adjusted American* (New York: Harper Colophon, 1966).

[3] Sidney Jourard, *Disclosing Man to Himself* (Princeton: Van Nostrand, 1968), pp. 109–110.

[4] Ernest Van Den Haag, *Passion and Social Constraint* (New York: Delta, 1965), pp. 289–298.

[5] Kurt Vonnegut, *Mother Night* (New York: Harper & Row, Publishers, 1966).

[6] Jourard, *op. cit.,* pp. 105–128.

[7] Bernard Farber, *Family, Organization and Interaction* (San Francisco: Chandler, 1964). And see also John F. Cuber and Peggy B. Harroff, *Sex and the Significant Americans* (Baltimore: Penguin Books, Inc., 1966).

[8] Philip Slater, *The Pursuit of Loneliness* (Boston: Beacon Press, 1970).

[9] *Ibid.,* p. 106.

[10] Carl R. Rogers and Barrie Stevens, *Person to Person: The Problem of Being Human* (Lafayette: Real People Press, 1967), p. 19.

[11] See José Ortega y Gasset, *The Revolt of the Masses* (New York: W. W. Norton & Company, Inc., 1960).

[12] Jourard, *op. cit.,* p. 154.

[13] William J. Lederer and Don D. Jackson, *The Mirages of Marriage* (New York: W. W. Norton & Company, Inc., 1968), pp. 35–36.

[14] Rollo May, *Man's Search for Himself* (New York: Signet, 1967), p. 56.

[15] Rollo May, "The Context of Psychotherapy," in Hendrik M. Ruitenbeek, *Psychoanalysis and Contemporary American Culture* (New York: Delta, 1964), pp. 79–80.

[16] Marian Radke Yarrow, Charlotte Green Schwartz, Harriet S. Murphy, and Leila Calhoun Deasy, "The Psychological Meaning of Mental Illness in the Family," in Thomas J. Scheff, *Mental Illness and Social Process* (New York: Harper and Row, Publishers, 1967), p. 27.

[17] *Ibid.;* see also Alan Watts, *Psychotherapy East and West* (New York: Pantheon Books, Inc., 1961), p. 193.

[18] Luis Kutner, "The Illusion of Due Process in Commitment Proceedings," in Scheff, *op. cit.,* pp. 104–105.

[19] For a discussion of this phenomenon, see Erving Goffman, *Asylums* (Garden City: Doubleday & Company, Inc., 1961).

4

the politics of indifference:
monopoly democracy

One of the chief considerations in any analysis of American society must be our inability, as isolated individuals, to solve social problems. For example, if we are concerned about poverty we may wish to start a poverty program; typically, we lack sufficient resources, and we find that those with resources to start such a program are unwilling to support us. In finding out why so little is being done, we must confront certain "political realities."

To some observers, politics in America is more a question of indifference than it is of adherence to ideology. The chief question asked by such observers is not "Who cares and why?" but "Who does not care and why not?" In fact, local and national politics often arouse as much interest as an average campus election. America is not a *participatory* democracy in the sense that the issues are presented and debated at the polls, and the citizens are given the maximum opportunity to examine the arguments and vote on the issues. There is a "credibility gap": what happens in politics bears little resemblance to the visible world. Do we care? Perhaps we are content merely to cast, or withhold, our vote. That we identify this process as democratic,

53

however, is a problem, if not for us, then for those who realize the nature of what is taking place.

If this political process is not democratic, then what difference does it make and to whom? First, if our form of government is not democratic, then the resulting lack of representation may be a cause of many problems such as poverty and war. Second, anti-democratic politics in America may be a logical extension of the value and action orientation discussed in the previous chapters; that is, politics may be more a symptom than a cause of the problem, and as such presents further evidence of the necessity of altering the entire system, rather than one aspect of it.

Political Decision-Making: "Who Does Not Govern"[1]

There are many theories about the American political process. The two most prominent theories may be described as the elitist and the pluralist. Those who maintain that American society is elitist claim that the country is governed by members of a composite privileged class, drawn from the economic, social, political and military fields. Perhaps the most famous statement of this idea is Mills' *The Power Elite,* which demonstrates the interconnected workings of the military polit- ical, and industrial complex and moreover shows that this complex recruits from the same socio-economic class. Mills argues that the control the elite exerts, directly or indirectly, prevents the average individual from having much influence in politics.[2] In *Who Rules America?* Domhoff has come to similar conclusions, albeit without Mills' explicit moral condemnation. Domhoff, however, modifies Mills' conception in pointing out that while elites may rule, they often disagree among themselves. He thus concludes that shifting coalitions within the upper classes may help maintain a semblance of democracy.[3]

Representing the pluralists are Riesman or Banfield.[4] Essentially, each argues that America is composed of various veto groups which cancel each other out in terms of political power. No one group can gain ascendancy over any other group or combination of groups. In a study of various decision-making situations in Chicago, Banfield found that, depending upon the issue, only those people who are concerned about an issue tend to participate and have influence with regard to that issue. Many of the economic, political, and social elite in the Chicago area often take little interest in the local decision- making process, since they are involved in more nationally-oriented concerns. This contradicts what Mills and Domhoff hypothesize, at least with regard to applying a power elite model to local decision-making practices. In a study of decision-making in New Haven, Dahl arrived at much the same conclusion.[5] Still, we should ask what might have happened in New Haven or Chicago had the issue really mattered to the members of the power elite. Would they then appear indifferent or be powerless?

At the local level, perhaps interest groups do tend to dominate the decision-making processes, if only because more powerful members of the larger society "can't be bothered." Nevertheless, to the average citizen it hardly matters whether a decision relating to local issues is fought out among a few strongly entrenched interest groups or is decided at a cocktail party given by the president of a large corporation? Either way, how much say will he have, and does he really want to have any say at all?

The two models are more complicated than this. In the Mills-Domhoff conception, there is room for those who are talented to join the power elite; however, the choice is usually not one of their making, it is the power elite which co-opts those who will help sustain it. Thus Richard Nixon made it from humble beginnings, backed by large business interests, to the White House. The elite does not change with the addition of new members from "below," because the new members already think like the old elite (or, if they do not, they soon will). In simple form, those who become higher managers or executives in large business concerns learn to think about the world in a certain way; they need to do this if they are to succeed. Those who are judged by the elite to be deficient in the qualities which make a good elitist are therefore denied the opportunity to move upward.

In the pluralist model, another kind of monopoly system is at work. Existing groups make the rules and then decide which other groups may be allowed to play. The two-party system works on the assumption that any other party would be superfluous and moreover an affront to the existing parties. Therefore, all other political parties are considered illegitimate and every effort is made to discredit them. Pluralism, in this case, exists to maintain the status quo.[6] But is the existing number of interest groups adequate protection of the public good? What about those people who are not represented?

Both the elitist and the pluralist theories ignore the fact that political power may reside in the given value framework, ideology, or "image" of American society itself, with the existing power elite or interest groups acting either openly or inadvertently to preserve this image.

Power may lie in the traditional system and the inequities which this system preserves, as articulated by those who purport to be the "legitimate" representatives of this system. Political power can and must, from this point of view, be shaped by the dominant economic and social institutions—the ideology that legitimates it, the structure of these institutions, and the actions of those persons who claim to represent these institutions. Why doesn't the American political system function as, in theory, it is supposed to, and why do those who articulate these theories often become inadvertent "apologists" for the system? The answer may be clearer if we elaborate how the power elite and pluralist conceptions work in practice.

The elitist and pluralist models are not so far apart as may appear at first glance. One has only to examine the electoral process in order to see many of the convergences. An individual can usually be elected to national political office only with the aid of large contributions of money.

The successful candidate who has accepted large sums of money from interest groups or individual contributors often finds himself owing them favors. In big elections, the price the candidate must pay for the essential services of his backers is reckoned in terms of his policies and programs. With increased TV coverage in campaigns and the "packaging" of candidates by advertising agencies (Nixon's 1968 campaign), we may soon have candidates who refuse to take a position on anything for fear of offending someone. Rising publicity costs increase the candidates' dependence on financial contributions as well. The question is then asked: Whom is one voting for, the candidate, the advertising firm, or the financial backers? [7]

Even if the electorate were represented in Congress by elected officials of their choice, would such officials be able to do anything? To put it another way, what power does Congress have left? There is much evidence to suggest that in the last few decades initiative and power in the government have shifted to the executive branch. This shift to more centralized control parallels similar shifts in industry, as large-scale organizations strive for greater efficiency and control over their "constituents." A prime example of congressional inadequacy in recent years is the way in which the "undeclared" war on the Vietnamese people has been extended to Cambodia and Laos, without the prior consultation, let alone the consent, of Congress. Why have a Congress at all? Perhaps the Constitution, which reflects the different economic and social conditions under which it was first framed, is outmoded, and no longer serves as a guarantee of democracy, let alone a balance of power in the federal government:

Whether guided by the more active or passive concept of the job, the President is now the central figure in the legislative process. The President's program occupies the dominant place on the congressional agenda. Most of the major laws are drafted in the President's office; the budget is put together there and presented to Congress as a packaged entity. A bill initiated by the individual congressman faces giant obstacles unless it has been submitted first to the President's Budget Bureau for "legislative clearance." [8]

If all this is true, then how are *the people* represented in national and international affairs? Interest groups and elitist politics come together to lobby in Washington to prevent passage of bills, for example, by threatening to withhold campaign contributions (ultimately votes). If you cannot get enough money to run for office, it is unlikely you can raise enough money to finance a strong lobby in Washington or at the state capitol. The expenses of the required wining-and-dining are often beyond the means of many groups which would question the political reality upon which much of the nation's legislation is based. Moreover, once outside this framework, such groups—migrant farm workers, ghetto dwellers, anti-war demonstrators—often find it difficult to get to see anyone and to make their case heard. And when other means are employed in order to dramatize their plight or position (for example, demonstrations by Vietnam Veterans Against the War), these groups are told that they should work through the system, and go through the "proper channels" if they wish to be taken seriously.

The national political conventions probably represent the system at its worst. After running in a series of primaries, the various candidates and their delegates come together to decide who will represent each of the two major political parties in the forthcoming presidential election. Both the costs of mounting a national campaign and the necessity of appealing to diverse interests combine to make the two political parties take similar positions. Furthermore, in the political arena there is no real debate between the two parties. It is the candidate who is least offensive to the largest number of people who is selected to be the standard-bearer. This is the man who is required to be the moral and political leader of the nation after election day. How can a man who is used to compromising himself at every turn or who refuses to take a stand on principle do more than guarantee the status quo?

Delegates to nominating conventions are, of course, not always (nor even almost always) chosen on the basis of primaries. Most states do not run primaries. How are delegates chosen, and what interests do they represent? Are the nonwhite and the poor fairly represented? While local party caucuses ostensibly determine the make-up of the delegation, state party officers and already elected officials have in the past had a disproportionate say in who ends up on the slate of delegates going to the conventions. The Democratic Party Convention of 1972 achieved a fair amount of equal represen- tation of youth, women, and minorities, much to the chagrin of tradi- tional party leaders.[9] Until the 1972 Democratic Party Convention, crucial issues were rarely debated live before television audiences. The more cynical among us may say this is because television censors most everything the least bit controversial, protecting the public from hearing about the things which most concern it. Another, perhaps more cogent, reason is that those interests represented at the conven- tions do not, for the most part, wish to offend potential voters who might be watching.

In contrast to 1972, the Democratic Convention in 1968 was alotted only about two hours to debate the war in Vietnam. At the same time, a sizeable number of youth sought to dramatize many of the problems facing American society by peacefully demonstrating in Chicago. They were not granted a permit to use a stadium, one which they had ap- plied for well in advance of the convention, they were not permitted to assemble peacefully in a park, and they could not make themselves *visible* to the delegates coming to Chicago to vote for the presidential nominee. The resulting clash between youth and local authorities was dramatized on television for the public, but not for the delegates. These youth movements will be examined to a greater degree below, but it should be noted here that those leading the demonstrations were later tried on conspiracy charges—that is, for crossing state lines to conspire to provoke a riot. Political speech became "inflammatory" only when spoken by a "leftist." When the conservative Vice President Agnew later used similar rhetoric, he was hailed as a "patriot." It is significant that in 1972, many of those who had been in the streets of Chicago had become delegates to the Democratic Convention, a rather radical transformation in a four-year period. It remains to be seen whether such party reform will result in a changed political cli- mate in American society, and greater political power for those long- denied seats in the executive, judicial, and legislative branches of the government. Certainly it is a step in the right direction![10]

The traditional American political structure results in what has been called a "mass society"; there is a great division between those who make the political decisions and those who must live under them. Few intermediary groups exist to mediate between the power elite or large interest groups and the masses, the "non-political society," average individuals, us. This political situation leaves individuals with a sense of powerlessness and an inability to "get up for" a political debate or election.

Does Voting Make a Difference?

If it is true that we have no say in deciding who is going to run for public office, if there is nothing to choose between any two candidates for office (a criticism often leveled at the presidential candidates), then why do we bother to vote? Lower voting turnouts are typically associated with the black, the poor, or other communities outside the "mainstream" of American society.[11] These people do not vote because they are not represented in the roster of "available" candidates and there is little chance of their having a say in this selection process.

When people have no stake in the electoral process there is little reason to show up at the polling places on election day.[12] If it makes no difference which way people vote then it is pointless for those people to spend time and energy on politics.[13] For most of us politics is something that happens at elections once every two or four years when we get the chance to exercise our constitutional rights.

Even if we feel we are voting for an individual who occupies a position we can support, we may wonder whether we shall hear anything more of the program for which we voted after election day. It will be remembered that during the 1964 presidential campaign Lyndon Johnson was the "peace" candidate with Barry Goldwater, representing the hawks, opposing him. Much to the dismay of many who voted for Johnson, it was *their* man who, in office, was chiefly responsible for escalating the war in Vietnam. Voting a straight party-line may yield similar contradictions. For example, a vote for the Democratic Party may be a vote for a candidate who, if he is a Southern Democrat, may be far more conservative than a moderate Republican. By the same token, many liberal Republicans often take traditional or even liberal Democratic stands. It would seem that since this is the case, there should be a realignment of party positions, with candidates for office standing as Democrats or Republicans according to how they represent given positions. In practice, such relabeling would not be a solution, because neither political party represents a fundamental challenge to the status quo, though there are some indications that this is changing.

Why Go into Politics?

Few of us want to get into politics because politics, at least the ideal sort of politics, is built on trust, and there is not much of that around these days. In an other-directed society, where much social interaction is based on manipulation and putting on a false front, how can trusting relationships develop? Why should we trust the politician if we cannot trust our neighbors or our friends? [14] Furthermore, how can we take a political stand if we are afraid of being "found out," of risking social position, of offending other people? Democratic debate implies that those debating have respect for themselves and the inherent worth of their own opinions; yet, few people can feel their worth and dignity in the types of work and consumption the society allows them. [15]

Moreover, in a society which is going through so many changes, durable attachments to political parties of the traditional kind, and steady agreement on the adoption of policies—or on the content of those policies—are proving more difficult to achieve. It is easier to change our ideas, to cease having any ideas at all, or to adopt the ones we receive from the mass media, our friends, and *existing* politicians. Without a "social identity," participation in politics becomes impossible. As Robert Lane points out:

> Where a man has achieved a clear and strong social identity, anything that affects a group he has embraced and incorporated in himself makes him a partisan. He enters politics as a group member, finds his rationale for activity in the (internalized) group goals, evaluates success and failure in terms of group (and therefore self-) advancement. Where the social identity is diffuse . . . individual goals and purposes must serve as political motives, and since the relation of politics to these individual purposes is often obscure, the drive to participate in politics is often weak. Political participation unsupported by a strong social identity is difficult for the amateur to sustain. [16]

In a society in which political parties are vast, diffuse, and stand for very little, there are few organizations to mediate between large, powerful interest groups and the ordinary citizen. There is therefore little motivation to enter the political arena. There are no such organizations because what interaction does take place is, for the most part, socially maintained on an informal basis, lacks a traditional or historical reference, and is neither morally nor politically "active." [17]

American society tends to insure the need for political elites while at the same time guaranteeing minimal participation in democratic politics. It is the political elites who are responsible for and take care of us, who make it possible for us to privatize our lives and concern ourselves only with matters that directly affect us. And, of course, it is such privatization which keeps us out of power, and the political elites in.[18] While the politician handles local, national, and international political events, we can focus on what we are going to eat, whom we will take out, and what we will watch on TV in the evening. (And as we saw earlier, even in these areas we have relatively little say or choice.) Is there any reason to believe that politics should be divorced from other social processes in American society, that is, that the political nature of the society should differ markedly from industrial and social aspects?

It has been noted that the development of democratic institutions coincided with a small-town and farming type of economic structure where each individual owned his own piece of land, his own cow, and his own ideas.[19] He was "his own man." But in a society dominated by big business bureaucracies, not small farms and stores, where are the foundations for democracy, self-esteem and independent thinking? As Lane has shown, the rise of "democratic" societies appears to coincide with industrial development—but not overindustrialization. He argues that belief in the omnipotence of big government could be a substitute for the function religion traditionally had.[20] Maybe our representatives in government are our new "high priests." We *do* want to believe in something. There are few heroes left in political life; all that remains is a vast bureaucracy, inhabited by nameless faces and empty rhetoric. There is little moral investment by most Americans in political debate—all that seems to matter is that the sham of "democratic" government is somehow kept up. What emerges from such an analysis is that we no longer really care who wins, because we know that whoever wins, we are the losers.

Let Everyone Speak—or Only Those Who Have Already Spoken?

Attempts to make the American political system more democratic often run into problems. For one, the legitimacy of a pressure or interest group, as we have already observed, is often decided by those who are themselves legitimate—and jealously so. Wolff has aptly characterized pluralistic political practices in America as composed of legitimate groups who reside at the top of a plateau surrounded by steep cliffs, at the bottom of which dwell the outcasts or those striving to achieve legitimacy. The plateau is only accessible to certain groups, and it is up to those groups who are already on the plateau to decide which other groups it will admit.[21] Such a system prevents the free-play of competing groups and interests. This comes out most clearly in terms of government support and regulation:

> The government quite successfully referees the conflict among competing *powers*—any group which has already managed to accumulate a significant quantum of power will find its claims attended to by the federal agencies. But legitimate *interests* which have been ignored, suppressed, defeated, or which have not yet succeeded in organizing themselves for effective action, will find their disadvantageous position perpetuated through the decisions of the government. It is as though an umpire were to come upon a baseball game in progress between big boys and little boys, in which the big boys cheated, broke the rules, claimed hits that were outs, and made little boys accept the injustice by brute force. If the umpire undertakes to "regulate" the game by simply enforcing the "rules" actually being practiced, he does not thereby make the game a fair one. Indeed, he may actually make matters worse, because if the little boys get up their courage, band together, and decide to fight it out, the umpire will accuse them of breaking the rules and throw his weight against them! Precisely the same sort of thing happens in pluralist politics.[22]

Control of "legitimate" and "illegitimate" protest has recently taken another curious turn: the creation of secret files on suspect citizens. Our bureaucratic, technological society has begun to employ sophisticated means to abridge our freedom. It is now an open secret that "the arrival of computer technology in government file-keeping is pushing the country toward a mass surveillance system unprecedented in American history." [23]

How much freedom should there be for dissent and protest? Should all interest groups be tolerated no matter how obnoxious, uninformed, or stupid? Can there be intelligent debate between those who are informed and can reason, and those who are not, and cannot? [24] Of course, this begs the question: How is the definition arrived at of "well-informed," and, moreover who is to define it? Again, is there a legitimate form and content of reality within which debate must take place, or can other forms and contents also make a "legitimate" contribution? Does tolerance of all ideas and opinions result in a "neutralization of opposites," as when the victims of napalm are treated with the same intensity of feeling as a soap commercial? As Marcuse has observed:

> A democracy with totalitarian organization objectivity . . . may foster a mental attitude which tends to obliterate the difference between true and false, information and indoctrination, right and wrong. In fact, the

decision between opposed opinions has been made before the presentation and discussion get under way—made, not by a conspiracy or a
sponsor or a publisher, not by any dictatorship, but rather by the "normal
course of events," which is the course of administered events, and by the
mentality shaped in this course. Here, too, it is the whole which determines the truth. Then the decision asserts itself, without any open
violation of objectivity, in such things as the make-up of a newspaper
(with the breaking up of vital information into bits and interspersed
between extraneous material, irrelevant items, relegating of some radically
negative news to an obscure place), in the juxtaposition of gorgeous ads
with unmitigated horrors, in the introduction and interruption of the
broadcasting of facts by overwhelming commercials. . . .[25]

There is a sense in which tolerance of different ideas and opinions is
indistinguishable from the chronic indifference which characterizes
the political process in general: it is all tolerated as part of the larger
reality framework—it does not matter what is in the newspapers, just
so there is a newspaper with newsprint on it; it does not matter what
the politicians say, just so they say something once in a while, particularly around election time. In all of this there is a pervasive anti-
intellectualism, an acceptance of idealistic statements without question
so long as they are in accord with "freedom" and "democracy," while
at the same time divorcing such statements from political realities.

The Mass Media: Communication of What to Whom?

What is the function of the mass media in the American political
process? Does the press serve a power elite, and if so, how is this
done? Part of the "legitimate" reality about American society is supplied to us by the mass media. Newspapers, radio, television and
other forms of media serve the function of structuring and interpreting
events for their audience. How they portray a given event in large
part determines the importance that event assumes in the eyes of the
American populace. Being only on the receiving end of mass media
communications we can only accept what they say as true (unless we
are among the very small percentage who read other divergent sources
of news information). To doubt the word of the mass media or that
of the "high priests" is to question the legitimacy of our reality and
to reject the security which this reality provides. Television can greatly
alter the character of a particular news event and can lead to a false
interpretation of the particular character of that event. For example,
during the early fifties, a parade was held in Chicago commemorating
General MacArthur. The television cameras presented a picture of

overwhelming enthusiasm for the General by showing certain types of closeups and picking up on only certain types of audience response, while the overall support for the general as witnessed by those actually attending or witnessing the parade in person was quite different. As the Langs point out:

> MacArthur Day is but one case of the "landslide effect" that results as media coverage of events and public responses to that coverage reinforce each other. Television disseminated an image of public sentiment that was overwhelmingly in favor of the general and, by implication, his politics. This effect gathered force as it was incorporated into political strategy, picked up by other media, entered gossip, and thus over-shadowed reality as it was experienced by observers on the scene.[26]

The news media not only interpret actual events; they may also serve to make up events, or they go along with politicians who stage events in order to gain publicity or notoriety. Such events are called "psuedoevents" [27] because they gain attention by the news coverage provided of them, rather than because of the actual event itself. Douglass Cater, a Washington correspondent, has commented:

> Television misused constitutes not simply a negative but a positive threat to the conduct of orderly government. Fragmentary reporting in this medium, even more than in printed journalism, tends to stimulate the staging of synthetic dramas. The politician cynical enough to fake an exhibition of histrionics manages to steal the few seconds of the nightly TV news roundup from the politician who has contributed sense to the public dialogue.[28]

The news media are increasingly able to control what is reported because so few people have direct access to actual events. This means, in effect, that these media can come to serve a propaganda function.[29] The more publicity given to an event, the more important that event comes to seem. Most of us do not really care if the reality we are reading about "exists" or not, just as we are not really interested, for the most part, in political decisions or in politics in general. What is important is that there is some news, that there are facts, that there is some type of reality. Yet, facts do little good unless we can use them, and since there is little we can do with the facts we pick up, why should we bother? Better to turn to the sports page and comics. Several studies tend to support this conclusion, demonstrating that particularly in regard to foreign affairs news, few people are interested. As Cohen notes:

The volume of international news is a small proportion of total news space in most newspapers, and small in absolute terms as well. If little foreign affairs news is published even less is read, on the average (a most important qualification.) The extent of such readership is suggested in the American Institute of Public Opinion's readership survey of 51 news-papers, conducted for the International Press Institute: of the daily average of 106 column inches of international news from home and abroad that was published, the average number of column inches actually read by adult readers came to 12, or about half a column. It was further estimated that only two and one-third minutes were devoted to reading this ma-terial.[30]

Other studies have shown that less than one-third of the electorate is interested in politics, let alone reading about such politics in the news media.[31]

There also seems to be a bias toward reporting violence and crises. In the spring of 1970, when many of the nation's college campuses attempted to re-direct their activities against the war in Vietnam and Cambodia, the newspapers focused on those few persons who burned ROTC buildings or threw rocks, rather than on the tens of thousands who participated in community action programs designed to mobilize local citizens against the war. Similarly, war news discusses body-counts and battles, not the less sensational issues over which the war is being fought.

We like to remain comfortable; we want to trust the politicians and the news media. When both the opinions in the news media and what politicians say coincide, we feel good: to do otherwise is to invite insecurity.

Some critics of the news media take a different stance. They do not speak of objective reporting or voluntary censorship. Instead, they accept that all news reporting is by its very nature biased and acknowl-edge the need for journalists to take responsibility for their opinions. The difficulty is that, as David Deitch has pointed out in *The Nation:*

> The notion still prevails among reporters that they should strive to be as objective as possible. It has a nice, clean-cut ring to it, but nobody has been able to tell them how to approach that elusive goal, much less what it really means. Most reporters and newspapers fall back on the idea that the proper solution is a kind of "balance," a presentation of pro and con that lends itself to mathematical analysis: that is, always try to get the other side of the story, even for just a couple of lines.
>
> It is a puzzle why reporters continue to insist that objectivity, or balance, is the key to good journalistic life, but one explanation may be that it permits a kind of psychological anonymity. A reporter need not

Courtesy of Gyula Szabo

Courtesy of American International News Service

Courtesy of Gyula Szabo

is POW
your brother!
..WELL, HE IS!
POW/MIA, WASHINGTON DC
v's
tive in S.E. Asia

reveal what sort of person he is, uncover his biases. More important, by clinging to the myth that he is indeed being as objective as humanly possible, he can evade personal responsibility for his work; he is only a technician of the news. Advocacy, on the other hand, openly admitted, requires an exposure of self, a willingness to undergo scrutiny, and a commitment to excellence that seems very demanding.[32].

Thus the mass media manage the news either by conscious editorial choice or by uncritically printing lies. Media define for the public what are and what are not the salient and important issues of the day.

As we are relatively powerless to confront large scale mass society politics, so too we are isolated by the mass media. There is little we can do about our situation—we cannot talk back to Associated Press reporters, for the news industry is big business, and, like any propaganda machine, no matter how subtle, it has reinforced itself with an elaborate technology. The spread of information costs money; most financial backing accrues to those representing "safe" investments— establishment news and advertising. Most news media are extremely reluctant to offend those taking out full-page ads or thirty minutes of television time to sell their products, and indirectly or incidentally pay for the evening's news. This is how the news media come to support the status quo, and the power elite. It is true that there are brief flurries of controversy here and there, but more often these degenerate into sensationalism and are soon absorbed into the thousands of other facts, pseudo-facts, and events reported daily to the selectively perceiving individual who tunes most of it out regardless of what the message is. Is this participatory democracy at work?

The New Left: Ideologically "In," Tactically "Out"

Outside of this political framework resides the "New Left." In this section, I do not propose to examine in depth the political tactics of the New Left or detail New Left activities on the campus. What I shall attempt to show is why the New Left has been unable to join other interest groups in "legitimate" political processes. In essence, the New Left poses a threat, for it attempts to practice what America preaches, and in so doing exposes the reality behind the clichés of "freedom" and "democracy." The New Left also challenges the traditional economic base of political power, for it has not relied on large financial contributions to support its position; rather it appeals to idealism for political sustenance. This has been one of its problems.

To the New Left the present political system is oppressive because it denies them adequate opportunity for representing their views as well as those of many other "minority" groups in the halls of Congress and in the executive and judicial branches of the government. Growing out of the civil rights movement in the late fifties and early sixties, the movement has focused its attention on community organizing, poverty programs and a concerted general attack on the war in Vietnam. Why do some youth feel American political conditions oppressive and attempt to do something about them, while others are seemingly content to accept injustice? What makes youth "radical"? Kenniston, in a study of youth working in Vietnam Summer in 1967, found several factors which seemed to contribute to participation in the movement: high academic performance, liberal parents, Judaism, association with Unitarians or Quakers, permissive, anti-authoritarian, child-rearing practices, and the desire to implement values inculcated, but not necessarily practiced, by their parents.[33] Though these factors may predispose youth to political activism, there are other factors whose presence is required if there is to be engagement in action. Among these are the type of situation (school) a youth finds himself in; the chance to meet and interact with those who feel much the same way he does; the types of issues which arise—whether or not he is "in the right place at the right time" (for example, Berkeley or Brookings, South Dakota); and the general political and cultural climate of American society—its apparent repressiveness or receptiveness to change.[34]

Once the movement began, many factors contributed to its growth. Perhaps the most important of these was the Vietnam war, with its concomitant domestic issues, most notably, the draft.[35] In general, the New Left has found itself dependent on factors outside of its control for political success because its growth has been in reaction to events. Often the reaction of the authorities makes any specific demonstration a success, not the actions of any New Left leaders themselves. A most dramatic example was the demonstration at the Democratic Convention in Chicago during the summer of 1968.[36]

In order to understand the New Left, many persons have contrasted it with the Old Left of the 1930s. The most outstanding comparison which can be made on this basis is that social conditions have contributed to essentially two different kinds of movements. For example, whereas the poverty which the depression wrought in the thirties made communist ideology and Marxian interpretations of history appealing, the affluence of America during the sixties has contributed to a sense of boredom and meaninglessness and a turn toward general humanistic ideals—justice, brotherhood, love, and peace. The means of the Old Left movements (discipline, party organization, and authority) could be adhered to, for the ends (planned economies, higher employment rates, and wages) justified whatever sacrifices were necessary. New Left advocates, on the other hand, rebel against bureaucracies, organization, discipline, and parental hypocrisy—if not control over them, and hence find their main attraction in a free-wheeling, "do your own thing" type of movement in which means and ends fuse. If the war cannot be ended tomorrow, then a community is established among those who are trying to end it. The ends —love, equality, justice—find themselves theoretically operationalized in this community. The Old Left used a rigid ideological frame of reference in order to justify its actions; the New Left finds its ideology in loose clichés which reflect a disenchantment with political programs and ideologies and a scepticism towards those who would attempt to implement them.

While the New Left is composed of a loose coalition of groups, there is a general split between those who follow given ideologies (the Progressive Labor Party, Weathermen) and those who do not (Yippies and the general cadre of demonstrators who turn out once every couple of months to picket, sit-in or march for civil rights and peace). The Old Left found justification and freedom to act within its political ideology; the New Left finds its freedom in the emptiness and hypocrisy of a system that no longer matters. In fact, in this sense the fewer the successes of the movement, the *freer* it is to create its own society, for it loosens its dependence on the actions and reactions of others outside the movement. Such an attitude leaves one hoping for a moral victory. Success would destroy the revolution, for it would demand bureaucracies, party organization, discipline and a program, the very things which many of the members of the New Left find anathema.[37] In this same vein, those groups on the Left who have tied themselves to party organization and strict ideological adherence have often found their tactics inapplicable to specific situations either because the people they were trying to influence were not "politically sophisticated," or because these people opted not to get involved in another political party, or because the ideology and tactics which followed from it resulted from faulty analysis. The end result of this has been that those groups on the Left who have sought political solvency on the basis of Old Left ideologies have found few followers.[38]

Members of the New Left want romanticism in a system gone sour, to die for ideals in a society whose ideology is characterized by television commercials and an indifferent populace. Until recently, many activists could find solace for the lack of meaning of their situation by going South and registering black voters, not an unworthy cause.

By eliminating Southern white oppression against blacks, they could work to free all peoples, a chance to put into practice an idealism seemingly not applicable to their own communities. In a remake of the frustration–aggression hypothesis, they perhaps inadvertently became party to a syndrome which might be labeled frustration–charity. The frustrations of living with an affluent middle-class white society without meaningful goals forced many youth to go to the blacks in order to find the meaningful goals their own community lacked. They wanted to find their white "soul" by giving aid and assistance to ghetto communities or southern rural poor. But when they returned from the South or from the ghettos, the problems germane to their own community remained—empty relationships, empty jobs, empty leisure, consumption and an educational system which appeared to reinforce the status quo. Solutions to these problems are more qualitative than quantitative—it's so much easier to get someone a job than to worry about the quality of that job; it's so much easier to register voters than to change the power structure of which you find yourself unwittingly a part; it's so much easier to picket than to canvass door-to-door among one's *own* neighbors in an attempt to convince them that their opinions are unsound.

The Weathermen, an offshoot of SDS (Students for a Democratic Society) have come to see their role as supporting a black vanguard which will end American imperialism. This ideology makes white radicals into elitists who deny problems germane to their own community in exchange for a new kind of "civil rightism." And blacks who reject this kind of "support" come to be called "revisionists." [39]

In essence, the New Left is outside the reality framework because it has not, until the recent McGovern Presidential campaign, made use of traditional tactics. The attitudes it manifests often challenge the ideological base and rationalizations which most members of mainstream America use to justify their existence. Members of the New Left often have beards or long hair, do not wear ties or suits, and, in general, cultivate an appearance which visibly distinguishes them from the "straight" society whose values they reject. Many in American society judge individuals on the basis of their appearance, taking little time to get to know them (in fact, not really wanting to know them since this would entail perhaps revealing certain repressed aspects of themselves). It is so much easier to stereotype. In its anti-organizational stance, the New Left finds itself in direct opposition to the organized life-style of many Americans.

Primarily, it is the moral stance of the New Left that poses its greatest threat to the American Way of Life. In a society in which most persons are politically amoral and indifferent, thinking its political leadership is adequately handling problems, the publicized realization that this is not the case can be a shattering blow, one to be avoided at all costs. The New Left, through attempting to practice the ideological tenets of the "founding fathers," challenges the omnipotence of the current high priests in power, and in so doing calls into question their religion (as well as religious tolerance). For the layman, such a challenge can only breed anxiety, either forcing him to retreat even further from political reality and responsibility, or to take a new interest in the political situation. In the latter case this new interest often means attempts to put down the insurgents, rather than coping with the questions raised by the New Left.

The New Left, at this writing, suffers from a crisis in leadership; it appears that the times themselves have bred the movement, that it does not need new leadership to stir it on to battle. For example, it has been said that the more conservative members of the movement made Gene McCarthy a candidate for the Democratic nomination for president in 1968; McCarthy did not make the movement. While the New Left draws its power from and basically represents an appeal to people *qua* people, the power elite appeals to entrenched institutions, an outmoded ideology, and the traditional system. As Paul Goodman observed, the struggle is between "people and personnel."

NOTES

[1] Robert Dahl, *Who Governs?* (New Haven: Yale University Press, 1961).

[2] C. Wright Mills, *The Power Elite* (New York: Oxford University Press, 1959).

[3] G. William Domhoff, *Who Rules America?* (Englewood Cliffs, N.J.: Spectrum, 1967).

[4] David Riesman, "Who Has the Power," in Reinhard Bendix and Seymour Martin Lipset, *Class, Status, and Power* (New York: The Free Press, 1964), pp. 154–162; and Edward C. Banfield, *Political Influence* (New York: The Free Press, 1961).

[5] For a discussion of this see: William Korhauser, "Power Elite or Veto Groups," in Peter I. Rose, *The Study of Society* (New York: Random House, Inc., 1967).

[6] Robert Paul Wolff, Barrington Moore, and Herbert Marcuse, *A Critique of Pure Tolerance* (Boston: Beacon Press, 1969), p. 52.

[7] Joe McGinnis, *The Selling of the Presidency* (New York: Trident Press, 1969).

[8] This is a quotation from Douglass Cater, as cited in Domhoff, pp. 84–85.

[9] For a discussion of the Chicago Convention see Norman Mailer, *Miami and the Siege of Chicago* (New York: Signet, 1968).

[10] Mark Levine et al., *The Tales of Hoffman* (New York: Bantam, 1970).

[11] Seymour Martin Lipset, *Political Man* (Garden City: Doubleday & Company, Inc., 1960), p. 189.

[12] Robert E. Lane, *Political Ideology* (New York: The Free Press, 1962), p. 353; Lipset, *op. cit.*, p. 191.

[13] Robert Lane, *Political Life* (New York: The Free Press, 1965), p. 47. Among the decisions which voting involves are the following according to Lane: "In the first place, voting should be understood as an *act* involving an expenditure of energy and time, the coordination of muscles and mind, scheduling the event among other events.. . . . Second, voting requires a *decision;* perhaps a decision on a very low level of decisiveness, but nevertheless a positive commitment to one side or the other (with ticket splitters committing themselves more to individuals than parties). Third, the voting decision implies a certain reading of the newspaper, an awareness of surroundings, a listening to radio and reading of the newspaper, an awareness that *this implementation of an emotion.* The emotion may be fear of nonconformity, a partisan loyalty to a symbol or group, a dedication to a program, but whatever it is, the act of voting goes beyond the stage of merely experienced feeling. The person who cannot do this remains to 'stew in his own juice.' Finally, the voting act is an *affirmation,* an interpretation that democracy is not a sham; the votes are counted; they do make a difference."

[14] Lane, *Political Life,* pp. 163, 168.

[15] Lane, *Political Ideology,* p. 231.

[16] *Ibid.,* pp. 398, 472.

[17] *Ibid.,* pp. 308–309.

[18] *Ibid.,* p. 75.

[19] *Ibid.,* pp. 246–247.

[20] *Ibid.,* p. 195.

[21] Wolff, Moore, and Marcuse, *op. cit.,* p. 45.

[22] *Ibid.,* pp. 47–48.

[23] "Secret Files on Suspect Citizens," *SF Chronicle,* July 1, 1970, pp. 24–25.

[24] Wolff, Moore, and Marcuse, *op. cit.,* pp. 94–95.

[25] *Ibid.,* pp. 97–98.

[26] Kurt Lang and Gladys Engel Lang, *Politics and Television* (Chicago: Quadrangle Books, 1968), p. 75.

[27] Daniel Boorstin, *The Image* (New York: Harper & Row, Publishers, 1961).

[28] Douglass Cater, *The Fourth Branch of Government* (New York: Random House, Inc., 1965), p. 106.

[29] Walter Lippmann, *Public Opinion* (New York: The Free Press, 1965), p. 29.

[30] Bernard C. Cohen, "The Press, the Public and Foreign Policy," in Bernard Berelson and Morris Janowitz, *Reader in Public Opinion and Communication* (New York: The Free Press, 1966), p. 135.

[31] Bernard Berelson, "Democratic Theory and Public Opinion," in Berelson and Janowitz, *op. cit.,* p. 492.

[32] David Deitch, "The Case for Advocacy Journalism," *The Nation,* November 17, 1969, p. 531.

[33] Kenneth Kenniston, "The Sources of Student Dissent," in James McEvoy and Abraham Miller, *Black Power and Student Rebellion* (Belmont: Wadsworth, 1969), pp. 318–320. For discussions of the New Left, see Kenneth Kenniston, *Young Radicals* (New York: Harcourt, Brace & World, Inc., 1968); Paul Jacobs and Saul Landau, *The Young Radicals* (Boston: Beacon Press, 1966); Seymour Martin Lipset and Sheldon S. Wolin, *The Berkeley Student Revolt* (Garden City: Doubleday, 1965); "Radicals Re-Visited," in *Change,* November–December, 1969; Richard Flacks, "Revolt of the Young Intelligentsia: Revolutionary Class-Consciousness in Post-Scarcity America," in Roelerick Aya and Norman Miller, *The New American Revolution* (New York: The Free Press, 1971).

[34] *Ibid.,* pp. 320–322.

[35] Jerome H. Skolnick, *The Politics of Protest* (New York: Ballantine Books, Inc., 1969), pp. 35–57.

[36] *Ibid.,* p. 33.

[37] For a discussion of this attitude, particularly among the Yippies, see Free, *Revolution for the Hell of It* (New York: The Dial Press, 1968). See also, Norman Mailer, *Armies of the Night* (New York: Signet, 1968); Abbie Hoffman, *Steal This Book* (New York: Pirate Editions, 1971).

[38] For a comprehensive discussion of a group's adherence to and resulting failure in attempting to apply a given New Left ideology, see Harold Jacobs, *Weatherman* (San Francisco: Ramparts Press, 1970).

[39] Michael P. Lerner, "Weatherman: The Politics of Despair," in Jacobs, *ibid.,* p. 402.

5

outside the image: poverty and discrimination

Amid much pomp and splendor, the United States launched a rocket to make the first manned landing of the moon, a project representing a 24 billion dollar expenditure. On the day of the landing, television broadcast live for over thirty hours, constantly replaying both the spectacle and interviews of people in the streets as to their thoughts on that historic occasion. A leading newscaster shed tears at the historic moment remarking, "I wonder what those youth think of us now?" He was referring to those who had criticized the moon landing as a misplaced adventure, a national ego trip to divert public attention while cities fell apart and millions went hungry within the United States.

The moon landing and the exploration of space in general, though in themselves remarkable technological achievements, are a clear demonstration of the difference in realities between those who inhabit the mainstream of economic and political life and those who do not. Did the rural black family living in the Mississippi Delta shed the same tears on that historic occasion? It is part of the irony of contemporary American life that the poor also gloried in the moon adventure; at least it served to take their minds off the daily problem of physical survival. Indeed, the day was considered of such importance that President Nixon made it into a day of national "participation" by ordering the closing of schools and the cancelling of some public employment. It is rare in the annals of American history that television viewing has been "required."

To the ghetto dweller and the black Mississippi tenant farmer, the question might have arisen as to why there had not been other such days of televised national participation, for example, of rat infested tenement houses, of migrant farm worker labor camps without any sanitary facilities, of children going hungry because their parents could not afford to buy food stamps, of men sitting on street corners day in and day out, not out of choice, but because there was nothing else for them to do. Were not these aspects of American life important too? Did they not make interesting and exciting viewing, enough for the President to interrupt his normally busy day to congratulate these members of society on their contribution?

The significance of this is not that 24 billion dollars was spent on the space race, but that the federal government did not have enough money left over to fund adequate anti-poverty programs. This is an apt illustration of the application of the "double standard." Poverty is not visible to most Americans: Only when riots tear apart the fabric of our cities do we sit up and take notice. "What happened?" we say to ourselves, hurriedly changing channels on the television set to a family soap opera, pretending to ourselves that the riots didn't occur, and hoping the National Guard will quickly restore order. Despite the publicity given to anti-poverty programs and the rebuilding of cities, landing men on the moon has exposed a contradiction in our society: It seems that America is more concerned with technological achievement than she is with ensuring the welfare of her people.

Poverty and Discrimination Related:
The Problem in Perspective

There are between 35 and 40 million members of American society who, on the basis of one criterion or another, have been judged to be poor.[1] This does not mean that all of these will die of starvation tomorrow; it does mean they suffer economic inequities which do not permit them to enjoy "the American way of life." They are not free to partake of the consumer and leisure goods discussed in Chapter 2, to worry about the meaning of work in the terms which were discussed in Chapter 1, or to concern themselves with the quality of interpersonal relationships in the ways which we discussed in Chapter 3. These poor people constitute what has come to be recognized as the "Other America." This "Other America" does not exist in a vacuum. To say there is an "other" America presumes that there must be an America encompassing it, and that there is a relationship between the two entities, some reciprocity of rights and obligations.[2] Moreover, what qualifies one for the category of "other American"? Does this word or definitions refer to all those earning less than, say, $4,200 a year? And given this cutoff point, can all those falling below it be classified and treated the same way, and under the same programs? Is there a difference between the aged, the handicapped, those who are black or brown or white, those in rural and those in urban areas who fall under our definition of "poor"? If so, what is the difference, and how does it reflect and influence our response? [3]

Obviously, to be one of the "poor" is to be placed in a negative or marginally acceptable category. Work is held in high esteem in our society; someone who does not work is considered to be unworthy of the goods, services, and success that result from such employment. If we do not work, we are not considered, in society's terms, to be full citizens. It matters very little whether we do not work because the job we could work at is tedious and dull, because we are black and no one will hire us, or because we are physically handicapped. The individual who does not work cannot enjoy the rewards of such labor or buy the goods he sees others enjoying. He is told, in effect, "Since you do not work you do not have any money, and since you do not have any money, you cannot live according to the life style you are *supposed* to live by: You are not an American."

If being poor is an offense against society, so, too, is being born black. That being nonwhite can have an effect on whether or not we will be born into and remain in poverty is revealed by the following statistics from the Kerner Commission report on civil disorders:

. . . 30.7 percent of nonwhite families of two or more persons lived in poverty compared to only 8.8 percent of whites. Of the 10.1 million poor persons in central cities in 1964, about 4.4 million of these (43.6 percent) were nonwhites, and 5.7 million (56.4 percent) were whites. The poor whites were much older on the average than the poor nonwhites. The proportion of poor persons 65 years old or older was 23.2 percent among whites, but only 6.8 percent among nonwhites. Poverty was more than twice as prevalent among nonwhite families with female heads than among those with male heads, 57 percent compared to 21 percent. In central cities, 26 percent of all nonwhite families of two or more persons had female heads, as compared to 12 percent of white families.

Among nonwhite families headed by a female and having children under 6, the incidence of poverty was 81.0 percent. Moreover, there was 243,000 such families living in poverty in central cities—or over 9 percent of all nonwhite families in those cities. Among all children living in poverty within central cities, nonwhites outnumbered whites by over 400,000. The number of poor nonwhite children equalled or surpassed the number of white poor children at every age group. 54 percent of all poor children in central cities in 1964 were nonwhites. . . .[4]

Despite such facts and the thousands of other such facts which continue to be disseminated by social scientists and government agencies, discrimination and poverty continue. Why?

Poverty and racial discrimination are related in more ways than the statistics cited above might lead us to believe. Both groups, the poor and the nonwhite, are constantly bombarded by the advertisements and slogans of middle-class white society and culture. They are exhorted to buy commodities they cannot afford and perhaps do not even want. Such inducements give way to rising expectations and temptations, often pushing poor families into chronic debt or theft in order to realize the expectations of being "American." Both groups stand outside the cultural and social framework, in a different reality, staring in through the window of television advertisements and textbooks: they are told that they may look, but may not touch. At the same time, the poor often aspire toward aspects of middle-class white culture that middle-class whites feel they should not have (for example, political power), yet are without the means of achieving such aspirations (except *through* political power).[5]

There are different types of poverty in American society. One distinction can be made between "case" and "insular" poverty, the former referring to the handicapped, and the latter to poverty areas in which everyone in a given section of the country (for example, Appalachia) is destined to be poor by virtue of the economic characteristics of that area.[6] The former are given aid on an individual basis, the latter in terms of community help. Another distinction has been made between the "new" and the "old" poor, or those who became poor because of the effects of automation, and those who experienced dire circumstances during and due to the Depression. The old poor differ from the new in that their condition was viewed as temporary in nature, they could afford a sense of optimism, and it was this optimism which the unions were able to capitalize on in creating more viable economic circumstances for the economically disenfranchised. The new poor have little hope; their poverty is ongoing. Forced out of jobs they have occupied for decades, these men are in many cases untrainable. Because of a history of being unable to find suitable (if any) employment, many lack the motivation to "pull themselves up by their bootstraps." For those who have grown up in insular poverty areas, there is no history of being punctual, of daily employment, or of responsibility to the company—when enough money is earned they quit or temporarily retire.[7] The owners of such companies come to feel that these men are lazy, good for nothing, and are reluctant to hire them. This clash in values represents only one of many between the two "cultures." In areas of insular poverty, those who do have hope or have the skills to get "ahead" leave the community—those who remain are hard to organize and to employ in any worthwhile occupation. It is those who remain behind who have lost hope of ever improving their situation. Also, while the old poor worked in factories where they formed a type of community, the new poor (for example, housekeepers and janitors) are either unemployed or lack a common base from which to unionize. The labor force is becoming a more white-collar one, but the skills that the chronically unemployed are being trained to perform through government programs are blue-collar jobs for which there is less demand. Ironically, it was these very jobs which provided the old poor a means of escape from poverty.[8]

If the old poor can be differentiated from the new, so too can the poor black be differentiated from his white counterpart. Whereas the poor white may be the offspring of immigrant parents who trace their ancestry to Europe, the poor black lacks any "ancestry." Stripped of his identity, first on the slave ship and then on the plantation, he had or has no viable or "accepted" culture on which to fall back.[9] Furthermore, blacks did not free themselves, and gained little power from the emancipation proclamation.[10] The son of a European immigrant could mingle with other whites if he wished, gradually extricating himself from an unwanted identity. The black could neither erase his color nor change how that color was treated by the "majority" white society. When most immigrants came over there were many unskilled jobs, albeit often in sweat shops. Today, for those whites on poverty lists and for blacks of rural descent who have migrated to urban areas, few jobs are open, and the trend is downhill rather than up. Finally, the black family was not best suited to educate its children in the values of "white" America. In the conditions within which black youth grew up, it was difficult for them to acquire an education and even if they did somehow manage to acquire skills, worthwhile opportunities which would have allowed them to practice those skills were few.[11] In the face of these differences, the black poor have a double strike against them, one that makes their situation all the more desperate.

There are yet other factors that serve to maintain racial discrim-

ination. Many whites discriminate against blacks for more than fear
that blacks will take away their jobs or cause a decline in property
values when they move into white neighborhoods. Whites use blacks
as scapegoats for frustrations engendered by adherence to an unsatisfactory white ideology. White men have fears concerning the supposedly superior sexual prowess of black men. Many whites feel
intimidated by the "black mystique." Black people are highly visible
and as such openly challenge the reality framework of middle-class
white America. They challenge, particularly, the contradictions inherent
in the Constitution and they show up the shamefully inadequate implementation of those pledges. There may be many more subtle causes
of discrimination than economic insecurity alone, and they should be
kept in mind when evaluating the problem of American society and
its inability to treat people as people.

Poverty is a problem for American society because the poor do
not like being poor and because middle-class white society often
feels threatened by actions on the part of the poor and nonwhite to
achieve those material and social rewards which they feel are right-
fully theirs as members of American society. The poor question the
validity of the middle-class white reality framework. Among the poor
there exist many different cultures, and, in fact, many variations *within
each of these cultures* (which we have grouped below, only to say that
they differ, in large part, from middle-class white society).[12] What is
it like to live on the "outside"?

Employment: Jobs Nobody Else Wants or No Jobs at All

Poverty is usually not temporary; if you are born poor, the chances
are you will stay poor. What helps to keep you "in your place" is the
difficulty of finding a job that offers worthwhile economic and social
rewards. The first problem you face is that you lack training, have no
skill to offer, and have little chance of getting such training or skill.
The existing job-training programs are able to handle only a small
percentage of those eligible for training; neither enough staff nor
money is allocated by federal or local governments. For example, in
New Haven, Connecticut, in 1967, there were only enough funds to
deal with 20 percent of the unemployed.[13] But what good is job training
if no jobs exist when the training is finished?[14] For the most part,
training programs educate the unemployed for blue-collar work in
private industry, the very jobs which are being phased out by automated plants. There are jobs to be had in the public sector, but such
jobs are mostly white-collar, or those that require technical and social

skills demanding the most education and "reculturation" of those residing in poverty cultures.[15]

If you do not get into a training program, what are your chances
of finding work from the state employment agency? How do those
who work at the agency see you? Regardless of the cause of your
unemployment, you are not considered a worthwhile and healthy
individual, because you do not have a job and because you have not
been able to find one yourself. The doctrine of self-help, of individual
initiative, and other such middle-class ideas are rooted in the hearts
and minds of those emissaries who are sent out into the poverty belts.
These messengers are neither tolerant nor neutral; they represent the
mainstream point of view, and this directly affects their perception of
the unemployment problem. Even if they have empathy for the jobless,
there is simply little they can do, given the jobs that are available and
the state of the American economy. The available jobs are temporary
and menial: maintenance men, janitors, dishwashers, or other such
occupations that require no skill, pay little money, and offer no incentive. Those jobs that do require skills are controlled by the unions
which often discriminate against the very persons (poor blacks) who
most need work.[16] The results are revealed in the following table which
contrasts income and type of employment between white and nonwhite employees.[17]

Type of Occupation	Percentage of Male Workers in Each Type of Occupation—1966		Median Earnings of All Male Civilians in Each Occupation—1965
	White	Nonwhite	
Professional, Technical, Managerial	27%	9%	$7,603
Clerical and Sales	14	9	5,532
Craftsmen and Foremen	20	12	6,270
Operatives	20	27	5,046
Service Workers	6	16	3,436
Non-Farm Laborers	6	20	2,410
Farmers and Farm Workers	7	8	1,699

Once inside the employment agency, other problems emerge. Being
for the most part understaffed, these agencies can spend very little
time with each applicant. They must adopt an attitude of "take it or

leave it," in terms of the jobs offered. Working in a system which rewards quantity (how many men a given agency placed) rather than quality (what type of employment was obtained for a given applicant), they keep unskilled and manual workers "in their place." It is much easier to find employment in temporary or unskilled work than to sit with an applicant for long hours going over jobs which may offer advancement and more permanency. Similarly, it is often easier to find employment for a woman, particularly a black or a brown woman, as a domestic, rather than for her spouse (in almost any capacity). This, of course, has a profound effect on the poor family, wherein often the husband must sit home with the children while the wife becomes the breadwinner. Often, the husband refuses to accept this status and leaves, relinquishing all responsibility for children and family problems to the mother, who must then assume the burden of working and taking care of her children.

It is hard to organize those found in temporary occupations, domestics, and manual or farm laborers, who are willing to accept whatever they can get. Such occupations do not have large central work areas where a significant number of workers may be reached, nor do they have the money to contribute to a union strike fund. Employers find it easy to fire "troublemakers" and hire other destitute persons who are just "begging" for a few dollars. Organizing such "industries" as those mentioned above has not appealed to existing unions who perhaps see little "glory" from such activities or have little interest in the jobs the poor work at.

Lacking suitable employment, the poor thus find it difficult to deal with their circumstances. If we were in charge of an employment agency, or owned a large factory which could employ those now classified as the hard-core unemployed, what would we do? How would we cope with this situation? If we were unemployed, lacked education and job skills, how would we find work? Would we feel that the type of work available was gratifying and worthwhile? If not, then why would we continue working, why would we show up to work on time? Why not simply earn a few dollars and then stop working, until we needed a few more? The employment factor, however, is only one of a constellation of factors which influence each other and create poverty cultures.[18]

Welfare: "Parasites" in the Land of Plenty

If you cannot find a job, then you must derive your income from some other source, such as welfare. One "statistical" aspect of your life which may disqualify you is being a single male member of society of working age who is employable. You may also be disqualified if you are the male head of a household, even if you are not working. In this case, your wife and children may be unable to receive any financial assistance until you move out.

The remote chance of a man's being able to gain meaningful employment thus makes his plight a particularly difficult one, as well as making unemployment the key to marital instability and destitution. If you do not work, you had better not live with your family or you will all suffer, at least according to the welfare program.[19] This law is reportedly being altered, but nonetheless it is indicative of the attitude taken toward "the poor."

Welfare is supposed to enable a family to physically survive, a goal which frequently becomes impossible when such a family cannot even afford the money necessary to buy food stamps. Furthermore, it costs more to live in a ghetto, where families often have to buy on credit and from smaller stores which charge higher prices.[20] Welfare payments are usually fixed, not according to existing prices and standards of living in a given area, but arbitrarily or on a national basis. Moreover, as the standard of living (or rather, the cost of living) goes up (5 percent per year), welfare does not go up at a corresponding rate. People on fixed incomes suffer most from inflation. Increases in welfare payments, if they are not dissipated by inflation, are often absorbed by other agencies—for example, increasing the rent paid to the public housing authority.[21] Such practices do little to raise incentive, or increase one's standard of living. If you are able to achieve some minimal type of employment, your welfare check may also be less. Thus your income may not ever really improve, though you are ostensibly more "self sufficient" or self-supporting. It is not difficult to see from the list of jobs available to the poor why they cannot "pull themselves up by their bootstraps."

What is far more important to the poor is the demoralizing relationship between the poor and the welfare agency. Recipients can and do have many aspects of their lives regulated through the welfare program: who you can live with and how your money will be spent, to give but two examples. Such regulations are particularly annoying when persons from the welfare department can come to your door at all hours of the day or night, peek through windows to see if you have a man in the house, or discover whether you have purchased some "outrageous" luxury items, ones which may be part of the "standard package" for most middle-class whites.[22] In becoming a "ward of the state," you run the risk of losing all privacy. Welfare agencies, in making these stringent regulations, assume that the poor are not capable of managing their own lives, that they will lie in vouching for how they spend their money or who is living with them (for example, how many children they have). This is particularly revealing when we assume that middle-class whites tell the truth when reporting their income for taxes (or, if they do not, are entitled to anything they can get), yet, at the same time, those who desperately need relief funds will supposedly take the chance of lying in order to get them.[23] Furthermore, the welfare program brings its own distinct value judgments to bear in considering what types of relationships are meaningful or "moral." In making common-law marriages "illegitimate," welfare agencies often end up discriminating against children. Similarly, agencies would like to limit the number of children a poor family brings into this world because those families which are largest often receive the largest welfare payment.[24] Few welfare agencies provide birth control information they are funded to provide.

Welfare agencies subsist within the same network of problems as do public employment agencies. They are understaffed, there is excessive paperwork, caseloads are too high, their employees are underpaid and lack suitable training to enable them to cope with the complex problems existing in ghettos and other poverty belts.[25] Under such conditions, case workers must do the best they can, often to the detriment of those whom they would serve. Furthermore, many of those eligible for welfare are not even served due to agency problems or misguided legislation.

Your welfare check then, for you and your children, is not a ticket out of the ghetto, for it hardly enables you to survive where you are. There is little sense in getting a minimal job (the only kind available), for your salary will be deducted from your welfare payments. So you sit and wait for each month's check, fighting off prying caseworkers, attempting to show them, though it is most often quite obvious, that you are poor, that you need their assistance, that you too are a member of American society and deserve some of its fruits. To the welfare department and much of middle-class white society, you are a parasite, but in your own mind, you cannot understand how to get out of where you are. Eventually, you too may come to take on the role assigned to you, to view yourself as they do, as a pathetic, dependent figure, pushed and pulled, this way and that, with no control over your own existence, with the message imprinted on your brain: Just stay out of the way, for we have more important things to do, and more important things to spend our money on. We'll leave you alone, if you leave us alone.

Do the poor have a right to survive? Or, must they live under the constant threat of annihilation? If they do not have such a right, why not?

A House Is Not Always a Home

So you find you cannot get a job, that you must rely on welfare payments. Such a situation also means you cannot afford adequate housing, but must take whatever is available, just as, if you want to work, you must take whatever job is available. If you recently arrived from a rural area there is a good chance you will find your way into the poverty belt or black ghetto, depending upon what color your skin is, because that is the only place you will find housing you can afford. Moreover, the ghettos, particularly for poor blacks, expand to occupy more space as the white middle class flees to tree-lined suburbs.

Almost all Negro population growth is occurring within metropolitan areas, primarily within central cities. Frm 1950 to 1966, the U.S. Negro population rose 6.5 million. Over 98 percent of that increase took place in metropolitan areas—86 percent within central cities, 12 percent in the urban fringe.

The vast majority of white population growth is occurring in suburban portions of metropolitan areas. From 1950 to 1966, 77.8 percent of the white population increase of 35.6 million took place in the suburbs. Central cities received only 2.5 percent of this total white increase. Since 1960, white central city population has actually declined by 1.3 million.

As a result, central cities are steadily becoming more heavily Negro, while the urban fringes around them remain almost entirely white. The proportion of Negroes in all central cities rose steadily from 12 percent in 1950, to 17 percent in 1960, to 20 percent in 1966. Meanwhile, metropolitan areas outside of central cities remained 95 percent white from 1950 to 1960, and became 96 percent white by 1966.

The Negro population is growing faster, both absolutely and relatively, in the larger metropolitan areas than in the smaller ones. From 1950 to 1966, the proportion of nonwhites in the central cities of metropolitan areas with one million or more persons doubled, reaching 26 percent, as compared with 20 percent in the central cities of metropolitan areas containing from 250,000 to one million persons, and 12 percent in the central cities of metropolitan areas containing under 250,000 persons.

The 12 largest central cities (New York, Chicago, Los Angeles, Philadelphia, Detroit, Baltimore, Houston, Cleveland, Washington, D.C., St. Louis, Milwaukee, and San Francisco) now contain over two-thirds of the Negro population outside the South, and one-third of the Negro total in the United States. All these cities have experienced rapid increases in

Negro population since 1950. In six (Chicago, Detroit, Cleveland, St. Louis, Milwaukee, and San Francisco), the proportion of Negroes at least doubled. In 1968, seven of these cities are over 30 percent Negro, and one (Washington, D.C.) is two-thirds Negro.[26]

Many more people per square mile live in ghettos than in the surrounding suburbs. The Watts area of Los Angeles, scene of the 1965 riot, had (for example) ten times the number of persons per square mile than did the surrounding Los Angeles metropolitan community.[27]

Not only are the ghettos crowded, but housing which does exist is often substandard, dilapidated, and owned by persons who either cannot afford to keep these houses up or by absentee landlords who care very little what the house looks like (or whether the plumbing works) so long as they get their monthly rent check. If you want to escape from these conditions, presuming you have the financial resources to do so—*and you are black*—there are very few places you can go. In many states, "open housing" exists more in word than in deed. Thus, the prospective black buyer often finds himself unable to move from the ghetto because no one in the surrounding suburbs will rent or sell to him.[28] Moreover, if you have lived off credit for a number of years, or even if you have not, there is little likelihood that banks would consider you a "good risk," a factor severely limiting your residential purchase opportunities.

Faced with this housing situation, the only way into "improved" housing is through public housing projects. Those who do move into these projects are often stigmatized in the same way as welfare recipients. Public housing merely means a shift in landlords, not a chance to own your own home. The fact that the government is the new landlord does not necessarily mean you will be treated any better than you were by "private" citizens you formerly rented from. Rather, the impositions are different. Whereas "private" landlords expected little of you, and did little for you in return, letting their property run down, government housing authorities impose minute restrictions and regulations on your every activity involved with the "home." Paul Jacobs comments:

> The "rules and regulations" which the Housing Authority attempts to use to control the tenants encompass nearly every detail of daily life. Tenants who do not put trash cans out alongside the house are charged for having it done by the maintenance crews; tenants who don't clean up their own yards are charged for having that done. If a maintenance man decides a lawn needs watering and turns on the hose, the tenant is charged for that; if a stove is broken and it is the property of the Authority, the tenant

is charged for the repairs. The tenants may put only those screen doors on the apartments which are supplied and installed by the Authority, and they must pay for both the door and installation at the usual commercial rates. . . . "The kids can't climb the trees and they can't play on the grass in front of the house," bitterly complains a mother. . . . "In the project no one is allowed to have a pet," explains the principal, "and so these kids come to school without having had much contact with pets. Dogs and cats are strange to them." [29]

It is this type of control or "close supervision" which breeds the very dependency and fear characteristic of the welfare agency. And both departments exist in a sense under the same "roof," for when welfare payments go up, so do rent payments to the Housing Authority.[30] The housing authority is run as a business, and those who are not good business risks, who do not conform to the rigorous standards, are promptly evicted. But bad as such housing is, there is not nearly enough of it, nor are there other adequately financed federal housing programs designed to serve low-income groups.

In Detroit, a maximum of 758 low-income housing units have been assisted through these programs since 1956. This amounts to 2 percent of the substandard units and 1.7 percent of the overcrowded units. Yet, since 1960, approximately 8,000 low-income units have been demolished for urban renewal.

Similarly, in Newark, since 1959, a maximum of 3,760 low-income housing units have been assisted through the programs considered. This amounts to 16 percent of the substandard units and 23 percent of the overcrowded units. During the same period, more than 12,000 families, mostly low-income, have been displaced by such public uses as urban renewal, public housing and highways.[31]

Such programs hardly fit the bill, and are mere token attempts to serve the needs of the populace. No wonder that the poor become frustrated, after having their expectations raised by false promises and catchy phrases.[32] Again, action speaks louder than campaign rhetoric. For those who cannot find a "decent" place to live, it is difficult to go to work or to achieve any kind of motivation at all, when you are forced to sleep in cramped, close quarters, with rats scampering to and fro in search of a meal. Housing is the base of community life. If that base is destroyed, or warped by insufficient "covering," then so too may much of what happens outside the home, in school, at work, and in our relationships. How would we feel living with eight other people in a one- or two-room apartment, knowing our livelihood depends upon the good graces of the welfare department or middle-

class white society, while at the same time we are constantly bombarded by advertisements urging us to dye our hair blond, drive a new Chevrolet, and take out life insurance. We might begin to ask ourselves whether or not we are a part of the "life" depicted on billboards and television commercials. While we ostensibly have our "own" society, this society is not necessarily one we take pride in or would choose to preserve if given an alternative: rather, it is a means of coping with frustration, of being "sold-out" by well-meaning white liberals who themselves find that there are in fact no suitable jobs or houses available, despite all claims on the part of the government to the contrary. We find ourselves reacting to the pressures exerted on us by middle-class America, and it is this reaction which becomes our reality and culture.

Bad Health: Cause or Symptom?

Living under adverse housing and occupational conditions, on streets where the garbage is seldom picked up, shopping at markets which offer low quality merchandise at high prices, the poor also suffer malnutrition and disease to a disproportionate degree. Such illness is more a symptom than a cause of central city and rural labor camp conditions. Moreover, even if you can get to a doctor or hospital to receive a prescription or cure, you still have to return to live under the very conditions which generated the illness in the first place. Cures can be only temporary unless the dilapidated and unsanitary conditions of poor neighborhoods are eliminated.[33] This is not to say that all physical illness can be purged simply by correcting living conditions: Members of the white middle class also suffer health problems. Still, many diseases common to slum conditions can be eliminated by doing away with slums.

The result of inadequate diets (inadequate either because you cannot afford food stamps or because such stamps do not even exist in the county in which you reside [34]) and constant ill health have made life expectancy among the poor considerably less than among their middle-class counterparts.[35] As the Kerner Commission report points out in discussing the black ghetto:

> To some extent because of infant mortality rates, life expectancy at birth was 6.9 years longer for whites (71.0 years) than for nonwhites (64.1 years) in 1965. Even in the prime working ages, life expectancy is significantly lower among nonwhites than among whites. In 1965, white persons 25 years old could expect to live an average of 48.6 more years; whereas nonwhites 25 years old could expect to live another 43.3 years, or 11 percent less. Similar but smaller discrepancies existed at all ages from 25 through 55, and these discrepancies actually became wider between 1960 and 1965.[36]

Given that these insanitary conditions exist, when illness does occur, the chances of finding a doctor or hospital are significantly less for the poor than for members of the white middle class. In Watts, for example, before the 1965 riot, there were no hospitals for the tens of thousands of persons living in the community. If no hospital exists, or if doctors are scarce (even if you can afford one), you must travel outside your residential area to find a doctor, or to receive hospitalization services. The lack of suitable transportation between ghetto areas and other neighborhoods often makes this alternative unfeasible or impracticable. Many persons who would like to avail themselves of public medical facilities and services are unable to do so and must rely instead on whatever "local" remedies they can come up with.

Should you find a hospital, it is usually overcrowded, understaffed, and forces people to wait for long periods of time. For mothers who must take care of numerous children this can become an undue hardship, in terms of babysitting fees or restless children forced to sit in hospital waiting rooms. Jacobs reports the following "case study," concerning a mother about to give birth to a baby at the General Hospital in Los Angeles:

"Now when I went into the General to have my baby," says another mother, "I didn't go in by myself, but they put me on a table because I was, you know, ready to have it but I wasn't in pain. And after they examined me they put me on a stretcher with a red blanket. Now, this is supposed to be an *emergency*. After they examined me, well, true, my pains did start, you know. And my baby was overdue and he was coming. And they're—I'm still layin' on the cart and calling somebody to come help me, and they're walking around like I wasn't even there. So when they came in, they finally took me around to X-ray and brought me back. I laid on the table and then they found out the baby was breech and they had to turn the baby around. But see, all this *time* elapsed in between. I'm waiting here for them to turn the baby around—waiting for X-rays. I'm still hurtin', you know, and the baby's still comin'. 'Oh, the baby's not comin', you're not ready,' but I *know*, I know when the baby's coming. But they tell you what you don't feel, like they're having the baby, you know, like they're feeling the pain.

"So, when they got—when they turned the baby around, the pains really started coming. The baby was almost here, halfway here, and I keep telling them—they didn't give me anything, they just turned the baby around, and that is hell, you know, that is hell. And they had strapped me down. And I laid there until the baby was born in the bed. I kept telling them the baby was coming. And they kept saying the baby wasn't coming, but the baby was there, laying right there. So that's General. But after that I swore off—I wouldn't go. I didn't care what kind of emergency

I had. I would borrow, beg, or steal the money before I'd go over to the big General. And I have been going to the General ever since my mother was takin' us. And I remember sittin' up in that long hall with all those beds with all the people, just sittin', sittin', sittin'. And I said—but when I had my oldest child, that's because I *had* to go—other than that, I am not going. If I have to beg, borrow, or steal the money." [37]

For the aged faced with these conditions, unable to work, lacking sufficient funds for medical aid (even with Medicare), and adequate housing, they must attempt to eke out a living totally dependent on the good will of their children or government agencies.[38]

The conditions faced by migrant farm workers are equally serious. Without a stable home base, often these workers do not even qualify for welfare or unemployment benefits. At the same time, their wages are among the lowest in the land. Living in makeshift work camps, often lacking even minimal sanitation facilities, from which they must move every six weeks or so, these "outcasts" almost never have the opportunity of medical assistance. Moreover, while it is they who pick the foods which appear in glorious supermarket displays, fruits and vegetables which we buy, they themselves are often close to starvation. At the same time they run the risk of DDT poisoning. While food rots in large silos in the Midwest, these *Americans* go hungry. Forced to depend on "company" stores for food and clothing, stores which charge exorbitant prices because they have a monopoly on the "market," migrants are unable to get out of the position they have been born into. There is little time for their children, who must work, to go to school. Moreover, even when in school, a hungry body does not usually make a "studious" mind. Always up to their necks in debt, these migrants can never save up enough to settle down in one area, and they lack the skills and training necessary to qualify for other employment. Finally, though American citizens, many are Spanish-speaking and cannot communicate their grievances or seek their rights from government agencies. This results in institutionalized racism.

Health, then, in the case of the poor, is one indicator of the differences between middle-class white "reality" and those residing on the "fringe." Even when programs do come into existence, piecemeal and temporary as they may be, it is difficult for a child or adult who has never *seen* a dentist automatically to become motivated to consult one —and to keep appointments, and follow prescriptions. Again, to assume that they will is to impose a middle–class value-system on a poverty culture—the two perspectives rarely match, for the conditions which give rise to each are considerably different.

Education for Whom?

If you are poor, but are not the son or daughter of a migrant farm worker, there is a good chance you will be able to enroll in school. There is not, however, a very good chance you will be able to stay there; frequently less than half of ghetto high school students graduate, and of those who do, it is the rare student who is able to go on to college.[39] Compare this to some middle-class high schools which send upwards of 80 to 90 percent of their graduates to college. Why should this be the case? Why are middle-class youth more strongly "motivated" to learn than their poor contemporaries? Is there any connection between lack of suitable employment, poor housing and health *and* school attendance, educational motivation, and graduation?

Suppose that you are young and black, growing up in a ghetto community, one in which your father has been unable to find a job and, subsequently, is not around the house very much, one in which your mother and you, as well as your brothers and sisters, survive by receiving welfare checks. There is not enough money, even with welfare checks, so frequently you are hungry. You have a hard time getting much sleep at night, what with your brother and sister, with whom you share a bed, constantly bumping into you. In the morning on the way to school you see jobless men, perhaps your father, sitting out on the street or shooting pool in one of the local halls. You arrive at the school and go to class. Your stomach begins to growl because there was little or nothing in the house for you to eat. You try to concentrate on what the teacher is saying, but your stomach keeps bothering you. Mrs. Jones, the nicely dressed *white* teacher, calls on you to recite from a homework assignment you were supposed to have finished last night. You haven't done the assignment and so you stare down at the desk top, hoping she will call on someone else.

But what *did* you do last night? You thought about the assignment, albeit momentarily, but the house was too noisy, your baby brother and sister were screaming for something, there wasn't any room for you to lay out your books and papers, and besides the books you had to read were about a world of which you are not a part. They just didn't seem to fit your situation. Moreover, it was hard to understand the *language* they were written in; it was surely not the same as the one you used at home, or while playing in the street every day. But then, maybe that was the idea. You were not supposed to learn about your own world; rather you were supposed to memorize examples from other environments.

What's the point, when you know you will never be a part of this other world? Why go to school at all when the only authority figures, the teacher, the social worker who checks up on welfare payments, are white? These are the only persons rewarded for memorizing these books, yet it's hard to see what kind of reward your mother is receiving. She has the authority, but she doesn't get much besides headaches from having it.

You could never be nor aspire to any of these positions; the world you will grow into revolves mostly around hustling: pimping, gambling, dope, peddling "hot" goods. These are the occupations to be "revered" by a young man of your caliber, this is where status in the community lies. Or, one day you might become a member of the Panthers and fight for black dignity and power. In either case, however, these realistic role models are not those celebrated in the textbooks you have to read, nor by the white teachers you have to listen to in the classroom. Suppose you do aspire to be middle class. What good will a high school degree do you when you won't be able to get a job and the money you earn will never be sufficient to buy the home of your choice? The way to get the goods the whites have is by stealing, or hustling—all you have to do is look around you to see that. School is just a waste of time.

You are caught in a kind of game, in which you do not expect to succeed, nor for the most part, do you want to, according to middle-class rules and regulations. But you're not the only one who does not expect you to make it; the entire school system is in a sense playing this game with you. Teachers do not expect you to get out of your situation, and they teach accordingly. The schools you attend are filled with broken blackboards, chairs, and windows. The classrooms are overcrowded. But most important, the teacher does not expect you to succeed, and so reinforces his or her image of you—as lazy, stupid, good-for-nothing. And the teacher's characterization tends to be self-fulfilling. You are expected to get bad grades, to not do your homework, and lo and behold, this is exactly the way you behave.[40] The school system itself aids in this prophecy by allocating the least amount of funds to your school district, reserving most of the money for school districts where the kids "have a chance," because they are white and middle-class. Similarly, only the poorest teachers find their way into the ghetto or central city, for who wants to teach unmotivated "troublemakers." The pay is also often less than one can get from the "better" districts.

Two programs initiated to cope with this situation—busing and

Headstart—have had mixed results. If a child is bused out of the ghetto, he must return there in the evening to confront an environment which may differ considerably from his school experience. Moreover, it is somewhat absurd to expect a child to forget everything he knows when he goes to school, to copy unfamiliar standards and values which do not match his personality or social situation. "You cannot eliminate all that is familiar to a child and expect him to learn." [41] Is it not the schools which have caused so much trouble for the child, rather than vice versa? [42] The issue must also be faced as to whether or not the child *must* memorize middle-class values (even if they are worthwhile) or can he take pride in his own culture and value system, no matter how diametrically opposed to middle-class values this system may be? And if he can, then why are these values not reinforced in the schools this child goes to? On the other hand, the busing of black children has improved their educational abilities in many areas—reading, math, English, as well as providing a greater opportunity for exchange of cultural values.

The Police: For the Protection of Whom?

One of the prime links between white, middle-class society and the poverty belt is through the police.[43] The police come to be seen by poor, black, and brown people as a force of repression rather than service. The middle-class community may perceive the police issuing traffic tickets, helping old ladies cross the street, arresting demonstrators, and generally serving their community, whereas in the ghetto the police give a quite different account of themselves. It is in the ghetto that police meet their arrest quotas. Persons having a record can be picked up on suspicion and "preventively detained"! That this may have a disastrous effect on their chances of employment or of receiving welfare is quite often ignored by the arresting officer.

The differential between *white* crimes and *black* crimes is also brought out in other ways. For example, when someone who is black commits a crime against someone who is white, the victim is usually able to initiate prompt action against his assailant, whereas if the crime is black against black, it is often ignored by the police.[44] Furthermore, police are more apt to employ violence in quelling crime in the ghetto than in middle-class white neighborhoods. In this context, it will be remembered that, in 1968, Mayor Daley instructed the Chicago police to shoot to kill arsonists and to maim looters. Someone stealing a chair from a store can be shot by police attempting to stop him, while this same person, if brought to trial, would certainly not receive the death penalty for his crime.[45] The important thing to realize is that the police have a "right" to shoot this person, for they control the "legitimate" use of violence in the community and nation.[46] How can we be sure that when a police officer or group of police officers kills someone in the course of duty (preserving law and order) that they are not expressing their own particular political or value orientation? [47] How do we know, when a police officer is killed, if it was in self-defense or a premeditated act on the part of someone habituated to poverty and urban squalor? The organized attacks, in 1971, by police on Black Panther headquarters in Chicago and elsewhere, help elucidate this issue. Part of the problem is that the police have a different conception of social problems, particularly ghetto problems, than does the ghetto dweller: "People, rather than social conditions, cause crime." This view helps justify the presumed "fact" that the police can "do little about the problems they are called upon to repress." [48]

That the violent force which police demonstrably have at their command can be a political issue is indicated by the interest which police associations have shown in backing political candidates or in lobbying for or against specific types of legislation (for example, civilian review boards). In 1969 a retired police officer was elected mayor of Minneapolis on a law-and-order ticket. Criticism leveled against one cop is taken to be an attack upon all cops. The police, moreover, tend to present a united front against any who would dare impugn their dignity. Further, the nature of their work often means that the only friends which cops have are other cops. Policemen also tend to live in the same neighborhoods, creating, in effect, their own "ghetto." These are, however, usually not the "ghettos" they police. It is in the face of these types of issues that the problem of Blue Power has been raised.[49]

A concomitant result of problems police have in coping with ghetto "disturbances" is their training program. In the first place, they often have a difficult time recruiting adequate personnel, due largely to the type of work they perform, and the kind of remuneration they receive for such work. Again, it appears that those governmental agencies which deal directly with the poor are those which are the most poorly staffed and inadequately paid. The type of training which the candidate for "policehood" must undergo reflects the "rotten apple" view of crime mentioned above. Little is taught about human relations, ghetto problems, or social problems in general (although there are instances where this is changing, particularly in some of the larger departments). Paul Jacobs notes, in discussing the Los Angeles police department:

"How to do it" is taught in 529 hours in 12 weeks. The curriculum, reflecting accurately what is considered important in the LAPD, emphasizes the technical aspects of police work: only a few hours each are devoted to the background of law enforcement and to race and human relations —although the department states that such questions are discussed in other classes, too—and the major emphasis is on such subjects as criminal investigation procedure, the care and use of firearms, physical conditioning and control tactics, and patrol procedures, which includes approximately two hours on race relations, two on press relations, and eight on public relations.[50]

In the same light, in a time in which urban problems are becoming more and more complex, requiring more sophisticated training and programs, there seems to be a reliance on what worked before and a particular resistance, especially on the part of older members of the police force, to adopting needed curriculum changes.[51] But training reforms in themselves may not be enough; perhaps the entire concept of police-community relations must be re-evaluated.

The courts tend to reinforce the police view of the world against that taken by ghetto dwellers. Not only can police arrest if they "suspect" that you did something wrong, but once arrested you are presumed guilty unless proven innocent, a particularly heavy burden to bear when you cannot afford to get a lawyer and know little of your constitutional rights.[52] The crime you are guilty of committing, however, may be that of being black or brown, or of living in poverty without a job, or expressing different values and beliefs—hustling, for example.[53] This type of situation is normal when you are black or brown, but becomes especially evident during a riot, when the courts do their best to enforce law and order, rather than serve the cause of justice. During such periods, bail is set particularly high—a tactic called, "preventive detention"—so that the individual presumed guilty cannot return to the streets.[54] This view of justice creates little respect for police or courts of law among poor and nonwhite people, and does more to create a police-state mentality and a fear of the government than perhaps any institution which deals directly with the poor.

In essence, the poor see the police as agents of the system whose function is to keep the poor in their place. The police do not serve the community of the poor, rather they represent middle-class interests insofar as they maintain law and order, which is to say, the status quo. Those who are not happy with the way things are and who challenge the system by attempting to control their own lives and who seek to check the abuse of police power in their communities, are shot or arrested and put away.

Effect on the Family: Middle-Class White versus Lower-Class Black Relations in Microcosm

One of the stark facts which emerges from a study of the poor black family, especially in relation to the middle-class white community, is that the poor black family cannot protect its members.[55] In their dependence on welfare for income, and on unemployment agencies for jobs, having their homes inspected (invaded) by case workers, their neighborhoods occupied by hostile police, their communities destroyed or revamped by urban renewal programs, poor blacks no longer have (if they ever did have) control over their family or the community in which the family resides. In relinquishing such control, the family ceases to serve one of its primary functions: the protection of its members. As the family loses control to welfare and other public agencies, its members becoming submissive to the dictates of these agencies, family members learn more about respecting whites (the representatives of these agencies) than members of their own families.[56]

Moreover, about one-third of these families are female-dominant (according to 1972 census data), for as the male cannot gain employment, he often leaves home, and the child finds his mother as his only adult model. For male black children, this can be disastrous. The mother in enforcing respect for her, regardless of whether or not it is due, implicitly teaches him how to respond to whites he will later come in contact with.[57] Of course, many black families do adjust adequately and cope with this matriarchal situation, and in fact, criticism has been leveled at those middle-class white researchers (the Moynihan Report) who apply their own value framework in attacking the instability of the black family.[58] Nevertheless, the significant issue remains that the family, as well as the single, poor, black or white ghetto dweller, is for the most part powerless in dealing with middle-class service agencies and commercial enterprises.

Poverty as a Way of Life

Not all members of the poverty cultures, however, are powerless in dealing with members of their own community, nor are all dependent on middle-class "charity" for survival. Many blacks become hustlers of one type or another—pusher, pimp, gambler—and through these activities are able to obtain the same commodities the middle-class white community values.[59] In the process, they create their own value system and means of maintaining self-esteem. But even here, the hustle assumes there is someone to hustle from; it is a kind of negative identity, flaunted in the face of middle-class power and dominance. When and if discrimination is ended, will this particular identity also perish? Is the culture of poverty and those identities and roles which grow up concomitantly with it only a reaction to white power? And if so, what will happen when this power is equalized? If one does not have the ability to hustle, poverty becomes a way of life largely built around responses to welfare and unemployment agencies, dilapidated schools, homes, and hospitals. For the majority of those living in ghettos and other poverty areas, this syndrome tends to foster dependence, lack of motivation and self-esteem, and a loss of identity. Many of the poor attempt to play it "cool" maintaining a "distance" between themselves and the chaotic world they live in,[60] identifying with their "oppressors," or playing at being "middle-class" in order to avoid psychologically the negative consequences of facing their actual situation.[61]

The problem of poverty, intermeshed with the problem of power in American society, also throws poor whites and blacks into direct competition for the same scarce jobs and the same substandard housing. Since the 1965–1967 riots and the attention lavished on the black community, poor whites have felt increasingly alienated and left out. They find themselves ignored by federal programs and projects.[62] It is this conflict that has fostered right wing political activity within the poor white community. Yet, regardless of who among the poor comes up with the scarce jobs, the poor in general remain outside the mainstream of American life. The communication process is one-way: the poor do not tell the middle-class white community how *they* should behave, nor are they able to gain a voice (except once in a while on the back pages) in the news media to tell their story and articulate their problems.[63]

The American Indian: Resurrecting a Past
That Has Disappeared Forever

The American Indian represents a special case of poverty and oppression. The reader is well aware that there are relatively few Indians left. Since the whites came West 150 years ago, the Indians have been driven both physically and culturally from the American continent. We have imprisoned them on reservations where they are largely forgotten. So long as they "kept their place," we did not further disturb them. These reservations do not match territories formerly held by Indian tribes; their boundaries are arbitrarily drawn and contain some of the worst land available. When there exists a group of people accustomed to living according to certain geophysical conditions, whose culure is based upon coping with these conditions (for example, hunting buffalo), there is a crisis when these conditions no longer exist. What happened, then, to the Indians who were forced to move away from lands—either because others wanted what the land had to offer, or because the land was destroyed by others and was no longer "worth" anything? Since what little culture was left no longer contained any practical referent, it began to lose its meaning; the Indian experienced a sense of anomie, or of value loss. Not surprisingly, then, on many reservations there is an exceedingly high rate of alcoholism, suicide, as well as problems similar to those we have described for the ghettos and "normal" poverty belts: hunger, unsanitary conditions, poor housing, and unemployment.

The American Indian is trapped in a seemingly untenable position. On the one hand, he desires to hold onto the traditional culture of his past, and to achieve "red power" and dignity; but, on the other hand, the traditional culture he tries to hold onto is no longer congruent with the sociophysical environment in which he now dwells. The pressures are toward assimilation and, ultimately cultural extinction. If the Indian is to survive in American society today, it seems he must, if he can, introduce capitalism to the reservations on which he lives. However, such economic development is not in keeping with his cultural traditions and it would only hasten their decay. There is, apparently, no alternative. The Indian must cease to be an Indian, at least, in any recognizable form. He cannot return to the past; for the past, in terms of physio-cultural environment, no longer exists.

Most Indians either have moved to cities, where they are assimilated, form their own ghettos, or go on welfare rolls; or they have refused to do anything, though reservations are increasingly bringing in small factories in which they can work. Many, however, are still under the influence of the "company" store, to which they must pay their monthly subsistence check, or to Indian Bureaus which exert a tremendous control over their lives. With the seizure in 1971 of Alcatraz Island in San Francisco Bay, many Indians hoped to regain their lost lands—yet this effort, when confronted with the power of white America, only achieved token and temporary success for reasons already alluded to.

Most whites, until recently, refused to recognize the existence of

Indians or Indian reservations except as tourist attractions. They could not or did not want to see the problems which the Indians face (which means that they refused to give the Indians any aid or assistance in getting them out of the untenable situation they were in). And such aid which was provided was on Anglo, rather than Indian, terms. In part, the problem was lack of visibility: Most of us were not even aware of the existence of reservations, let alone the conditions on these reservations, as most of us are not aware of the conditions or location of migrant farm labor camps. But ignorance is no excuse for society's treatment of minority groups outside its reality framework or value perspective.[64]

The Chicano

The Chicano (Mexican-American) finds himself in a position similar to that of the American Indian. Growing up predominantly in the rural Southwest in lands adjacent to Mexico, Chicanos trace their heritage both to Mexican and Indian cultures. Relegated to a position near the bottom of the social scale because they have their own language and, for the most part, do not speak English, and because their skin is brown, they are treated as "exiles" in a land they formerly owned. Though five million strong, many Chicanos will face the same loss of culture and heritage as the Indian if they are to economically survive in contemporary American society. Rural America is vanishing and the ability of our agricultural economy to sustain a large work force is declining.

Despite the victories of the United Farm Workers under Caesar Chavez in the grape fields of California, the way out of poverty for most Chicanos is through middle-class education and jobs, while much of their culture continues to become bastardized in Taco stands and advertisements for Frito corn chips. Chicanos face many of the problems most other poor and nonwhite persons face in terms of their education, health, employment, housing, and political opportunities; yet, the crucial issue will still be the ability to maintain their culture in the face of the poverty, material goods, mass culture, and occupations held out by white America. Cultural pride is a force for raising consciousness and building power within the community. Such "equality" as may be achieved, however, poses a threat to the cultural identity which helped achieve it.

Chicanos have long suffered not only because of the above conditions but also because of the difficulty in overcoming a fear of authority inculcated by the Patron (landlord) system and the Catholic Church.

It is difficult for the fatalist to feel that he has control of his destiny in a world fraught with insecurity. In addition, the Chicano's distrust of strangers and leaders outside of his own community and church has made it difficult to organize on a regional or national basis.[65]

Riots

In the face of the conditions described above, what would you do? How would you respond to programs which raise expectations without really raising much else? How would you respond, if you had little or no "legitimate" power, to a situation which you could no longer stand to live within? Many blacks have had no choice but to express their indignation and frustration by taking to the streets, by rioting against the manifestations of white middle-class society which stand visibly before them. As Bob Dylan has so aptly said, "When you've got nothin', you've got nothin' to lose"—a phrase which accurately characterizes the feelings and thoughts of many ghetto blacks:

> Men reduced to the status of non-persons and removed from the protection of the social code can hardly be expected to honor the responsibilities imposed by that code. And men (now emancipated) excluded from all benefit of the social order, indeed preyed upon by that social order, may wear lightly the injunction that (a white man's) property is sacred. No, we grant that it is likely that blacks steal more than whites, but we suggest that there is no more efficient way to produce a thief than to steal a man's substance and command that he hold his peace.[66]

Ghetto riots have proven that property rights are valued more highly than human rights—it is more important to save and protect existing property holdings (pawn shops, markets, clothing stores), than to deal with the condition of the human lives affected either directly or indirectly by those who own and manage this property. This phenomenon should not surprise us, for as we noted in Chapter 3, human lives themselves are often treated as property by members of the middle class. The ghetto resident who has never owned or had access to middle-class commodities experiences little guilt in stealing or burning down a store.

The Kerner Commission delineated three main causes of riots: pervasive discrimination and segregation, black immigration and white exodus, and black ghettos. These three conditions when combined with frustrated hopes, powerlessness, and a feeling that violence is a legitimate form of social action, generated this form of protest [67] during the years 1965–1968. The American white middle class appeared

particularly shocked by the violence and destruction which characterized the riots, not because violence is not a part of American life, but
rather because individuals outside the mainstream of American society
—nonwhites—were responsible.[68] Indeed, violence has always been a
part of the American way of life; witness the founding of labor unions
in this country, the Haymarket riots, and the long string of wars we,
as a nation, have participated in. Violence is a staple of our television
diet (for example, Vietnam), which conditions latent patterns of response and makes violent behavior a viable option in a conflict situation.[69] If riots are destructive, why is the constant poverty and depriva-
tion experienced by ghetto residents and other "members" of the
poverty belt not viewed in the same way? Are these conditions not
equally, if not *more*, destructive? To assume, as many have done,
that riots are the results of only a few troublemakers, the "riffraff," is
to miss the essential causes of riots, the conditions which have already
been discussed. Equally, to assume that the Vietnam war is being
waged by a few high-placed government officials and the military-
industrial complex is profoundly to misunderstand the nature of
American society.

> Is it conceivable that . . . several hundred riots could have erupted in
> nearly every Negro ghetto in the United States over the past five years
> against the opposition of 98 or 99 percent of the Black community? And
> is it conceivable that militant young Negroes would have ignored the
> customary restraints on rioting in the United States, including the com-
> mitment to orderly social change, unless they enjoyed the tacit support
> of at least a sizeable minority of the black community? [70]

Why don't urban whites riot? In part, the urban white represents a
fragmented, privatized world, for it is the impoverished urban white
who has not made it in a *white* society. He tends to view his problem
as an individual one, rather than one which calls for group solutions.
Those that do have either the skill or talent to make it out of the ghetto
never come back; there is nothing to remind them of a boyhood spent
in poverty. Lacking race or color as a unifying symbol, the urban
white has difficulty organizing with other whites into a political community, whereas the black can easily see whose side he is on, and
who is on that side with him. Even if he should escape the ghetto, the
color of his skin is a constant reminder (as are "closed" housing
laws), as to who he is, and where his real interests lie. But probably
one of the main differences is that the poor urban white, frustrated at
being unable to find a job, housing, or status blames his failure on his
black ghetto neighbors, rather than focusing on the real cause of his

frustration, the economic and political system which has disenfranchised him. It is this resentment which is tapped and drained by rightwing and racist political movements: the Klu Klux Klan, the American Independent Party (George Wallace), and the Christian Anti-Communist Crusade. It is these whites who resent the recent attention which they suppose has been lavished on blacks, the anti-poverty programs and "integration" efforts. The Skolnick report summarizes:

> American social and political institutions have not found ways of accommodating both the legitimate grievances of aspiring minorities and the grievances of those who feel the threat of displacement. Nor have those institutions succeeded in substantially lessening the dangers of physical violence or criminal victimization which accompany life on the fringes of the slum. The result has been a pervasive insecurity for the white, urban dweller, which, while frequently exaggerated, nevertheless has a basis in the rather grim realities of contemporary urban life. Under present conditions, property values may indeed be threatened when blacks move in numbers into white areas; whites living near black ghettos do have to cope directly with the problem of "crime in the streets"; and the failure of American institutions to commit themselves decisively to the eradication of racial injustice means that the root causes of white insecurity as well as black discontent are likely to remain with us. It is in the context of these conditions that urban white militancy is nourished. Politically ineffective, educationally limited, and uncommitted to the finer distinctions regarding civil liberties and minority rights, the urban white of ethnic working-class background is increasingly disposed to resistance.[71]

While it appears we are equating the working-class and white "slum" dweller, even middle-class whites do not want change to occur as rapidly as ghetto blacks, nor do they perceive the urgency of the problem.

The War on Poverty: Rising Expectations, Empty Budgets

The War on Poverty was centered essentially on community-run programs—or the poor with some staff (accountants, social workers, teachers) and monetary aid would deal with poverty as they saw the problem. They would pull themselves up through community development programs—the community, rather than the individual, was the target. By enabling the poor to participate, it was felt they would gain a sense of involvement and motivation toward improving their lot, for they would have a psychological investment in the program. Again, however, the program was geared to those who ostensibly stood a good chance of making it out of the ghetto, "the young, rather than the old or handicapped." [72]

Almost immediately this program ran into difficulties, for it appeared that the poor were being left out of the very program which was designed for their participation.[73] There were few poor persons involved in the design and executive aspects of the war on poverty, precisely those positions to which the poor could lend their experiential judgment so lacking in former programs composed of middle-class service workers:

> Generally speaking, two arguments are put forward by advocates of placing the poor on these influential bodies (commissions to end poverty). They say that long-term users of public and private agencies (whether as clients of public welfare or of private family service agencies) can provide a unique insight into the effectiveness of social services—a perspective free of bias stemming from considerations of career, political interests and the public relations needs of agency representatives. It is further argued that the poor can best define their own needs and suggest appropriate uses of federal funds to meet them. Inclusion of the poor, it is said, will help to overcome a long-standing colonialism in the welfare field (both public and private).[74]

Many participants in these programs were required to sign loyalty oaths —a means by which "troublemakers" (often those most critical of traditional programs) could be barred from effective leadership roles and involvement.[75]

The primary issue revolved around who would control power in the community. To give poor people, particularly nonwhites, more power over urban politics and finances would be to change the scope and structure of urban politics—who controls jobs, where money is spent, and who benefits. Around this issue can be seen conflicts between groups which have a vested interest in existing programs and those which desire change.[76] The War on Poverty ended up giving money, for the most part, to existing or already operating organizations and government units, rather than creating new ones. Thus welfare and unemployment agencies, already staffed with middle-class social workers, were apt to receive much more aid than, for example, the Panthers, though many of the former group's programs had proved of little or no use to many poor persons.[77] Or, existing boards of education, many of which were already discriminating against the poor and nonwhite, were given the job of operating Headstart programs. Finally, the War on Poverty missed the essential point: Involvement of the poor in the "war" had psychological and motivational significance far beyond actual financial gain or loss, or, in fact, above what was actually accomplished by such a war.[78] If the poor could be involved, which they were not, they would at least get the feeling that they too counted, that they too had a say and a stake in what programs involved them, and that they too could do something about their lives and community.[79]

There were still other problems which community actions programs ran into, many of which, perhaps, are irreconcilable. Nathan Glazer has pointed out:

> The decisions the administrators of these programs must make are too difficult for any mortal. Does one offer jobs in the program to the newly aroused leaders of the poor—and if so, is one strengthening the program or buying off the leaders of the poor and reducing the pressure? How much pressure does one put on the mayor to include the representatives of the poor—and is one seeking easy demagogic victories by posing as the leader of the unfortunates against the soulless bureaucracies, or is one really trying to improve the workings of the bureaucracies? And what about the representatives of the poor one is trying to place on C.A.A.'s— is one simply aiding one faction in the Negro community or the civil-rights struggle as against another? Or is one truly changing the fundamental constitution of American local government? [80]

Who speaks for the poor? How can one expect the poor to practice participatory democracy when most middle-class Americans don't? How can we expect the poor to follow the tenets of orderly constitutionalism when it has always served to discriminate against them? Can the poor be expected to be any more democratic than their middle-class counterparts, those who are fiscally operating these programs behind the scenes, who ostensibly provide the models for the poor to follow? [81]

Some people are managing to leave the ghetto, but the ghetto does not altogether leave them; for the poor are sharing less and less of the economic pie, if not in actual percentage of the number of poor, then in the buying power of the poverty income (32 percent of the nation's blacks were below the official poverty level in 1971 [34 percent in 1970], while the income level remained static for 1969–1971).[82] Moreover, those programs which do exist to aid the poor, often aid only the "deserving" poor, or those not actually on the bottom, those who are able to work.[83] The others presumably do not come forth, would not look good on the record—their prognosis or chance of failure in existing programs might be too high, and their participation would also thus not make very good political capital. Many of those entitled to aid also do not receive it because of pride or fear of bureaucratic entanglements.

At bottom there is a pervasive fear which seems to exist in middle-class America about "rocking the boat." "Other-directedness" and privatized insecurity rear their heads; everyone waits to see what everyone else is going to do, and while the middle class is waiting, the poor are starving.

Black Power: Taking Care of Business

In response to the continued failure of poverty programs, efforts at integration, eradication of discrimination, and the lack of impact countless private and governmental commissions have had on the problems of poverty and race, many blacks have developed a new attitude and taken a political stand. Defined by Stokley Carmichael as "Black Power," this movement assumes that blacks will gain an equal share of the American pie only if they have the power to back their claim—whether this be political power (votes), economic power (ownership of stores and businesses), or military power (ability to protect themselves against police and white brutality).[84] This position tacitly accepts the idea that America is a politically pluralistic society. It adds that if you are not going to be swallowed up by other groups in the coalition, you must be able both to define who you are and to bring something to the coalition. If you cannot do so, then there is little chance of getting others to listen to and recognize your position. Furthermore, as opposed to most integrationist postures, Black Power does not assume that white is superior because it fosters pride in being black, a pride that can serve to motivate the poor and the oppressed regardless of their material circumstances. You do not have to work to be a black person, nor do you have to copy or strive to live up to a middle-class white television image; rather, you just are.

In contrast with other minority groups which have asserted their claim to power, the Black Power movement is seen as a direct threat to the middle-class white. The threat revolves around a challenge to traditional roles and relationships between white and black worlds, or as some have put it, between a colonialist and an anti-colonialist position. "As colonialism disappears, the previously unquestioned authority of the white world likewise disintegrates, and with it the capacity of a predominantly white society to maintain its privileges." [85] As black people in American society have watched their brothers and sisters in Africa and Asia throw off white colonialist regimes, they too have agitated for the same freedom and power. In so doing, they have adopted many of the revolutionary (anti-colonialist) attitudes of their African and Asian brothers.

Black Power represents a threat to the established "reality" of the American power structure, for some blacks no longer wish to remain in the position that has been assigned them for hundreds of years, nor can they wait for long-delayed legislation to be enacted and implemented. Nonviolence, a tactic traditionally employed by the civil rights movement, has cost too much time, with too few rewards. In any case, what little progress has been made in the field of civil rights has not been consolidated in recent years. And the Nixon administration's record will show that every effort has been made to appease "middle Americans" while the rights of black Americans have gone by default.

To be a member of the black community may mean becoming a Panther or a Blackstone Ranger, or being active in some other community program or black solidarity movement.[86] ROTC may be used to train for resistance and national liberation, rather than as a tool to enforce "the man's" values and power position.[87]

How may black, brown, red, or yellow persons gain an equal opportunity in American society? Must they continue to rely on the good will of a largely recalcitrant white society, a society which, as we have seen, is afraid to practice the values it preaches, while extolling models of material comfort impossible for most poor persons to meet? If we were outside the system—because we were born outside the system—what would we do, how would we respond?

NOTES

[1] Michael Harrington, *The Other America* (Baltimore: Penguin Books Inc., 1964), p. 9.

[2] Georg Simmel, "The Poor," in Chaim I. Waxman, *Poverty: Power and Politics* (New York: Grosset and Dunlap, Inc., 1968), p. 6.

[3] Warren C. Haggstrom, "The Power of the Poor," in Waxman, *ibid.*, p. 119.

[4] Otto Kerner et al., *Report of the National Advisory Commission on Civil Disorders* (New York: Bantam Books, Inc., 1968), p. 259.

[5] Sterling Tucker, *Beyond the Burning: Life and Death of the Ghetto* (New York: Association Press, 1968), p. 8.

[6] Harrington, *op. cit.*, p. 18.

[7] For a general discussion of this subculture see Elliot Liebow, *Tally's Corner* (Boston: Little, Brown and Company, 1967).

[8] Haggstrom, *op. cit.*, pp. 186–190; also Harry M. Caudill, "The Permanent Poor: The Lesson of Eastern Kentucky," in *Atlantic Monthly*, June, 1964, pp. 49–53; and Michael Harrington, "The Politics of Poverty," in Jeremy Larner and Irving Howe, *Poverty: From the Left* (New York: Dissent Publ., 1969), pp. 13–38.

[9] Tucker, *op. cit.*, p. 59.

[10] *Ibid.*, p. 56.

[11] *Ibid.*, pp. 57–68.

[12] Studies of these different cultures, however, often lack validity due to the researcher's own biases, most often resulting in unwarranted generalizations. For a discussion of these see Charles A. Valentine, *Culture and Poverty* (Chicago: University of Chicago Press, 1968).

[13] *Ibid.*

[14] C. M. Miller and Pamela Roby, "The War on Poverty Reconsidered," in Larner and Howe, *op. cit.*, p. 74. See also Harrington, "The Politics of Poverty," *op. cit.*

[15] James Ridgeway, "The More Glorious War," in Waxman, *op. cit.*, p. 203.

[16] William B. Gould, "Discrimination and the Union," in Larner and Howe, *op. cit.*, pp. 168–185. See also S. M. Miller, "*Poverty, Race and Politics,*" in Waxman, *op. cit.*

[17] Kerner, *op. cit.*, p. 254. See also Liebow, *op. cit.*

[18] Paul Jacobs, *Prelude to Riot: A View of Urban America From the Bottom* (New York: Random House, Inc., 1966), p. 109.

[19] *Ibid.*, p. 94.

[20] Alan Batchelder, "Poverty: The Special Case of the Negro," in Arthur I. Blaustein and Roger R. Woock, *Man Against Poverty: World War III* (New York: Random House, Inc., 1968), p. 67.

[21] Jacobs, *op. cit.*, p. 72.

[22] *Ibid.*, pp. 61–96.

[23] *Ibid.*, p. 69.

[24] Robert Lekachman, "Can More Money End Poverty?", in Larner and Howe, *op. cit.*, p. 65.

[25] Jacobs, *op. cit.*, pp. 63–84.

[26] Kerner, *op. cit.*, p. 243; also Jacobs, *op. cit.*, p. 133.

[27] Jacobs, *op. cit.*, p. 146.

[28] *Ibid.*, p. 145.

[29] *Ibid.*, pp. 160–161.

[30] *Ibid.*, p. 165.

[31] Kerner, *op. cit.*, p. 142.

[32] Chester W. Hartman, "The Politics of Housing," in Larner and Howe, *op. cit.*, p. 153. For further discussions of the housing problem see Lawrence M. Friedman, *Government and Slum Housing* (Chicago: Rand-McNally & Co., 1968).

[33] Jacobs, *op. cit.*, p. 195.

[34] Joseph S. Clark, "Starvation in the Affluent Society," in Blaustein and Woock, *op. cit.*, p. 92.

[35] Kerner, *op. cit.*, p. 271.

[36] *Ibid.*, pp. 270–271.

[37] Jacobs, *op. cit.*, pp. 188–189.

[38] Ben B. Seligman, "The Poverty of Aging," in Larner and Howe, *op. cit.*, pp. 107–123.

[39] Jacobs, *op. cit.*, p. 213.

[40] For an interesting presentation of this phenomenon see Jonathan Kozol, *Death At an Early Age* (New York: Houghton Mifflin, 1967).

[41] Deborah Meier, "Head Start or Dead End?", in Larner and Howe, *op. cit.*, p. 135. See also Edgar Z. Friedenberg, "An Ideology of School Withdrawal," in Robert Perrucci and Marc Pilisuk, *The Triple Revolution: Social Problems in Depth* (Boston: Little, Brown and Company, 1968), pp. 494–505.

[42] *Ibid.*

[43] Jacobs, *op. cit.*, p. 58.

[44] Robert Pearman, "Black Crime, Black Victims," *The Nation*, April 21, 1969, p. 502.

[45] Jacobs, *op. cit.*, p. 33.

[46] Jacobs, *op. cit.*, pp. 30–35; See also, Stephen H. Wildstrom, "Mugged by the Sheriffs: An Anecdote," *The Nation, op. cit.*, pp. 496–497.

[47] Roldo Bartimole, "Bad Day in Cleveland," *The Nation*, July 14, 1969, pp. 41–45.

[48] Jerome H. Skolnick, *The Politics of Protest* (New York: Ballantine Books, 1969), p. 257.

[49] Hans Tock, "Cops and Blacks: Warring Minorities," *The Nation*, April 21, 1969, p. 491.

[50] Jacobs, *op. cit.*, p. 47.

[51] Skolnick, *op. cit.*, p. 257.

[52] Jacobs, *op. cit.*, p. 50.

[53] Skolnick, *op. cit.*, p. 270, 301.

[54] *Ibid.*, p. 315. See also Jacobus ten Broek, *The Law of The Poor* (San Francisco: Chandler, 1966).

[55] William H. Grier and Price M. Cobbs, *Black Rage* (New York: Bantam Books, Inc., 1968), pp. 69–71.

[56] *Ibid.*, p. 144.

[57] *Ibid.*

[58] Laura Carper, "The Negro Family and the Moynihan Report," in Perrucci and Pilisuk, *op. cit.*, pp. 461–468.

[59] Jeremy Larner, "Initiation for Whitey: Notes on Poverty and Riot," in Larner and Howe, *op. cit.*, p. 98; also, for an interesting personal point of view and case study see Malcolm X, *The Autobiography of Malcolm X* (New York: Grove Press, Inc., 1966).

[60] Grier and Cobbs, *op. cit.*, p. 57.

[61] Haggstrom, in Waxman, *op. cit.*, pp. 122–128.

[62] Robert Coles, "The White Northerner: Pride and Prejudice," in Perrucci and Pilisuk, *op. cit.*, pp. 398–406.

[63] William L. Rivers, "Jim Crow Journalism," in Judson R. Landis, *Current Perspectives on Social Problems* (Belmont: Wadsworth Publishing Co., 1959), p. 173.

[64] Stan Steiner, "The American Indian—Ghettos in the Desert," in Blaustein and Woock, *op. cit.*, pp. 136–145. See also, Edgar S. Cahn, *Our Brothers' Keepers: The Indian in White America* (Washington: New Community Press, 1969). Many researchers assume they can go into a ghetto, barrio or reservation, ask questions, and find out what is going on. Despite the often good intentions of the scholar, what "data" he is able to derive is more a result of his own expectations and cognitive outlook than that of his respondents. For example, it is "fashionable" to spend a summer on an Indian reservation doing research and helping out. While the researcher may not expect to find Indians sitting around waiting to play in the next John Wayne cowboy film, they do expect to find Indians suffering from anomie and white infiltration of their culture. They also expect to find Indians who will respond accordingly. And, unfortunately, many Indians attempt to live up to white expectations by giving them the answers they seek. Such a symbiotic relationship, besides creating a false picture, has Indians role-play away their pride and dignity, in exchange for attention and perhaps better "treatment." It is far better, under such circumstances, to have Indians do research on Indians, and so forth; or if impossible, to adopt a phenomenological approach, letting the situation and culture determine the questions and answers according to the categories which they supply.

[65] See Stan Steiner, *The Mexican Americans* (New York: Harper and Row, Publishers, 1970); Joan London and Henry Anderson, *So Shall Ye Reap* (New York: Thomas Y. Crowell Company, 1970); V. Deloria, *Custer Died for Your Sins: An Indian Manifesto* (New York: Avon Books, 1970).

[66] Grier and Cobbs, *op. cit.*, p. 93.

[67] Kerner, *op. cit.*, pp. 203–204.

[68] *Ibid.*, p. 230. See also Hugh Davis Graham and Ted Robert Gurr, *The History of Violence in America* (New York: Bantam Books, Inc., 1969).

[69] *Ibid.*

[70] Skolnick, *op. cit.*, p. 148.

[71] *Ibid.*, p. 226.

[72] Deborah I. Offenbacher, "The Proper Study of Poverty; Empirical versus Normative Perspectives," in Waxman, *op. cit.*, p. 52.

[73] Charles E. Silberman, "The Mixed-up War on Poverty," in Waxman, *op. cit.*, p. 83.

[74] Richard A. Cloward, "The War on Poverty—Are the Poor Left Out?", in Waxman, *op. cit.*, p. 161.

[75] Varvara Carter, "Sargent Shriver and the Role of the Poor," in Waxman, *op. cit.*, p. 206. For a discussion and case study examples of community action programs stemming from the War on Poverty see Ralph M. Kramer, *Participation of the Poor* (Englewood Cliffs, N. J.: Prentice-Hall, Inc., 1969).

[76] Cloward, in Waxman, *op. cit.*, p. 166.

[77] Silberman, in Waxman, *op. cit.*, p. 93.

[78] *Ibid.*, p. 84.

[79] Joseph Froomkin, "The Poor Program," in Waxman, *op. cit.*, p. 220.

[80] Nathan Glazer, "The Grand Design of the Poverty Program," in Waxman, *op. cit.*, p. 290.

[81] For an excellent discussion of poverty–community action programs see Kenneth Clark and Jeannette Hopkins, *A Relevant War Against Poverty* (New York: Harper and Row, Publishers, 1970).

[82] Stephen Thernstrom, "Is There Really a New Poor?", in Larner and Howe, *op. cit.*, p. 83–93.

[83] Paul Jacobs, "America's Schizophrenic View of the Poor," in Larner and Howe, *op. cit.*, p. 54.

[84] Stokely Carmichael and Charles V. Hamilton, *Black Power* (New York: Random House, Inc., 1967). For other discussions of this phenomenon, see Nathan Hare, "The Case for Black Separatism: 'Black Perspective'," in James McEvoy and Abraham Miller, *Black Power and Student Rebellion* (Belmont: Wadsworth Publishing Co., 1969), pp. 233–234; Roy Wilkins, "The Case Against Separatism: 'Black Jim Crow'," in *op. cit.*, pp. 235–236. For a discussion of "Black Capitalism," see "Black Capitalism: Problems and Prospects," *Saturday Review*, August 23, 1969. See also Sondra Silverman, *The Black Revolt and Democratic Politics* (Boston: D. C. Heath & Company, 1970).

[85] Skolnick, *op. cit.*, p. 143.

[86] *Ibid.*, p. 171.

[87] *Ibid.*, p. 170.

6

pax Americana: tread heavily and carry a B-52

"I got me a VC, man. I got at least two of them bastards." The exultant cry followed a 10-second burst of automatic weapons fire yesterday, and the dull crump of a grenade exploding underground.

The Marines ordered a Vietnamese corporal to go down into the grenade-blasted hole to pull out their victims. The victims were three children between 11 and 14—two boys and a girl. Their bodies were riddled with bullets. . . .

"Oh, my God," a young Marine exclaimed. "They're all kids. . . ." Shortly before the Marines moved in, a helicopter had flown over the area warning the villagers to stay in their homes.[1]

Many people around the world have become victims of American foreign policy. Our seemingly unrelated domestic problems of housing, of poverty, of employment and of education, can also be traced to that same foreign policy. At the heart of the problem is the ethnocentric point of view that American social reality is the only reality of which everyone would like to be part. Such a view ignores different cultural and socio-environmental circumstances which do not lend themselves to "Americanization." In spite of this, substantial capital investments continue to maintain overseas military installations and

Courtesy of The Atomic Energy Commission

large nuclear weapons stockpiles, when the money might better be used to cope with America's pressing domestic social problems.

There are yet other issues here. For one thing, the very existence of our military arsenal is of material interest to the rest of mankind; either by conscious effort (pushing the button) or by accident (due to technological failure) the earth could easily become a billion radio-active molecules each distended from the other. Another crucial question that needs to be asked is: Does the United States have the right to intervene in the domestic affairs of other nation states in order to preserve what it refers to as its "security"? More specifically, how does American foreign policy relate to social change in the developing nations? (That is, does America have the right to influence or control such change, especially revolutionary change, if it appears to be in our interest to intervene?) And on another level, do we have a right to conscript young men against their will to fight in wars or to enforce policy decisions they do not believe in?

Let us consider a broader perspective. Is war and the preparation for war any longer (if it has ever been) a viable means of settling conflicts between nation states in the age of the nuclear deterrent? If it is not, then what impact would such an analysis have on American foreign policy? To put it another way, is American foreign policy an anachronism supporting an outmoded view of and structural relation to the international community? Is our policy based on a narrowly economic view of other nation states, that is, does it rest on what markets are available to us and how "friendly" those markets are? Or rather, do we conceptualize the world in ideological terms, communist–democratic, moral–immoral, free–imprisoned, and so on, and formulate our policy accordingly? Finally, how does American foreign policy affect us? How does our own attitude affect the problems which it has created both domestically and in the world community?

American foreign policy is shaped by a given view of the world that conceives of outside forces that may be either "real" or perceived as "real." We not only react to the actions of other nation states, we also initiate actions (for example, in seeking out new markets), and these actions have a profound influence on the world community. This chapter will focus primarily on the problematic aspects of American foreign policy. In order to conceptualize these, it is necessary to ask what the purposes of our foreign policies are. Such purposes, however, are not often easily analyzed, for such goals may be implicit as well as stated; and conflicting policy statements by different public and private officials do not make it easier to conclude what our intentions are. However, critics of American foreign policy have tended to fall into one of three groups and evaluate the goals and problems of our foreign policy accordingly. Perhaps the mildest critics are the "liberals," those who see certain aspects of our policy as either unworkable, misconceived, or "not well thought out" (for example, American involvement in Vietnam) but who find our overall policies essentially correct. Such a critic might view containment in Europe as a proper response to "communist aggression," but improper in Southeast Asia.

Another group, whom we shall call the "Cold War" critics, find American policy (at least since World War II) based on a misperception of the communist threat. They argue that this has been exaggerated and that the series of reactions and offensives to this threat have resulted in the Cold War. In other words, the Cold War is the fault of American foreign policy. This so-called moral crusade, these critics would claim, has resulted in the creation of a "counter-empire and ideology of anti-communism," [2] one much more of a threat to the world's populace than the ideology toward which the Cold War was supposedly directed.

A third group, the anti-imperialists, consider American foreign policy to be dictated by the imperatives of capitalism—the necessity for constantly expanding markets, raw materials, cheap labor, and strategic power—and that we have created a situation in which the United States is the leading purveyor of imperialism in the world today. We intervened in the Dominican Republic in 1965, according to these critics, because of the threat posed to our economic investments in that country as well as to our political supremacy throughout Latin America, just as we remain hostile to Cuba because they nationalized many of the factories we formerly owned and controlled, and her revolutionary example is one which the United States cannot afford to see copied by other Latin American countries.

American foreign policy is vulnerable to all these charges. Since the most widespread and serious critiques come from the cold war and anti-imperialist critics, we shall examine these "attacks" in some detail, pointing out, at the same time, how such criticisms might be modified or questioned by the liberal critic's views.

The Cold War: Self-Fulfilling Prophecy or Reaction to Foreign Aggression?

So-called "traditional" or "legitimate" views hold, as most of us are well aware, that the Cold War was initiated through aggressive actions taken by the Soviet Union, particularly in Eastern Europe shortly after World War II, and that developments on our side—the building of nuclear arsenals, the stationing of half a million men in Europe, ringing the USSR and China with nuclear bomber bases—can only be construed as a protective reaction. However, "Soviet aggression" can be viewed in another light, as a response to our actions. As Henry A. Wallace, Secretary of Commerce shortly after World War II, pointed out at the time:

> How do American actions since V-J Day appear to other nations? I mean by actions the concrete things like $13 billion for the War and Navy Departments, the Bikini tests of the atomic bomb and continued production of bombs, the plan to arm Latin America with our weapons, production of B-29's and planned production of B-36's and the effort to secure air bases spread over half the globe from which the other half of the globe can be bombed. I cannot but feel that these actions must make it look to the rest of the world as if we were only paying lip service to peace at the conference table.
>
> These facts rather make it appear either (1) that we are preparing ourselves to win the war which we regard as inevitable or (2) that we are trying to build up a predominance of force to intimidate the rest of mankind. How would it look to us if Russia had the atomic bomb and we did not, if Russia had 10,000-mile bombers and air bases within 1,000 miles of our coastlines, and we did not. . . .[3]

More specifically, it is often thought that after World War II we dismantled our armed forces unilaterally. The fact is that, to a considerable extent, Soviet forces were also disbanded—this in the face of having to protect long, potentially hostile borders.

Moreover, Soviet expansion into Eastern Europe did not take place until after NATO was formed:

> The difficulty in maintaining the thesis that immediate unambiguous and "remorseless" expansion by the Soviet Union, even prior to the armistice, was solely responsible for what followed, is that it fails to account for certain key facts, and that it depends on certain assumptions which are untenable. The thesis fails to explain, for example, the fact that it took the Russians four years (from 1945 to 1949) to effect a remorseless expansion *behind their own military lines.*
>
> Similarly, the thesis overlooks the contrast between Russian conduct in Hungary, where a free election was allowed to take place in 1945, and in Bulgaria and Rumania, where the Red Army installed Communist Regimes almost at once. In point of fact, Soviet machinations in these latter two countries were carried out under the terms of an agreement between Churchill and Stalin, made in October 1944. While Stalin was given what amounted to a free hand in Bulgaria and Rumania by the accord, Churchill was given a free hand in Greece, which he used to forcibly suppress the anti-fascist resistance movement and to establish his own preferred regime, a rightist monarchy. The fact that Stalin kept his side of the agreement is of key significance, since Churchill could in

no event have affected matters in Bulgaria or Rumania, whereas Stalin's refusal to provide aid to the Greek Communist and leftist forces in their battle with the British, was of critical, even decisive importance.[4]

Thus what appeared to Americans at that time as merely the actions of "free peoples" helping other "free peoples" could only be construed by the Soviet Union as American aggression along its borders. American claims to take not one inch of land to the contrary, the U.S. was left in occupation of Japan, the Philippines, most of Western Europe, as well as economically involved in Iran, Turkey, and a host of other countries on Russian borders.

While we tend to view aggression only in light of physical troop movements, other nations view aggression along economic as well as other lines. When the United States initiated the economic Truman Doctrine and Marshall plans, ostensibly to aid Western European countries to get back on their feet in order to be prepared for the next war (against Russia)—the Soviet Union could only interpret such actions as a direct threat to their Eastern European hegemony and sovereignty. They responded accordingly by tightening up their "buffer" zone with the West. It is of interest to note that, even before the development and formation of NATO, United States power was evidently sufficient to deter Soviet intervention in Yugoslavia, a nation which, under Tito's leadership, openly challenged the monolithic communist world centered in Moscow. What, then, was the need for NATO?[5] Again:

Try to imagine . . . what the world of 1945 must have looked like from the viewpoint of this Russian nationalist. Before him towered a demanding United States, history's most violent nation (Hamburg, Kassel, Dresden, Tokyo, Hiroshima, Nagasaki—unparalleled), in the prime of its superpower. Behind him lay the unburied bodies of 20 million Russians and the burned farms and gutted factories of the Soviet economy. In his mind was the memory of unambiguous Western opposition to the Soviet Union. What were his choices? It appears he had two: (1) He could accept the American plan of European partition, take no action to close the door on East Europe and hope that the inevitable American penetration of the Danubian economy would be carried forward with a sympathetic eye on the U.S.S.R.'s economic needs and political sensitivies; or (2) he could accept the partition and close the door. Two unappealing alternatives. Given Western diplomacy since 1918 and such current clues as the abrupt termination of U.S. lend-lease to Russia (but not to France and Britain), the first was probably out of the question. . . . The second alternative was also bad. It destined Russia for conflict with the United States at a time when peaceful relations were very much in Russia's practical interest.[6]

There is neither the space nor is this the place to do more than pose questions relating to our early involvement in the Cold War. But there is some evidence to suggest that Eastern Europe went communist as a response to our policies vis-à-vis Western Europe, and that, had we not so massively "intervened" in Western Europe, many Eastern European countries, now communist, would have been allowed to remain capitalist.[7] As it was, however, our policies generated a self-fulfilling prophecy, we expected the Russians to build an "iron curtain," and we did everything in our power to make sure they did so.

What is apparent from the early Cold War period is that we were building a moral crusade against communism. The United States took upon itself a latter-day "white man's burden" to save mankind from the scourge of communist hordes threatening the "Free World." [8] However, what we defined as the Free World often constituted the support of outright dictatorships—Franco's Spain, Greece, half the Latin American States, and many others. It appeared to many nations, when viewing American foreign policy, that there was a distinct contradiction between stated policy—support of the Free World—and the actions taken in furtherance of that policy. This became particularly clear during the Korean War when, under pressure from the United States, United Nations forces intervened in the Korean conflict. The contradiction was apparent in the fact that UN forces were used to prevent South Korea from going communist, while such force had not in previous years been employed in the settlement of other such conflicts:

> The UN was brushed aside in Greece, and independent action taken to defeat Communist guerillas. In Indonesia the United States had brought strong moral pressure to bear on the Netherlands in the Security Council, but no troops and planes were sent to fight the Dutch when they defied a UN cease-fire order. Nor did the United States mobilize the UN to save the infant Israeli Republic when five Arab states invaded Palestine in 1948 to overturn by force the partition plan adopted by the UN General Assembly. Defiance of the UN could not have been more flagrant, but the United States moved no troops and planes to save the victims of Hitler's hate who had gathered in Israel and who appeared to be on the point of being destroyed by the armies of UN members converging on them from all sides. . . .[9]

Even after North Korean troops were pushed back within their own borders, no attempt was made to hear the North Korean case. In fact, UN troops led mostly by American forces under General McArthur wanted to push the war to China and were horrified when, with American troops on Chinese borders, the Chinese intervened in the war. What might have happened if several hundred thousand Chinese troops were stationed in Mexico poised and threatening to cross American borders? How might we have responded?

United States policy came to be defined by President Truman as "you're either with us or against us." [10] There were no shades of gray. The price of economic aid or military assistance was solidarity with the United States. The Free World came to be viewed as composing those nations who were fanatically anti-communist. And the free world defensive took on global proportions. Ronald Steel notes:

> From the seeds of the Truman Doctrine and the precedent of NATO came the Middle East Resolution, under which Congress gave President Eisenhower permission to protect the Arabs against communism; the CENTO and SEATO treaties that John Foster Dulles constructed to fill in the alliance gap from Iran to the Philippines; the ANZUS treaty with Australia and New Zealand; special defense arrangements with Japan and Korea; an unwritten obligation to protect India; the pledge for the defense of the entire western hemisphere under the Rio Pact; various peace-keeping functions under the United Nations; and, most recently, the Tonkin Gulf Resolution, a blank check given by Congress, allowing President Johnson to intervene as he sees fit in Southeast Asia. Early in 1968 the United States had 700,000 soldiers stationed in 30 countries, was a member of four regional defense alliances and an active participant in a fifth, had mutual defense treaties with 42 nations, was a member of 53 international organizations, and was furnishing military or economic aid to nearly 100 nations across the face of the globe.[11]

When looked at from the other side of the world, what we term defensive can easily take on offensive proportions. As Steel has demonstrated, while we may claim we have no imperialist ambitions, we nevertheless employ imperialist methods or means.[12] To the victims of our policy, what is the difference? Action speaks louder than rhetoric. This type of benevolence, in fact, results in a kind of "welfare imperialism," under which the underdeveloped nations are aided so long as they are anti-communist. The emergence of any new "communist" state, no matter how nationalistic, is a threat to our security. In confusing "Soviet imperialism" with rapid economic development in underdeveloped nations, we often end up supporting dictatorships which do not have the support of the local population, thus forcing a choice between "freedom" and modernization.

Even if we concede for a moment that the Cold War was, as many liberal critics contend, unavoidable in the European community after World War II, the political realties which fostered this conception no longer exist. The NATO countries have been rebuilt. Moreover, with nuclear weapons as a deterrent to the threat of communist expansion, the stationing and arming of troops in Europe makes little sense, especially in light of the fact that many former enemies would as soon resolve their differences. Most of our European allies trade with the communist bloc and recognize and trade with the People's Republic of China and Cuba. They have their own problems to contend with; they just don't need us the way they used to. Finally, there is some real question as to whether policies, developed in response to an ostensible or perceived Soviet threat in Europe, can be applied to a similar perceived threat in Asia, Africa, and Latin America.[13]

According to our critics, our actions have been dictated by a particularly ethnocentric view of "freedom" (that is, democracy) and what we understand to be the answer to "human needs." We expect all peoples to think as we do. As Steel comments:

> The freedom Americans are called upon to defend by the sword takes on an abstract ring when applied to societies outside the Western tradition. In the West "freedom" means the ability of men to choose, to change, and to reject the governments under which they live. To an Angolan rebel, however, it means independence from Portugal; to a Cuban revolutionary it means release from American economic control; to a Rumanian it means the defiance of the Soviet Union; to white Rhodesians it means the right to dominate a Black majority; to the Ibo tribesman of Nigeria it meant independence from the government in Lagos; and to the peasants of Brazil's northeast it means bread and a patch of land. These are not all freedoms which it is in America's power to grant, nor even necessarily freedoms which we would value.[14]

In essence, we assume that other peoples are faced with the same problems as we are and apply our foreign policy accordingly. We assume other nations fear communism as we appraise it, just as we do, or that they are willing to devote the same priorities to fighting it as we are. Many nations, however, are faced with issues, which are for them far more crucial: how to feed and house their people, how to win independence from a colonial power, how to overthrow the dictatorships they are forced to live under. For these states, our fear of communism often appears absurd.[15] The problem of Red China is a specific example:

> The world looks very different from Peking and from Washington. From our point of view, American interventions in Asia have been noble and divorced from national advantage. With no territorial ambitions ourselves,

we have sought through our intervention only to protect free peoples against Chinese communist aggression. This is why we fought a war in Korea for three years, why we guard Chiang Kai-shek's army on Formosa, why we are furnishing military aid to most of non-communist Asia, and why our own soldiers are fighting in Vietnam. We are there because, in the official view, only American military power prevents the Chinese from dominating Asia.

But to China's eyes, shaded by the spectacles of Marxist orthodoxy and of historical suspicion of the West, the United States is a threatening foe which nearly invaded Chinese territory in the Korean war, which uses her military power to prevent Formosa from being returned to China, which has rimmed China with military bases from Pakistan to Japan, which has kept her out of the United Nations, which continues to participate in the Chinese civil war by supporting Chiang Kai-shek, which is fighting a war with a communist ally on China's southern frontier, and which seeks to deny China her sphere of influence in Southeast Asia.[16]

Given China's historical experience with the West—the Open Door policy, the Opium Wars, her exploitation by Western powers, and her historical view of the world which saw China as the center of a universe filled with barbaric hordes, it is little wonder that Chinese leaders show signs of paranoia. Again, though the Chinese threaten to destroy the West, Chairman Mao making great oratory addresses, actions speak louder than words and not one Chinese soldier has set foot on foreign soil (Tibet here being construed as historically part of China). And, while Americans declare they are preserving freedom and self-determination, the United States has troops in thirty nations. Actions speak louder than words.

Not only do many nations not endorse our order of priorities, but, as we have seen, they are also aware of the contradictions in our policies. This is particularly the case in our policies toward Latin America. Under cover of the Monroe Doctrine, which guarantees any nation in the Western hemisphere the *right* to protection by the United States, we tend to treat all American peoples as the same when they are not. The Latin American culture is vastly different from that of the United States. Latin Americans face different problems in terms of priorities: poverty, dictatorship and overpopulation. We declare they have the right to self-determination, then promptly intervene in their internal affairs, often on behalf of corrupt dictatorships or to topple popularly elected governments (as we did in Guatemala, the Dominican Republic, Brazil). If a government which we suspect of being socialist comes to power, we do everything to make sure it does not last. The armed invasion of Castro's Cuba is a case in point, as is the intervention

of ITT in the election of Allende in Chile. Again, these activities occur
even though the United Nations Charter specifically makes such action
illegal, the OAS (Organizaiton of American States) agreements specifically prohibit such action, and we condemn other nations (the Soviets)
for intervening in the internal affairs of their own so-called allies
(Czechoslovakia):

> For the nations of the Caribbean who had had the big stick used against
> them, and for all those who fear that their turn may be next, the possibility
> of American military intervention is a good deal more real than the remote
> danger of a communist take-over.[17]

However, the most dire consequence of our foreign policy is the
adverse effect it is having on much of the world's population. This is
perhaps best exemplified by what has happened in Vietnam.

Vietnam, during and before World War II, was part of Indo-China,
a colonial possession of the Dutch and subsequently the French. Vietnamese fought against Japan during World War II and expected to
receive their independence from the French, a colonial power which
controlled much of Vietnam's small economy and did little for the
average Vietnamese peasant. While the French considered granting
independence after the war, they reneged and reinforced the small
number of troops they had in the country after World War II. Faced
with severe problems of poverty and desiring independence, the Vietnamese formed an independence movement under Ho Chi Minh, a
communist but primarily a nationalist.

The French were defeated in 1954, and at a conference held in
Geneva agreed that Vietnam should be *temporarily* divided until elections could be held in 1956 to reunite the country. This time period
was essentially to give the French a chance to withdraw their troops
from Vietnam. The United States had financially backed the French
during their brief war; in fact, having been devastated by World War
II, France would have been unable to carry out such a war effort without United States aid. When the French withdrew in 1954, American
policy makers felt a vacuum was left in South East Asia, a vacuum
which could either be filled by us or the communists. Thus the United
States came to replace the French by supporting a series of puppet
regimes in Saigon.

When 1956 came, the United States refused to permit elections,
knowing that Ho Chi Minh—acknowledged as the George Washington
of his country—would clearly win, and Vietnam would fall to the
"communists." With this refusal came the formation of a group com-

posed of communists and liberal democratic elements in South Vietnam who had formerly fought against the French. This was the National Liberal Front. The United States during this time was supporting a man by the name of Diem, a dictator who had imprisoned thousands of persons for their political beliefs, who had been slow to initiate land reform, and who supported a small wealthy group of landowners in Saigon. The National Liberation Front, operating in rural areas, began large-scale land reform, set up schools and hospitals, and in general bettered the lot of the Vietnamese peasant. Within a few years, the Front had gained control of most of South Vietnam except for the larger cities.

In the face of this "threat," the United States sent in massive commitments of troops (550,000 at one point), dropped millions of pounds of bombs on South and parts of North Vietnam, defoliated millions of acres of land, poisoned crops, and created at least 4 million refugees in the South. At the same time, neither the United States nor the regime in Saigon which it sponsored initiated any land reform or sought to implement the ideals of freedom and democracy, ideals for which it claimed international support. Such support was never forthcoming. In fact, the only "allies" fighting on the side of the Saigon government were a contingent of 50,000 troops from South Korea, armed and paid for by American money; a small contingent of Thais fighting under a similar agreement; and a medical corps from Australia. In other words, these allies were mercenaries.

The democracy which the peoples of South Vietnam were supposed to rally around was represented by newspaper censorship and a prohibition aginst permitting even neutralist candidates, who were slightly critical of the war effort, to run for election. Even under these restrictions, the runner-up candidate in the national elections held in 1967 was sentenced to five years at hard labor by elected President Thieu.

The United States has initiated wholesale urban renewal projects, leveling thousands of villages. One particular village (Ben Suc) studied by Jonathan Schell was moved from its rich agricultural area to a desert-like spot in which nothing could grow. Originally a village that leaned toward the National Liberation Front, a follow-up to his earlier study showed that 50 percent of the villagers had changed to hard core communists. American actions in Vietnam have almost totally destroyed the local cultures, besides killing perhaps several million persons. In Saigon, Vietnamese women often earn more than their husbands, working as prostitutes and call girls, or running off with American GIs. This has destroyed the Vietnamese family structure, causing many Vietnamese men to commit suicide. In the heat of the

Tet offensive, the logical absurdities of American military power were revealed when a city was destroyed "in order to save it."

What has the Vietnamese peasant gained from all of this? Having no history of democratic government or participation as we define it, poor, ill-clothed, and undernourished, wanting to be free from foreign control or merely desiring to be left alone, he now finds himself called upon (at point of death) to support a colonial power, one with similar aims and intents (at least as he sees them) as other colonial (white) powers have had. How can he readily distinguish between the French and the Americans? What have the latter done for him which the French did not do—except destroy his fields, his home, and many of his relatives? Why should he not support the National Liberation Front, a movement whose primary effort has been to liberate Vietnam from foreign control? Since the border with North Vietnam is and was only designated as a temporary one, the only foreigners in Vietnam are the Americans and the mercenary troops they call their "allies." [18] What has happened in Vietnam is now happening in Cambodia and Laos, although the publicity given to the wider war is almost nonexistent.

This is our foreign policy in action. According to Cold War critics, this policy ignores the realities of nationalism and the economic problems which underdeveloped nations must face. Moreover, it neglects cultural differences which exist between the United States and Asian, African, and Latin American peoples. In so doing, it does little to serve the peoples it would "save"; rather, it supports the status quo, existing "stable" governments, and economic conditions—all in the name of American security.

But what is the real threat which ideological communism presents to Americans or American policy makers? What have the so-called communists done that we should get involved? Why does change frighten us? In order to answer such questions, we should be aware that American foreign policy does not function independently of domestic conditions or those factors which I have described in the first five chapters of this book. If Americans are other-directed, if they are unable to trust but have got to rely on others who will ostensibly give their lives meaning. If their jobs are empty and unsatisfying, if they feel powerless in the face of the American political and economic system, such problems are bound to affect our relationships with other people in the world. This does not mean that shortly after World War II most Americans necessarily supported the Cold War. Rather, given the desire of a few key officials to invoke the communist threat it was easy for their policy to gain acceptance since there was little information to challenge this interpretation. Moreover, most Americans wanted to believe this interpretation was the correct one, they wanted to believe in the infallibility of their government and of an American way of life which was ostensibly threatened by alleged communist expansion. They wanted to believe, because there was nothing else which would give them a meaningful ideology (albeit of a negative kind) in face of the emptiness of American traditions, the "Protestant ethic" and the "spirit of capitalism." By focusing on outside forces they could repress many of their own problems; in their anti-communism they could hope to give meaning to those traditions they no longer practiced.

The existence of another world ideology is also a challenge to the supremacy of one's own belief. We are no longer the center of attention, and many of the people (nations) we had looked to for support are no longer to be relied upon. When one's world view is based on securing such support, even the threat of withdrawal of support is hard to face. It then becomes necessary to eliminate the competition, rather than examine those factors which cause the competition to exist and thrive in the first place.

When we cannot trust anyone, we also come to fear them. We feel not only that they no longer love us, but that they threaten our existence. Again, they either love us or hate us, they are either communist or capitalist. There is no middle road. We come to fear them because they question the security of our world view—in this case, by challenging our assumption that the American way of life is the only way of interpreting the demands of human existence. Our drive for popularity means that Americans must continually be reassured of their place in the world, for they cannot define such a place themselves. Having undergone, without having successfully concluded, a period of rapid social change, our ideology lags behind our actions, and empty rhetoric often takes the place of facing crucial problems. Rapid social change produces insecurity. As Senator Fulbright has pointed out:

> The missionary instinct in foreign affairs may, in a curious way, reflect a deficiency rather than an excess of national self-confidence. In America's case the evidence of a lack of self-confidence is our apparent need for constant proof and reassurance, our nagging desire for popularity, our bitterness and confusion when foreigners fail to appreciate our generosity and good intentions. Lacking an appreciation of the dimensions of our own power, we fail to understand our enormous and disruptive impact on the world; we fail to understand that no matter how good our intentions—and they are, in most cases, decent enough—other nations are

alarmed by the very existence of such great power, which, whatever its benevolence, cannot help but remind them of their own helplessness before it.

Those who lack self-assurance are also likely to lack magnanimity, because the one is a condition of the other. Only a nation at peace with itself, with its transgressions as well as its achievements, is capable of a generous understanding of others. Only when we Americans can acknowledge our own past aggressive behavior—in such instances, for example, as the Indian wars . . . will we acquire some perspective on the aggressive behavior of others; only when we can understand the human implications of the chasm between American affluence and the poverty of most of the rest of mankind will we be able to understand why the American "way of life" which is so dear to us has few lessons and limited appeal to the poverty-stricken majority of the human race.[19]

The real threat of communism, even if the whole world (aside from the United States) were to go "communist," is perhaps to our place in history, to the importance with which we feel we as a nation deserve to be treated.[20] The real threat to the other-directed person is to be thrown out of the group which defines his importance and gives his life meaning. Out on his own, he is forced once again to examine his life, and the values by which he has lived.

When an individual (or nation) is afraid of losing something—its place in the sun, its ideology, investments, possessions—it seeks to hold onto them ever more closely, even though the threat may be imaginary. All actions are interpreted as threats; the "enemy's" activity no matter what it is, if it can be interpreted as aggression, serves to justify the policy. Each new perceived threat causes a tightening of security (in national terms, the production of more and more missiles) until eventually war breaks out.

Why is there paranoia on a national scale? If American values are all that we say that they are, we should have no fear that they will be subverted by, say, the Communist Party.

American Imperialism: Oil or Ideology?

Other factors may provide a more ready explanation for the fear of communism, the foremost of which is the economic ties which the United States has with many of the world's nation states. Imperialism has usually been defined as the building of an empire by military conquest—Rome, Germany, France under Napoleon. Yet, today we recognize other, more insidious, forms of imperialism. Before we turn to these, it is important that we understand that what has been called

American isolationism, as distinct from post-World War II internation-alism, may in fact, be a misnomer. Throughout the eighteenth and nineteenth centuries Americans expanded westward, conquering lands held by Indians and Spaniards. In part, this also meant agrarian ex-pansion. Could this not be considered a form of traditional imperialism rather than of isolationism? How is one to differentiate continental and overseas expansion? Doesn't the difference merely represent a change in tactics, rather than in strategy? How is one to gauge the distinction made between agrarian and industrial expansion—is it a tactical or fundamental difference? [21]

Americans have a significant stake in the economic, and conse-quently, the political futures of many nations. Today, for example, many of our large oil companies are dividing up perhaps the world's largest offshore oil reserves in South Vietnam. It is not hard to make the connection between this exploitation and the larger one of the war in Vietnam. Many of our large corporations rely on the importation of raw materials—tin from Bolivia, oil from the Middle East and Latin America, to give but two examples—in order to ensure production. The exportation of such commodities requires the presence and the support of stable and friendly governments to guarantee production and to ensure that factories will not be nationalized, that taxes and wages will not be raised, in short, that nothing will erode the margin of profitability. Over fifteen years ago, C. Wright Mills gave some indi-cation of the extent of our foreign investments:

> American export of goods and services amounted to $26 billion in 1957; in addition, twenty-five hundred U. S. firms with branches or subsidiaries abroad sold some $32 billion. The U. S. "foreign market" is $58 billion a year. "Foreign earnings," *Fortune* wrote in January 1958, "will more than double in ten years, more than twice the probable gain in domestic profits." [22]

And such investments are profitable:

> Department of Commerce figures show that in the period 1950–61 there was a direct American foreign investment outflow of $13.7 billion. In the same period, returned income was $23.2 billion, a profit of $9.5 billion. For profitability, the underdeveloped world is at least Europe's equal, more probably its superior. Standard Oil of New Jersey *reports* a 17.6 percent return on its Latin American investment and a 15 percent return on Eastern Hemisphere investments for 1962, compared with a 7.4 percent return on domestic. Commerce Department figures show Americans putting $516 million (new investment and unreturned earnings) into Europe in 1956

and taking home $280 million. By 1961 the nearly 2-to-1 investments–earning ratio had dropped toward 3-to-1: $1.5 billion new investment, $525 million returned earnings. Compare the figures for Latin America, remembering that the stakes here are the real wealth and real labor of Latin American people, not just so many numbers in a book: In 1956 we invested $500 million and returned a profit almost half again as big, $770 million, for a net capital loss to Latin America of $270 million.[23]

To keep the money rolling in entails support of the status quo—which, in turn, often means active support of poverty; dictatorship, of course; and the exploitation of other countries' resources.[24]

A country is drained of its raw materials which are then processed elsewhere, and sometimes later returned to that country as finished products. By charging high tariffs on finished commodities, the United States manages to keep many nations operating on an agricultural economy, which means dire poverty for the majority of the population, insufficient capital to industrialize, and few markets for the products of those countries with industries. One-crop economies such as those of most Latin American countries are governed by these laws. Should the price for the crop drop, the entire nation goes into a depression.[25] United States foreign aid has many strings attached; countries receiving aid are prohibited from nationalizing American industries and are obliged to use the money to buy United States products.[26] In addition, aid is often spread so thin that it amounts to token interest in a specific country, rather than full-scale economic investment.[27]

Finally, it should be said that most of our foreign aid finds its way into the hands of corrupt dictatorships which spend it on military hardware purchased in the United States. The people who need our aid rarely feel the full force of America's good will unless it be at the other end of a bayonet. In Latin America, military expenditures for protection against foreign attack (ostensibly by communists) are little needed: Everywhere guns and napalm are purchased to keep dictatorships in power—for example, Batista in Cuba, Duvalier in Haiti, Franco in Spain, Salazar in Portugal, Chiang Kai-shek on Formosa, and Park in South Korea. While it may appear to the American people that "free elections" are taking place in some of these countries, what happens is that there is usually only a reshuffle of men at the top. The frequency of coups in Latin America signifies merely a power struggle among the ruling élite.

Foreign investments and aid amount to "welfare imperialism." Through these investments, countries are encouraged to align themselves politically with American policies, often to the detriment and neglect of their own peoples. One example of this deplorable trend is Guatemala, where from 1950 to 1954 a duly elected government carried out land reform, expropriating some of the "unused" soil of United Fruit Company. In 1954, troops supported by the CIA invaded Guatemala and placed the country under military rule. Since that time, the land has been given back to United Fruit and the people live in worse poverty than ever. Green Berets have been trained for action in Vietnam in Guatemalan jungles and Cuban "freedom fighters" supported by the CIA have also received similar training on Guatemalan territory. As Eduardo Galeano has commented:

> By every standard Guatemala's extreme poverty is appalling. Only 15 percent of the federal land is under cultivation. Only 750 tractors are in use in the entire country. The country is short one million housing units. In the province of Quiche, there is only one doctor per 120,000 people. A shortage of clinics, hospital beds, and medicine extends throughout the entire country. But ironically, Guatemala is one of the seven Latin American countries that is repeatedly praised by the State Department for having joined the U.S. in shipping medicine to South Vietnam. Out of every 10,000 children born alive, 1,200 die before the age of four. Most of the remainder are condemned to a life without schools, shoes, milk and toys. . . . Guatemala's Army is probably the only one in the world which has one colonel for every thirty men. . . .[28]

By aligning ourselves with dictatorships and oligarchies, our actions again speak louder than our vain words for the hungry and powerless masses of the Middle and South American continents, as they do in Asia and Africa. We force nations to choose between having "democratic" (anti-communist) forms of government and socialist forms of government, between acute poverty and modernization.[29] Why can't our policies support socialist forms of government, land reform, and progressive legislation? Is it in our long-term interests to do otherwise? Most of those actions which we label communist are more often forms of national socialism, with the emphasis on nationalism. As many writers have pointed out, "communism" is usually tempered by friendly trade agreements and political neutrality, rather than hostility. What are the impoverished to do; how can they cope with the severe physical problems of survival which they must face every day of their lives? Apparently, the only way to rapid industrialization for many of these nations is through a planned socialist economy. Yet, we continue to block the growth of socialist economies in the Third World, and instead support those very forces which serve our economic interests (and keep the masses in their place). Would it not be better in the long run—if we are going to intervene anyhow—to support the forces of change against the status quo? Can the masses of these countries wait forever, knowing that we are not the revolutionary society of textbook history? Ultimately, of course, if these nations do develop socialist economies, depriving us of cheap raw materials and labor, then capitalism will no longer be able to survive, and consequently we will have to transform our own economy from capitalist to socialist. In the same vein, perhaps only if America becomes a socialist nation will the nations of the Third World be able to deal effectively with their problems.

Fear of communism can be construed as a fear of losing political and subsequent economic control over many nation-states. We seem only too ready to rush to the aid of corrupt and despotic governments who cry "communist," though what they really fear is change and a loss of power. As Donald Wells has perceptively observed, "The nation that leads the world in foreign investments also leads the world in foreign military bases." [30] Or perhaps we are merely protecting our tourists who venture abroad in strange and far-off lands to learn of other cultures and peoples—or are they really inspecting the empire they secretly feel is theirs?

> One reason Americans abroad may act as though they "own the place" is that many places they very nearly do: American companies may dominate large segments of a country's economy; American products are advertised on billboards and displayed in shop windows; American hotels and snack bars are available to protect American tourists from foreign influence; American soldiers may be stationed in the country, and even if they are not, the population are probably well aware that their very survival depends on the wisdom with which America uses her immense military power.[31]

As friendships may be bought and sold in the open marketplace of suburban America, so too may the friendship of nations be bought and sold; there is little difference in the way many Americans view either. Those nations which dare to challenge the types of friends or the number of friends the United States allows them, must confront American military and economic power. American foreign policy is a burden rather than a help to most of mankind. This is the problem which we must face up to, for the world will change, whether Americans like it or not. Is it because we are unsure of our own value system that we fear others? Do we have the moral right to demand of other nations that they satisfy our own needs and give us the security we appear to lack?

Revolutions: In Spite of All We Do

In spite of all Americans have done to maintain the status quo in other countries, revolutions do occur. In order to understand the effectiveness of America's foreign policy, we must examine why they occur and what role we have had in their formation. In their study of revolution, Leiden and Schmitt found five preconditions for the development and success of a revolutionary movement. First, in underdeveloped societies the people must feel a sense of foreign oppression. It is not enough for such oppression to exist—rather, "powerful sectors of 'dependent' elements (must) first of all conclude that they are dependent; secondly, that the dependency is somehow unjust or impropre; and thirdly, that they can do something to change that relationship." [32]

The sense of foreign oppression of which Leiden and Schmitt speak is felt by many Vietnamese, other Asians, and Latin Americans, if not in an overt military sense, then in fundamental economic relationships.

Leiden and Schmitt next discuss the failure of the economy to meet the needs of a nation's population and confront pressing questions of poverty and industrial development. Revolution usually occurs when segments of the population are "on their way up" but find the path blocked.[33] It is in the frustration of these rising expectations that American economic dominance and tokenism in foreign aid do more to foster revolutionary conditions than hinder them. Furthermore, the showcase of shiny new American commodities juxtaposed with the poverty which much of the world's population must daily face is a constant sore point. We say, in effect, "Why can't you be like us?", and, at the same time, we support dictatorships and oligarchies that maintain the very conditions which must be overcome, and our companies drain developing countries of the very raw materials their economies need.

A third precondition of revolution is the lack of congruence between the social and political systems in a given society, or between what certain significant segments of the population expect and what the political system delivers.[34] In many of the developing nations, intellectuals are demanding a change in form of government which will be more commensurate with the socio-economic realities of their society. Responding to their nation's poverty and American "welfare imperialism," they insist on a change from the "puppet" governments supported by the United States to more socialistic forms of government, which can more readily respond to the needs of the "people."

A fourth factor which Leiden and Schmitt discuss is that certain defects in a specific regime may predispose it to revolutionary overthrow. Here they speak of a government which can command neither respect nor support, which is trapped by outmoded traditions and vested interests.[35] Dictatorships that imprison thousands of political dissenters, that levy high taxes while keeping the population illiterate and ill-fed and that follow the dictates of foreign powers (the United States) against the interests of their own people are prime examples. It is usually only with military aid or the promise (threat?) of military support from the United States that such governments are able to put down potential revolts and stay in power. The final result of all this is that in a prerevolutionary situation the government copes with demands by tightening rather than loosening its control. Instead of permitting gradual peaceful change, it allows no change at all.[36] This usually insures a bitter confrontation between the haves and the have-nots, for there is no longer any way of reaching an agreement except by force. By refusing to recognize the need for social reform, the United States places itself in an antirevolutionary and counterrevolutionary posture, regardless of the dictates and public statements of its political leaders—that we stand for "freedom" and "justice" for all peoples.

In sum, revolution appears to be the result of a gap between aspirations and achievements.[37] Revolutions do not begin at the moment newspaper headlines broadcast their existence to the world. Nor do they begin at the moment a dictator cries "communist threat." Their source is years of poverty, discrimination, injustice, and colonial rule. Most Americans do not empathize with such conditions, and given our own relative material wealth, we find it difficult to understand. Seeing revolutions only as an end product, we wonder why they have occurred. We fail to see the role American foreign policy has played in creating them. We contemplate the violence of revolutionary upheaval without considering the violence—which we have by our actions often endorsed—of poverty, of disease, of political terror, and social injustice. Why does a nation with revolutionary tradition shun revolution?

Perhaps revolutions are distasteful to us because they are a threat to the hypothetical "stability" we seek to foist on each other—a "stability" behind which we hide our insecurity and lack of confidence and trust in ourselves and those around us. Revolutions scare us, just as do hippies and war protesters, because they threaten and challenge our reality structure, our "law and order," our image of the world. They question the validity of the opinions of those whom many of us thought we could rely on and trust—Washington politicians and newspaper men. If you cannot believe the President, then whom can you believe? If a revolution occurs, therefore, we find it difficult to find fault with those to whom we have entrusted the task of maintaining a secure world view and ideology. It is so much easier not to see any connection between a revolution in another country and our policy towards that country; it is so much easier to blame communists and other agitators—so much easier to blame them, and then send in troops to destroy them—in defense of the "free world." By subsuming nationalistic drives under the simplistic heading of "communist subversion," we limit our options in a revolutionary situation.[38]

War: A Reflection of American Society

War is often thought of as a prime means of enforcing or defending America's foreign policy. The effects of such a policy on both the psychological health of the American people as well as its domestic policies are many. The most obvious effect is the dehumanization which results from playing "the war game." In Vietnam our forces dealt in "body counts" and "kill ratios," and success in battle was gauged by the response to the question "How many Cong you get today?" The numbers of dead built up to a level which was incomprehensible to most people. This was a result of the psychological process known as "extinction": If a threat, for example, of nuclear war, is repeated often and over a long period of time, it loses its meaning or is repressed totally from the world of perceptual experience.[39]

One recent example of the dehumanization process can be observed in the incident at My Lai in which American soldiers massacred innocent Vietnamese peasants:

> In other parts of My Lai 4, GIs were taking a break, or loafing. Others were systematically burning those remaining homes and huts and destroying food. . . . Charles West recalled that one member of his squad who simply wasn't able to slaughter a group of children asked for and received permission from an officer to let them go.
>
> West's third platoon went ahead, nonetheless, with the killing. They gathered a small group of about ten women and children, who huddled together in fear a few feet from the plaza, where dozens of villagers already had been slain. . . . A few men now singled out a slender Vietnamese girl of about 15. They tore her from the group and started to pull at her blouse. They attempted to fondle her breasts. The old women and children were screaming and crying. . . . An old lady began fighting with fanatical fury, trying to protect the girl. . . . One of the GIs finally smacked the old woman with his rifle butt; another booted her in the rear. . . .

Nineteen-year old Nguyan Thi Ngoc Tuyet watched a baby trying to open her slain mother's blouse to nurse. A soldier shot the infant while it was struggling with the blouse, and then slashed at it with his bayonet. . . . Le Tong, a 28-year-old rice farmer, reported seeing one woman raped after GIs killed her children. . . . It was estimated that between 450 and 500 people—most of them women, children and old men—had been slain and buried. . . . "After the shooting . . . all the villagers became Communists." [40]

One of the chief consequences of this is that human beings are treated as objects, a process which has been defined in the following terms:

Increased emotional distance from other human beings . . . a diminished sense of personal responsibility for the consequences of one's actions . . . an increasing involvement with procedural problems to the detriment of human needs . . . inability to oppose dominant group attitudes or pressures . . . (and) feelings of personal helplessness and estrangement.[41]

And the media contribute powerfully to the dehumanization by conditioning our responses:

In the same bland voice with which the news announcer reports the imminence of the Christmas season, he reports the wiping out of enemy villages. We can watch a television program relating the efficiency of the ambulance units in picking up wounded soldiers, patching them up, and sending them back to the front lines and the common response is "How nice that they are so efficient, helpful, and humane." [42]

This is all part, albeit an insidious part, of the propaganda battle waged in order to sustain the wider war between two nations. We are able to expose ourselves only to such information as supports this point of view; information which may disturb the security of the public mind is either not printed or censored. And the publication of the Pentagon Papers and the Nixon administration's response are proof that our society is not free to make up its own mind.

Conditioned to buying anything which is plentifully advertised, most of us are ready to buy the government's version of the war.

Just as American foreign policy cannot be considered apart from domestic attitudes and conditions, so too, war and the preparation for war on an international scale has repercussions at home. In the United States, the most pervasive result of war has been the creation of a military-industrial complex. This complex employs millions of persons and has, in effect, created its own technological imperative.[43] Once war is accepted as a means of furthering foreign policy, technology, as the most efficient and effective tool of handling other problems, takes over. Just as in other industries a technological solution to one problem only leads to more technological problems; here, small bombs lead to ever larger ones. The "inner logic" of the system requires endless refinements of weapons and stockpiling. What may have started as a national need rapidly becomes a bureaucratic one as ever newer weapons must be sold to Congress in order to keep the economy and the war machine in operation.[44] And the more weapons produced, the greater becomes the need for Vietnams to test these weapons out and to justify a constant increase in the military budget.

The preparation for war breeds the expectation of war and legitimizes its use in the settlement of international disputes. Are those who wage and prepare for war, therefore, those best able to wage peace? [45] In other words, when warfare and the preparation for war so dominate our economy, can such an economy readily adjust to a "peacetime" situation? When the Vietnam war ends, the money now being spent on the war will in all likelihood, according to President Nixon, continue to be spent on the nation's "security." Antiballistic missile systems and other such technological deterrents will readily eat up the annual thirty billion dollars all too recently expended on Vietnam.[46]

One reason is the apparent collusion between the Pentagon and large defense contractors: Thousands of retired generals and admirals serve on boards of directors and act as consultants. It is not surprising then that the United States sells annually at least a billion dollars worth of guns to foreign nations.[47] This can sometimes be embarrassing when, as in the Arab-Israeli or the India-Pakistani confrontations each side makes war on the other with weapons manufactured in the United States. Congress can vote billions for war or defense in a matter of minutes, but takes months to debate spending a few million dollars for a "war on poverty." [48]

A translation of how much money *could* be spent on domestic programs is supplied by Melman in the following listing: [49]

One TFX airplane: $5,000,000
    = 13 elementary schools, or
    = 570 dwelling units in low-rent public housing projects, or
    = 278 hospital beds
One Polaris submarine with 16 missiles: $122,600,000
    = 331 elementary schools, or
    = 6,811 hospital beds, or
    = 13,723 dwelling units in low-rent public housing

Military space program (military astronautics and related equipment), 1965 estimate: $1,283,714,000
  = 71,317 hospital beds, or
  = 3,469 elementary schools, or
  = 143,688 dwelling units in low-rent public housing
Civil Defense Budget for fiscal year 1965: $358,000,000
  = 40,071 dwelling units in low-rent public housing projects, or
  = 967 elementary schools, or
  = 249 secondary schools, or
  = 19,900 hospital beds, or
  = 32,545 nursing home beds, or
  = 795 miles of highway in rural areas, or
  = 223 miles of highway in urban areas
Atomic Energy Commission, Nuclear Weapons Program, 1965:
$1,800,000,000
  = 4,864 elementary schools, or
  = 201,477 dwelling units in low-rent public housing projects, or
  = 100,000 hospital beds
Based upon domestic equivalent of military spending, 1965:
    elementary school: $370,000
    secondary school: $1,433,000
    1-mile rural road: $450,000
    1-mile city road: $1,600,000
    1 hospital "bed": $18,000
    1 nursing-home "bed": $11,000
    1 low-rent apartment: $8,934

One consequence of the limited debate on defense spending is gross
corruption. Galbraith has pointed out that "firms with the poorest
performance in designing highly technical electronic systems [used in
missiles]—and the failure rate was appalling—have regularly received
the highest profits." [50] Moreover, the defense industry is a parasite on
the economy. Melman comments:

> Whatever worth may be attached to the defense and space program,
> this much is clear: The work of these men, when completed, does not,
> by its very nature, contribute to economic health, or to further pro-
> duction. From an economic standpoint defense work only expends
> manpower and materials. That is why the growth of defense work is
> parasitic growth, regardless of the fact that the workers buy groceries
> and services with their salaries. Since we use about two thirds of our
> prime technical research talent for military-oriented work, the result is

a short supply of comparable talent to serve civilian industry and civilian activities of every sort.[51]

The defense industry, then, is a "brain drain" on the rest of the economy.[52] "Over-kill" in Vietnam likewise has been lethal to domestic programs.

Does the heavy reliance on such military production "guarantee" our policies of "welfare imperialism" or of military intervention? Does such production necessitate these activities? Will our economy collapse without preparation for war? Does Southern California go into acute economic depression when one of their larger defense firms fails to get a specific missile contract? Is this how our foreign policy is determined by the defense industry with its lobby in Congress? When we rely so heavily on armed conflict as a means of solving social problems in other nations, can we hardly criticize black Americans for seeking to redress their real grievances through direct action? Why is it easier to cry socialism in the field of public medicine, but to see no such connection in dealing with military contracts? Why is it easier to pay men to kill than to think? [53]

Modern Weapons of War

In the next sections, we will examine two sets of weapons: nuclear and chemical-biological. Emphasis is placed on these weapons not only because of the increasing part they are coming to play in the development of foreign policy, but also because of their impact on domestic defense spending.

Chemical-biological warfare—in which lethal viruses are introduced into the environment—is a "defense" in the unlikely event of a country's resistance to external attack by radiation and TNT. Since there are many international agreements and treaties prohibiting the use of chemical or biological weapons in wartime, governments take care to "prove" or justify the fact that they are not employing such methods. However, once a degree of chemical warfare is approved by a government, whether by means of stated policy or by public acquiescence:

It is an easy progression from justifying the defoliation of jungle so as to deprive guerrillas of cover to "treating" hundreds of thousands of acres of rice-crops to deprive guerrillas—and the people—of food. And to awarding the highest U. S. civilian medal to a woman scientist who discovered a better rice blast fungus—more effective, that is, than the natural disease which has in the past destroyed Asian rice crops and killed millions by famine.[54]

CBW (chemical/biological warfare) has many advantages over more conventional methods. For one thing, such weapons are relatively cheap to produce and do not require elaborate delivery systems. Furthermore, most CBW weapons only destroy people, leaving much of the urban structural environment intact:[55] CBW is often quite difficult to detect, being either invisible or tasteless, and (the biological weapons) can be spread fairly easily and are difficult to defend against.[56] Serious disadvantages exist, however. CBW weapons are difficult to control—a disease element introduced into a specific environment may last longer than anticipated or spread outside the target area to contaminate large sections of "friendly villages." Certain agents, such as tear or mustard gas, are designed to be used in wide open spaces where they will remain nonlethal. If thrown into caves where the gases cannot dissipate, such nonlethal weapons may often prove deadly.[57] Will a battlefield commander worry about such things as concentration of gas when caught up in winning a war? There are other aspects to this argument:

> Even if a "humane weapon" is developed, its humanity will require the delivery, as in the laboratory, of a precisely measured dose to a standard victim. Both these requisites have thus far been impossible to obtain in the field. Chemical and biological weapons are notoriously uneven in their dispersal and therefore in the amount absorbed by each recipient; to ensure that every person receives an incapacitating dose, some will have to receive an overdose. Furthermore, the young, the elderly and the infirm will be the particularly susceptible victims.[58]

That such control, in fact, has proved impossible to achieve was only recently demonstrated at the Dunway CBW testing grounds in Utah, where a small amount of nerve gas escaped, killing 6,000 sheep grazing several miles away.

Is any one actually being hurt by the implementation of such weapons? The use of defoliants in Vietnam has, in some cases, upset the ecological balance of the environment, and some chemicals are expected to stay up to one hundred years. Nothing edible can grow in these locations. Moreover, saturation bombing from the air has turned tens of thousands of acres of once fertile land into a "moonscape." The effects on the civilian population are obvious. When crops are poisoned and forests defoliated, is it not the women, old men, and children who bear the brunt of the attack? Starvation most affects those who cannot fend for themselves, and with starvation the threat of disease is increased. With an already overwhelming shortage of doctors in Vietnam, the result is clear.[59] Do such tactics win the "minds and hearts" of the populace? A recent report released by a group of Stanford University scientists reached the following conclusions in terms of our efforts in the Vietnamese War:

> No one can conclude, after looking carefully at the impact of our military strategy in Southeast Asia, that we are fighting a war against an army. Instead, we are waging a war against people and the land they live on. The central question is now a simple one: How can we claim to be acting on behalf of people when our action itself is prohibiting a future for them? . . . Defoliants have now been sprayed on more than 5 million acres of Vietnam land, and uncounted acres of Cambodia. Effects of these chemicals include long-term destruction of forest vegetation; widespread heavy damage to rubber plantations in both Vietnam and Cambodia; transformation of Vietnam from a rice-exporting country to an importer of rice; decrease of overall agricultural production by 30 per cent. . . . There is also strong evidence that the spray campaign is leading to a growing number of birth defects in Vietnam. . . . Our government claims to aid a country and its people by destroying both.[60]

Under the guise of good citizenship, many corporations are contracted to produce CBW weapons—for example Dow Chemical, once the producers of napalm:

> Dow accepted this contract because we feel that simple good citizenship required that we supply our Government and our military with those goods they need when we have the technology and capability and have been chosen by the government as a supplier.[61]

In other cases "pure science" has been used as a cover under which men produce deadlier weapons, claiming they do not know how their research will be employed. It is further presumed, of course, that they do not know who is funding this research. Yet, it is not only within private enterprise that such research is enacted: Universities contribute directly to measuring the effectiveness of and production of CBW weapons.[62]

The end of production of CBW weapons will not make the world safe and secure, for such weapons are only a symptom of our attitude toward war.[63]

Nuclear warfare, our other scientific achievement in this area, is based on a system of deterrence: We don't expect either side to use the weapons; rather, each side threatens the other with their *possible* use. Nuclear war has been compared to a chess game. At the RAND corporation, it is calculated how much *we* or *they* can afford to lose in a nuclear confrontation. Often it appears that we are willing to gamble everything (Cuba, 1962). These nuclear deterrence systems are expensive, with a single system often costing well beyond 30 billion dollars.

The nuclear war game is played essentially with two types of deterrent: deterrent against an all-out nuclear attack (Type I) and deterrent against an extremely provocative act (Type II). However, what we assume to be Type I deterrent, the Soviets may consider to be Type II deterrent and act accordingly. Such a mistaken judgment could result in a devastating nuclear war no one really wants. As Falk explains:

> Imagine, for example, that the Soviets had done some very provocative things, such as invading Western Europe with conventional armies, on such a large scale that we felt that we could not stop the invasion by any limited actions, and that we would not be able to rescue Europe at a later date. We might still not be willing to strike the Soviets with our SAC [Strategic Air Command], in view of the terrible price we would have to pay to their retaliatory blow, even if we struck them first. However, we could evacuate our cities and place our forces on a super-alert status, and thus put ourselves in a much better position to strike first and accept the retaliatory blow. We might then present the Soviets with an ultimatum. We would in effect be presenting the Russians with the following three alternatives: to initiate some kind of strike; to prolong the crisis, even though it would then be very credible that we would strike if they continued to provoke us; or to back down or compromise the crisis satisfactorily. We would hope that the Soviets would prefer the third alternative, because our Type I Deterrence would make the first choice sufficiently unattractive, and our Type II Deterrence would do the same for the second; but we might be wrong, and they might take the first alternative. Or they might take the second alternative on the assumption that we would back down, and we might not.[64]

Our nuclear war strategy is developed on the basis of such calculations. Not only may there be a miscalculation of the intentions of the other side which may set off a war, but as the films *Fail Safe* and *Dr. Strangelove* attested, such a war can be set off by human or technological accident. In fact, we have already lost "unarmed" nuclear bombs off the coasts of Spain and Greenland. Nuclear stockpiling has extended to a point where we can speak of "over-kill." Both American and Soviet arsenals contain enough weaponry to wipe out the earth and its population 100 times over. Each side states that the reason they need such an abundance is that the other side has similar amounts and is prepared to use them if we should fail to keep up the pace. It is ironic that after the 1972 arms limitation agreement concluded between the United States and Russia, Defense Secretary Laird asked for a 4 billion dollar *increase* in the defense budget in order to develop a new bomber. But would the other side really use the weapons? Would not such an unleashing contaminate the entire earth with radioactive material so that no one would be the victor? [65] Is it necessary to destroy the earth in order to save it?

The assumption of rationality during actual, rather than "play," nuclear attack may also be a false one. In the case of an attack, leaders would have to make almost instantaneous decisions. Such decision-making only comes from the inculcation of past experience. Since the nature of warfare has changed, what worked in a conventional war situation may no longer hold for decision-making in a nuclear confrontation. Reliance on tradition, then, may not be a sufficient guide to present action.[66] Moreover, the President usually surrounds himself with men who tend to agree with him—in a "war council" he would find few who would dare to challenge openly whatever becomes the Chief Executive's decision. Human beings may prove quite incapable of responding to and making decisions on the use of nuclear weapons. Should decision-making be taken over by machines, the mistakes and accidents which might occur can readily be imagined. We would have even less say in whether we lived or died.

It is often held that we could save ourselves in a nuclear conflagration by burrowing deep into the earth. This "civil defense" program is predicated on the assumption that a certain percentage of the population will be able to survive a nuclear attack. If we grant that a certain percentage will escape the immediate nuclear holocaust, the question of survival on a planet filled with radioactive air and soil, its industrial plants destroyed, rampant with disease due to millions of rotting bodies still needs to be answered: Where will the survivors find enough uncontaminated food to sustain themselves? It must be remembered that these are not cavemen, nor are they "equipped" to survive as cavemen once did, nor will the planet look the same as that cavemen once faced.

Even more important, how would individuals living in fallout shelters for years even be able to tolerate each other? Living in cramped, close quarters, disputes would no doubt frequently arise. What would prevent them from resorting to the same means—killing —to settle their conflicts? Several years ago, a television play showed what might happen during a nuclear attack if there were not enough shelters to go around—neighbors shooting neighbors to keep them out of *their* shelter. The entire civil defense program breeds an atmosphere of fear and distrust, for it falsely assumes we can survive a nuclear attack. Children go through air-raid drills as though this were World War II. What happens after they duck under their desks, "safe and secure" from flying glass: Do they then go outside and play? This program also subtly conditions us to the "inevitability" of war and acts as a break on the initiative to consider peaceful alternatives. Thinking about the unthinkable, on the other hand, is not something that we care to do, like the visitor to the museum at Hiroshima:

> Four times at the museum in Hiroshima.
> I saw the people walking around.
> People walk around, lost in thought,
> Among the photographs, the reconstructions,
> For want of something else, among the photographs,
> The photographs, the reconstructions, for want of
> Something else, the explanations, for want of
> Something else.[67]

The nuclear war game is only the logical extension of the rest of our foreign policy, a policy which seeks to deter us from examining the issues, our own outmoded values. By building walls around our other-directed transparent relationships, around a largely "empty" economic system, we pretend that, somehow, the problems on the "inside" will go away, and are entirely the fault of those on the "outside," the "communists." Can a nuclear arsenal give meaning to our relationships, make our occupations worthwhile, allow us a real choice at election time, solve the "race" issue? Can war or the preparation for war solve world poverty and population problems? Can it bring about a recognition that there are different cultures and peoples with different needs and ambitions? If it can do none of these things, there can be no justification for continued support of such a system.

NOTES

[1] Cited in Felix Greene, *Vietnam, Vietnam* (Palo Alto: Fulton Publishing Co., 1966), p. 163.
[2] Ronald Steel, *Pax Americana* (New York: The Viking Press, Inc., 1967), p. 16.
[3] David Horowitz, *The Free World Colossus* (New York: Hill & Wang, Inc., 1965), pp. 62–63.

[4] *Ibid.*, p. 28.

[5] Carl Oglesby and Richard Shaull, *Containment and Change* (New York: The Macmillan Company, 1967), pp. 41–2.

[6] *Ibid.*, pp. 84–85.

[7] Horowitz, *op. cit.*, pp. 90–94.

[8] Steel, *op. cit.*, p. 3.

[9] Horowitz, *op. cit.*, p. 124.

[10] *Ibid.*, pp. 102–103.

[11] Steel, *op. cit.*, p. 10.

[12] *Ibid.*, p. 17.

[13] *Ibid.*, p. 19.

[14] *Ibid.*, p. 317.

[15] *Ibid.*, p. 165.

[16] *Ibid.*, pp. 134–135. See also Felix Greene, *China* (New York: Ballantine Books, Inc., 1962), and A. Doak Barnett; *Communist China and Asia* (New York: Random House, Inc., 1962).

[17] Steel, *op. cit.*, p. 16.

[18] For discussions of the Vietnam War, see David Schoenbrun, *Vietnam: How We Got In, How To Get Out* (New York: Essandris, 1968); Marvin E. Gettleman, *Vietnam* (Greenwich: Fawcett, 1965); Robert Shaplen, *The Lost Revolution* (New York: Harper & Row, Publishers, 1966); American Friends Service Committee, *Peace in Vietnam* (New York: Hill & Wang, Inc., 1966); John Gerassi, *North Vietnam: A Documentary* (New York: The Bobbs-Merrill, Co., Inc., 1968); Johnathan Schell, *The Village of Ben Suc* (New York: Alfred A. Knopf, Inc., 1965), and *The Destruction of Quang Ri Province* (New York: Alfred A. Knopf, Inc., 1968).

[19] J. William Fulbright, *The Arrogance of Power* (New York: Random House, Inc., 1966), pp. 21–22.

[20] Robert L. Heilbroner, "The Revolution of Rising Expectations: Rhetoric and Reality," in Neal D. Houghton (ed.), *Struggle Against History* (New York: Washington Square Press, 1968), p. 122.

[21] William Appleman Williams, "Rise of an American World Power Complex," in Houghton, *op. cit.*, p. 3.

[22] C. Wright Mills, *The Causes of World War Three* (New York: Ballantine Books, Inc., 1958), p. 73.

[23] Oglesby and Shaull, *op. cit.*, pp. 82–3.

[24] Seymour Melman, *Our Depleted Society* (New York: Delta, 1965), pp. 253–255.

[25] Gabriel Kolko, *The Roots of American Foreign Policy* (Boston: Beacon Press, 1962).

[26] Horowitz, *op. cit.*, p. 230; Kolko, *ibid.*, p. 81.

[27] Steel, *op. cit.*, p. 265.

[28] Eduardo Galeano, "With the Guerrillas in Guatemala," in Arthur I. Blaustein and Roger R. Woock, *Man Against Poverty: World War III* (New York: Random House, Inc., 1968), pp. 367–368. See also Steel, *op. cit.*, p. 208; Norman Gall, "Letter from Peru"; and Sam Schulman, "Latin American

Shantytown," also Blaustein; and for a discussion about Guatemala, specifically see Eduardo Galeano, *Guatemala: Occupied Country* (New York: Modern Reader, 1969).

[29] Steel, *op. cit.,* p. 281.

[30] Donald A. Wells, *The War Myth* (New York: Pegasus (Publishing), 1967), p. 208.

[31] Fulbright, *op. cit.,* p. 10.

[32] Carl Leiden and Karl M. Schmitt, *The Politics of Violence: Revolution In the Modern World* (Englewood Cliffs, N. J.: Prentice-Hall, Inc., 1968), p. 39. See also James C. Davies, *When Men Revolt and Why* (New York: The Free Press, 1971). Roderick Ayar and Norman Miller, *National Liberation: Revolution in the Third World* (New York: The Free Press, 1971).

[33] *Ibid.,* pp. 42–43. See also Crane Brinton, *Anatomy of a Revolution* (New York: Random House, Inc., 1965); and Henry Bienen, *Violence and Social Change* (Chicago: University of Chicago Press, 1968).

[34] Leiden and Schmitt, *op. cit.,* p. 44.

[35] *Ibid.,* p. 48.

[36] *Ibid.,* p. 50.

[37] Ivo K. Feierabend, Rosalind L. Feierabend, and Betty A. Nesvold, "Social Change and Political Violence: Cross National Patterns," in Hugh Davis Graham and Ted Robert Gurr (eds.), *Violence in America* (New York: Bantam Books, Inc., 1969), pp. 636, 647.

[38] Fulbright, *op. cit.,* p. 72.

[39] Viola W. Bernard, Perry Ottenberg, and Fritz Redl, "Dehumanization: A Composite Psychological Defense in Relation to Modern War," in Robert Perrucci and Marc Pilisuk, *The Triple Revolution* (Boston: Little, Brown and Company, 1968), pp. 17–34. See also Fullbright, *op. cit.,* pp. 136–137.

[40] Seyman M. Hersh, *San Francisco Chronicle,* June 2, 1970, p. 21.

[41] Perry et al., pp. 25–28.

[42] Wells, *op. cit.,* p. 59.

[43] John Kenneth Galbraith, *How to Control the Military* (New York: Signet, 1969), p. 55.

[44] *Ibid.,* p. 35–36.

[45] Wells, *op. cit.,* p. 69.

[46] Galbraith, *op. cit.,* pp. 12–13.

[47] *Ibid.,* p. 30.

[48] Melman, *op. cit.,* p. 38.

[49] *Ibid.,* p. 37.

[50] Galbraith, *op. cit.,* p. 25.

[51] Melman, *op. cit.,* p. 7.

[52] *Ibid.,* p. 11.

[53] *Ibid.*

[54] Lord Ritchie-Calder, "Introduction," to Steven Rose, *CBW* (Boston: Beacon Press, 1969).

[55] I. Malek, "Biological Weapons," in Rose, *Ibid.,* p. 53.

[56] J. Perry Robinson, "Chemical Weapons," in Rose, *Ibid.,* p. 31.

[57] *Ibid.,* p. 25.

[58] M. F. Kahn, "Vietnam," in Rose, *Ibid.,* p. 98.

[59] A. W. Galston, "Defoliants," in Rose, *Ibid.,* pp. 64, 71.

[60] David Perlman, "Report on the War to Kill the Land," *San Francisco Chronicle,* June 24, 1970.

[61] Elinor Langer, "United States," in Rose, *op. cit.,* pp. 125–126.

[62] *Ibid.,* p. 129.

[63] *Ibid.*

[64] Herman Kahn, "The Arms Race and Some of Its Hazards," in Richard A. Falk and Saul H. Mendlovitz *Toward A Theory of War Prevention* (New York: World Law Fund, 1966), pp. 23–24. The interested reader should also see Herman Kahn, *On Thermonuclear War* (Princeton: Princeton University Press).

[65] Melman, *op. cit.,* p. 45.

[66] Jerome Frank, *Sanity and Survival* (New York: Vintage, 1968), pp. 165–190.

[67] Marguerite Duras, *Hiroshima Mon Amour* (New York: Grove Press, Inc., 1961), p. 17.

7

the depleted structure:
ecology of the sewer

If we are what we eat, what exactly are we? The foods we consume have in the past been (and some still are) saturated with DDT or nitrates, monosodium glutamate, or other additives which can fundamentally alter our body chemistry. Consequently, it is quite possible that our very perception of the social and natural world around us has been distorted or disturbed. If we live in Los Angeles, New York, or any of over a dozen other cities, we are forced to breathe the equivalent of two to three packs of cigarettes per day. We have employed technology to make life easier and more comfortable, to enable people to live free of mental and physical disease, and to live longer. The elimination of disease, however, has meant that more people are able to live, and to live longer, thus creating shortages of food and other commodities in many parts of the world. In response to this upset in the balance of nature we introduce still more artificial elements into our environment to enable us to survive.

Environmental pollution is the product of Western man's attitude toward nature. In essence, man is not viewed as a part of nature—rather, nature is there for man to use as he sees fit, be it in the construction of houses or parking lots, or in the manufacture and dropping of napalm bombs. Nature exists as an interdependent system of organisms; destroy one and we change the relation of each to the other.[1] Not only must man be viewed as a functional part of this ecosystem (that is, that he is like other animals—he must eat, eliminate, reproduce), but also he must *feel* himself a part of this environment.[2] Unfortunately, most of us do not. On the contrary, the Western idea is one of man *versus* nature, conquering his environment, shaping nature to fit his needs whatever these may be. A clear case of rape—the word is not too strong for the crime that has been committed against the land—has been followed by repeated acts of even greater barbarity. However, the evidence of degradation has accumulated slowly and quietly, giving most of us time to adjust to the consequences of our actions.

There is no immediate personal, life-and-death crisis in most individuals' minds, for no one appears to have been obliterated by smog, pesticides, or artificial additives. Rather, the effects are in the long run, in what is accumulated. This does not alleviate the problem; it only makes it more difficult to raise public concern about it. Just as there are ecological chains of life, where each organism depends on countless others for survival, so too are there chains of death, where destruction of one part of the environment destroys others.[3]

One problem has been that there is no land or *environmental ethic*. Land for Western man means property, and may be treated as such. Any other organisms residing on such property automatically become the property of their human owner who can in turn do whatever he wishes to them. As with most property, there are *rights* but few *obligations*.[4] Moreover, property is a means of identifying status; it can be bought and sold. If it is not worth much according to our economic system, then why preserve and take care of it? For example, why cherish what we define as a weed? What is its worth? Yet, even if something is valuable, it is valuable because of our economic values, not necessarily because of its place in nature. Corn is cultivated because we can use it as a food commodity, yet, in the process of growing corn, the spraying of various insecticides to root out annoying weeds, grasses, or insects fundamentally alters the place of corn in the natural environment.

Some critics point out that what is "natural" depends upon the period of history: Was it natural for bubonic plague to exist during the Middle Ages? Is it not natural for man to use his environment to suit his purposes? Then could it also be that if the destruction of our environment is natural, the demise of humanity may also be natural (and shortly upon us)?

Destruction of Habitat: Changing the
Environment To Fit the Needs of Whom?

We noted in Chapter 2 that many Americans are preoccupied with consumption, not necessarily out of need for the commodities themselves but rather out of the symbolic meanings attached to them. What do we do with all these goods when we are done with them? What happens to that car we wanted so badly, only to tire of it after a year or so? We sell it, right? Then what happens to that car when it can no longer command a market value? It turns into apparently worthless junk and is moved to a massive junkyard somewhere. What happens to the "no-deposit, no-return" bottles and cans which are consumed by the millions? They go to large garbage-disposal locations —"out of sight, out of mind." But not out of nature. Nor are their effects completely disposed of.

Let's look at this process in another way. In order to produce a car, certain depletable raw materials (for example, iron ore) have to be mined. Once the car is completed and purchased, it joins millions of other cars on the nation's highways, with each car giving out some unburned fuel. The resulting smog pollutes the environment, often making it difficult to breathe, killing trees and plants, and in the long run shortening human lives. Yet, the production and consumption of new model automobiles continues, not because our lives are really improved by them, but simply because we just have to have them. The "throw-away society" means "progress" for the economy. In fact, there is a planned obsolesence for many commodities in terms of their desirability, quality, and function.[5]

This process is bound to have an effect on the way people interact, and on the way human beings view themselves. The idea of being able to throw away what we no longer want, *and of being able to treat people as objects,* leads to the throwing away of people: When we tire of someone, all we have to do is discard him. Yet, when we get tired of the environment we have created, and long for the grass and trees we have replaced with concrete freeways and parking lots and tract homes, we may be quite unable to change it back to what it was before the freeways, lots, tracts—and junk yards, and polluted lakes and streams. Can we play with ecological forces in the environment the way we play with the production and consumption of new material goods, and with people? Are these ecological forces even ours to play with? Who owns the mountain that is turned into a ski resort?

Besides the glut of material goods on the market, there are currently alterations of the habitat which must be considered as irreversible and which can have lethal effects on man. Perhaps one of the major problems is that of chemical pollution—the use of insecticides, and other such "equalizers" to alter the environment making it more "suitable" for human beings to survive. Again, the "engineering" attitude is taken: Do whatever you want to plants, streams, or soil, and "to hell with the side effects." [6] This same attitude is taken on the part of those who use insecticides. They divide the world into useful and useless plants and trees. Those plants which are not useful, as defined by man, are eliminated. Little effort is made to see how a condemned "weed" fits into the ecological process. Insecticide users ignore some vital considerations:

> Two ecological ideas are at the heart of these pollution problems: First is the principle that substances released into environment move in pathways loosely described as "cycles" and often return, concentrated, to threaten man himself. Second, the poisons used to control pests have effects on many populations, not merely the pest; effects of these poisons include: (a) killing some wild animal populations, especially those of predatory animals which regulate populations of other animals; (b) causing population eruptions of other species which may become new pests; while (c) the old pests remain and evolve new ability to survive the poisons.[7]

What happens in practice is that we go to the market and buy a can of pest spray to eliminate flies and weeds. Suppose we pick weed killer. The average person may not follow the directions on the side of the can; perhaps he will use ten times the amount necessary to kill a particular set of weeds which are threatening his rose bushes, thinking that "more is better." While wiping out the weed, this poison is then carried into the soil with the decomposition of the weed, from which it is picked up by various other plants which feed on an underground water supply.[8] The water transfers this poison to edible plants and in turn to animals. We eat the plants and animals, and the poison is returned to us, but not in the same concentration as that which we applied to the weed we were spraying.

In terms of large-scale agriculture, therefore, appropriate or "nonlethal" spraying of DDT on grass is concentrated when eaten by animals, and is in turn concentrated again when men eat these animals or the products of animals—milk, butter.[9] The last person in line gets the highest concentration. These so-called food-chains turn "harmless" dosages of insecticides into potentially deadly dosages. The concen-

tration of DDT increases because a cow eats so much grass containing the DDT residue. People drink milk from many cows, so again the addition of several different sources of DDT.[10]

There are other effects of the introduction of chemicals such as DDT into the soil. They may stay in the soil a long time, even for years, so that their effects on other parts of the ecosystem can continue for the same period of time.[11] We know that such build-ups occur in man. For example, we have a difficult time passing on some of the insecticides and additives we accumulate from eating food. Thus, the synthetic additives in packaged and frozen foods, each of which may be harmless if taken by themselves, may accumulate harmful concentrations within our bodies. We don't eat just one box of frozen fish—we may eat the same fish with the same additive twenty times per year.[12]

Another problem with the pesticides is that often they must be used in ever heavier dosages, for the plants and insects they are used against may develop immunities to the sprays. Carson concludes:

> The whole process of spraying seems caught up in an endless spiral. Since DDT was released for civilian use a process of escalation has been going on in which ever more toxic materials must be found. This has happened because insects, in a triumphant vindication of Darwin's principle of the survival of the fittest, have evolved super races immune to the particular insecticide used, hence a deadlier one has always to be developed—and then a deadlier one than that. It has happened also because . . . destructive insects often undergo a "flareback" or resurgence, and after spraying, in numbers greater than ever before. Thus the chemical war is never won.[13]

These heavier dosages, of course, mean higher concentration. The amount of DDT used between 1940 and 1966 increased eight times, and predictions are that, had it not recently been banned, usage would have increased four more times by 1975.[14]

Perhaps equally important is that in the process of increasing the dosages the ecosystem is simplified and fundamentally altered. In fact, critics have suggested that pesticides be renamed "biocides," a word similar to "genocide" in its connotations.[15] We fail to ask what the relationship is between weeds and grass, between one insect and another, or between insects and plants. When insecticides eliminate one species, there can be a rapid increase in another that formerly had to do battle against the destroyed insect. While a complex ecological system is able to maintain its own balance, in a simplified one such as those we frequently create, balance is at best temporary.

The same process can happen when we introduce new species into a formerly stable environment.

> Some keen gardener, intent upon making Hawaii even more beautiful than before, introduced a plant called *Lantana camara,* which in its native home of Mexico causes no trouble to anybody. Meanwhile, someone else had also improved the amenities of the place by introducing turtle-doves from China, which, unlike any of the native birds, fed eagerly on the berries of *Lantana.* The combined effects of the vegetative powers of the plant and the spreading of seeds by the turtle doves were to make the *Lantana* multiply exceedingly and become a serious pest on the grazing country. Indian mynah birds were also introduced, and they too fed upon Lantana berries. After a few years the birds of both species had increased enormously in numbers. But there is another side to the story. Formerly the grasslands and young sugar-cane plantations had been ravaged yearly by vast numbers of army-worm caterpillars but the mynahs also fed upon these caterpillars and succeeded to a large extent in keeping them in check, so that the outbreaks became less severe. About this time certain insects were introduced in order to try and check the spread of *Lantana* and several of them . . . did actually destroy so much seed that the *Lantana* began to decrease. As a result of this, the mynahs also began to decrease in numbers to such an extent that there began to occur again severe outbreaks of army-worm caterpillars. It was then found that when the *Lantana* had been removed in many places, other introduced shrubs came in, some of which are even more difficult to eradicate than the original *Lantana.*[16]

Certain natural "agents" (for example, wind and water) serve to spread insecticides from one species to another, and there is little we can do to control this spread, no matter how controlled the particular spraying. Polluted waters eventually end up in the oceans, in seafood, and ultimately, according to some scientists, in our drinking-water. Fundamentally, the ocean forms a primary link in the oxygen process through the marine diatoms which grow there. When the pollutants kill the diatoms, they also destroy our oxygen supply. Fortunately, the earth has for the present an abundant supply of polluted oxygen (smog) and is in no danger of running out.

Several questions must be raised in light of the poisoning of the ecosystem and the ultimate self-destruction of man. First, do those who manufacture and produce such chemical agents have the right to do so? Who is to protect the consumer of synthetic foods? Who is to protect the inhabitants of the environment being destroyed? As Carson has asked: Where is the bill of rights governing such issues?[17] Did the population of the United States ever consent to have its food polluted in this manner? How can we continue to trust our government when it permits chemical poisoning to continue without adequate checks or evaluations on the use of such poisons? What happens when we discover that the milk we drink contains high amounts of DDT? What type of control do we have over our lives? [18] Again, the decisions being made for us, without our consent (unless our silence is our consent), are often irreversible. The "cyclamates" are off the market, but how many other "cyclamates" exist, which we have yet to find out about?

Another critical problem is the type of world these poisons, this engineering mentality, is creating. Technology is relied on to solve all problems.[19] We have created an asceptic world:

> In this careful, cosmetic [germ-, bug-, and insect-free] world there are no gnarled people, no mature or older men and women whose faces, bodies and hands have been formed and indented through direct contact with the brines, caustics and tannins of elder nature. When these people, in response to vestigial urges, penetrate the wilderness briefly on summer vacations, they do so sheltered in their hydromatically propelled perambulators, cared for and distracted by the multitude of gay gadgets such as folding stoves, shirt pocket radios, collapsible plastic furniture; nourished through the umbilical cord of intricate transport and communications. The Grecian exposure to sun and wind is after all achieved only in carefully selected beaches, resort spots or dude ranches, guaranteed free of chiggers, abrasive gravel and black flies. Painful effort, sweat other than that which can be quickly removed in the locker room showers, gruelling and permanently disfiguring contacts with the elements —such elements are discreetly missing.[20]

Finally, though the engineers keep building, almost because this is the only way they, and we, can relate to nature, the question must be asked: Who needs it? Is this the result of a profit-oriented economy, where any means are justified to increase such profits? Have our lives been fundamentally improved by elimination of all our "enemies" in nature? The problem also must be seen as more than a conservation of resources or a question of aesthetic efforts to "beautify" America; rather, it is a question of ecosystems and our place in them.

Pollution: The Breath We Take May Be Our Last

Most of us are familiar with smog and its effect on our own immediate life. We breathe, and after a while it becomes difficult to take any more deep breathing. Our chest hurts. Sometimes our eyes tear.

Smog is the result of having more than a normal number of particles in the air. Approximately 2000 pts/mil is considered normal. Los Angeles has been reported to have up to 15,000 pts/mil, with 35,000 pts/mil being considered lethal. Auto emissions, factories and airplanes are its major sources. The process works in the following way:

> Traveling combustion chambers [cars], like any other combustion devices, spew forth a certain amount of unburned gases—ingredients for the airy stew. Sunshine serves as the cooking element in the photochemical process. The container, for all intents and purposes, are weak winds which prevent the ingredients from being lost out the sides. And the lid is provided by a phenomenon known as "temperature inversion."
>
> Temperature inversion is produced when a layer of warm air sits atop a layer of cooler air, thus inhibiting the normal process of vertical ventilation from the rising of warm air.[21]

It is said that the average New Yorker breathes the equivalent of smoking thirty-eight cigarettes per day—and at this writing, perhaps more.[22] The Rienows have stated the problem bluntly:

> In a civilization whose air may be composed of 21 percent natural gases and 79 percent automobile and other combustion gases, we shall be burdened with lungs that demand an outmoded mixture of some 79 percent plain nitrogen and 21 percent oxygen. We are trying to adapt a prehistoric physiology to an ultra-modern technology and losing on every front. Paleontology tells us that unless we switch and learn to adapt our technology to our prehistoric bodies, we shall perchance pay the price of the dinosaur and the other unadaptable life species which have preceded us.[23]

In Osaka, Japan, in 1960, twenty-second whiffs of oxygen were distributed through public vending machines for the equivalent of three cents.[24] Soon, perhaps, people in Los Angeles will be walking around with gas masks on, or will be unable to emerge from their air-conditioned homes for fear of dying of asphyxiation. Yet, air-conditioning processes that also clean the air need increasing amounts of water which is already in short supply in smog-choked areas such as Los Angeles and New York. The energy needs of air conditioning can also exacerbate air pollution.

Air pollution has also affected the amount of sunlight which reaches the earth's surface. When, as on a smoggy day, there are a tremendous number of particles in the air, less sunlight reaches the animals and plants which dwell there. This has a decided impact on the weather, and, in the long run, on which animals and what types of vegetation exist. At the same time, smog has had a considerable effect on plant leaves by destroying the photosynthesis process.[25] If plants are destroyed, then so too is one link in the making of oxygen which we need to breathe; and perhaps of a more immediate concern, the destruction of plants means the destruction of sources of food both directly (vegetables) and indirectly (through animals). Any such alterations mean changes in the ecosystem, an upset in the "balance" of nature.

In line with air pollution is water pollution, which also results from the deposit of certain waste materials, except in this case the materials are solid. The most common method of disposing of such materials in the past has been to dump them into the water system—any nearby stream, lake, or ocean will fit the bill. The trouble with this method was that these materials soon killed everything in the particular lake or stream. Lake Erie is a prime example, but there are thousands of others.[26] Burying and burning garbage has also been employed, the latter technique, of course, contributing to smog. In communities which place certain restrictions on how much sewage can safely be dumped into a specific river or lake, these limits are soon passed.[27] Some cities have begun to experiment with sewage treatment facilities in an attempt to reuse the water which was being polluted. However, where this has been attempted, one of technology's modern miracle workers, detergents, have come back through the taps in kitchens, for the suds were nearly impossible to destroy. These same suds played havoc with sewage plant operations.[28]

Another fundamental problem has begun to affect disposal operations. There is just too much waste being produced. The following citation from Gene Marine gives some idea of the magnitude of the problem:

> An urban unit of 1,000,000 people produces . . . 500,000 tons of sewage a day. . . . Sewage aside, that same urban unit produces, every day, another 2,000 tons of solid waste that has to be disposed of. On top of that, it throws into the air, every day, 1,000 tons of particles, sulfur dioxide, nitrogen oxides, hydrocarbons and carbon dioxide. In 1963, American mines, every day, discarded 90,400,000 tons of waste rock and tailings. In 1965, every day, more than 16,000 automobiles were scrapped. . . . Every one of us in the United States generates about 4.25 pounds of solid waste a day, in one form or another (in the cities it's about 6 or 7 pounds per capita). . . .[29]

With so much to get rid of, and industry producing more every day for us to consume and eliminate through our overfed systems, the problem is approaching a crisis. Yet, little is done about it, for we rarely see the garbage dumps, and we rarely associate a tin can lying on the beach with a chronic pollution problem, nor, for that matter do we see the link between profit-making, employment, production, consumption, and pollution. It all stops somehow at the consumption stage. Is there place to put it all? (Outer space?) With the world's population on the rise, we cannot put waste out of sight much longer. The "unsafe for swimming" signs may soon proliferate into "unsafe for drinking or breathing."

Too Many People and Not Enough Zoos

Many scientists would argue that a very large part of the pollution problem we have been discussing is due to the population explosion which the world has been undergoing for the last 100 years or so. The population of the world has been doubling approximately every thirty-seven years, and the rate at which the doubling occurs is in itself accelerating—by some estimates, at from 1 to 3 percent per year.[30] Thus, the number of years it takes to double the population will continue to decrease, so that by the year 2000 we should have roughly 6.25 billion persons living side-by-side. Why has there been such a sudden increase in population? For one thing, modern medicine has been able to almost eliminate many diseases (including yellow fever, malaria, and small pox) which formerly struck children during the first few years of their lives. As this neo-natal mortality rate decreased, more persons were able to survive into the reproductive years, and, in fact, live to a ripe old age.[31] We arrive at the population growth rate by subtracting the death rate from the birth rate.[32] As medicine has aided in a reduction of the death rate, then, the growth rate has accelerated even more as most of those born have survived.

The increase in population has also been related to the increased ability to produce and transport greater quantities of food. In the so-called underdeveloped countries of the world, however, modern health measures have reduced rather than increased the standard of living, for increased food production cannot hope to keep up with increased population.[33] The old adage "the rich get richer and the poor get poorer" applies here, for the rich, industrialized societies increase their population at a much slower rate than do the underdeveloped countries. The former have greater birth-control sophistication and the desire for smaller families. In many underdeveloped countries, women are continually pregnant, for in the past perhaps half of all their children died in infancy.

With the introduction of modern medical and health measures, more of those born survive, while attitudes toward pregnancy and birth control have not altered accordingly. Nor have birth-control programs in these societies been very successful to date. (An interesting exception is Japan, where the use of abortion has recently caused what they consider to be underpopulation.) For perhaps two-thirds of the world's nations, numbers of people form a "pollutant." "Under-developed" then comes to mean starving at the rate of 3.5 million per year,[34] because most of these nations cannot handle their population problem, given a low Gross National Product, illiteracy, and primitive agricultural techniques.[35] Some of the population doubling times for these countries and what they mean is revealed in the following:

> Doubling times in the UDCs (underdeveloped countries) range around 20–35 years. Examples of these times (from the 1968 figures just released by the Population Reference Bureau) are Kenya, 24 years; Nigeria, 28; Turkey, 24; Indonesia, 31; Philippines, 20; Brazil, 22; Costa Rica, 20; and El Salvador, 19. Think of what it means for the population of a country to double in 25 years. In order just to keep living standards at the present inadequate level, the food available for the people must be doubled. Every structure and road must be duplicated. The amount of power must be doubled. The capacity of the transport system must be doubled. The number of trained doctors, nurses, teachers, and administrators must be doubled. This would be a fantastically difficult job in the United States—a rich country with a fine agricultural system, immense industries and rich natural resources. Think of what it means in a country with none of these.[36]

It is no wonder that the starvation rate is increasing. Still, it is difficult to measure the true starvation rate as many countries do not keep adequate demographic information. People already weakened by starvation often die of disease, and their death, by starvation, therefore, does not always get reported.[37] Scientists estimate that at the present time approximately 40 percent of the world's population is under 15 years of age, which is the reason for immense population increase predictions in the near future. And, as Ehrlich pessimistically points out, it's just too late for half the world's population at the present time. Most will starve.

While we may have the capacity to prevent such starvation from taking place, we don't really care to do anything about it. Although concern is expressed, there is little financial substance behind these outcries, for it is not *we* who are overpopulated.[38] And besides, more people mean more markets, do they not? The only difficulty is, as the present world revolutionary climate testifies, will the half of the world's population which is starving permit the other half of the world to live in affluence, while it dies? Do we have the right to become "overdeveloped," to grow fat off the natural resources and labor of others? Developing nations, with more than two-thirds of the world's population, consume little more than one-seventh of the world's energy output; the developed nations use six times as much energy with less than half as many people.[39]

Another interesting issue raised by the population explosion is that it has always seemed to be socially acceptable to reduce the death rate, but socially unacceptable to reduce the birth rate. Let's face it: regardless of the economic circumstance, most people like living. We do, don't we? Why shouldn't the Chinese peasant or the Calcutta slum dweller? The key question, of course, is not how many people survive, but what quality of life will those that do have.[40] Again, the problems are complex, for with increased numbers of people, more medicines must be produced to protect their health from the ever-present threat of new diseases which grow out of an altered ecosystem. As the drive for increased production of food intensifies, people will forget about the dangers of DDT spraying, or of additives in fresh and packaged foods; when people are starving, they do not care whether the crops have been sprayed. In mortal combat no one watches to see that the correct amount of "safe" gas is employed.[41]

In the United States, population problems have taken another form. Cities are growing at a rapid rate largely due to a type of self-fulfilling prophecy. Land is cleared for housing tracts, airports are constructed, freeways and dams are built—all in order to make it possible for greater numbers to survive in a given urban area. Why not just refuse to build a new airport or freeway? Would this not limit population growth? Why support the expansion of a given area beyond its ecological capacities, such that it would have to rely increasingly on artificial means and dependence on other areas to survive? A prime example of this kind of urban growth is Los Angeles, a city dependent on the natural resources of other states in order to satisfy its water and power needs. Of course this question is rarely asked, and if so, only rhetorically, for it goes against the desire for progress as measured by quantitative growth. But do we want that many more people in a given area; that many more freeways; that much more smog? In the past, population supposedly limited itself by natural contingencies. Have not these same limits already been reached in many urban areas, as well as nations? Then why aren't they recognized?

Perhaps a key question here is what increased numbers of people will mean to other social problems we have been faced with. What type of government and economy will be necessary in order for these increased numbers to survive? For one, a planned economy will be a requirement, for the world's resources are limited, and their use will have to be planned for, unless we all wipe each other out in a debate over who should sit where at the planning table. Moreover, this type of planning would necessitate a drastic revision of our ideology, particularly those aspects relating to "free enterprise" and individual freedom and liberty. Privacy will decrease as will the ability to own or maintain private property. Think of what twice the number of people presently living on the earth would mean.[42] The problems of consumption, leisure, work, education, mental illness, war, and poverty can only increase with increases in population.

A brief scenario provided from Ehrlich's book *The Population Bomb* best presages the possible crises:

SCENARIO II. In 1979 the last non-communist government in Latin America, that of Mexico, is replaced by a Chinese-supported military junta. The change occurs at the end of a decade of frustration and failure for the United States. Famine has swept repeatedly across Asia, Africa, and South America. Food riots have often become anti-American riots, as our enemies claimed we were withholding food from the starving. In Southeast Asia the Vietnam, Thai, and Laotian wars have resulted in massive casualties, economic crises, and eventual withdrawal to the MacDougal line. Behind that line Australian, Malaysian, and American troops face the growing power of Red China and her allies. As the massive famines swept across Latin America, a series of armed interventions by the United States had proved inadequate to stem the revolutionary tide. During the Mediterranean crisis of 1978 the joint Mexican–United States expeditionary force had been withdrawn from Costa Rica, and the last American "volunteers" had withdrawn from Chile. Only the outbreak of a particularly virulent strain of bubonic plague killing 65 percent of the starving Egyptian population had averted a direct Soviet–American clash in the Mediterranean.

In 1977 both superpowers had withdrawn all aid and influence from the Indian subcontinent as India fell apart into a large number of starving, warring minor states. In her entire history the United States has never faced such a generally hostile world as she does in 1979. Western European nations, living in ever-greater austerity, side with the Soviet Union, accusing the United States of waging biological warfare against the Egyptians. They are joined in their denunciation by Pope Pius XIII who also accuses the United States of "eating meat while the hungry of the world lack bread." In the United States there is actually less meat to eat than at any stage in our history, and price and wage controls and dollar devaluation are an old story. Food and water rationing are standard. Many cities are cycling regularly between riots and uneasy peace under martial law. Nearly complete polarization of opinion exists between the far left groups advocating a complete withdrawal from the international scene and the far right advocating more military action. The government, now virtually a left–right coalition, is under extreme pressure from both sides. It finds any effective action difficult to take.

The Mexican Coup hits President Montgomery at a time of profound internal crisis. The third Los Angeles killer smog in two years has wiped out 90,000 people. Troops holding the city under martial law are under constant attack by rioters. The President's Environmental Advisory Board has reported a measurable rise in the sea level due to melting of the polar ice caps. The Board states further that the decline in fisheries in both the Atlantic and Pacific is now irreversible due to pollution and recommends the immediate compulsory restriction of births to one per couple, and compulsory sterilization of all persons with I.Q. scores under 90. It says that, unless the population size in the United States is reduced rapidly, it too will be facing massive famine by the year 2000. The Emergency Agricultural Commission Report indicates that additional desperate efforts to increase agricultural output would . . . reduce production. It recommends a moratorium on the now "over-kill" synthetic pesticides. This is required if there is to be any chance of restoring reasonable soil fertility in devastated areas of California and the Middle West, and if biological controls are to be used against resistant pests. Pollution and pesticide poisonings have supplanted cardio-vascular disease as the number one killer of Americans.

In early 1980 the Chinese and Russians jointly begin to establish missile bases and other military facilities throughout Latin America. They announce a new policy of containing American aggression. In the United States right-wing pressure to launch preemptive nuclear strikes against both China and Russia becomes extreme. Sino–Russian intelligence, estimating that the President will yield to pressure, recommends a first strike by communist forces. This advice is acted upon, and a general thermonuclear war ensues. Particularly devastating are the high altitude "flash" devices designed to set fire to all flammable materials over huge areas. At one point 15 monster fires rage in the Northern Hemisphere. Each covers an average area of 400,000 square miles—four times the area of Colorado. Inside and outside these areas, wherever conditions permit, huge fire storms are generated. The effects include rising radiation levels and climatic catastrophe resulting from the addition of enormous amounts of debris and carbon dioxide to the atmosphere. These and general sterilization of the soil (followed by massive erosion) make the northern two thirds of the Earth uninhabitable. Pollution of the sea is vastly increased. Small pockets of *Homo sapiens* hold on for a while in the Southern Hemisphere, but slowly die out as social systems break down, radiation poisoning takes effect, climatic changes kill crops, livestock dies off, and various manmade plagues spread. The most intelligent creatures ultimately surviving are cockroaches.[43]

The Supermarket Will Soon Be Empty

Many problems of population size and density are due to the depletion of natural resources. As our own resources become scarce, we will increasingly have to rely on other nations to fill our needs. As the Rienows point out, in ten years 9.5 percent of the world's population will be consuming 83 percent of the world's raw materials.[44] By extracting and exporting these raw materials from underdeveloped nations, we hinder their chances of ever industrializing, for these resources are non-renewable.[45]

The population problem also revolves around the production and distribution of food. It has been calculated that the average person needs 2800 calories per day in order to survive.[46] As the following chart shows, much of the world's population falls substantially below

Proportions of Population Living at High, Intermediate, and Low Per Capita Caloric Intakes

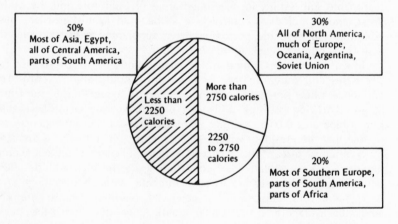

this norm.[47] In fact, vitamin deficiencies are so common in many areas that entire populations are readily susceptible to numerous disease agents.[48]

Most of the good land is already being farmed, and most of that land which was formerly in use can no longer be employed for farming due to past practices of neglect, such as overgrazing, removal of trees, and lack of fertilizers.[49] Since the good soil has been removed in many areas, large amounts of phosphorous and other additives are needed to make it farmable. Unfortunately, most of these lands lie in countries with insufficient economic resources to do so. And the future looks equally bleak, for in countries such as India better than 90 percent of the population is engaged in farming, while only 4 percent is involved in manufacturing or industrializing. With such a small industrial base, there is little room to develop the amount of capital necessary to manufacture soil additives or trade for them.[50] Those lands which could be developed lie largely in the northern parts of Africa and South America, and would little effect food shortages in already over-crowded Asia.[51] As the world's population grows, the amount of food that can be produced remains limited. And when food resources are increased it seems to do little good as the population only increases that much faster. Shipments of food to starving nations then does little to alleviate the basic problem, even if we find the money and the ships to transport it. In fact, because of resulting increases in popula-tion some believe that such a "solution" may exacerbate the problem.[52] Other stop-gap measures such as CARE packages seem to have the same result.[53]

Consider again water as a basic resource. We have already noted that much available water has been polluted beyond repair. But even the so-called "clean" water that is available is rapidly diminishing in quantity and quality, and often has to be imported hundreds of miles to serve large urban areas. Furthermore, this water is increasingly being loaded with chemicals.[54] The Rienows give an example of how rapidly our water supply is being used up. Beginning in Texas, they find:

> In its high plains the citizens are drawing 7 million acre feet from the water table that nature is recharging at the rate of only 50,000 acre feet per year. In one 25,000 square-mile area in New Mexico and Texas, natives have been pumping it out 140 times as fast as it is trickling in. The Mississippi basin wells are 400 feet deeper on an average than they were ten years ago. Nebraska has dug 27,000 wells since World War II, sucked down its fossil water table more than 15 feet, and will run completely dry in from 50 to 100 years.[55]

Moreover, when concrete is put down, water can't drain off into wells; it runs instead into gutters that lead it to a polluted lake or ocean.[56] More optimistic viewpoints look to desalting operations to satisfy our

thirst. But Ehrlich has argued that the maximum world desalting capacity will by 1984 be able to supply only one thirtieth of our *own*
nation's needs.[57]

Fossil fuels (coal and oil) and many metals are rapidly being depleted. In fact, Brown has stated that should present industrial capacities be destroyed in a war we would never be able to rebuild them
since raw materials required now lie too deep within the soil, and in
too bastardized a form to permit access by less than highly technologically sophisticated means.[58] There is no turning back. Again, it is
obvious that we need highly centralized planning in order to distribute
the available limited resources.[59] This all-pervasive social organization
will limit our freedom, particularly our freedom to consume the number of trinkets presently being offered us. Yet, as we have noted, without such consumption our economy would soon collapse because of
the monopolist capital imperative on which it thrives. As a result, the
waging of war to maintain control over available resources will become one of the problems facing the world's peoples.

We should think about this the next time we are lured into a department store. We should ask ourselves who is going hungry because
of the luxury items we are buying. We should ask ourselves about all
the cans lying beside the highway and the raw materials which went
into these throwaway commodities. *We are part of the problem.*
Though large corporations may produce these materials, we purchase
them, and we benefit and will eventually suffer from their production.
The next time an anti-American riot occurs in one of the underdeveloped nations, reflect on the probable cause of instability. We look
to technology to solve our problems. None the less there is a limit
to the amount of population the earth can support, and technology
can only affect this in a minor way, even if we wish to employ it for
this purpose. At present we seem more intent on using it to send
men to outer space and develop our nuclear weapons defense capacities.

Where Do We Start? What Must Be Changed?

In summary, there are essentially five points at which the environental
crisis can be fixed, all of which lead to different courses of action.

1. Many critics, most notably Ehrlich, place the blame on larger
populations. A reduction in population size, therefore, will not only
relieve the pressure on the earth's vanishing resources, but will also
reduce pollution, over-crowding, and the general eco-catastrophe that
we are facing. The solution, from this perspective, is to engage in

massive birth control on a world-wide scale, including the use of pills, abortions, and sterilization techniques.

2. Other critics see the problem in terms of the economic system under which the Western nations, chiefly the United States, currently exist. Capitalism, it is felt, through its demand for constantly expanding markets, creates a never ending drain on raw materials and the need to sell these as finished products which then end up polluting the environment. Moreover, such production necessitates the cutting of costs—items need to be mass produced. Mass produced commodities, such as plastics, are not biodegradable (they cannot be put back into nature). Competition for markets results in economic imperialism (see Chapter 6) in which the poor nations are drained of their raw materials to support the conspicuous consumption economies of the rich nations. Consequently, they cannot industrialize. The rich nations often attempt to retain dictatorships ("stable" governments) in these poor nations so that this economic relationship is not altered. This places the have-not nations in a position such that they have to use high amounts of substances such as DDT on their land to make it more productive and enable their increasing populations to survive. The result, of course, is increasing pollution.[60] "Socialist" nations (Russia) often end up doing the same thing vis-à-vis underdeveloped countries. Yet, *they do not have to maintain expanding markets;* it is not a socialist imperative. Production does not have to be for profit. It is argued that under a socialist system, all of the people can have a say in what is produced and what will be consumed, and that they will come to desire those things which are less polluting and less of a drain on natural resources. Such a system will also be more equitable.

3. Regardless of the economic system under which goods are produced, some critics see the problem as primarily one of increasing consumption. If people would stop buying the many fads and gadgets daily turned out by corporations and lavishly advertised on television, much of the environmental problem could be eliminated. The solution, then, lies in shifting our need for these excess consumer goods (see Chapters 2 and 3) and placing these needs elsewhere—that is, in better interpersonal relationships. The result would be less pollution and less drain on natural resources, plus there would now be enough to go around.

4. Some critics, notably Commoner, see the problem in terms of the way goods are produced, rather than the number which are produced. If our production could be more in tune with our environment, more biodegradable, then we can go on producing as much as we like and the earth will still survive. Taking phosphates out of detergents

is one such effort. Viewing the problem in this way involves harnessing technology to more humanistic concerns.

5. Finally, there are those who argue that the environmental crisis cannot be effectively dealt with unless we change our general value framework. This means not basing our identities on the number of material possessions we have collected, nor wanting to prove our individuality by our behavior in the supermarket. It also means learning to live ecologically with other people and with the land, seeing ourselves as part of an interlocking collective unit—not just picking up beer cans in the street.[61]

It can be said that the problem probably lies in a combination of all these factors, as does the solution. One of the things we will have to face is that we can never go back to nature, because the nature we would desire to return to no longer exists. We have tampered with nature and must continue to do so; the only question left to us is how are we going to continue as a technological society and survive. Moreover, coming to grips with the environmental crisis must ultimately mean realizing that the world itself is an ecological unit—not only biologically, but socially as well. World-wide economic and social integration is therefore inevitable. There can no longer be any such thing as isolation.

NOTES

[1] Paul Shepard, "Introduction: Ecology and Man—Viewpoint," in Paul Shepard and Daniel McKinley, *The Subversive Science* (Boston: Houghton Mifflin Company, 1969), p. 7.

[2] Edward S. Deevey, Jr., *"The Human Population,"* in Shepard and McKinley, *ibid.,* p. 42.

[3] Robert Rienow and Leona Train Rienow, *Moment in the Sun* (New York: Ballantine Books, Inc., 1969), p. 46.

[4] Aldo Leopold, "The Land Ethic," in Shepard and McKinley, *op. cit.,* p. 402.

[5] For an extensive discussion of this see Vance Packard, *The Waste Makers* (New York: Pocket Cardinal, 1967).

[6] Gene Marine, *America the Raped* (New York: Simon and Shuster, Inc., 1969), p. 17.

[7] Frank E. Egler, "Pesticides—in Our Ecosystem," in Shepard and McKinley, *op. cit.,* pp. 230–231.

[8] *Ibid.,* p. 256.

[9] Rachel Carson, *Silent Spring* (Greenwich: Fawcett–Crest, 1962), pp. 30–31.

This same process can be applied to nuclear weapons testing: see G. M. Woodwell, W. M. Malcolm, and R. H. Whittaker, "A-Bombs, Bugbombs and Us," in Shepard and McKinley, *op. cit.,* p. 233.

[10] *Ibid.,* p. 139; see also Earle L. Reynolds, "Irradiation and Human Evolution," in Shepard and McKinley, *op. cit.,* p. 301.

[11] Carson, *op. cit.,* p. 50.

[12] *Ibid.,* p. 157.

[13] *Ibid.,* p. 16.

[14] Rienow and Rienow, *op. cit.,* pp. 195–196.

[15] LaMont C. Cole, "The Impending Emergence of Ecological Thought," in Shepard and McKinley, *op. cit.,* pp. 273–274; see also Harmon Henkin, "DDT and the Constitution," in *The Nation,* March 10, 1969, p. 310; Marine, *op. cit.,* p. 24; and Paul R. Ehrlich, *The Population Bomb* (New York: Ballantine Books, Inc., 1968), pp. 49–53.

[16] This is a quote from Charles Elton cited in Garrett Hardin. "The Cybernetics of Competition: a Biologist's View of Society," in Shepard and McKinley, *op. cit.,* p. 290.

[17] Carson, *op. cit.,* p. 22.

[18] Rienow and Rienow, *op. cit.,* pp. 59, 204.

[19] Marine, *op. cit.,* p. 114.

[20] Peter van Dresser, "The Modern Retreat from Function," in Shepard and McKinley, *op. cit.,* p. 366.

[21] Mitchell Gordon, *Sick Cities* (Baltimore: Penguin Books Inc., 1965), p. 94.

[22] Rienow and Rienow, *op. cit.,* p. 141.

[23] *Ibid.,* p. 151.

[24] Gordon, *op. cit.,* p. 91.

[25] Louis J. Battan, *The Unclean Sky* (Garden City: Doubleday & Company, Inc., 1966), p. 75.

[26] Marine, *op. cit.,* p. 105.

[27] Gordon, *op. cit.,* p. 114.

[28] *Ibid.*

[29] Marine, *op. cit.,* pp. 106–108.

[30] Deevey, *op. cit.,* p. 43; Ehrlich, *op. cit.,* p. 18.

[31] Harrison Brown, *The Challenge of Man's Future* (New York: Compass, 1956), pp. 75–80.

[32] Ehrlich, *op. cit.,* p. 25.

[33] Paul B. Sears, "The Inexorable Problem of Space," in Shepard and McKinley, *op. cit.,* p. 80.

[34] Ehrlich, *op. cit.,* p. 17.

[35] *Ibid.,* pp. 22–23.

[36] *Ibid.,* pp. 36–37.

[37] *Ibid.,* pp. 81–94.

[38] Marine, *op. cit.,* p. 196.

[39] Ehrlich, *op. cit.,* p. 34.

[40] Sears, *op. cit.,* p. 80.

[41] Ehrlich, *op. cit.,* p. 49.

[42] Rienow and Rienow, *op. cit.,* p. 227.

[43] Ehrlich, *op. cit.,* pp. 74–78.

[44] Rienow and Rienow, *op. cit.,* p. 21.

[45] Brown, *op. cit.,* p. 55.

[46] *Ibid.,* p. 107.

[47] *Ibid.,* p. 112.

[48] *Ibid.*

[49] *Ibid.,* pp. 130–135.

[50] *Ibid.,* p. 58.

[51] *Ibid.,* p. 135.

[52] Rienow and Rienow, *op. cit.,* p. 25.

[53] William Paddock and Paul Paddock, *Hungry Nations* (Boston: Little, Brown and Company, 1964), p. 23.

[54] Rienow and Rienow, *op. cit.,* p. 71.

[55] *Ibid.*

[56] Edward Higbee, *The Squeeze* (Toronto: William Morrow, 1965), pp. 268–270.

[57] Ehrlich, *op. cit.,* p. 97.

[58] Brown, *op. cit.,* p. 233.

[59] *Ibid.,* pp. 218–220.

[60] For a discussion of capitalism and its influence on the environmental crisis see Barry Weisberg, *Beyond Repair* (Boston: Beacon Press, 1971).

[61] For a general discussion of all of these factors see Barry Commoner, *The Closing Circle* (New York: Alfred A. Knopf, Inc., 1971).

8

mass education: memorizing the rules of the game

Many of the problems dealt with so far in this book may seem hard to visualize and identify with. Their locus is far away and it is easy to say, "that's their hang-up, not mine." The problem discussed in this chapter is very much our own. As Alan Watts might say, "we are it." We are it because we are the ones waiting for the professor to define what is worthwhile to know, to memorize, and to forget after exam week. We are it because we are waiting for someone else to speak, hoping our name won't be called. We are the ones who have "voluntarily" enrolled in a four-year course in the "American Way of Life." Actually, we are bored with what's going on in the classroom and spend most of our time daydreaming or doodling in our notebooks. We are it because we are either afraid or unwilling to question our position, to find an alternative.

Let us restate the problem by stating its opposite. You are a professor. One day you come into your lecture class and take a seat approximately half way toward the front of the room. While you wait for the lecture to begin, you read the student newspaper or discuss the approaching exam with the student sitting next to you. The bell rings and the students wait for you to end your little game and tell

Courtesy of Gyula Szabo

them what they're supposed to know for the test—some even go so far as to turn their heads around to stare at you. You refuse to move. Five minutes pass, then ten. A few students begin to squirm in their seats; others take out a book and begin to read the day's assignment; no one questions your action.

Finally, one student, at the urging of several peers, asks, "Is there going to be a class?" (meaning "Why don't you end this silence already and get up to the front of the room where you belong?").

You return the question with "What question do you want answered? What do you want to learn?"

"How should I know?" comes the reply—"You're the teacher!"

Five more minutes pass in silence, a few students begin to leave. Everyone seems embarrassed. Suddenly another student asks, "Where's this class going, anyway?" When again you say "Where do you want it to go?" he shrugs his shoulders. A few others yawn.

Educational institutions exist, for the most part, to socialize young people, and to get them to conform to the dominant norms and values of American society. Accordingly, they reflect rather than challenge "the way things are" because those who run the schools *represent* society, and, for the most part, want to preserve the status quo. What has been valued in the past is assumed, for the most part, to be what will be valued in the future. As the Protestant Ethic ostensibly serves to justify work in the greater community, so too, this same ethic is used to keep students at their books, in school, memorizing facts, and acquiring values that have little relevance to their situation. Those who refuse to conform, to sit and listen and memorize and obey are made to feel guilty about their failing to live up to their "commitments" as American citizens. Just as those who do not work have difficulty establishing a worthwhile identity in a work-oriented society, so in school, character is judged in terms of competitive achievement, the number of books read (input), the number of pages written (output), the number of examinations passed.

The schools also unwittingly reflect certain "negative" attributes of American society, particularly its other-directedness. Although American ideology is emphasized in textbooks and lectures, the way the schools are run makes it virtually impossible for the student to gain practical knowledge of participatory democracy. The lack of its existence in the larger community, of course, helps reinforce this situation. Students who are given to understand that free enterprise is the American way of organizing the economy must reconcile this information with a corporate economic structure, in which the individual has little to say over what he produces, or over how such production is to take place. The essence of school lies in the fringe benefits—sexual exploration, athletic events, and friendships; the rest, the classroom activity, is just a game we play because we're supposed to. It matters little whether or not what goes on inside the classroom is related to the outside world. Most students seem to care very little whether the values inculcated by the university, college or high school are of relevance to the community, nor are they encouraged by society to doubt and to question. Students accept definitions of what *is,* as defined in school by the teaching staff, or in the community by the advertising media and political elite. For the students who do not accept, the task remains for them to alter the traditional role of the schools so that they accord with their personal expectations and are responsive to their needs.[1]

If the school curriculum is lacking in content and if the ideas promulgated by the school system have little application to the community, they must be challenged. Do schools indoctrinate rather than educate? What do we *mean* by "education"? How do we educate people with the will to transform society? The question is a very real one because, as I shall attempt to show, the school system is responsible for many of the problems which beset society today. The schools, perhaps even more than our parents, tell us who we are and who we are supposed to be, what is right and what is wrong, what we can question and what we cannot. That this system has proved dysfunctional for American society is revealed in the types of interpersonal relationships we maintain, the types of jobs most of us do, the types of commodities most of us will be urged day and night to consume, the type of foreign policy the United States currently maintains, and the types of attitudes we have toward the black and the poor of our society.

The Many Worlds of Educational Illusion

1. *We are learning something from a teacher who has answers that are true and meaningful.*

Most students expect that all teachers somehow have a corner on the market of truth. If a teacher were to say "The world is really square," many students would write it down and believe in it, just as they might believe that the sun will set in the evening. We don't expect a teacher to lie to us or to be mistaken in his or her analysis. This is one of the reasons why teachers are rarely challenged. Not only do we believe, the teacher also for the most part believes that he or she is infallible. The idea is inculcated early in our educational career that it is better to go along than to be hassled or flunked for our insubordination. Jerry Farber notes:

> Students don't ask that orders make sense. They give up expecting things to make sense long before they leave elementary school. Things are true because the teacher says they're true. At a very early age we all learn to accept "two truths," as did certain medieval churchmen. Outside of class, things are true to your tongue, your fingers, your stomach, your heart. Inside class things are true by reason of authority. And that's just fine because you don't care anyway. Miss Wiedemeyer tells you a noun is a person, place or thing. So let it be. You don't give a rat's ass; she doesn't give a rat's ass.[2]

Since these are the teacher's facts or the textbook's facts, rather than our facts, it makes little difference to us whether we learn them or not, except in terms of passing exams or being rewarded for being a "good pupil." We learn to memorize a foreign environment. But how do we know that what the teacher says is true? How do we know that the information printed in this book has any modicum of truth to it? It may all be a lie. Does this make any difference to us? Suppose the facts that most teachers rattle off are true; is there anything we can do with them, do they open up new worlds for us to explore? Most of us have discovered the difference between relevance and truth. Many facts are true, but irrelevant because they cannot be related to our lives. Much of our education consists of learning these facts, for they are, almost by definition, uncontroversial. They are boring, but they serve the purpose of filling our heads with trivia, and keeping our critical faculties unexercised.

The compartmentalization of the educational system into different areas and conceptions of knowledge means, particularly at the college level, that once we decide to specialize (and ultimately we must specialize), our study will be limited to a certain area of knowledge. This makes for what Joseph Royce has called "encapsulated men," or the belief that one's own special discipline represents "the whole truth and nothing but the truth, so help us God." [3] If we study sociology, for example, we come to believe that only sociology can truthfully define reality. Such compartmentalization places severe limits on learning, for it arbitrarily cuts us off from other facts and ways of knowing. Can a compartmentalized teacher, therefore, be expected to have *the* answer?

What is the value of grades if all they measure is the memorization of meaningless, insignificant, and perhaps inaccurate facts? Demanding that the instructor have the answers seems to mean too that the instructor have positive answers—are not negative opinions just as good? Cannot one learn just as much from a wrong answer as from a right one? [4] In a final sense, however, facts which are unlived, which are not personally experienced, are not real facts to us at all, but only empty words. If facts are to be a reflection of our life, then both the negative and the positive must be presented and experienced. The teacher can only answer for himself, and although other people, older people, often try to answer for us, they cannot.

2. *We want to be free to learn on our own, to find our own truth. A meaningful curriculum would make a difference.*

The facts do not make a difference, but, for the most part, we are not willing to seek out any that do. We are unsure of our intellectual capabilities outside the structured classroom situation and "doing it on our own and in our own way" has never been emphasized by the school system, or by American society in general, except in the fantasy world of advertisements. Very early in life we discover that others define what is and what is not meaningful behavior. Given the freedom to develop our own curriculum, few of us would take advantage of it, for we have been convinced that this is not our responsibility, not our place or role in American society. Our role is a passive one. As a patient in a mental hospital, we have become convinced that what the doctor tells us to do is in our own best interest, that we will continue to place our confidence in him and give up all responsibility for our actions while in the institution.[5]

We are afraid of freedom, of time (at least during school hours) that is not being spent in "useful" activity. If given freedom, how would we know what we are supposed to learn, when there have always been other people around to tell us? We care very little, then, when told what our rights are and even less when told we have lost them. This freedom is of the kind which we find off campus—the "Don't bother me, I won't bother you" sort of freedom. Much experimentation has taken place in recent years on college and on some high school campuses. Yet, this experimentation is, typically, quite academic (theoretical), for it can only be put into practice in safe isolated units —that is, on the campuses. Take such experimentation off campus and into the community and this freedom disappears.

Experimental courses and schools within a given college or university community often serve as means of filtering out those students who might become easily disenchanted with more traditional curriculums and teaching methods. In becoming disenchanted, they would begin to cause trouble both for the teaching staff and the administration. These experimental programs thus give prospective "troublemakers" a chance to let off steam without really ever affecting the "system." They are given whatever they desire to keep them "entertained." Through this process some of the more subtle forms of cooptation are often unwittingly used to maintain the status quo on college and university campuses. "Academic freedom" then becomes just that—academic—and is treated accordingly by the larger community which controls the budgets and often the hiring and firing procedures. Should any faculty members take such freedom too seriously (that is, challenge the elite interests in the surrounding community and state), they will soon learn the hypocrisy of the term.

How much safer though, just to go along; how much freer we feel. But this is freedom *from* being hassled, from having to take responsibility for our own actions, much as our parents have freedom from communism, from having to practice values they pledge allegiance to, from having to question policies the government makes in their name. Is this not the freedom most college and high school students want? This is the very type of freedom that is reconciled with classroom practices of authority and conformity. The professor has told us that we are free. We smile to ourselves, feeling warm and comfortable, proud to be an American. Meanwhile the lecture continues and we write down other facts.

3. *We are being taught to be free and democratic individuals.*

The textbooks we read may talk about freedom and democracy, but there is little resemblance between the written word and what goes on in high school and college classrooms. Jerry Farber has said that students can best be seen "as niggers." [6]

> School is where you let the dying society put its trip on you. Our schools may seem useful: to make children into doctors, sociologists, engineers—to discover things. But they're poisonous as well. They exploit and enslave students: they petrify society; they make democracy unlikely. And it's not *what* you're taught that does the harm, but *how* you're taught. Our schools teach you by pushing you around, by stealing your will and your sense of power, by making timid square apathetic slaves out of you—authority addicts. . . . The medium in school truly is the message. And the medium is, above all, coercive. You're forced to attend. The subjects are required. You *have* to do homework. You *must* observe school rules. And throughout, you're bullied into docility and submissiveness. Even modern liberal refinements don't really help. So you're called an underachiever instead of a dummy. So they send you to a counselor instead of beating you. It's still not your choice to be there. They may pad the handcuffs—but the handcuffs stay on.[7]

Thus, as a "make-believe" ideology is passed on, what really counts is the *method,* and this method enables a mass-automaton, other-directed society to continue.

In these educational institutions youth become their own commissars. No one has to tell them to obey; they feel guilty when they do not. No one has to tell them not to experiment or to do the assignment; they are afraid to do otherwise. John Holt, a well-known educational critic, has asked what happens to the seeming intellectual curiosity and creativity found in very young children:

> We destroy this capacity by making them [children] afraid, afraid of not doing what other people want, of not pleasing, of making mistakes, of

failing, of being *wrong*. Thus we make them afraid to gamble, afraid to experiment, afraid to try the difficult and the unknown. Even when we do not create children's fears, when they come to us with fears ready-made and built-in, we use these fears as handles to manipulate them and get them to do what we want. Instead of trying to whittle down their fears, we build them up, often to monstrous size. For we like children who are a little afraid of us, docile, deferential children, though not, of course, if they are so obviously afraid that they threaten our image of ourselves as kind, lovable people whom there is no reason to fear. We find ideal the kind of "good" children who are just enough afraid of us to do everything we want, without making us feel that fear of us is what is making them do it.[8]

The attitude that is inculcated in our schools is hardly one which is synonymous with democratic government. There is the feeling, particularly on college or university campuses, that though students may realize what is taking place, they will respond by saying "Indeed a diploma; once I get it, *then* I'll do my thing, challenge the authority structure, fight the government." Only they never do, for then it is too late; they have already been too indoctrinated to even want to challenge the system. Or they lack both the courage and the knowledge as to how to challenge it. Besides, after graduation there are more "practical" things to worry about: a family perhaps, or travel plans, or waiting to gain power before acting. But by then. . . .

Is this education or indoctrination? Can you educate a "slave?" No — you can only "train" him.[9] The radicals on campus watch for police raids and internment in modern-day concentration camps while "Miss Jones does her quiet thing with the kids in the third grade." [10] The subversion takes place within the minds of students, and to such a large degree that most will never even think about the real enemy. This is not to say that there are not real police on many campuses, but that the problem is more complex.

But freedom also entails having a choice, and this is precisely what we don't have. Admittedly, if we are taking freshman English we may have a choice of instructors, but we are unable to choose whether to go to school or not, or whether to take freshman English or not, or whether to attend class or not, or whether to take the exam or not. We have pseudo-choices, but the real decisions have already been made for us.[11] We cannot drop out. Without a choice, we are not in any sense free. While we may think we are being educated for freedom, we are really being educated *from* freedom, *from* having to make choices, and *for* conformity.

4. *The larger community cares whether we learn anything or not.*

Quite possibly the larger community has no use for whatever "knowledge" we may pick up in our sixteen or so years of schooling. This is almost certainly true for our college education. Naturally, the community wants us to be literate, to understand what a 10–1 body count ratio means, or know how much we will save if we buy now, pay later. Much of the knowledge gleaned from textbooks and professors, if taken too seriously, can be dangerous for the community, for it may force this community or nation to practice what it preaches. Even harmless tracts such as the Constitution begin to stir awkward questions relating to civil rights, the rights of free speech and assembly, and other such "subversive" ideas. This does not apply so much to the hard science area of engineering, physics and chemistry, or even to the life sciences of biology, physiology, and medicine. It does apply to the social sciences and humanities.

In the sixties, with the escalation of the Vietnamese war, numerous teach–ins were held around the country. Speaking at these teach–ins, which were largely designed to raise consciousness about the war, were many anthropologists, sociologists, and political scientists who had spent years, perhaps their entire careers, studying Vietnamese society. There was an outcry, especially from government officials, that these educators of public opinion had no business to question the country's foreign policy. After all, it was argued, didn't the government have *all* the *relevant* facts? Furthermore, these speakers would never have consented to giving "aid and comfort" to the enemy if they only had the facts the government had. These arguments implied that professors did not have a right to speak publicly with the knowledge they had gathered from their chosen and life-long professions or specialties and that what they said was not the "truth." The facts and opinions they held were not worthwhile facts and opinions, because they contradicted government arguments. In essence, much knowledge gained through liberal arts disciplines was not considered by segments of the larger community, government, and public to be knowledge at all, but rather "subversive opinion."

What does such an attitude do to men who have spent their lives gathering such "subversive opinion"? Why, in fact, should a liberal arts student bother to listen to these instructors when what they say is held by the larger community to be blasphemous? Why, in other words, bother to learn at all, when we care very little, and the larger community cares even less about what we are learning? Equally important, what does such an attitude do to the people from whom this educated opinion is withheld?

Even if we should "learn" something, it may not mean anything unless it is "legitimate" knowledge.[12] Knowledge gained in the liberal arts is not legitimate because there is nothing we can *do* with it. In a pragmatically-oriented culture and in a society such as ours, it is important to be able to *do* things and make things; quantity often takes precedence over quality. With nothing to show for all our years of effort in the liberal arts curriculum, why should they take us seriously? What have we contributed to the community?

The message is clear: Even if we manage to learn something, there are few referents in the larger community for the words we have memorized. Thus, knowledge can easily be forgotten. And without reinforcement, it is.

5. The knowledge explosion means something; it is better to have more data and fewer values.

Education must gauge its ends according to the values of the larger community it serves. Perhaps the most influential community value is the technological imperative, whereby technology itself generates a demand for more technology. Consequently there is a high demand for more and more scientists and technocrats. This is equated with the production of "facts"—the scholar must produce "data" if he is to claim equal status with his managerial and scientific counterparts. Computers tally IBM cards, while human hearts swell, eyes excitedly await the results. Any problem will do, so long as one can quantify it. How else might the contribution a sociologist makes be compared with the design and production of a new toaster? The public is conditioned to want the facts—all the facts. "Ninety-eight percent of those who brush with peyote get stoned; 42 out of every 57 persons will die sometime during their lives. . . ." Facts themselves are not unimportant. Rather, it is the premium put on facts that is at issue here: What do all these facts mean? Who is responsible for them? Might the energies channeled into producing them be better spent elsewhere?

In terms of dollars invested in education, by far the largest number of grants for research go to the hard sciences, for they make a tangible (quantifiable) contribution to American life. They aid in the search for more and "better" consumer goods. As the GE commercial used to say, "Progress is our most important product," and such progress is judged by what we can see, rather than by the philosophical questions we might have pondered in class. There is a contradiction, however; for as ever greater numbers of commodities are produced, fewer people want to seek gainful employment producing them—all they seem to want to do is to be able to buy. Yet, as least *ostensibly,* education is not for consumership; it is for becoming a respectable productive component of the American economic structure. However, the "method" of education *is,* inherently, for consumers—the teacher tells us what the facts are, as the advertiser will later tell us what to buy. Consumption becomes our most important product.[13]

The ultimate question is, to what ends are these facts put? Scientific discovery and technological development have produced atomic bombs which have wiped out whole cities, and have despoiled and polluted the earth. Who is responsible? Do the universities, especially those which have corporate interests and defense research programs, bear a share of the responsibility? We are consumed with anxiety about the goals to which most of our lives have been directed. The system assumes the necessity of more data. Indeed, we would feel cheated if a new paperback, a new textbook, were not always forthcoming at the campus bookstore, if we did not continue to receive the latest journals in the mail, if. . . . What the facts mean matters very little, their function is to assure us that our society is moving somewhere. The direction in which we are moving is hardly ever discussed because open discussion of the values of society might result in the kind of change which would replace our consumer economy.

6. *We want to be in the classroom.*

Perhaps the biggest illusion of all is that we want to be right where we are, that we enjoy school, and if given a free choice we would still attend classes. In fact, many of us (particularly those of us who are at small liberal-arts colleges) are perfectly happy with our position, but there are many more living a lie. We sit in class and day-dream; we avoid confrontations with the professor; we write pages which do not contain a single opinion of our own. Yet no amount of pressure—exams, grades, or platitudes—will get us to admit we are just not interested. So we are learning to please someone else, to be other-directed. Then why play the game, why waste our time? Is it because, as Farber puts it, we "won't get to put [our] hands in the gigantic goodie-box," [14] unless we do?

Many of us are afraid of confrontations. Other-directedness teaches tolerance, an acceptance of the bland. Our inability to confront our situation as it actually is, to ask what it means, to consider alternatives, places us in the same category as the student who has not yet realized that it is all without meaning. Through our very inaction we give aid and comfort to American society; we tacitly support the system. But, then again, we may want to be in school, if only for fringe benefits: It's where the action is (sexual freedom, drugs, freedom from parental control); it's where our friends are; it's a place for us to stall away four years of our life, so we won't have to make any immediate decisions. We won't have to confront the world and support ourselves. Education is a privilege. We owe it to society to be in school, so we're only fulfilling our obligation. We ignore that in so doing we may be copping out and becoming a victim of the very system we may some day desire to have a say in.

Rest assured, this is not to say that many students do not gain something, however intangible, from their sixteen years of education from hard-working, dedicated teachers. Nor is this to say that in areas outside the liberal arts, there is not a ready link between classroom knowledge and application in the larger community. Yet even here the question of who is responsible for what science produces is largely ignored. And it is the rare business school which asks "why bother to work at all?"

We cannot escape answering the question of *who* should determine the goals of education: students? faculty? the community? government? business?

7. The illusion that this is an illusion.

Not everyone, however, goes along with our educational institutions. Some students never make it out of high school; countless others drop out of college. According to Friedenberg the real question may be: What kinds of people with what kinds of values *stay in school?* [15] Perhaps we have already answered that question. In any case, dropping out is considered a "bad thing" in American society. Those who refuse to work are called bums; those who refuse to consume are labeled cheapskates; those who refuse to vote (because there is no one to vote for) are "subversives"; and, those who refuse to conform are "undesirables."

Dropping out of high school, and even college, means, in society's eyes, that we will be unable to find a decent and productive job. It is with such a justification in mind that society urges its younger members to complete their schooling. With respect to high school education, however, this argument is fallacious. As Friedenberg has shown, it is only because a few drop-outs have been lured back to get their high school diplomas that such programs have proved successful.

The number of blue-collar jobs, as we have noted in Chapter 1, is steadily diminishing. If all the drop-outs went back to school, there would not be nearly enough jobs to go around, because blue-collar work is the only type of job a high school diploma brings.[16] And what types of jobs *are* these? Are they worthwhile? Yet, even for the student who is lured into or back to college with the promise of a better job, can society really deliver? Or is the real lure more pay and fringe benefits? All this assumes there is some relationship between the job we will eventually do and the education we receive. But Keats notes:

> There are more than 20,000 different kinds of jobs offered in our society, and only a small fraction of them actually require specific college preparation. It would seem that the longer one considers the alleged relationship between job and diploma, the less real reason one finds for assuming there *is* a relationship between the content of a formal education and the humdrum demands of the daily work we actually do. If this is the case, are we being realistic when we say that a man must have a diploma to get a job?[17]

Again, the real reason for requiring a college diploma as a prerequisite for performing certain occupations is the type of mentality which education breeds, rather than the knowledge which may incidentally be acquired.[18] This is why school comes to be viewed as a privilege, rather than a right. It is a privilege because it enables us to make money. Most of us do not realize that *society needs us;* for without our participation, society, as most of our parents' generation understands it, would cease to flourish.

Given that schools fail to guarantee a worthwhile career, students begin to look for meaningful identities outside the educational system. This is particularly the case for the minority child, or anyone not raised according to middle-class values.[19] If a child can see nothing to gain by conforming to the educational system, he either drops out or becomes a high school rebel. For the lower-class or minority student this may be due to an inability to conceive of the prospect of a worthwhile future job and to a general alienation from middle-class values. Unable to find a suitable place in the school system, such a student begins to look for one outside that system.

Consider the possibility that, rather than schools being geared to middle-class values, they are geared to no values at all. And, while producing a relatively small minority of physical drop-outs, most of its students are mental drop-outs. Paul Goodman puts the issue this way:

Numerically far more important than these overt drop-outs at 16, however, are the children who conform to schooling between the ages 6 to
16 or 20, but who drop out internally and day-dream, their days wasted,
their liberty caged and scheduled. And there are many such in the
middle class, from backgrounds with plenty of food and some books
and art, where the youth is seduced by the prospect of money and
status, but even more where he is terrified to jeopardize the only pattern
of life he knows.[20]

Perhaps we should not blame the school system; maybe it is only
a middle-man operation. It keeps people off the streets. School acts
to keep people off the labor market until the market is ready to
employ them.[21] But for many youth the streets become the more attractive option, job or no jobs, for at least on the streets they can be
their own person. It is this prospect that presents such a challenge to
our traditional conception of authority. Thus dropping out is characterized by many parents and school administrators as "short-run hedonism," or "negativism." [22]

Street life gives a youth an opportunity to find his own identity
and self-esteem, one which he can feel comfortable with.[23] If we do
not fit in with formal school processes, whether with classes themselves or the extra-curricular activities provided, there is little reason
for us to keep taking up space, unless we want to "subvert" the
system. Schools cannot guarantee that we will be able to get a good
job; they also attempt to structure our personality along middle-class
lines. Students read standardized textbooks written to deemphasize
individual differences. Thus the individual student cannot find out who
he or *she* is, but only what the standardized man or woman is. Moreover, schools take elaborate measures to deny creative and rebellious
students the chance to build self-esteem along lines not recommended
by the local school board. Such measures may vary from building
fences around school grounds, to simply "letting the school do its
thing."

Why are we afraid of letting students drop out? Can they not learn
as much in the street and countryside, as much or more that is relevant
to their lives, as they can in the classroom? Are we afraid they will
get into "trouble?" What kind of trouble and why? Is the old adage
"An idle mind is the devil's workshop" true? Do street people necessarily have idle minds? Must everyone work, and work at jobs as they
have traditionally been defined, or should there be an education for
leisure and political participation? And where is it better to achieve
such an education—in school or in the community?

Education for Whom?

Much of the drop-out problem, if it is a problem, is due to the irrelevancy of many of our educational materials and techniques to the student's interests. This, of course, raises a fundamental question: Who decides what is relevant? Furthermore, schools force lower-class, minority, and ethnic youth to give up their cultural heritage and conform to a foreign set of values and even a foreign language. Middle- and upper-middle class counterparts may openly flaunt what many poor students desire for themselves—money, a decent meal, smart clothes, perhaps a car. Since school boards are often dominated by members of the upper-middle class, other segments of society are frustrated in their attempts to change school policies. Many poor and minority students have a difficult time finding status in their own communities, where, for example, the "hustler" may be esteemed. In school they have a difficult time learning "the man's" culture, and attempts to achieve self-esteem (for example, by blacks wearing their hair "naturally"), are often denied them.[24] Too, deviant behavior on the part of minority group members is often viewed as criminal, while the same behavior by middle-class youth is considered as a harmless prank. The poor and minority students thus find themselves in a position without power, forced to learn irrelevant material and plan for a future which will not be theirs to have, meanwhile receiving few gratifications in terms of grades, self-mastery, or the dignity which could motivate them toward the further pursuit of educational goals.[25]

Teachers and administrators consciously sort out and refuse to educate these students. As Arthur Pearl comments:

> The teacher's responsibility is to teach, but instead we engage in self- fulfilling prophecy. We decide that certain people cannot be educated; we refuse to educate them; they grow up uneducated; and we pride ourselves on our exceedingly accurate predictive index. This sorting prin- ciple puts a stamp on pupils very early in the game which follows them all the way through the production line until they come out labeled "dumb" or "smart" because there has been very little done to change the initial judgment . . . In a school where middle-class white students go, where the median income for the parents is over $10,000 a year, 92 per cent of all students are in college–bound tracks. In another school in Washington, D.C., where 100 per cent of the students are Negro and parents make less than $4,000 a year, 85 per cent are in non–college bound tracks. In other words, almost 9 out of 10 of the Negro youth are being told they are not college material (and thus they cannot get a

credential). In effect, these youth are being told they have no future except possibly in menial service occupations.[26]

It is a result of such processes that our schools are often labeled racist.[27]

Those who desire an educational system that is relevant and which challenges the values of the community are ignored or chastised, almost as much as members of minority groups. Any "radical" education is not conceived as legitimate. Not only is this true for classroom innovation, it also holds for what are considered worthwhile extracurricular activities. For example, at Berkeley in 1964, university authorities held that those who sat at tables with information on anything from the war in Vietnam to legalized abortion were somehow disturbing the educational system—they were making "illegitimate" protests. On the other hand, pep rallies, the selling of homecoming buttons, homecoming parades, football and basketball games were all perfectly acceptable because these activities help to foster the traditional values of competition, fair play, and sportsmanship.

Similarly, student government gives realistic opportunities for those who will later participate in the decision-making process of American government. Such governments, for the most part, are not really concerned with problems crucial to its student constituents, just as the American government often ignores those issues the citizenry considers most important.

Radical education is not legitimate because it challenges the status quo, the way of life which many comfortable middle-class Americans assume all other Americans have. Those radical elements who pose a threat to the community must be eliminated, either through dismissal or by denial of financial aid to those who protest, no matter what their constitutional rights may be.[28] Expelling students, however, will not solve the problem, for they are only a symptom of the larger issues posed above. One of the real tragedies of this conflict of interests is that student radicals who seize campus buildings may gain very little. What has a revolution that seizes a specific university profited? [29]

Presumably, of course, the revolutionaries will do something to change the educational system, but such a change must inevitably clash with the real power interests, the technological society itself. And this is where the basic problem lies. The enemy is the entire system, the entire social reality. Whom can the radicals attack—those fellow students around them who have already been brainwashed by the system? They must fight against the affluent, the bland, the racist, and the sexist elements—the content of education itself. Above all, they must fight against a system that co-opts and defuses, that lets them scream as loud and as outrageously as they can, knowing full well that they will soon exhaust themselves against the billboards and TV commercials which run electrically because it is a penny cheaper than gas.[30]

What Makes Teachers the Way They Are?

Teachers are the product of the very institutions that will later employ them. For elementary and high school teachers, the curriculum itself is a clear enough indication of what will be expected of them in the classroom. For example, there may be a course called, quite bluntly, "classroom control." Other courses which are required are: "writing on the blackboard," "how to make up exams and give out grades," and "how to win over your students without whipping them." If you think this is an exaggeration, go over to the education department and inquire into what it takes to get a credential.

Perhaps just as serious a problem as the curriculum is the kind of people who go into teaching in the first place. Who is it that is willing to put up with courses like "classroom control"? How can such courses attract and create challenging and interesting teachers? At the college level, the problem never arises. At this high altitude the professor rarely cares about teaching, is not trained to teach, and if given the opportunity would gladly do what he has been trained for—namely, research.

This is not to say that at numerous small liberal-arts schools and state colleges teaching is not emphasized. But even here, there is rarely a workshop on how to conduct a relevant and meaningful course —academic freedom may mean only that you are free to bore the students to death. Little effort is spent on teacher evaluation, either by fellow faculty or students in schools where teaching is held to matter. *Publish or perish* is not a fiction for those at top universities, where those who do not publish enough may be said to be on their way to both publishing *and* perishing.

Major universities gain their reputations, for the most part, on the basis of the research going on at their schools and, subsequently, on the basis of the papers and books published by their faculty which bring government and private grants. Given that this is so, there often develops a conflict between the interests of the student and the interests of the professor and university. Does the university want to hire good teachers or good researchers, for there is rarely financial support to hire both?

Just what is a professor? He is supposed to possess enough knowledge to present a modicum of "truth" in a given area while provoking students into considering the meaning of the subject. It follows that students must hold some interest in gaining this knowledge. If they attend the professor's lecture for auxiliary reasons, then what the professor has to say does not really matter—he becomes popular by putting on a good performance, by being funny, by being a "ham." The quest for knowledge ceases to be important for both him and the student.

Research is often accompanied by specialization which helps eliminate responsibility for the uses to which knowledge is put. Professors thus appear to be professional apologists and "buck passers." If a given area of research becomes controversial, they can say it's outside their field of interest. They avoid getting their names associated with unpopular positions or controversial research projects. They prefer problems that may be easily shaped into articles and published. Particularly in the social sciences such problems often have little to do with the larger community. For one thing, many issues which are crucial to the larger community are just not relevant to the professor's specialty as he defines that specialty. In essence, he has compartmentalized himself out of any responsibility for community issues.

Secondly, he is worried about his job. Controversial issues are by nature public issues. Since the public is deeply concerned about what direction such issues may take, they do not want people doing jobs and given authority (which they are reluctant to recognize) to tell them what to do. Those involved in these issues become *persona non grata*. The public asks state legislatures to be alert to any state-employed faculty who take positions not consistent with contemporary public policy. Since those of privilege have final say in the education budget, their power to stifle outspoken opposition is considerable.

The department to which a professor belongs, in order to guarantee its prestige among other departments around the country, sanctions its faculty by urging them to keep their research to the "field," to use traditional methodological and theoretical formulations. If they do not, then a faculty member runs the risk of being disenfranchised. He is no longer a "legitimate" specialist. He is no longer a professional; he is giving the university and his profession a bad name.

Finances are also relevant here. In order for the professor to do research, he needs a grant-in-aid of some type. Such money is usually made available through the government or a large foundation. Since this is the case, the professor is unlikely to get money to investigate a given area if his hypotheses run counter to either governmental policy or local public opinion. Since the mass media and the public at large rarely get a chance to debate public policy, particularly that clouded in controversy, such policy becomes preconceived, and the professor thus aids, though perhaps inadvertently, in preserving the status quo. Having remained all his life in the ivory tower, the professor cannot tell his students how to solve or even attempt to solve problems which face the community. This separation of academia from the community is, in large part, responsible for the boredom and frustration which many students experience on campus.

Who Should Control the Schools?

Do radicals have a right to determine their own education, to control the campuses they seize, or even to seize campuses in the first place? The public debate on school control has centered mainly on elementary and high schools. Here, arguments have ranged back and forth between community controlled schools, and those which should be federally controlled, and even academically controlled. Arguments for community control point out that only the community can know what is relevant for their own children. But which community—the youth community or their parents who pay school taxes and vote on bond issues? It has also been felt that if the community has a say in the educational process, that it will become more involved in what the children are doing.

Arguments against this position question the ability of a community to educate their children—won't most parents simply opt for a maintenance of the status quo? How can they possibly promote schools which question their own values, their social reality? But even more important, without federal financial aid and support, many school districts will become quite unequal, unable to support quality education, even if they want to. Federal support, however, often ignores individual characteristics of school districts such as between a black and Chicano area of a given city. Many argue that the teachers themselves are the only ones who are qualified to determine what should be taught in the schools, especially at the elementary school level. This recommendation is seldom satisfactory to taxpayers who want some say on how their money is being spent.

A similar type of conflict is taking place in higher education, where community means "state legislature" or "board of trustees." Within a college or university itself, many students are arguing for control over the method and content of their education. College administrators, caught between students, faculty, and state legislators, attempt to reach some sort of compromise. But where does the real authority lie? How can students respect an administration and faculty which represent an often outmoded value system and educational process? How can a faculty respect the knowledge of "radicals" who have neither the educational experience which the faculty has, nor as much at stake (financially and occupationally) as that faculty?

Behind this issue lies the question of academic freedom—can a faculty be forced by its students to teach what it does not want to teach? And if they refuse, can such students then replace these faculty with those who do offer "relevant" instructional materials? And whose side is the administration to take—that of the faculty, whose rights they would defend, those of the students in whose name the college theoretically operates, or the state legislature and larger community who demand the elimination of faculty and student "subversives"?

Schools as Factories

Schools have come to resemble their counterparts in the business community: corporations and factories. Production is the prime consideration: The number of students turned out, not the quality of the students, is what counts. With even larger classrooms, and increasing calls for everyone to have the benefit of a college education, such a trend cannot seemingly be avoided. Underlying this is an anti-intellectualism which takes pride in numbers.[31] In order to handle these increased numbers efficiently, colleges must hire more administrators and install large computers. Students are so many IBM card numbers and are treated accordingly.

The university resembles a corporation in yet more elaborate ways for it has economic ties that make it dependent on corporate connections. University trustees often represent large business interests, interests which cannot always be divorced from the goals of higher education. However, such conflicts of interest are rarely preceived by either the public at large or by the students.[32] In addition, some faculty members find their time more rewarded if spent on consultantships than in doing "pure" research or in teaching. While many hide within the walls of academia, removing themselves from the ongoing society, these consulting faculty constitute a reinforcement of the status quo in the community.

The number of administrators who serve on boards of directors is on the increase, as is the number of faculty members employed to testify before Congress on the worthiness of a particular product. Government too employs faculty members in counter-insurgency research,[33] as well as in the production of other types of classified data.

The National Student Association (NSA) has even been used by the CIA for its own purposes, and many former officers of NSA have been employed full-time by the CIA.[34]

All of this raises crucial questions as to the functions of a university. Is the university just another "front" for corporate capitalism? How can the university provide a means of controlling and evaluating the technological society if it has become, in fact, a prototype of that very society? Moreover, how impartial is the knowledge a university produces, if such research is constantly dependent on corporate and governmental influences in terms of funds and other financial remunerations? It may be objected that the very function of a university *is* to serve the needs of society—but *who* determines these needs? Is not one of society's requirements the existence of an institution that constantly challenges society's goals and means of achieving these goals? If not from the universities and colleges, then from where else is such an evaluation and challenge to come? If the faculty and the lay community are unwilling to address themselves to these issues— then to whom can the student turn but those "radicals" who represent his neglected interests, how can he not be radicalized himself?

If the college and the university are viewed as part and parcel of the technological society, then the students who fail in such a system believe they do so because of failures *in themselves*. The system is omnipotent and cannot be criticized. The goals of education are then determined by corporate directorates and faculty members held in bondage by such directorates—they are top-down directives (Shape up or ship out!"). The student resembles his bureaucratic counterpart, the white-collar worker. He is compartmentalized. He occupies a position, and the rules and obligations cannot be tampered with. The student is expected to work diligently and not to question. Where are the enterprising creative young executives to come from (or has the computer replaced them)? For the bureaucratic student meaning exists not in learning but in the fringe benefits—for example co-ed dorms, a three-day class schedule, a course with no exams.

NOTES

[1] Edgar Friedenberg, *The Vanishing Adolescent* (New York: Dell Publishing Co., Inc.), pp. 187–188.

2 Jerry Farber, *The Student as Nigger* (North Hollywood: Contact Books, 1969), p. 117.

3 Joseph R. Royce, *The Encapsulated Man* (Princeton: D. Van Nostrand Co., 1964); see also C. P. Snow, *The Two Cultures* (Cambridge: Cambridge University Press, 1960).

4 John Holt, *How Children Fail* (New York: Delta, 1964), p. 34.

5 Farber, *op. cit.*, p. 40.

6 *Ibid.*, pp. 114–128.

7 *Ibid.*, pp. 14, 17–18.

8 Holt, *op. cit.*, pp. 167–168.

9 Farber, *op. cit.*, p. 15.

10 *Ibid.*, pp. 27–28.

11 *Ibid.*, p. 23.

12 Paul Goodman, *Compulsory Mis-education* (New York: Horizon Press, 1964), p. 87.

13 John H. Schaar and Sheldon S. Wolin, "Education and the Technological Society," in *The New York Review of Books,* Vol. XIII, Number 6, 1969, pp. 4–5; see also Holt, *op. cit.*, p. 169.

14 Farber, *op. cit.*, p. 23.

15 Friedenberg, *op. cit.*, p. 49.

16 Edgar Friedenberg, "An Ideology of School Withdrawal," in Daniel Schreiber, *Profile of the School Dropout* (New York: Random House, Inc., 1968), p. 18.

17 John Keats, *The Sheepskin Psychosis* (New York: Dell Publishing Co., Inc., 1967), p. 23.

18 Farber, *op. cit.*, p. 30.

19 Arthur I. Stinchcombe, *Rebellion in a High School* (Chicago: Quadrangle, 1969), p. 9.

20 Goodman, *op. cit.*, p. 29.

21 *Ibid.*, p. 70; see also Stinchcombe, *op. cit.*, p. 179.

22 *Ibid.*

23 Morris Rosenberg, *Society and Adolescent Self Image* (Princeton: Princeton University Press, 1965).

24 Arthur Pearl, "Slim and None—The Poor's Two Chances," in Schreiber, *op. cit.*, p. 319.

25 *Ibid.*, pp. 320–321.

26 *Ibid.*, p. 317.

27 For discussions of minority group education see Jonathan Kozol, *Death at an Early Age* (New York: Bantam Books, Inc., 1968); James Hearnden, *The Way It's Supposed To Be* (New York: The Viking Press, Inc., 1969); Herb Kohl, *36 Children* (New York: W. W. Norton & Company, Inc., 1968); and Holt, *op. cit.*

28 Schaar and Wolin, *op. cit.*, p. 3.

29 *Ibid.*

30 *Ibid.*, p. 4.

[31] Richard Hofstadter, *Anti-Intellectualism in American Life* (New York: Random House, Inc., 1964).

[32] James Ridgeway, *The Closed Corporation* (New York: Ballantine Books, Inc., 1968), p. 18. See also for a similar type of discussion Paul Goodman, *The Community of Scholars* (New York: Random House, Inc., 1962).

[33] For example see Irving Louis Horowitz, "The Life and Death of Project Camelot," in *Transaction*, Vol. III, No. 1, November, 1965, pp. 3–7.

[34] Sol Stern, "NSA and the CIA," in *Ramparts*, March, 1967, pp. 29–37.

two

where can we go?: American society reconstructed

9

stop the machine,
I want to get off:
toward the elimination of
work and consumption

Solutions to the problems of American Society described in the first part of this text are often of a piecemeal variety—that is, while attempting to focus on specific issues, critics tend to ignore the relationship of parts to the whole. Even more important, such solutions are often based on outmoded premises and unwarranted assumptions. An example of one such solution is the War on Poverty (reviewed in Chapter 5). This ongoing program essentially trains men for jobs which, in a few years, will be obsolete, because it discounts the effects that automation and technology are having on the occupational structure. The program assumes that all men will *have* to work—at least as "work" has traditionally been defined. But is this necessarily the case now, and will it be the case in the future?

In much the same way, solutions to international problems have been viewed in terms of larger armies and more deadly armaments, strategies which have repeatedly proven only temporarily effective. The question is: How many would-be reforms take the underlying value system for granted, accept the reality structure, and attempt to

195

adapt solutions which will fit into that value framework? The purpose of this chapter is to evaluate solutions to the problems of work, consumption, and leisure by questioning the basic premises on which many of these solutions are founded. Can the values of work, consumption, and leisure be salvaged, or are they outmoded concepts of another era?

Toward a New Industrial System: Is There Really a Difference between the United States and Russia?

In Chapter 1 we considered the meaning that work holds for most Americans, and the increasing dependence on technology. At the same time, we noted that most of us work in order to be able to consume, and that this has created a shift from a production- to a consumption-oriented society. In the future, however, shall we continue to work in order to consume, and must we pile up consumer goods in order to "survive"? Before examining this question, let's again look briefly at the economic structure. Predictions are that the giant corporate business enterprises which already dominate American society will grow even larger and demand increasingly large amounts of capital. Corporate enterprises will further require increasing specialization of personnel and technology. The time lag between the decision to produce a certain commodity and the advent of that commodity on the open market will become longer, this whole process will require an increasing amount of planning and consequent inflexibility.[1] For the average worker, it matters little whether he lives in Soviet society where the state ostensibly does the planning, or American society where planning is handled by a small number of large corporations. For both, real control of the economy rests in the hands of the technostructure and its imperatives. This technostructure is the real target for those who would deal with problems of alienating work and superfluous consumption. As Galbraith has stated:

> The enemy of the market is not ideology but the engineer. In the Soviet Union and the Soviet-type economies, prices are extensively managed by the state. Production is not in response to market demand but given by the overall plan. In the Western economies, markets are dominated by great firms. These establish prices and seek to insure a demand for what they have to sell. The enemies of the market are thus to be seen, although rarely in social matters has there been such a case of mistaken identity. It is not socialism. It is advanced technology and the specialization of men and process that this requires and the resulting commitment of time and capital. These make the market work badly when the

need is for greatly enhanced reliability—when planning is essential. The modern large corporation and the modern apparatus of socialist planning are variant accommodations to the same need. It is open to every free-born man to dislike this accommodation. But he must direct his attack to the cause. He must not ask that jet aircraft, nuclear power plants or even the modern automobile in its modern volume be produced by firms that are subject to unfixed prices and unmanaged demand. He must ask instead that they not be produced.[2]

Not only do Western economic spokesmen feel this way. Predrag Vranicki, writing out of Yugoslavia, notes:

We dare not close our eyes to . . . the fact that socialism is not a magical leap from an alienated to a de-alienated society; to the contrary, it is a new historical process which also contains certain alienated forms; nor can one ignore the fact that its historical import and mission is precisely the conquest, not the increase, of alienation. In terms of the contemporary level of human development, regardless of specific countries, socialism is also a hierarchical society . . . bureaucracy is a constant accompaniment to socialism. . . . Socialism has not yet abolished the production of commodities, hence the market, money, or any of the fetishes which inevitably appear at this level of economic and cultural development of mankind. Regardless of the possibility of much stronger intervention on the part of the socialist state or society itself to prevent the occurrence of the various deformations originating from such a pattern, the occult power of the market and of money, and the hierarchy of status, are bound to have an alienating effect on the unstable structure of contemporary man. Egocentricity, the division of the personality into an official and a private component, and various other resultant moral aberrations are nothing more than manifestations of human alienation, even under socialism. . . .[3]

This is not to overlook certain fundamental differences between the goals of the two societies. For example, production in Soviet countries is ostensibly aimed at satisfying "basic" human wants (food, clothing, and shelter), while industries in the West must create consumer demand. Yet, Eastern European societies are increasingly asking for the more luxury types of consumer goods, such as television sets, fashions, and so forth. Therefore these countries will probably come more to resemble Western economies in fulfilling such desires. Another similarity is that the larger Eastern European nations import raw materials from many of the underdeveloped nations just as the United States and other Western European nations do. Thus "Welfare Imperialism" exists on both sides of the Iron Curtain, and is motivated by the same factors.

Focusing again on the West, what motivates large American corporate firms? Most of us would probably point to the profit motive. Galbraith suggests that this is no longer true:

> The members of the technostructure do not get the profits that they maximize. They must eschew personal profit–making. Accordingly, if the traditional commitment to profit maximization is to be upheld, they must be willing to do so for others, specifically the stockholders, what they are forbidden to do for themselves. It is on such grounds that the doctrine of maximization in the mature corporation now rests. It holds that the will to make profits is, like the will to sexual expression, a fundamental urge. But it holds that this urge operates not in the first person, but in the third. It is detached from self and manifested on behalf of unknown, anonymous and powerless persons who do not have the slightest notion of whether their profits are, in fact, being maximized. In further analogy to sex, one must imagine that a man of vigorous, lusty and reassuringly heterosexual inclination eschews the lovely, available and even naked women by whom he is intimately surrounded in order to maximize the opportunities of other men whose existence he knows of only by hearsay. Such are the foundations of the maximization doctrine when there is full separation of power from reward.[4]

The real goal becomes maximizing the success of the organization, which is measured in terms of organizational growth and technological development. Motivation for many workers, especially the white-collar group, comes to be seen in terms of adaptation of the worker's goals to those of the corporation and identification of the worker with the organization.[5] The more scientifically oriented and technically specialized the work force becomes, the easier this is.

Adaptation means that our goals become those of the organization and are seen as one and the same. "What's good for General Motors is good for the world." Moreover, such goals identify progress with size and quantity of production. And size necessitates continued consumption of material goods, so that further production and concomitant growth can occur. It is here, of course, as we noted in Chapter 2, that advertising comes to play such a significant role.[6] Many white-collar workers feel important by identifying with (for instance) Lockheed, not with their specific occupational task. And the consumer, for his part, feels he is a free man in an open market, that he can buy what he wants, when he wants. Ostensibly, everyone lives happily ever after, presuming that we ignore the problems which this type of industrial system creates for those who are a part of it.

Corporations which go around the world in search of raw materials, then, do so not only to increase profits (the motivation perhaps of a board of directors), but because of technological imperatives. The economy needs oil in order to continue the operation of millions of cars, and these cars must continue to run if the majority of the work force is to be employed (and the image of America supported).

Other economists have argued that the profit motive does in fact exist, that profits are the personal goals most executives match with the goals of the companies they are part of.

It may be that both motives coexist, with the profit motive becoming increasingly important as one goes up the hierarchy. Whether the goals of corporations are growth and technological innovation or increasing profits, the end result is the same. Competition may not be ruthless, but the need for expanding markets still remains.

What Will Happen to the Blue-Collar Worker?

The increasing efficiency and technological sophistication of automation is eliminating blue-collar jobs. Those now unemployed and those who will soon lose their jobs must either be retrained or receive some sort of guaranteed income.

Retraining may be undertaken by the government or by private corporations. But one must consider that for someone who has spent over twenty years on an assembly line, retraining includes extensive psychological changes as well. A retraining program could create professional and pre-professional employment for currently unemployed, uneducated, and occupationally unskilled members of American society. These jobs would be mainly in the area of public service; individuals can be hired as social workers and community organizers. Such a plan has been developed by Riesman and Pearl. It would make current credential requirements obsolete and consider in their place an individual's ability and motivation to aid his own particular community.[7] Other types of retraining facilities involve reorienting workers toward computer and automated industries in which the individual watches dials instead of bolting on fenders. One major drawback of these various programs is that they do not train workers for middle-management positions, which depend more on social than physical skills. Primarily, this type of socialization is what a college education is all about: not what is taught but what is almost inevitably learned— the techniques of manipulation, the "glad hand," the toothpaste smile. This same barrier in the past kept the blue-collar worker from advancing beyond foreman; the skills required to enter management were not learned on the assembly line.

Another problem resulting from the decline in the number of jobs is that leisure time is being forced on those who seem most incapable of handling it and do not really want it. Those who have occupied the most inflexible job situations, assembly line work and whose lives are time-oriented around such work, often have little conception of what to do with their newly "earned" free time. Nor can they afford it. Those who do have some conception of what to do with their time are, somewhat paradoxically, the ones most needed by the corporate structure. If blue-collar workers are not immediately laid off, they do not have the time or the financial ability to undertake retraining even if they desire to do so. In order to cope with this problem, Suhm has devised a cumulative earned leave plan in which employees can earn time off the job to be used as they desire—either in undertaking further retraining or in some type of leisure-time activity.

Principal Features of the Cumulative Earned Leave Plan

1. A system by which all employed persons covered under Social Security earn time off from their jobs in addition to regular vacations.

2. Leave time earned would be determined by increases in national productivity as measured by output per man-hour in the over-all economy caused by labor efficiency and improved technology.

3. Individual leave time accumulations would be based upon actual time worked, up to a maximum of 40 hours per week.

4. Accumulated leave time would be transferable between jobs and could be saved indefinitely for use in a single period of extended leave or utilized in short but more frequent periods of leave.

5. The schedules for using leave time would be determined by agreements between employers and employees or their representatives.

6. Job benefits, seniority, and other rights of employees would be protected while on leave.

Principal Features of the Employment Adjustment Fund

1. A centralized system for financing the Cumulative Earned Leave Plan.

2. Equal contributions to the Fund by the employee, the employer, and the federal government and maintained in individual employee accounts.

3. Contributions to the Fund to be based upon a percentage of

      the employee's wages or salary on incomes up to $10,000 per
      year.

4. Percentage contributions to the Fund to be determined by productivity increases in the national economy.

5. Funds in an employee's account could be used only in conjunction with the Cumulative Earned Leave Plan or paid to survivors
   in case of death.

6. Employees on leave under the program would be paid from the
   Employment adjustment fund on a monthly basis. The amount
   of payment would be determined by dividing total months of
   accumulated earned leave by the total amount in the employee's
   Employment Adjustment Fund account.

7. Employees drawing earned leave benefits would not be allowed
   to work at other paid employment covered under the program.[8]

Assuming that employees want more leisure or desire retraining, such
a plan could solve some of the unemployment problem since it would
necessitate a continuing rotation of the labor force.

    An alternative to retraining is the guaranteed income. This program
could work in several ways. In conjunction with retraining efforts, a
living wage would be supplied until an individual got back on his feet,
until he was retrained and reemployed.[9] Another form of guaranteed
income provides funds for those already employed but unable to make
enough to survive.[10] This would be a type of supplementary wage. In
terms of the way the welfare system currently operates, a recipient
would not lose his welfare payments or benefits because he got a job
which paid him only slightly more than his welfare check. As it now is,
there is little incentive to seek any employment at all. Moreover, family
responsibilities make it difficult to accept such a job unless one has a
substantial amount to profit and can afford baby sitting services, etc.[11]

    Perhaps the central issue is why not *just* a guaranteed income with
no strings attached? Why concentrate on getting people jobs? [12] I shall
return to these questions later in the chapter.

What if the Means of Production
Are Not Worth Owning?

Many ways have been suggested to make jobs more interesting, challenging, and worthwhile. Among them are profit-sharing and a role
in planning company operations. Profit-sharing, while seemingly worthwhile in small companies, loses much of its appeal when applied to

large corporate organizations, for the profit shared amounts to very little. To what degree does a General Motors stockholder feel he has a stake in the company's future? In terms of decision-making, again, small companies have the most to offer. Yet, as we have noted, the trend in our society is toward larger corporate units. To talk about making company decisions in such organizations is to talk about being the one who feeds the computer and carries out its dictates. With the increasing amounts of planning and control that are necessary, corporations must maintain a degree of certainty in decision-making which can only come from reliance on computers. To leave decision-making in the hands of mere mortals, assuming that these mortals have the necessary knowledge and skill, is almost out of the question. Too much is at stake. Fromm has noted that while one can still accept or reject the recommendations of computers, "he would have to be out of his mind to take the risk, since there is not a greater source of certainty than God—or the computerized solution." [13]

The problem with plans which have the worker share in decision-making is that the worker himself often does not necessarily want to participate. He does not want to be responsible for his own actions, nor for the actions of others. He would rather be told in polite, discreet, and subtle terms what to do. Security, yes, but not freedom, anxiety and ulcers. If poverty is defined as "a lack of power to command events," then most people as conditions are now will always be poor, and they will want to remain so.[14] The personality characteristics we defined in Chapter 3 will continue to make this the case, unless such characteristics are fundamentally altered.

Given the size of business enterprises in Western and Eastern Europe and in the United States, would it make a difference if "the people" owned the means of production, as such production is now conceptualized or carried out? Would the goals of such enterprises be fundamentally altered? Would we still not demand that such enterprises produce washing machines, newer and more stylish dresses, deodorants, hair dyes, and cars? If the corporation does not exist to make a profit—at least as its primary motivation—then would not the same commodities cost approximately as much as they now do? And, even if they cost much less, what difference would this change in ownership make in solving the basic problem at hand? If votes were taken on what should be produced, demands *might* be made that such necessary life-support items as cars and washing machines and light bulbs last much longer than they now do. Perhaps this would give workers more pride in what they produce. Then again, they might become bored with producing the same almost indestructible item,

Courtesy of Gyula Szabo

year in and year out; and certainly, as consumers themselves, they could become as bored as any other consumer if all they could purchase was the same item, year in and year out.

In an affluent society such as ours, most physical wants are being met. How then can one take pride in and measure his contribution to society by material production if that society does not need any more material and is bored with what it has? None of this is altered by the people owning the means of production. What if the means of production are not worth owning? We own the public corporations, does it make any difference to us? We own the government. Does it give us a feeling of worthiness, of participation in the national economy and the future of American society? Putting ownership of the means of production in the hands of "the people" can enable all of the people to share in the fruits of technology, but will it guarantee that these

Courtesy of Gyula Szabo

fruits will change, or that the rest of the world's people will get an equal share of them? Of course, the private corporations would likely have to be eliminated in order even realistically to pose these questions, unless existing ones become philanthropically oriented and cease producing superfluous commodities.

In order to answer these questions *we must want* to answer them. We must want to change the types of commodities our industries currently produce; the distribution of goods and services; and ownership of the means of production. Do we? Most employees would rather exchange places with managers or stockholders; few would, at this writing, want to nationalize the economy.

Regardless of who owns the means of production, if such production is to be efficient, planned, and circulated so that the maximum number of people are able to benefit, and given scarce natural resources, we must ultimately have to face up to the fact that these types of industries can only be run by computers and automated machines. Most workers will have very little say in the production process at all. Most of us seeking meaningful and worthwhile work will have to do so outside the scope of basic survival needs. This will not necessarily mean that these machines will run our lives; rather, food, clothing, and shelter will come to be taken for granted in the same sense that we accept the fact that each of us does and has a right to breathe. How can we bring such a situation about? What types of work and occupations would we then participate in? Would these be defined as "work"? In other words, would there be a difference between work and leisure?

There are other ways of making existing jobs more interesting and worthwhile. In some businesses (particularly in factories today) individuals work at more than one job, so they don't have time to get bored. Yet, each task in itself remains the same: uninteresting. Toffler has spoken of "adhocracies," in which groups of people from different occupations are temporarily brought together to produce a given commodity, and after which the team disbands to be grouped in another configuration with other people.[15] In order to bring more creativity into the marketplace, it has been suggested that an income floor be established so that individuals would be free to do what they wanted—in terms of production—without risking loss of salary.[16] This might only bring fancier types of deodorants, but, optimistically, it could also serve to free persons to experiment in relating to one another in value changes, and in other types of artistic endeavor. The former product could easily be co-opted by business enterprises; while such co-optation and subsequent bastardization would prove much more difficult in the latter case.

An End to Alienating Work and Superfluous Consumption: Getting Off the Treadmill

We pointed out in Chapter 1 that there are just not enough jobs to go round and, most certainly, there are not enough worthwhile jobs. Why continue to attempt to employ everyone, especially when many industries are performing at less than 50 percent capacity? Moreover, most of our industries produce non-essential commodities—clothing we don't need, cars whose only advantage over last year's model is that they have a new tail-fin. If we no longer purchased these superfluous goods, then even more people would be out of work, and we would have to find something else for them to *do*. If the defense industry were dismantled, unemployment would increase still further. Yet a change in priorities can re-employ many of these persons in social service occupations, as teachers or doctors, in building schools, and so forth—in occupations outside the traditional factory-corporate apparatus.

As noted in earlier chapters, consumption is often used as a substitute for empty occupational tasks; it gives us a chance to show who we are as defined by what we can buy. It gives us a sense of power which is lacking in the hours spent at work. Constant consumption relieves anxiety. As Fromm states:

> Here is an individual who is powerless to have any influence—beyond a marginal one—on the affairs of the state or the enterprise in which he is employed. He has a boss, and his boss has a boss, and the boss of his boss has a boss, and there are very few individuals left who do not have a boss and do not obey the program of the managerial machine—of which they are a part. But what power does he have as a consumer? There are dozens of brands of cigarettes, toothpastes, soaps, deodorants, radios, television sets, movie and television programs, etc., etc. And they all woo his favor. They are all there "for his pleasure." He is free to favor the one against the other and he forgets that essentially there are no differences. This freedom to give his favors to his favorite commodity creates a sense of potency. The man who is impotent humanely becomes potent as a buyer and consumer. Can one make any attempt to restrict this sense of potency by restricting the freedom of choice in consumption? It seems reasonable to assume one can do so only under one condition, and that is that the whole climate of society changes and permits man to be more active and interested in his individual and social affairs, and hence less in need of that fake freedom to be the king in the supermarket. The attempt to question the pattern of unlimited consumption meets with another difficulty. Compulsive consumption compensates for anxiety . . . [stemming] from the sense of inner emptiness, hopelessness, confusion, and tension. By "taking in" articles of consumption, the individual reassures himself that "he is," as it were. If consumption were to be reduced, a good deal of anxiety would become manifest. The resistance against the possible arousal of anxiety would result in an unwillingness to reduce consumption.[17]

Given that it would be possible to reduce the factory, corporate, and in some cases, the civil service work week to 10–15 hours per week, before finally eliminating it for most persons, and given that we could stop consuming at our present rate, why not do so? We know that material possessions do not really give our lives meaning. Moreover, such commodities are inherently limiting, and a restriction on our freedom, for we must always carry them around with us—if not physically then in our heads to show who we are. It is a problem of *having* versus *being*. When one has things, he is constantly afraid of losing them; he is fundamentally insecure; he is afraid of being vulnerable; he is static. Fromm comments:

> The increasing emphasis on ego versus self, on having versus being, finds a glaring expression in the development of our language. It has become customary for people to say, "I have insomnia," instead of, "I cannot sleep"; or, "I have a problem," instead of "I feel sad, confused" or whatever it may be; or, "I have a happy marriage" (sometimes successful marriage), instead of saying, "My wife and I love each other." All categories of the process of being transformed into categories of having. The ego, static, and unmoved, relates to the world in terms of having objects, while the self is related to the world in the process of participation. Modern man *has* everything: a car, a house, a job, "kids," a marriage, problems, troubles, satisfactions—and if all that is not enough, he has his psychoanalyst. He *is* nothing.[18]

Thus we come to spend our lives defensively, protecting what we have, rather than concentrating on *living* as a *process*. In the same way, then, when we define our existence by the job we do, we become desperately afraid of losing that job, because we do not know who we are without it. In order to be free we must let go of our possessions, and say not "I have *values*," but "I am *living* these values."

By refusing to buy what is produced, consumers have power to force corporations to produce durable consumer goods. At the same time, it is technologically possible for computers and automated machines to crank out simple foodstuffs, clothing, and pre-fabricated housing units—to make these available and free as the air we breathe (and, unfortunately, often of the same polluted quality). If we no longer found it necessary to seek employment, or buy thousands of excess commodities, then what would we do? For one thing, we could devote much of our time toward what has been called "self-actualization"—that is, fulfilling whatever potential we, as human beings, now have. Freed from the necessity of superfluous consumption and alienating work, we could experiment with the society we now occupy, altering its basic institutions, changing the way decisions are arrived at, and thus, we could transform our social relationships. We might find satisfaction in *being ourselves;* we could come to see ourselves as processes rather than as static, pre-directed things whose lives have been programmed by advertisers and middle-management computer analysts. Out of such re-evaluation we could seek other types of occu-

pational endeavor—as teachers, architects, artists; create new occupational categories—political activist, professional student; even help
others self-actualize themselves, deal with national and international
social problems, solve the dilemma of the haves versus the have-nots.
Individuals could measure their contribution to society by being "paid"
for relating to each other, for participating in the decision-making
process, for their artistic works. When we are doing what we want to
do we're not preoccupied with job status or the amount of money
we are being paid; thus the dichotomy of work and non-work, or
occupation itself, could become a misnomer. Some seventy-five years
ago Bellamy (in his celebrated novel *Looking Backward*) described a
society in which everyone was paid the same amount, yet performed
the tasks they wanted to perform. What if there is no real difference
between one's work and leisure activities, if work *is* leisure, if we
are doing what we want to do? [19] In other words, what does it matter
if they will pay us more money to play baseball when we really like to
play football? If our basic needs are taken care of in either case, then
we can do what we want. Does it make any difference if baseball has a
higher status?

How can the gap be bridged between this type of work and that
which we now know?

How can our priorities be redirected, our defense plants closed
down, our shopping centers made into areas of art display and recreation?

How can the Protestant Ethic be eliminated as a guiding force in
our work activities? How can we let people know that they don't
have to work?

How can production be directed toward serving the needs of all
the world's peoples instead of as a means of polluting American
society with excess material goods?

How can workers be convinced to leave their jobs in defense and
superfluous consumer goods industries and enter other occupations,
or refuse to work at all? In either case, how can a guaranteed wage
be established so that monetary considerations are not the prime
motivation for seeking employment?

We have the power as consumers to refuse to buy, and—as producers—by refusing to participate in factory and corporate enterprises,
to alter the economy regardless of who now owns the means of
production. But first *we must want to!* We must be able to see
something better, an alternative—not only outside of ourselves, in the
structure of American society, but inside as well.

NOTES

1 John Kenneth Galbraith, *The New Industrial State* (New York: Signet, 1968), pp. 24–27.

2 *Ibid.,* pp. 44–45.

3 Predrag Vranicki, "Socialism and the Problem of Alienation," in Erich Fromm, *Socialist Humanism* (Garden City: Doubleday & Company, Inc., 1966), pp. 309–311.

4 Galbraith, *op. cit.,* p. 128.

5 *Ibid.,* p. 146.

6 *Ibid.,* p. 220.

7 Frank Riessman and Arthur Pearl, "Poverty and New Careers for Non Professionals," in Arthur Blaustein and Robert Woock, *Man Against Poverty: World War III Reader on the World's Most Crucial Issue* (New York: Random House, Inc., 1968), pp. 216–227.

8 Lawrence L. Suhm, "Cumulative Earned Leave: New Tool for Economic Planning," in Robert Theobald, *Social Policies for America in the Seventies: Nine Divergent Views* (Garden City: Doubleday & Company, Inc., 1968), pp. 109–110.

9 Garth L. Mangum, "Guaranteeing Employment Opportunities," in Theobald, *op. cit.,* p. 38.

10 F. Helmut Weymar, "The Poor Should Be Paid Bonuses," in Theobald, *op. cit.,* pp. 57–59.

11 *Ibid.,* pp. 60–61.

12 *Ibid.,* p. 72.

13 Erich Fromm, *The Revolution of Hope* (New York: Bantam Books, Inc., 1968), p. 50.

14 John R. Seeley, "Progress from Poverty?", in Steven E. Deutsch and John Howard, *Where It's At* (New York: Harper & Row, Publishers, 1970), p. 430.

15 Alvin Toffler, *Future Shock* (New York: Random House, Inc., 1970).

16 Suhn, *op. cit.,* p. 119.

17 Fromm, *op. cit.,* pp. 123–124.

18 *Ibid.,* pp. 87–88.

19 Mangum, *op. cit.,* pp. 55–57.

10

why grow up?: youth culture—the new societal model

Critics of the contemporary scene have argued that given problems of population, pollution, and the threat of nuclear war, we have at best ten or fifteen years left. Perhaps this is the case; yet, such a viewpoint tends more to symbolize the "generation gap" than to strike fear in the hearts of those close enough to listen. In this instance, the gap is between those who view the problems we have considered in the first part of this book and then throw up their hands in dismay saying: "There's nothing I can do; it's all hopeless," and their children, who view the future in the present, and attempt to plant beauty and love in a desert of despair. Before going further, it should be understood that not all adults are defeatist, and certainly not all youth are shining examples of love and beauty. But many are. Do youth represent a new societal model, a different reality, an alternative? Can they, or aspects of their culture, provide us with a guide to the future and solutions to present problems? Or, rather, do they not represent more of the same hidden behind a façade of flowery clichés and beaded hearts?

Youth have in large measure become societal models because no one else seems to want the job—it has fallen to them by default.[1] Some fifteen years ago, Goodman pointed out that youth were "growing up absurd" because the jobs which awaited them were not worth performing.[2] This absurdity was to become even more apparent when adults themselves began to realize that they occupied the very jobs their children were repelled by. In essence, as consumption and other-directed types of relationships became ever less satisfying a life style, these same adults began to look to their children as prophets of a more meaningful society. The traditional relationship between parents and children was reversed, and for perhaps the first time in history, youth culture became the dominant mode of orientation for society. What happens when adults begin to imitate and worship the culture of their children? Where does this leave the youths themselves? How do they handle their new role? What *is* their new role? And if adults are imitating their children, why all the talk about a generation gap?

In order to consider these questions it is necessary to discuss briefly what growing up, particularly the adolescent period, means in contemporary American society. Adolescence, a term only relevant to Western industrialized nations, refers to an ill-defined period falling between childhood and adulthood. The fact that there is no ready connection between childhood and adulthood forces many youth into a state of ambiguity; they don't know exactly what role they are supposed to be playing. Seemingly they are too old to be children or at least be treated as children, and so they are waiting to become adults.[3] But what are they supposed to be doing while they are waiting? Preparing for the future? As we have already seen, the schools they attend do not really prepare them for any occupation, so it is difficult to use this as a motivational ploy. Moreover, parents once provided role-models. We could look to our fathers and see what they did with their time and say, "That's what I want to do when I grow up." Today, however, most adult work is largely invisible, and that which is visible is not acceptable.[4] Adults are not proud of the work they do and spend little time elaborating on it while at home. Furthermore, many occupational tasks are so specialized that adolescents have difficulty understanding what their parents actually do, let alone wanting to perform such tasks themselves.

Parents may fail as models in many more important respects, and as they fail, so too does the family as an orientational and stabilizing unit. Primarily, as American ideology—the Protestant Ethic, individualism, and so on—has been emptied of meaning, those parents who continue to expound these concepts become hypocrites in the eyes of their children. Actually, much conflict between generations, or "across the breakfast table," results because youth take the proclaimed values of their parents seriously, while their parents do not.[5] One of the results of this is an attempt by some youth to treat and judge their parents as they would anyone else, on their individual merits, rather than because they happen to occupy a specific role. For example, the respect for authority that parents often claim simply because they are parents is no longer justified in the eyes of many youth. Rather, such respect must be earned, rather than assumed.[6]

Moreover, families are constantly on the move, being transferred to new locations, new jobs, new friends, new advertisements, and new fads. In a period of rapid social change, the family is beginning to come apart, and other institutions—educational institutions—take over those functions which the family, almost by necessity, has abdicated. Instead of forcing teenagers and adolescents to grow up faster, this mode of socialization serves to perpetuate the adolescent stage through such functional substitutes as "in loco parentis." [7] Schools treat adolescents as children, giving them little responsibility for determining their own destinies, while at the same time pampering them and not providing them with any tools to combat the hypocritical world that adults represent. Such institutions prepare youth to be "advertising fodder" or "political fodder." While the family is unable to provide a stable locus of identity, an anchoring function, parents seek to substitute acceptable role models. They use overindulgence to make up for all the things they, as parents, lacked when they were kids, and for the lack of love they find in their own relationships.[8] Their children, at least those growing up in white middle-class affluence, find little meaning in a constant bombardment of things, though they may gladly accept them, as well as anything else their parents wish to give up.

In a sense, the more parents find themselves unable to influence and command the respect of their children, the more they seek to make up for their guilt through reparation payments. This attitude, in effect, creates and perpetuates the very feelings of emptiness and loneliness which many adolescents are seeking to fight against. It leaves youth with no concrete responsible or acceptable roles to play; rather, they become the "playthings" of their parents, upon whom parents lavish all their unfulfilled dreams and unspent guilt, in promise of a forgiveness for they know not what. Such living through their children results in such psychological syndromes as Phillip Wylie's "Momism" —mothers who take out their frustrations on their children, often through quite subtle means.[9]

This gap between an unwanted adult world and the situation many youth find themselves involved in means that peers, rather than parents, must be depended on for knowledge and meaningful relationships.

The world comes to be related "horizontally" rather than "vertically." Such horizontal relationships occur not only between persons, but through underground newspapers and radio stations as well, and, as such, creates its own culture. Dependence on one's peers also helps produce a similar type of "other-directedness" as that experienced by "parents."

Growing up largely in this emotionally insecure position, youth have become quite susceptible to fads and to the consumption ethic. They literally create fashion and have a tremendous amount of buying power. Yet, youth is caught between two worlds—the one which they define and the one their parents define for them. On the one hand, society seeks to define youth and, on the other hand, youth seek to define themselves. This conflict in definitions makes itself felt in how the future is conceptualized and how the present is handled. While much of the adult world expects their children to grow up into nice, well-mannered consumers and workers, many youth have another conception. This clash becomes most apparent when, after remaining in ambiguous roles for approximately ten years, graduation brings the necessity of a job and a world most youth are ill-prepared to encounter.

> The permissiveness of postwar child-rearing has . . . been sufficient to arouse expectations. As babies, the middle-class young got picked up when they bawled. As children, they got their kindergarten finger paintings thumbtacked on the living room wall by mothers who knew better than to discourage incipient artistry. As adolescents, they perhaps even got a car of their own (or control of the family's), with all of the sexual privileges attending. They passed through school systems which, dismal as they all are in so many respects, have nevertheless prided themselves since World War II on the introduction of "progressive" classes having to do with "creativity" and "self-expression." These are also the years that saw the proliferation of all the mickey mouse courses which take the self-indulgence of adolescent "life problems" so seriously. Such scholastic pap mixes easily with the commercial world's effort to elaborate a total culture of adolescence based on nothing but fun and games. (What else could a culture of adolescence be based on?) The result has been to make of adolescence, not the beginning of adulthood, but a status in its own right; a limbo that is nothing so much as the prolongation of an already permissive infancy. To be sure, such an infantization of the middle-class young has a corrupting effect. It ill prepares them for the real world and its unrelenting if ever more subtle disciplines. It allows them to nurse childish fantasies until too late in life; until there comes the inevitable crunch. For as life in the multiversity wears on for these pampered youngsters, the technocratic reality principle begins grimly to demand its concessions. The young get told they are now officially "grown up," but they have been

left too long without any taste for the rigidities and hypocrisies that adulthood is supposed to be all about. General Motors all of a sudden wants barbered hair, punctuality, and an appropriate reverence for the conformities of the organizational hierarchy. Washington wants patriotic cannon fodder with no questions asked. Such prospects do not look like fun from the vantage point of between eighteen and twenty years of relatively carefree drifting.[10]

Following this line of reasoning, the only "occupation" left which offers a chance of maintaining fantasy is to become a "hippie." Yet, the educational system all too well prepares many youth for the transition to occupational boredom. While they are, indeed, pampered by their parents, it is within the limits of a well-defined reality framework: what passes for individualism and permissiveness can, under a different lens, be seen as co-optation and mass conformity. Nor, in disagreeing with the adult model which awaits them, are most youth prepared for combat or rebellion. Their heads are filled with many slogans, but their feet often say it all.

Caught essentially between two world views, both of which are attractive, most youth find they cannot get behind either. Wanting food, money, material possessions, and cars, as well as "free love," "poverty," community, and travel, they desire the best of both worlds, without fully knowing or understanding what each entails. It is no wonder, then, that most youth, after several years of social schizophrenia, take the easiest way out and find a job, get married, and settle down to living with the syndrome of problems we have already dealt with.

But not all youth get caught up in the half-and-half world of playing adolescent in American society. Many go other ways, at least for a while, and it is these youth who have perhaps provided us with a possible model for dealing with the problem of American society.

Do Your Own Thing: An Alternative Life Style or Subtle Co-optation?

Once committed to an alternative life style, there are essentially two ways to go: (1) become a revolutionary and *actively* fight the system, or (2) become a pacifist and seek to change it by example. The former leads to a variation of the politics loosely described as "New Left," the latter to the tribal anarchy of the hippies. There are, of course, modifications of both types. Let us give two impressions of the alternatives. The first is from Abbie Hoffman's *Woodstock Nation* and relates to a speaking engagement Hoffman had at a small college town in Ohio:

The recreation hall was packed when we walked in. It was a clankety old wooden building that I immediately loved, having just spoken in about a hundred ultra-modern paneled, soft-lighted mechanical mind-traps designed to rot your brain. The guys I was with, Steve Troyanovich and Jeff Gleiss, were shaking with ecstasy. Everybody had come out, even the mayor. It was as if Bevo was back in town! They didn't believe their eyes but there were ball players, black students (ten of them) . . . hillbillies, hippies (one), straights, ex-marines, teachers, six or seven hundred out of a one thousand student body. A teacher who had been thrown out last year had even come back. They had never seen a conspiring yippie–hippie–communist–drugged–sex-maniac, never mind one who had done all that in Chicago and gone to Russia for instructions and punched the head of HUAC and was taking LSD and they say he's gonna show obscene movies! "This we gotta see!" And they settle back in their seats ready for the show. I turned down an introduction (which I always do), jumped up on the stage and announced, "This is a fuckin movie about Pigs and Yippies. If you're stoned real good you can see the people fuckin in the grass. It cost me and my friends twelve bucks to make it and it ain't won no awards." Lights out, "Here's Yippie!" Bong! Mayor Daley appears. There is applause but wait—here come the Yippies pouring through the gates of the city, jumping to Phil Ochs and "I ain't marching anymore." The crowd was yelling for the Freaks. By the end of the film, everybody was jumpin up and down, hissing the cops, laughing their asses off. There ain't nothin SDS got that coulda worked that night at Rio Grande but that raggedy-ass movie did it. I jumped up at the end. They were all cheering like it was a basketball game. "I'm Huey Newton and I'm here to burn down the school!" It's a wild-ass rap, throwing away the mike, ripping off my shirt, yelling about how we are getting stepped on. "This is General Motors and you are the cars. Does General Motors ask the cars if they want all that fuckin chrome?" Dig it! Fun and sadness and sittin on the edge of the stage, cryin about how we are gettin gassed and beaten and arrested. Somebody held up the sissy V sign and I yelled, "Fuck that! We are at war!" I challenged the Klan, calling them chickenshit.

It's sweet talking about cupcakes and freedom and new ways of living the FUTURE. Because WE ARE THE FUTURE! It was the best since Lincoln Park and I was happy cause I knew the winter was over. It ended on a down-beat, suspenseful-like-hanging-slow-in-the-air, "The freak show is over . . . what are you going to do??? Hum???" I mumbled as I walked down the steps of the stage and up and down the rows of stunned students. . . . "What are you going to do now, hum? Why don't somebody else get up there and say what is on his mind! . . . No commies in this school? . . . No agitators? . . . No cat hangers? . . . SILENCE . . .

Then one kid stuttered up to the front and the place went wild. "I'm gonna take a few books out of the library tomorrow and sit out on the steps and read 'em and if they don't let Mr. Christopher stay [he was thrown off the teaching staff for making a minor criticism of the local system] . . . (gulp) . . . I might just not bring em back." Yippie! Then another and another got up. A jock even. A hillbilly drawled out one of the most beautiful raps I ever heard. A teacher gave an old-fashioned rap about what education means; then a kid got up and challenged one of the members of the administration who was sitting in the audience to answer the complaints. Everyone was screamin and stompin but he didn't say a word. A black cat got up on the stage. A chubby guy with his shirt hanging out. . . . "I'm one of those drunkin niggers you see around here every once in a while. . . . you gotta be drunk to go to this school. . . ." Everybody's hootin and yellin. Another black got up, an athlete, "I'm goin out to the library and take some books out too. . . . I gotta two-thous-and-dollar-a-year scholarship at stake but they can shove it if I can't have my dignity." And then the call for commitment. "How many comin out tomorrow?" And four hundred Freemen jumped up with their fists in the air. Steve and Jeff were ballin and I must admit I ain't felt that good for quite a while either and I was ballin too.[11]

This is when things go good. When they do not (and they did not for Hoffman at the Chicago conspiracy trial), then something is taken away—something which takes the ends seriously and employs original means to do away with hypocrisy.

Here is an example of one other alternative—perhaps a polar opposite, perhaps not, depending upon where in the bleachers you happen to be sitting:

Compare these empty alternative rituals [as put on by the establishment, planned, bureaucratized, holidays] with such rites as our hippies improvise for themselves out of potted anthropology and sheer inspiration. . . . The tribalized young gather in gay costume on a high hill in the public park to salute the midsummer sun in its rising and setting. They dance, they sing, they make love as each feels moved, without order or plan. Perhaps the folklore of the affair is pathetically ersatz at this point—but is the intention so foolish after all? There is the chance to express passion, to shout and stamp, to caress and play communally. All have equal access to the event; no one is misled or manipulated. Neither kingdom, nor power, nor glory is desperately at stake. Maybe, in the course of things, some even discover in the commonplace sun and the ordinary advent of summer the inexpressible grandeur that is really there and which makes those who find it more authentically human.

It would be easy to dismiss such merry displays as so much marginal *joie de vivre,* having no political relevance. But I think this would be a mistake. Here, in such improvised rituals, there is something postulated as sacred—and it is something worthy of the designation; the magnificence of the season, the joy of being this human animal so vividly alive to the world. And to this something sacred which stands above all men, causes, regimes, and functions, all are allowed equal access. Could this not be the ultimate expression and safeguard of a participative democracy, without which the popular control of institutions might always be corrupted by partisan interest or deference to expertise? These embryonic rituals may very well be an approximation of the no-politics Norman Brown speaks of. For what might this "no-politics" be if not a politics that doesn't *look* like politics at all, and which it is therefore impossible to resist by conventional psychic and social defenses? [12]

A happening at its best. A counter-culture: an alternative life-style. DO YOUR OWN THING. And so will everyone else DO *YOUR* OWN THING, all the department stores will DO *YOUR* OWN CLOTHING, and at ten times the cost because they want to *help* you DO *YOUR* OWN THING, and so will your friends do your own thing until you can't breathe, cramped for space to meditate and grow organic vegetables and other edible crops for harvesting and growing green upon, with the land but must keep from getting
    CO-OPTED
    USED
    MANIPULATED
and while doing my own thing, what things are other people doing, but if think about the things other people friends neighbors relatives, are doing cannot do my own thing
even though they may not like what things they are doing
like starving
but then they can do their own things if they want, if they are AWARE that they can
do their own things, I mean I don't want to bum other peoples trips not while they are falling in love with each other rolling round out in the grass pasture where society has put them
effectively out of the way of the bulldozers and marching bands of police and indignant citizens
of "Amerika"
put them OUT OF THE WAY on unused turnip patches where hassles can be avoided at all cost
to EVERYONE and confrontations cannot even be heard about since there is no electricity to plug the radio in-to

herded together in great numbers every once in awhile to listen to
SOUNDS and wait for the messiah to arrive or a bomb to drop
ALL OF US GATHERED TOGETHER brothers and sisters
TO GROOVE (must not be cynical, or present value judgement to
student who may inadvertently be reading between the lines, the space
gets wider all the time, symbols separate, begin to fall apart, left to
their own devices to survive the test of being without structure, but
all the same underneath, nevertheless, all just letters in the alphabet
when it comes down to it, and it will—come down to it) UNLESS
at Altamont speedway while DOING YOUR OWN THING 300,000
watch hells angels kill knife stab a body to death forever,
whose child is lost while DOING MY OWN THING do not wish to
bum anybody's trip but what's going on in town, in the ghetto, in
the little classrooms while we're out in the woods here listening to the
night running naked through the wind feeling
BEAUTIFUL, all of us BEAUTIFUL PEOPLE doing our own thing saying
it to ourselves over and over till we are convinced of our new
ideology of LOVE and TRUST for ALL
if only these others, these PIGS would come around so that we could
love them to be FREE and OPEN to EVERYONE but not to misconstrue
this as a sign that we are ready to be manipulated for
WE HAVE OUR OWN VALUES WE HAVE CREATED THEM IN OUR
OWN IMAGE if only everything would straighten out in our heads,
these guilt feelings which come now and again,if only everything would
ALWAYS be as simple and beautiful as they are sometimes when
everyone pitches in to help and commun-i-cate their feelings and
hassles which may be going through their heads every once in a while
like if everyone could just take each minute as it comes NOW in tune
with NOW in tune with the tears and laughter which float out of our
bodies and through all of us to UNITE us does unite us
ONCE IN A WHILE but why not more often?

But what do these youth want anyway? A chance to grow into
flowers? Who wants to be a flower? Give them power, if that's what
they want, give it to them, and see what THEY can do with it. But
they already have power, it's just that they don't realize it, it's just that
they can't seem to get themselves TOGETHER. AND THEY DON'T
KNOW WHAT TO DO WITH IT—THE POWER, like playing hot
potato, so why not give it away, surely someone must want it, maybe
take out an ad in the local paper. POWER TO THE PEOPLE. Power
to the people. WHAT KIND OF POWER?

As the spell of scientific or quasi-scientific thought has spread in our culture from the physical to the so-called behavioral sciences, and finally to scholarship in the arts and letters, the marked tendency has been to consign whatever is not fully and articulately available in the waking consciousness for empirical or mathematical manipulation, to a purely negative catch-all category (in effect, the cultural garbage can) called the "unconscious" . . . or the "irrational" . . . or the "mystical" . . . or the "purely subjective." To behave on the basis of such blurred states of consciousness is at best to be some species of amusing eccentric, at worst to be plain mad. Conversely, behavior that is normal, valuable, productive, mentally healthy, socially respectable, intellectually defensible, sane, decent, and practical is supposed to have nothing to do with subjectivity. When we tell one another to "be reasonable," to "talk sense," to "get down to brass tacks," to "keep one's feet on the ground," to "stick to the facts," to "be realistic," we mean that one should avoid talking about one's "inner" feelings and look at the world rather in the way an engineer looks at a construction project or a physicist views the behavior of atomic particles. We feel that worthwhile things come of such a state of mind— knowledge, solutions to problems, successful projects, money, power— whereas only some manner of unproductive self-indulgence comes of wallowing in "mere feelings." The more sophisticated may admit the legitimacy of allowing artists to moon and daydream. But the world, as every practical man knows, can do without poems and paintings; it can scarcely do without dams and roads and bombs and sound policy. Art is for the leisure hours; the time left over from dealing with realities and necessities.[13]

DON'T PLAY THEIR GAME! DON'T PLAY THEIR REALITY. We are both
means and end for WE ARE. LOVE and COMMUNITY. CAN YOU DIG
IT? what? what? what? everything fading in and out, so simple, so
complex, all or nothing, choice or chance, which is why, if
could just make sense, figure it all, passing through us, a gigantic
bubble bath and we cannot choose between the bubbles popping
within us
popping
within us, between the fingers outstretched to grab hold, the
eyes outstretched to grab hold passing through us these
sensations and other things look at the blade of grass staring at us, I'll
do the dishes without anyone having to tell me because I want to I love
to each dish washing each dish they will thank me but perhaps
not but I know anyway it was a good thing to do the
BAD VIBRATIONS coming on again and again but must keep looking,
searching getting things together, working things out, because there

"is nothing else" there's no going back we have found a new
innocence amongst the tire tracks and television eyes which go on
watching
THE SEARCH IS ALL THERE IS. And everyone can share in that or
the love that comes from just holding hands
for a little while. . . .

Every Man His Own God: A Church in Every House

There is something spiritual about all this, and the little pills or puffs
which are ingested from time to time by the organism for its own
well-being and self-preservation do not make it seem any *less* so
(though this is a touchy point even now for some people not wishing
to be identified with corruption or arguments of the ancients). Does
HE or doesn't HE exist and how much do we have to pay to keep him
in our church? HIS existence notwithstanding—a new Doctrine of
the Elect perhaps? A new communion with nature, with other people,
all other people and plants and bumble bees, can for one point in
time and in that moment for all points in time as Wolfe has spoken of
the Merry Pranksters, a group which first became renowned for setting
up a series of "acid-tests" and also for freaking people out by taking
them into their movie, the pranksters a kind of religious group:

> There was no theology to it, no philosophy, at least not in the sense of
> an *ism*. There was no goal of an improved moral order in the world or
> an improved social order, nothing about salvation and certainly nothing
> about immortality or the life hereafter. Hereafter! That was a laugh. If
> there was ever a group devoted totally to the here and now it was the
> Pranksters. I remember puzzling over this. There was something so . . .
> *religious* in the air, in the very atmosphere of the Prankster life, and yet
> one couldn't put one's finger on it. On the face of it there was just a
> group of people who had shared an unusual psychological state, the LSD
> experience. . . .
>
>   But exactly! The *experience*—that was the word! and it began to fall
> into place. In fact, none of the great founded religions, Christianity,
> Buddhism, Islam, Jainism, Judaism, Zoroastrianism, Hinduism, none of
> them began with a philosophical framework or even a main idea. They
> all began with an overwhelming new *experience* . . . "the experience of
> the holy." . . . At the very outset the leader did not offer his circle of
> followers a better state hereafter or an improved social order or any
> reward other than a certain "psychological state in the here and now."
> . . . What they all saw in . . . a flash was the solution to the basic pre-
> dicament of being *human*, the personal *I, Me,* trapped, mortal, helpless,

in a vast impersonal *It,* the world around me. Suddenly!—all-in-one—
flowing together, *I* into *It,* and *It* into *Me,* and in that flow I perceive a
power so near and so clear, that the whole world is blind to . . . that the
rational work-a-day world is blind to. . . .

Following a profound new experience, providing a new illumination
of the world, the founder, a highly charismatic person (Ken Kesey) begins
enlisting disciples. These followers become an informally but closely knit
association, bound together by the new experience, whose nature the
founder has revealed and interpreted. The association might be called a
circle, indicating that it is oriented toward a central figure with whom each
of the followers is in intimate contact. The following may be regarded
as the founder's companions, bound to him by personal devotion, friendship and loyalty. A growing sense of solidarity both binds the members
together and differentiates them from any other form of social organization. Membership in the circle requires a complete break with the
ordinary pursuits of life and a radical change in social relationships. Ties
of family and kinship and loyalties of various kinds were at least temporarily relaxed or severed. The hardships, suffering and persecution that
loomed for those who cast their lot with the group were counterbalanced
by their high hopes and firm expectations. . . .[14]

A new religion with new high priests and new followers: If only
the high priests this time could be on the *inside* rather than the *outside,*
and perhaps they were in little LSD time capsules, each with his own
Jesus Christ, each becoming his own God.[15] Not only the leadership,
but *everyone* feeling at one with the universe and all living things, and
even with things not so alive. And this is what is so attractive about it
all—from complete alienation to complete unity.[16] Perhaps this religion
takes us beyond YOUTH, beyond any kind of class, no matter how
concentrated we are on college campuses and department store
salesrooms or even during rock festivals; takes us into a new reality,
a oneness with nature. *What* identity crisis?

At least for the time being, a chance to *feel* your existence, to find
a subjective place among objective statuses and positions, amidst the
rationality of the human condition, the emptiness, the nausea and
regurgitation of *who* we are when in the long run, and even in the
short run all that one can really say is we are in the back seat of
oblivion necking with fate and a chance to be ourselves, a Libra or
Scorpio; are they a good match? While at the same time, there can
be no ideology, no formalization of the thing; just thousands of minute
situations which we daily encounter and flow through transient worlds,
for the present is all there is, a kind of situational ethics; and existential
decisions which are largely being made for us, at least sometimes:

You have to live for right now because if you live in terms of what might happen to you, what you expect will happen to you a number of years from now, you end up doing nothing but anticipating. I used to invest a great deal in anticipation. . . . I thought you could make more of an occasion by going through a long period of anticipation. What usually happens in a case like that—ok you're a kid in high school and someone groovy has asked you to a dance and you spend two weeks in a state of excitement about this dance, you go through a whole scene and the dance is a drag. It always is a drag. Or a party. You invest far too much in it and expect far more than you can ever get from it. If you just take it for what it is—you're not going to be disappointed.

If I make (a date) Monday night for Friday night—all right by Friday night I won't be for it. Because I'll be involved in something. I might be in Los Angeles. I might be in New York, you know, cause things happen that way. But it's always, but you're always falling into scenes kind of thing. You walk out of the house, you just got tired writing or something so you decide to go to Berkeley to have some coffee and maybe see some people and on the way you run into somebody and somebody else and it just keeps happening that way, you know but it's so hard to schedule. I have no long range plans. I don't know what I'm going to do the end of this week.[17]

But we're not victims of our situation either; rather we're just *with* our scene whatever it happens to be, flowing with it, and we can pick up the good or bad vibrations either way because we're in-tune, so we don't stop living even if we're sitting still.

Who's in the Zoo?

The big question though, is: "Who's in the zoo—we or they?" (Or are we both locked behind steel bars through which we must peer and which prevent us from seeing everything?)

When we stick flowers into rifle barrels are we co-opting the other side or are they co-opting us? For when have flowers ever been able to stop tanks, or to stop children from starving? But the big question is: "Have we really escaped into a new reality, or do we experience the same hassles, the same games, the same status system? Only it's all under disguise because "I've dropped more acid than you" and "I've been to Woodstock" and "Look at my hair and clothing and how many followers I have." If only we could forget everything we've been raised under, in, between, but still bring problems, advertisements with us, so deeply ingrained since early childhood, TV patterns to be hung-up and up-tight when it comes right down to it, unable to accept the planting of corn in the spring like everyone else:

No doubt many a "revolutionary festival" will degenerate into a mere mindless frolic—even as the militancy of "serious" demonstrations has been known to degenerate into fistfights . . . and then nobody convinces anybody of anything. But before we decide that the strategy of "no-politics" cannot possibly work, with it's recourse to indirection, involvement by seduction, and subliminal persuasion, let us be honest about one thing. If violence and injustice could be eliminated from our society by heavy intellectual research and ideological analysis, by impassioned oratory and sober street rallies, by the organization of bigger unions or lobbies or third parties or intricate coalitions, by "the flat ephemeral pamphlet and the boring meetings," by barricades or bombs or bullets . . . then we should long since have been living in the New Jerusalem. Instead, we are living in the thermonuclear technology. Given the perfectly dismal (if undeniably heroic) record of traditional radicalism in America, why should the dissenting young assume that previous generations have much to tell them about practical politics? [18]

For every one of us that is pure, there are five or ten or a hundred who are plastic,[19] seeking security in a new fad, next year it will be something else—seeking or *running from*—being open to freedom or manipulation or just BEING, in this case, in this case, not being able to put up with, to put up with, to-put-up-with. The counter-culture provides a sanctuary for many otherwise disturbed youth who would otherwise be in a *real* zoo,[20] but who now find themselves situated in a human zoo where they can nevertheless still be observed and their activities recorded but without much chance of a cure, it should be noted, it has been noted; they seem to reinforce each other's paranoia, to reinforce each other's mental disturbances and fantasies—about love and community and trust while Mr. Jones is beginning to get a wee-bit envious of all that free-love and food and companionship, and the values he never took seriously.

A ballroom surrealistically seething with a couple of thousand bodies stoned out of their everlovin' bruces in crazy costumes and obscene makeup with a raucous rock 'n' roll band and stroboscopic lights and a thunder machine and balloons and heads and streamers and electronic equipment and the back of a guy's coat proclaiming Please don't believe in magic to a girl dancing with four-inch eyelashes so that even the goddamn Pinkerton Guards were contact high.[21]

ACTION, NOT WORDS: Mr. Jones, it's all there is! And youth hungry for a little love, someone to talk to, to rap with, to screw, small change, spare change, spare feelings, spare tears to lend or soften the pain of BEING alive.

Can the New Consciousness Transform America?: The Selling of a Counter-Culture

While a small minority of the youth of America have, in fact, become totally immersed in the new consciousness, the majority have only adopted it as a new game to play. Contrary to what Roszak and Reich have predicted in their recent books,[22] because of this superficiality, the new consciousness cannot transform America, nor will it make the future much different from the present, except perhaps in providing a new circus for the children of Barnum and Bailey fans recently deprived of an afternoon's entertainment. Indeed, *the creation of a counter-culture has made such a revolution impossible,* for the counter-culture has become just another consumer product, a fad, and as such will be ineffective and impotent in creating a dialectic between itself and the mainstream. In many ways, the counter-culture *is* America, as American as apple pie, smog, and napalm, but is peddled under another name. And the small minority who do believe in a new consciousness are becoming totally neutralized and sterilized by the vast numbers of fellow travelers who claim counter-culture status, while failing to act out the rhetoric they mouth so easily.

American society has not been fundamentally altered by the counter-culture; rather, in a stroke of political and economic genius, the counter-culture mystique has made it seem *as if* everything were all right. The future will take care of itself, for we have the counter-culture, the new consciousness to save us. In this way, the New Generation, except for a small percentage, has been bought off from having to *do* anything. Rhetoric and fashion take the place of action because in most youth's heads, rhetoric is all there is; and the gap between knowing America is a problem and doing something about it widens. This is perhaps the most tragic part of all: It is in this very lack of motivation that the counter-culture consciousness sells out and betrays itself as being little different from the old consciousness, as being susceptible to marketing techniques and mass manipulation, as having the very mentality those in new Corvettes and false eyelashes manifest.

Is there a new consciousness or merely a change in rhetoric? Blacks often call Uncle Toms "Oreos" (after the cookie)—black on the outside, white on the inside. What word should we use to call most members of the counter-culture—hip on the outside, establishment on the inside—*nouveau groovy?* Is there a fundamental change in consciousness between attending a rock festival and watching the New York Jets or L. A. Rams play football? Is the relationship between Joe Namath and his seventy-five thousand fans sitting passively in the stadium significantly different from that which exists between Mick Jagger and his fans, except that the former will be watching through a haze of suds and booze, and the latter will be stoned on acid or grass? Both Namath and Jagger are necessary; the audience would quickly dissolve in despair without them.

Let's put it another way: If there were a coup d'etat at the White House and the Weathermen got in, would the nature of political participation have been fundamentally altered? Or would we still have political leaders telling us what to think, memorize and regurgitate at the polls—even better, not to think at all since they have the situation well under control. Is there an essential difference between sitting at the rock festival at Altamont Speedway watching passively while the Hell's Angels beat someone to death, and the case of Kitty Genovese in New York, whose screams for help could not arouse the thirty-seven persons within range of rendering assistance, but who were somehow intimidated by whoever was stabbing her? During the Cambodian demonstrations thousands of youth attended rallies protesting the war. But even on the most radical of campuses—Berkeley, for example—when finals and summer vacation came, the protests suddenly ceased, everybody went his own way (a prediction Nixon had made) while the war continued, our planes saturating villages in Cambodia and Laos our troops had only dreamed of visiting.

Why did the protests die so suddenly? For many students, demonstrations became a kind of fad, a happening, a thousand Woodstock Nations, a consumer product which could be treated in much the same light as a rock festival, and with the same type of participation. And after the happening was over, the crowds disappeared, leaving behind their commitment to end the war, the napalm, the Nixon administration. How effective can a counter-culture be which makes alienation a national pastime, a new fraternity whose sweatshirts proclaim HOSTILITY and ESTRANGEMENT, on sale at Sears for $4.95? But while the games change from dance marathons to fifteen-hour encounters (the truth shall make you free and immobile), from getting drunk to getting stoned, they are still games. So much depends on what you bring to the situation, and if all you bring is an "entertain me" type of mentality, then that's really all you'll come out with. If one expects to be manipulated because that's all he's really known, then he will be manipulated, call it counter-culture, democracy, or fascism.

Many in the youth counter-culture have deceived themselves into believing that they *are* free, that consciences *can* be salved by attending a demonstration twice a year, that the guilt they feel about the ghettos *can* be alleviated by registering Black voters or living in communes which play at poverty as if being poor was a union card to salvation. They have tricked themselves into thinking that because they shout slogans denouncing war that this eliminates the American presence in Vietnam; that "Pigs off campus!" solves the problem of community-college interaction; that interpersonal alienation ends when one has identified the fact that he is alienated. Most youth are insecure and look to the new consumer goods and slogans of the counter-culture as a means of finding an identity, a place in an all-too-hostile world. But they are still, to use a familiar cliché, other-directed, having others tell them who they are, what to buy, whom to protest against—as the TV commercials tell their parents.

Problems such as Vietnam, poverty, discrimination, consumption, and alienating work have to be memorized because few of these white youth experience them as problems and therefore find it difficult to become motivated to do anything about them. Those who do feel these issues deeply must fight against the intertia of countless others, fellow travelers looking for kicks and attention, who fade into the woodwork of empty verbiage once the reporters have gone and there is no longer anyone to listen to, applaud or hiss. A new consciousness may exist, but for most youth it's just more of the same, and it's comfortable and secure that way. Should we have really expected anything different, given the type of schools and the commercialism that most youth are raised on?

Madison Avenue might not be in control, they might not have created a conspiracy to sabotage the very values the counter-culture holds most dear, but in the end, what is the difference? In the name of keeping the economy functioning smoothly without increasing the labor force, and at the same time preventing it from blowing apart over Vietnam and Civil Rights, the "straight" society has capitalized on the superficial commitment of many youth to the new consciousness and has used the weakness of this commitment to pacify and control potentially disturbing elements and conflicts in America today. By using a "whipsaw" effect, Madison Avenue is able to turn disaster into profit—damned if they do, damned if they don't. They attack hippies for their long hair, shiftlessness, and lack of responsibility toward the good things about American society, while at the same time they give these youth an identity, a label, something to assuage the estrangement they already feel, a cause to unite around. And these youth take pride—like, "wow! I'm a member of a *counter*-culture!"

Everyone is a member of the counter-culture—shop at Macy's, buy an identity, become an individual, a reincarnated Marlboro man. The whipsaw encourages youth on the one hand to assume a distinct status and on the other insures that such a status acts as a form of political and social control, rather than subversion. Thus getting stoned is a major counter-culture activity, but so too is attending rock concerts and grooving on nature. While thousands of heads lie passively zonked out of their minds in some cow pasture, they are in self-imposed concentration camps, far from the power centers of America, out of the way; while the war goes on, and the VFW marches proudly in Portland, Oregon. Grass remains illegal, and thus all the more appealing to those who would rebel against that which *is* legal. Rock festivals are "dens of iniquity," while those who use these labels know full well that such hedonism inadvertently supports the status quo and enables the American Dream to ride rein over a new generation. Cops periodically raid college communities in search of anarchists and communists, keeping students busy finding bail money, defending *academic* freedom so they won't have time to launch an offensive in the surrounding community.

The counter-culture is preserved and solidified; it is made powerless, for it only reacts, only buys; what it sells is easily turned into profit, but by the other side. Sometimes such game playing helps preserve outmoded industry: raiding a few Panther headquarters, for instance, while millions of white parents go out and buy guns to defend themselves. After all, the war in the Far East is bound to end sometime, and then what will happen to our munitions plants? And finally, academics like Roszak and Reich legitimate the whole effort by declaring the existence of a counter-culture, thus making it respectable and impotent; making it "in" to be "out"—nouveau groovy.

But who needs these youth anyway? What difference does it make what they do so long as they don't bother the "American way of life." As Goodman pointed out some time ago, the economy can well afford to keep youth unemployed because there just aren't any jobs; not now, not in the near future, maybe never. So why get a generation all worked up over their future? Let them do their thing, and we'll do ours. And we'll make sure their thing stays popular. Give them experimental colleges to do whatever they want in, free land for communes a million miles from Disneyland, $2000 apiece to go to school, self-regulated baby sitting services, for the rest of their lives if need be, even free dope and birth control pills to keep them pacified on the reservation.

Yet these steps will probably never be necessary, for most members of the counter-culture are perfectly satisfied where they are. Those who are not are outnumbered 10 to 1 and are ethically opposed to putting their trip on someone else. They want to get their heads straightened out, but most of the time this is where it stops, with *their* heads. But just as important, who wants to "win," to change the theoretical détente with mainstream America? To win is to lose. To win means not being counter anymore. It means having to act, to make decisions, to assume responsibility, and who wants to do that? This is why the new consciousness is a noun rather than a verb. Being in the counter-culture often means staying where one is, rather than changing America. Let *them* act, and we'll protest whatever *they* do. And, as we have seen, the new consciousness is not really new, rather it is still on the receiving end of the commercial, consumers rather than creators of the new products and rhetoric. This is fundamental, because it is why the movement can so easily be co-opted, and why it is so little different from the culture we have known.

Consumership leads to a purchasing type of mentality, having one always on the lookout for new products in which to sink one's insecurities, hoping that in the next bargain one's ego will be repaired and made everlastingly secure. But it never is, since these products are not of one's own creation and are grafted onto the self. Like clothing, they are easily discarded when a new fashion comes along, a new drug, or building to burn down. In purchasing the symptoms (slogans and apparel) or by-products of the new consciousness, rather than creating it themselves—since such creation must originate in the self—most youth never get to the base of their own estrangement, the factors which generate their frustration with American society and with their own lives. As such, their rebellion is superficial and becomes easily manipulated by others. They become scapegoats for America's ills, but are not taken seriously; forced into a much sought after identity, they don't even realize when that very identity is used to let off pressures that would otherwise destroy the flag and the corporate and political giants on which it flies.

Those who readily identify with the new consciousness or counter-culture are caught in a kind of double bind, a type of social schizophrenia, represented by the conflict between where they are, and where they'd like to be. On the one hand, they would like to create an alternative to contemporary American society, and on the other, they don't want to play for keeps, destroy the society which supplies them with material possessions, rhetoric, and purpose. They daydream about a new society, yet sit in college classrooms, listen to the latest release, or walk the beach stoned out of their minds, their bodies adorned with the newest fashions. And Madison Avenue urges this very dichotomy, for caught between two places at once, one becomes apathetic and passive towards either. I don't want my cake, but I want to eat it, while Betty Crocker reaps the rewards. Thinking about that alternative society while your hand takes notes or rolls another number is much the same as the automobile worker on the assembly line daydreaming about one of the cars he is putting together.

The counter-culture cannot have it both ways. Daydreaming about freedom will always be just that as long as their bodies can be used by advertising executives to sell its products, by Washington to pacify the larger population, and by the hip-priests to push conformity to new rules and games. A few members of the counter-culture have stopped being hypocrites; they have refused to play the games others tell them to play, whether these be professors, executives, or counter-culture gurus. They are creating their own rules and values, making these rules and values a part of themselves so that they cannot be disassociated from them during calls for action. No one has to tell them to become motivated; it is an assumption on which their lives rest. While discarding American society as presently constituted, they actively construct a new society, their identities based on a positive affirmation of values they have thought through themselves, rather than as a purely negative reaction to decadent America.

It is only on this basis that a counter-culture can become more than just another consumer product, to be purchased and discarded, whenever is convenient. Starting over again is not easy; it never has been, but then neither is assuming responsibility for one's actions and making one's own choices—whether or not *you* want to drop acid, go to class, or burn down the Bank of America. Yet, this is the only way the gap between rhetoric and commitment, so apparent today, can be bridged. It is the only way that the counter-culture can be taken seriously, that youth can pose a threat to the America where to buy a Buick is the only thing which will give one's life meaning. If there is to be a new consciousness in America, then doing one's own thing must mean creating one's own values, no matter how uncomfortable such a process becomes for *each* and *every* counter-culture member. On the other hand, if youth's orientation toward the world around them—their values, beliefs, and actions—do not change, then neither will America, no matter how many lids are sold or posters painted shouting POWER TO THE PEOPLE.

NOTES

[1] Theodore Roszak, *The Making of a Counter Culture* (Garden City: Doubleday & Company, Inc., 1969), p. 22.

[2] Paul Goodman, *Growing Up Absurd* (New York: Random House, Inc., 1956).

[3] Hans Sebald, *Adolescence: A Sociological Analysis* (New York: Appleton-Century-Crofts, 1968), p. 8.

[4] *Ibid.*, p. 33.

[5] Roszak, *op. cit.*, p. 257.

[6] Sebald, *op. cit.*, pp. 34–35.

[7] *Ibid.*, pp. 38–39.

[8] Philip Slator, *The Pursuit of Loneliness* (Boston: Beacon Press, 1970), p. 74.

[9] Philip Wylie, *Generation of Vipers* (New York: Holt, Rinehart & Winston, Inc., 1942).

[10] Roszak, *op. cit.*, pp. 31–32.

[11] Abbie Hoffman, *Woodstock Nation* (New York: Random House, Inc., 1969), pp. 36–38.

[12] Roszak, *op. cit.*, pp. 149–150.

[13] *Ibid.*, pp. 52–53.

[14] Tom Wolfe, *The Electric Kool-Aid Acid Test* (New York: Bantam Books, Inc., 1969), pp. 113–115.

[15] Lewis Yablonsky, *The Hippie Trip* (New York: Pegasus, 1969), p. 292.

[16] *Ibid.*, p. 314.

[17] Quoted in James J. Carey, *The College Drug Scene* (Englewood Cliffs, N. J.: Prentice-Hall, Inc., 1968), p. 154. For other descriptions of the scene see, J. L. Simmons and Barry Winograd, *It's Happening* (Santa Barbara: Marc-Laird, 1968).

[18] Roszak, *op. cit.*, p. 154.

[19] Yablonsky, *op. cit.*, pp. 33–36.

[20] *Ibid.*, p. 330.

[21] Quoted in Wolfe, *op. cit.*, a statement by Paul Krassner, editor of *The Realist*, p. 225.

[22] Roszak, *op. cit.*; Charles Reich, *The Greening of America* (New York: Random House, Inc., 1970).

11

reality - busting

To bridge the gap between where we are and where perhaps we should be, between adhering to outmoded rules, values and institutions and starting over again, it is necessary to have a slightly different conception of our relationship to American society. Getting out of the present predicament in which we make piecemeal, stagnating efforts to deal with crucial social issues involves breaking out of the image or reality framework in which we are immersed; or, busting reality. Most of us resist radically altering the social system because we are caught in a "reality bind." A reality bind develops when individuals come to exist in two or more realities at the same time; instead of shifting from one reality to another, or even co-opting one reality into another, two or more realities are maintained concurrently. The resultant problem is a type of *social* schizophrenia. The dual personalities not only exist at the same time, but the individual is *aware* of their concurrent existence. This problem finds it generation in social rather than psychological causes.

The reality bind comes into play in a variety of ways and involves most of the social problems we have dealt with in this book. A prime example is the assembly-line worker who daydreams through his job while at the same time performing whatever tasks the factory requires of him. In this instance the bind represents a gap between our situa-

231

tional reality (the job we hold and the place of that job in the larger social system), and our orientational reality (how *we* view our situation and job). These two realities might better be described as representing a gap between objective and subjective world views—the objective being that manifested by the situational self, and the subjective being that manifested by the orientational self. When our situation is evaluated from "outside" we appear to be adequately involved in our work and satisfactorily performing our task. When viewed through our eyes, however, our task may be seen as repetitive and meaningless—we are not really there, although our body may be. The situational self should not be conceptualized strictly in terms of how others see us, and the orientational self is not meant to refer only to our view of ourselves; rather, we manifest both of these selves. However, in the situational self we are putting ourselves in the role of those who define our situation and viewing ourselves accordingly—we are seeing ourselves in our objective situation—as a worker on the assembly line.[1] Now, so long as we are performing our task up to par, why might this be considered a problem? Must the situational and orientational selves match?

A job is a role one performs, a role which *legitimates* one's existence in the overall value framework of American society. There are many ways to perform such a role, but the central idea, as we have noted earlier (in Chapter 1) is that one must work, regardless of which occupation he chooses to become involved with. This is to say that, psychologically, we would feel guilty if we did not work, and that we have rationalized the fact that society supposedly *needs* us to work. By playing certain societally specified roles, the overall social structure and social reality come to be and maintain their legitimacy. Moreover, it is through the performance of given roles that one casts his vote for the particular social reality he has been socialized into. He wants to and actually does believe it, often assuming it is the *only* possible reality. Furthermore, it is through the playing of roles and the validation of such role performance in the eyes of one's peers and associates that identities are formed and maintained.

What happens when we no longer believe in the role we are playing, yet continue to perform such a role? What happens when we no longer believe in the society we are playing? This condition was discussed in Chapter 3, and labeled "role-disinvolvement." When one is role-disinvolved, he can ostensibly be programming two (or more) often dichotomous roles at the same time—for example, assembly-line worker, and lover in a daydream. In such a case, can it be said that the role we are performing legitimates the social reality, or does it detract from it, legitimating another reality? The problem lies in the fact that we *want* to believe that our occupational task—our objective situation—is a meaningful and worthwhile one (that it is legitimate), while our subjective orientation, our daydream, belies such a claim. We want to believe that such a role is still legitimate because in our society we have not been permitted any alternative—we must work to be legitimate. Since we must maintain our objective situation or orientation, we cannot develop or fully believe our subjective or orientational reality; we can only play a type of "make believe." It should be noted that this phenomenon is not the same as the gap between doing what we have to do and doing what we want to do, for we *want* to play both roles at once. The clash is *between societal and subjective definitions* of what we should be doing; or of what roles we should be playing and which social reality we should be supporting through such roles. The fact that the worker is not able to become totally involved in either social reality creates the reality bind, for he begins to question which is the *real* reality? Which role expressing that reality should be maximized?

Every day examples of this phenomenon abound. There is the student who daydreams through most of his classes, but when asked to define who he is, maintains that he is, in point of fact, a student. There is the man who must decide which love is real: that which he feels for his wife and children, and that which he holds for various women he is extra-maritally involved with. The problem is often compounded when other social realities come to seem more attractive than the one we are in—the "greener grass" syndrome. Hence there is a constant proliferation of reality binds, yet these other realities only maintain their attractiveness in that they can never be entered into totally. Television advertising helps to maintain this proliferation by presenting the consumer with dual images of who he is and who he can be. The negative consequence is that we always feel we are missing something. If we go to work, we are missing sensual pleasures; if we don't go to work, we are missing the social sanctions and rewards of "being a good hard-working citizen."

The problem may be placed in a larger perspective. It can be viewed as a function of a type of ideological lag that occurs when there is a transformation of legitimation from one ideology to another. Traditional American social reality and ideology, which may no longer be relevant to the objective needs of the present, is enacted out nonetheless through roles one is no longer involved in. The very fact of acting out these roles prevents the social structure and social reality from being transformed and hinders realization of alternative roles and social realities. The status quo and its accompanying social problems continue. This is readily seen in terms of the assembly-line worker who refuse to acknowledge the fact that he may no longer need to work, and could make better use of his time by pushing for a guaranteed wage, seeking education for another type of occupation, or pursuing leisure activities.

Alienation: The Reality Bind Reaffirmed

Essentially four types of alienation result from being part of different social problems: alienation from the political and economic structure (minority groups and the New Left); alienation from other persons (middle-class whites); alienation from self (middle-class white and some minority group members); and alienation from nature (virtually the entire American population). Alienation—our subjective orientation —results because of our place in certain objective situations, much as the assembly-line worker manifests a type of alienation because of his objective situation. Finding ourselves in distasteful surroundings—large classes, worthless jobs, a nonrepresentational political structure, poverty, an immoral and meaningless war—we take subjective ways out, while at the same time maintaining the objective situation. This is not to say that some groups and some individuals are not working toward dealing with some of these alienating situations—but their efforts are largely doomed to failure because they are piecemeal and accept for the most part the assumptions of the objective situation they find themselves in. They accept the rules of the game, only they want to play the game better; they want to win. For example, Chicanos want jobs and their ethnicity but for the most part they accept the necessity of working in middle-class corporate and civil service enterprises.

This is a direct manifestation of the very bind we have been describing: We are caught between wanting to be someplace else and being where we are, and we do not want to give up either reality. Most of us do not wish to give up the games and their rules and the security they present; nor, however, are we satisfied with them. But instead of having the best of both worlds, the alienated have the worst. It becomes easier to daydream about getting oneself out of a situation, than to do something about that situation. When members of minority groups seek to fill the same jobs and buy the same goods as their middle-class white counterparts (as laudable as these goals may be from their point of view, they having never had these things), they

are playing the game of an outmoded social reality and value framework, and the very fact of their playing this game serves to keep this
reality framework legitimated. And so long as these rules and games
are legitimated, the basic structure of American society can never be
altered, and attempts to deal with problems become frustrating piecemeal efforts going no place—efforts which keep one alienated. For
the real cause of the problem is the reality bind, the conception of
ourselves in two worlds, each of which keeps the other from dominating, but each of which also keeps the other from granting fulfillment.

This problem will become clearer in a moment when we discuss
what must be done to alleviate it. But first let us consider some of the
other ramifications of this bind. Walter Kerr has interpreted the problem in this way: "We are vaguely wretched because we are leading
half-lives, half-heartedly, and with only one-half of our minds actively
engaged in making contact with the universe about us." [2] Many Americans come to be marginal men, existing not between two groups or
with role conflicts, but rather between two or more reality frameworks;
wanting to do something about a specific social problem, but unwilling
to give up other comforts, to put themselves on the line, caught without their material possessions on, without their value system, rules and
regulations, which have brought on the problem in the first place.

Other consequences of this can be seen in terms of everyday social
interaction in which there develops a gap between word and mood;
individuals find themselves saying words they cannot "get behind,"
telling someone how much we enjoy their company when, in actual
fact, we detest their presence. There are two selves, or realities: a real
self, which we hide from public view (which shows how we actually
feel), and an imaginary self, created by how others want us to act and
feel. Of course, these two can be reversed, and it can be claimed that
our public self is in fact our real self since it is the one which is acting,
while the self we hide from view is the imaginary one since it, for
the most part, only plays out its life in fantasy—we could have stopped
the war; we could have told the President what we really thought, we
didn't have to compromise.[3]

In large measure, we often refuse to admit the presence of this
subjective self, because it is rarely condoned by the objective situation
(value framework) we find ourselves in. It is not legitimate.[4] We can
sit back and watch our "objective" self, knowing we are not really
there: watch it play out roles and games which society feels are
legitimate. We can remain free by not really acting, not really showing
who we are, hiding under a security blanket in which we protect our
real feelings, our subjective reality, our individuality. Interactions be-

come designated not by who we are with but what are they doing for us, a type of conquest—how much do they help us maintain our objective reality, how much can we control them, buy them, have them as possessions? Of course, the reverse is also true—how much are we doing for them? In the end we become split apart; an identity for *ourselves* and an identity for *others*.

In essence, what often happens is a separation between feeling and cognition in which words or linguistic constructions cannot be taken seriously, just as lack of total involvement in either of two realities may mean that neither is taken seriously. Yet, we remain trapped within each of these two worlds; they are rarely seen as games in our eyes because we have a difficult time finding out their boundaries. We are unable to get outside of them to *create* other games and rules. We come to see ourselves as victims rather than commanders of our situation. Whereas our mood or feelings may exist in one reality, our words speak of another. In an interaction situation, which of our selves are we to believe, which can we take seriously—in short, who are we? Can one really be all things to all people? Or rather, in trying to be, does he lose his sense of conveying any one thing to any one person? How can one receive a consistent image of himself from his social world? He cannot, and thus becomes alienated from both himself and from others.

Fear of Commitment: Freedom from Acting

We have noted the roots of insecurity in Chapter 3 which make it difficult for individuals in American society to "be their own person." We wish to maintain both realities, unwilling to let go of one reality until fully convinced we can have or achieve the other. All bets are covered—there is no sense taking a chance if we might lose anything at all. But in so doing, we relinquish all chance for commitment. For how can we take a stand—even if we were secure enough in our own self-concept to be able to do so—if we have to consider a dual world, one which often presents contradictory demands? Yet, if we are not committed, can we gain satisfaction from our social reality or realities? If there is no *one* reality, how is commitment possible? Without commitment how will we change American society and how will we find out who we are?

There are other complications. If we make a commitment, then in our minds we are no longer free to choose. On the other hand, such freedom as we now claim is largely a myth, because we are caught between a well-defined objective situation we do not wish to be in, and a subjective reality we think about being in. All actions thus become equivocal so that we do not become trapped, but as a result, are paralyzed more than ever. This also means that we are not *responsible* for our own actions, since we are merely responding to the demands of others, our objective situation, or to a hypothetical subjectivity which only exists in fantasy.

In order to satisfy ourselves in any one reality then, to become fully involved, we would have to make an existential choice: Which world do we want to live in? The difficulty (as we have noted) is that such a choice would not be beneficial since the pains of insecurity are ostensibly greater than the potential satisfaction we may gain from becoming involved. There is another possible difficulty in choosing: Can we in fact do so of our own "free will," or must such a decision be left to alterations in the social structure? Which must be changed first: objective or subjective realities? Again, are we victims or creators of our own social reality framework—of the alienation and social problems we find ourselves a part of, of American society? Do we have control over the realities we find ourselves encapsulated within?

Beyond the Reality Bind:
Putting the Pieces Back Together

In Chapter 9 we pointed out that the means of production as presently constituted may not be worth owning; nor for that matter may much else that has traditionally passed for American society. The bind which we have discussed can be seen in terms of a gap between what and who we are—or, in Fromm's words, between "having" and "being." What we are, as we have noted, is what America wants us to be: our public image, our objective situation. Who we are is, simply, who we are: [5] all that is left when we subtract what we are, when we subtract our objective identity. Since this objective situation, or what we are, is largely outmoded, false, and decadent, the idea becomes to subtract or eliminate this objective self from our subjective situation, from our social framework, our thinking processes. In this case, it means starting over, with new rules which we can constantly change, rather than carrying around an objective self which does not fit the environment of contemporary American society. In this way we eliminate the bind, for there need be no difference between our subjective and objective selves—it is just that our social structure and ideology have created this difference and the social problems which follow from it.

Since it is our objective situation that places us in one or all of the four alienating positions, if we subtract out this objective situation then we take away one of the prime causes of our alienation, whatever type it may be. The idea is to deny the legitimacy of being placed in such an alienating position by refusing to go along, by refusing to legitimate the assumptions on which much of American society is founded, by refusing to play the roles which this society offers, by starting over.

Now, we have seen that if we subtract out the *what* we are, we are left with the *who* we are, our subjective self cut off from its social past, its possessions, insecure because there is ostensibly no one to define who it is, that it exists. And we have also seen that such an insecure position is largely untenable for much of the population of American society. In fact, this is the same position the aged find themselves in when they are separated from their children, forced to retire from their jobs, and placed in old age homes to wait to die. But this will become the social reality for most Americans when they are no longer needed at the factory or corporation. And this is now the situation for many of us, though we continue to refuse to recognize this fact.

Our objective situation is outmoded. It can no longer give our lives the meaning that can come only from us and through our direct interactions with others in an extremely fluid rather than relatively static society. It is the personal aspect of such interaction, the fact that we have little to gain from conforming to societal expectations, that comes to distinguish these interactions from our previous orientation; our mental reference has shifted from maintaining what is to creating what should be, what can be. The objective situation, the image, is dead; it's just that the burial rights are taking a long time. So as we face the fact that we have to die, this knowledge does not deny our efforts to live; instead it frees us to see that anything is possible. In casting off the *what* we are—consumer goods, material possessions, persons as possessions, and jobs—we also cast off much of our personal history which made these possessions and jobs seem so important. And in so doing, we alter our attitude toward those who come to face the world in the same way—for example, members of minority groups whom we may have formerly discriminated against because we were worried about property values. Since there is no longer any private property, there is little reason to maintain such a stance toward other persons.

Much of our bind can be conceptualized in terms of dichotomies: insecurity versus security; instability versus stability; impermanence versus permanence; no games versus I win–you lose. In order to escape these limits we must step out of them by destroying the structures, ideologies, and images which preserve them. This is not to deny that we are a product in large measure of our past experiences; rather, it is to keep ourselves open to infinite possibilities, much as the youth counter-culture in many of its aspects is ostensibly attempting to experiment and open itself up to new realities, new ways of living and relating. We become, in the words of Hampdon-Turner, "radical men" (or women), those who are free to create new images and ideologies, rather than conservatives, those who hold rigidly to past structures and values.[6] In such a conception many Marxists, some social scientists, and others typically associated with the Left, lose their claim to the banner of "radicalism," for the ideologies they worship cannot be tempered by current experience. They are not open to "change."

Placed in a situation in which the task is to create a new society— not one founded on unchangeable laws, but one in which rules are experimented with, added, and discarded, in which one's life is not based on whether or not a rule was broken, but on the idea that life is a process and rules must constantly change and that it is up to each individual to accept or reject *all* rules and to participate in the creation of different forms of living and relating—placed in such a situation no doubt we will immediately think of the chaos, insecurity, instability, and impermanence which would result. But why must these necessarily be considered negative attributes? What of the freedom such a situation would offer, the challenge?

In such a society, we could not sit back and let others make rules for us, tell us what to do, how to relate, whom to be. We would have to choose for ourselves—for the only manifestation of objective society which would remain would be automated machines which passed out food, clothing and shelter. Perhaps some individuals would be experimenting with food growing devices to feed large numbers of people and would build space ships. But the new frontier would be within our heads and in our interactions with others.

Walking out on American society, refusing to let that society define who we are, that we are alienated, would leave us in an insecure position. The task would then become to find out what we want—to act out some of our fantasies and subjective realities, to experiment, and to find out *who* we are. We can never really know what we want in the present so long as we are saddled by our past and use that past to limit present actions. The idea is that we are what we are—there is nothing we can do about our past—and that we can only change through the choices we make. The bind is a result of fragmented selves; it is difficult to choose because not only is choice not necessary, but we do not know which self is doing the choosing. If our own selves are fragmented, then we can only know or come to love fragments of others, because these others come to be viewed in the same way as we view ourselves. In trying to find out *who* we are—the first step being to subtract *what* we are—we also come to know why we are alienated, and how such alienation can be eliminated.

Objective and subjective selves merge; personal commitment leads to social commitment because our lives become political acts in that we must create our own rules to live by, and these rules affect other people. As American society is a social problem because of the interdependent nature of its outmoded institutions and images, so too do we create a new society by realizing the interdependent nature of our relationship with other people. Breaking away from the image of America does not mean living in isolation, doing our own thing to the exclusion of other persons. It means understanding how both the problems and hassles which we will go through as well as solutions to these problems are a product of our interactions with other persons in our society. So too is the joy, love, and community which can only be derived through such interaction. We cannot survive alone, nor, for the most part, can we find out who we are, or what rules we want to live by without the counsel and interaction of other persons. Man is a social animal: social problems lead to social solutions. To act in isolation without knowing our relationship to other persons, and to their problems, is to try to alter one problem in American society without knowing its relationship to other problems. It is to act in a piecemeal fashion, and to never arrive at any solution, since we are not attacking the root cause of our frustration.

As objective and subjective selves merge there is no longer any fragmentation. In discarding America as a mental construct, we are free to create a new society, and we must create such a society, for there is no longer anyone to watch after us, to tell us how we can live, what is meaningful and not meaningful. We cannot *not* decide, for such a decision is a decision. The only way we stop being a victim of the system, and an enemy of those who would try and change it, is to change it ourselves by discarding categories it forces us to live within and by creating a new society as a positive affirmation of the way we live our lives. Beginning with the anti-organizational bias of the youth counter-culture, we proceed to define ourselves in terms of *people,* not structures, *change* and *process* rather than permanence and stability. Security is seen in accepting and being open to and in creating change, not in holding on to past forms knowing that we are destroyed if these forms are destroyed. For such a turn of events to come about, a complete reconstruction of our educational and governmental institutions will be necessary, a strategy which will be discussed in the following chapters. From this viewpoint, then, *we* are the key to the future of American society.

We have found ourselves in a dark room. It takes a while for our eyes to adjust to the light, and we grope around the room with our hands, attempting to feel where the boundaries lie. We start off in one direction but can't seem to find any walls, the darkness seems to extend infinitely. Soon we run into other people whose hands are also groping out into the darkness and we begin to converse with them. We try to speak, but the words we use do not make any sense; they do not seem relevant to the situation at hand. We try to see what the other people are wearing but it is too dark to tell; perhaps they are wearing nothing at all, it makes little difference. We attempt to find out what role we are supposed to be playing, but there does not seem to be any specific role to play. We find someone's hands and they find ours. In the darkness everything is a possibility. Preconceptions and presuppositions do not work; we are without guides and guidelines. But we are.

Many of us will at first refuse to acknowledge the fact that the room is dark; but as more and more people cease to recognize existing forms and rules, we will have a difficult time ignoring the lack of light. At first, fewer and fewer of us show up for work, go to department stores, are drafted, vote. Even today businesses report that they are having difficulty attracting the most creative college graduates. As we realize the possibilities, it makes it more difficult for traditional institutions to continue to function and the more envious they become of us and the more fearful. But they are powerless, for if they destroy us, they destroy the future of American society, the bodies they will need to operate their commerce, to purchase the commodities they produce.

ALL WE HAVE TO DO IS STOP: SAY NO!

If we want to. What is the alternative; whom can we now trust, whom can we be vulnerable before? If we take away the TV advertisements, the material commodities, the pronouncements of government officials, the evening news, are we still alive without these other things to define that we exist? What we now consider so important—work, home, material possessions—will they mean the same in, say, ten years? Can we continue to plan as if nothing is going to change, except the style of the automobiles we drive? We know the consequences of our present attitudes toward life, toward each other; why not try another way?

Some of us will strike out on our own, or with some of our friends, in the dark of the night, without moon or stars or footpath to guide us. And for many of us, the challenge will first be as we have noted, to discover who we are, what is inside of us. For some, this will take the form of actively creating and exploring our social environment. For others this will mean a more inward trip. As Laing relates:

> The person who has entered this inner realm . . . will find himself going, or being conducted—one cannot clearly distinguish active from passive here—on a journey.
>
> This journey is experienced as going further "in," as going back through one's personal life, in and back and through and beyond into the experience of all mankind, of the primal man, of Adam and perhaps even further into the beings of animals, vegetables and minerals.
>
> In this journey there are many occasions to lose one's way, for confusion, partial failure, even final shipwreck; many terrors, spirits, demons to be encountered, that may or may not be overcome. We do not regard it as pathologically deviant to explore a jungle or to climb Mount Everest. We feel that Columbus was entitled to be mistaken in his construction of what he discovered when he came to the New World. We are far more out of touch with even the nearest approaches of the infinite reaches of inner space than we now are with the reaches of outer space. We respect the voyager, the explorer, the climber, the space man. It makes far more sense as a valid project—indeed, as a desperately and urgently required project for our time—to explore the inner space and time of consciousness. . . . The situation I am suggesting is precisely as though we all had almost total lack of any knowledge whatever of what we call the outer world. What would happen if some of us then started to see, hear, touch, smell, taste things? We would hardly be more confused than the person who first has vague intimations of, and then moves into, inner space and time.[7]

As we come to view ourselves as processes, means and ends will merge, change will be a constant, the journey will never end. Lagerkvist said: "Perfect love exists and the Holy Land exists; it is just that we cannot reach it. That perhaps we are only on our way there—only pilgrims at sea."[8] For the search could be all there is.

Confronting Infinity: Other Realities, Other Worlds

Beyond freeing oneself from a priori rules and games and institutions can come the realization that there is no distinction between us and the world we inhabit, that any such separation is a false one. As Watts put it:

A scanning process that observes the world bit by bit soon persuades its user that the world *is* a great collection of bits, and these he calls separate things or events. We often say that you can only think of one thing at a time. The truth is that in looking at the world bit by bit we convince ourselves that it consists of separate things, and so give ourselves the problem of how these things are connected and how they cause and effect each other. The problem would never have arisen if we had been aware that it was just our way of looking at the world which had chopped it up into separate bits, things, events, causes, and effects. We do not see that the world is all of a piece like the head-tailed cat.[9]

Thus, when we die we are merely changing molecular form, for everything is interconnected, a kind of social and physical ecology—if the "world is our body," then only part of that body is changing form. In this case, there is no reason to fear death, just as there is no reason to fear life, for they are both part and parcel of the same entity. Death is merely life without the lights on. We are not dropping out of society if we refuse to recognize its rules, for we can never drop out. Rather, we readdress the relationship between ourselves and the world, which is also a part of ourselves; we are bridging the dichotomy. Rules are then placed in perspective—they are created, made-up, no matter how long they have been with us, or how permanent and unchangeable they may appear. Since we have created them, we can alter their form.

But Watts is on to something even more important. In a world in which man is not conceived as a separate entity, but only as a manifestation of the whole, there can be no cause and effect, there is only *being*. Since there is no outside and no inside, since everyone is part of us and we are a part of everyone, all action is action with or against ourselves. To destroy another human being is in effect to destroy a part of our "body." In this case, "both win" or "both lose"—there cannot be "one-win and one-lose." All action is social because everyone is in fact related. Competition ceases to become important, because there is no one to compete against, no one role to fight for, no specific material possession to have. In a self-fulfilling society, co-operation takes precedence, for everyone has their own role, *as defined by them,* as members of a team. They may have to compromise, but it is *they* who will make that choice—society will no longer issue directives and status positions.

In reading these words, we assume that there are spaces between the lines, between the letters, but to look at these words in another way we might just as well look at the spaces and assume that there are letters which divide them, to look at the spaces between people and assume that they are nonexistent, nonliving, when in fact it may be people who are nonexistent entities separated by spaces. As Brockman has commented, human beings may be dead, all that remains are relations.[10]

All that remains are relations. . . .

Sypher, in another context, remarks:

> The organization man . . . still supposes he has a self; at least he is try-ing to heal it, or to find it, as he lies babbling on a couch in offices licensed to practice our new catechism and confessionals. But the man in the gray flannel suit, though he survives by camouflage, may have little to camouflage. His one care is to fit in, he must fit in to survive. His protective color is a last phase of Darwinian survival by adaptation —an adaptation that is total in an age of total togetherness. The irony is that the nineteenth century thought of survival as a struggle between rugged individuals. This was another romanticism. The rugged individuals forgot that an easier way to survive is to vanish, to avail one's self of an adjustment so total that at last there is nothing to vanish.[11]

What if all that remains are relations, lines between entities that no longer exist, criss-crossing back and forth like paths which circle the earth with no cause and effect? End the war that causes so much money to be diverted from giving everyone food, a sturdy shelter, and clothing. Let us declare that we will no longer put up with these games; we will simply stop playing, for a game cannot go on unless there are persons to play it—but the CHAOS!

Cage says: "Here we are. Let us say Yes to our presence together in Chaos." [12]

He also says:

> You want to know what we're doing?
> We're breaking the rules, even our own rules.
> And how do we do that?
> By leaving plenty of room for X quantities.
> We're putting art in museums, getting it out
> of our lives. We're bringing machines
> home to live with us. Now that
> the machines are here so to say to
> stay with us, we've got to find
> ways to entertain them. If we don't
> they'll explode, but as for going, we're
> going out. Did we just notice the moon

Courtesy of Gyula Szabo

or was it there always? Where we're
going is not only to the moon but out into
space. Home is discrete points. Space is an
infinite field without boundaries. We are
leaving the machines home to play the
old games of relationships, addition and
who wins.[13]

There are, of course, ways of dealing with the system, tried and
true methods, but they all assume
SANITY
when most of us know that this is an impossible prerequisite
to take the whole thing seriously, cause and effect and effect and
cause, that we are all merely particles, the whole earth one tiny particle
in some large

STOMACH which is in the process of digesting materials, only we are so small and insignificant that we cannot even feel the digestive processes except when there is perhaps a

HURRICANE or tornado

or, and, nevertheless, to fill up this page, these silences, nevertheless

there may be UNIVERSES with our own stomachs which are too small to know about and which do not feel our

DIGESTIVE processes with their own social problems and infinite possibilities

but do they know about us if we do not know about them, in other words, is anyone listening on the other end of the phone, on the other end of the space ship, on the other end of each sentence so desperately laid down

THAT IS TO SAY, we may have conceived of the world in the wrong way, from the beginning—but then the beginning is the end, and the end is the beginning—we may have been wrong to keep track of time, to ask why. . . .

AND

"Where am I?" said Billy Pilgrim.

"Trapped in another blob of amber, Mr. Pilgrim. We are where we have to be just now—three hundred million miles from Earth, bound for a time warp which will get us to Tralfamadore in hours rather than centuries."

"How—how did I get here?"

"It would take another earthling to explain it to you. Earthlings are the great explainers, explaining why this event is structured as it is, telling how other events may be achieved or avoided. I am a Tralfamadorian, seeing all time as you might see a stretch of the Rocky Mountains. All time is all time. It does not change. It does not lend itself to warnings or explanations. It simply *is*. Take it moment by moment, and you will find that we are all, as I've said before, bugs in amber."

"You sound to me as though you don't believe in free will," said Billy Pilgrim.

"If I hadn't spent so much time studying Earthlings," said the Tralfamadorian, "I wouldn't have any idea what was meant by 'free will.' I've visited thirty-one inhabited planets in the universe, and I have studied reports on one hundred more. Only on Earth is there any talk of free will." [14]

We can't take it

TOO SERIOUSLY (life, that is), but then again, we can take it too seriously, as we all well know, but at least we do know what the

Courtesy of Gyula Szabo

games are and can somehow get above them, or see them for what
they really are
    as any good Democrat will tell you there are many better
solutions than this, many sounder theories of what to do like
        electing congressmen who represent our point of view, if we

knew what our point of view was so they could pass legislation to deal
with some of the issues such as
        alienating jobs and relationships and giving poor people more
money to spend on consumer products, TVs and wrist watches, to
bring our troops home now so that they can be used in Latin America
and the money deposited in some type of anti-ballistic missile system
or OUTER space effort
        ARE YOU AFRAID? I AM. BUT IT DOES NO GOOD
                        TO BE AFRAID
                        OF STARTING OVER.
WHEN YOU LOOK AT THE ALTERNATIVES
        there is no longer a dichotomy between the individual *and*
society,
        that is, there does not have to be such a dichotomy
for one can sit on the beach with Lao Tzu feeling at one with nature
letting the waves pass over his head or
one can swim in with the tide, in and out, and still
be at one with nature. . . .

        Regis Debray said that for revolution to be successful in Latin
America the people had to develop their own ideologies, and not rely
on what worked in another revolutionary situation, China, Vietnam,
or the USSR for example.[15] But Debray almost served thirty years in a
Bolivian jail, thirty years in a Bolivian jail:
        IF I BECAME PRESIDENT—WHAT WOULD I DO? IF I WON,
    WHAT WOULD I DO WITH MY VICTORY, WITH ALL THAT I
                        HAVE INHERITED?
Would I change the game, or merely change the name of the game,
while keeping the same rules?
        For does understanding make a difference—to you, to the ocean?
Thousands of ways to communicate, but nothing to say, except
"wait till I get my color TV set, then you'll see, mother. . . ."

        . . . to which I answered in return that if the contents of the thousands
        of books in that irreplaceable library had been impotent to prevent things
        like the bombing which destroyed them from happening, I didn't really
        see what loss to humanity was represented by the disappearance of
        those thousands of books and papers obviously devoid of the slightest
        utility.[16]

But there are different ways to bust reality, just as there does
not have to be anything in its proper order, yesterday might become
today or tomorrow, time is not a deciding factor if you unplug yourself
                        from the clock

no space between one minute and the next, between one
action and the next, between one syllable, time speeded up and slowed
down
one can bust *the* reality by proliferating realities, that is, tiny
conflicts, that is, the tinest conflict, until we cannot keep up, until

it becomes too absurd, until we must just
                                    STOP
or one can achieve a synthesis between realities that is, by altering the
objective situation enough, and the subjective
                                    ENOUGH
    so that there would be a kind of compromise, but can we really
compromise with technology, if we have no control over even our own
lives, if we have no idea what we want, what we feel
                    without someone telling us that we can
EXIST WITHOUT "REALITY" BUBBLES if we understand what the
bubbles are and where they are sold.
    And the purpose of education will be to pose just such questions,
to force us out of the reality bind, to
    BLOW OUR MINDS so to speak, opening up each little crevice
WIDER AND WIDER
    as shall soon be noted
tactics must change, because the situation will be different both on the
OUTSIDE
            and inside our heads, the subjective reality

We were lying in successive rows heads touching feet like those lead
soldiers stacked in a box, but when we first came it was still virgin un-
defiled so I threw myself on the ground dying of hunger thinking the
horses eat it why not me I tried to imagine to convince myself I was a
horse, I was lying dead at the bottom of the ditch devoured by the
ants my whole body slowly turning by a thousand tiny mutations into
a lifeless substance and then it would be the grass that would feed on
me my flesh nourishing the earth and after all it wouldn't be so much
of a change, except that I would merely be on the other side of its
surface the way you pass from one side of a mirror to the other where
(on the other side) things may go on happening symmetrically, in other
words up above it would go on growing still indifferent and green just
as they say hair goes on growing on dead men's heads the only difference
being that I would be eating the dandelions by the root . . . but did I
really see him or think I saw him or merely imagine him afterwards or
even only dream it all, perhaps I was asleep had I never stopped sleeping
eyes wide open in broad daylight lulled by the monotonous hammering
of the shoes of the five horses trampling their shadows not walking at
quite the same gait so that it was like a crepitation altering catching up
with itself super-imposing mingling at moments as if there were now
only one horse, then breaking apart again disintegrating starting over
apparently running after itself and so on over and over, the war somehow stagnant, somehow peaceful around us, the sporadic cannon fire
landing in the deserted orchards with a muffled monumental and hollow

sound like a door flapping in the wind in an empty house, the whole landscape empty uninhabited under the motionless sky, the world stopped frozen crumbling collapsing gradually disintegrating in fragments like an abandoned building, unusable, left to the incoherent, casual, impersonal and destructive work of time.[17]

a different type of REVOLUTION.

This is not to say that this is the only alternative, that we *only* exist within "reality" bubbles or that the entire process must be changed, for it has been slowly changed, piecemeal, just pick up your newspaper, there is no sense in relating the various programs for they will be outdated by the time

you read this, if you have come this far for the earth is

CIRCLING US faster and faster, can we keep up with it, or it with us.
FALSE FALSE FALSEFALSEFALSE. . . . TRUE TRUE TURETEUTRUE
dichotomy perhaps, let us turn to the authorities:

Assuming that by competently reforming only the environment instead of trying to reform man, a favorably designed environment can be realized which will both permit and induce man to accomplish the same logical degree of physical success in universe as is manifest, for instance, by the hydrogen atom, how then can the economic and technological capability of all humanity to enjoy freely all of its world be accomplished exclusively by design science, without any individual interfering with another and without any individual being advantaged at the expense of another, with a design that will also induce its spontaneous adoption by world industrialization's managers? [18]

WHAT?
Becoming "water brothers," so to speak (that is, drinking from the
same cup), sharing the same bed, letting one's (that is, mine; that is,
your) sexual fantasies be acted out even in such serious context,
mingling our universes, intercoursing in front of the Bank of America,
or on the steps of the library, or everywhere staring into each other,
everything is possible logic being only another rule we use to design,
to rigidify, to hasten the collapse, to manipulate and use and bastardize
OUR LYING TOGETHER ON THE GRASS
touch-ing touching touchingtouchingtouchingtouching
WHAT
It has been proposed that the income tax be expanded,
    that the monies be used to give more people jobs;
it has been proposed that people
    love each other;
it has been proposed that the people take over all government and
private corporate offices—but what will we do when the poor have
been fed and work on assembly lines, what will we do to enhance
participation in government when no one wants to participate since
they are afraid?
                A PREDICAMENT! and we are a part of it
            for
                what's happening
        in the
            going on
and there are of course other means of busting reality
        as well as other solutions to the myriad of problems mentioned
herein

just as there are many other ways of making love
so
STAY TUNED. . . .

NOTES

[1] John O'Neill, "Self Prescription and Social Machiavellianism," paper presented at Institute International De Sociologie, Rome, September, 1969, pp. 15–21.

[2] Walter Kerr, *The Decline of Pleasure* (New York: Simon & Shuster, Inc., 1965), p. 12.

[3] R. D. Laing, *The Divided Self* (Harmondsworter, Middlesex: Pelican Books Ltd., 1966), pp. 84–85.

[4] *Ibid.*, p. 97.

[5] James Bugental, Lecture at California State University, San José, November, 1969.

[6] Charles Hampdon-Turner, *Radical Man* (Boston: Schenkman, 1970).

[7] R. D. Laing, *The Politics of Experience* (New York: Ballantine Books, Inc., 1968), pp. 126–127.

[8] Par Lagerkvist, *Pilgrim At Sea* (New York: Random House, Inc., 1964), p. 116.

[9] Alan Watts, *The Book* (New York: Random House, Inc., 1966), p. 27.

[10] Cited in *Whole Earth Catalogue,* The Portola Institute, California, 1969. For a discussion of a wide variety of building and philosophical reviews of how to survive and how to expand your awareness, the interested reader should purchase a copy of this catalogue.

[11] Wylie Sypher, *Loss of Self in Modern Art and Literature* (New York: Random House, Inc., 1962), p. 86.

[12] John Cage, *Silence* (Cambridge: M.I.T. Press, 1966), p. 195.

[13] *Ibid.*, pp. 197–199.

[14] Kurt Vonnegut, Jr., *Slaughterhouse-Five or the Children's Crusade* (New York: The Delacorte Press, 1969), p. 74.

[15] Regis Debray, *Revolution in the Revolution* (New York: Grove Press, Inc., 1967).

[16] Claude Simon, *The Flander's Road* (New York: George Braziller, Inc., 1961), p. 238.

[17] *Ibid.*, pp. 253, 320.

[18] R. Buckminster Fuller, *Utopia or Oblivion; The Prospects for Humanity* (New York: Bantam Books, Inc., 1969), p. 3.

12

revolution for what?:
models for an
alternative America

We have all undergone reality-busting. Let us say there are now 225 million of us who are prepared to create a new society. What should that society look like? What roles will we be expected to play? How will necessary goods and services be distributed? What values must we adhere to, if any, and how will conflicts between individuals be resolved? While most social institutions will have been destroyed in the process of reality-busting (the government, family, economic and religious structures no longer being operative), there will still be some givens we must take into account. Perhaps the primary legacy is that of reality-busting itself. We must be able to create a society where change is the norm rather than the exception, and where individuals continually question existing values and institutions, create new values, and explore alternatives to what is. Under such circumstances we can expect no racial, ethnic, or sexual discrimination. There are, however, another set of givens, those supplied by our physical environment.

As we have noted, there are 225 million of us who must be fed, have some amount of shelter and protection against the elements, who must have their clothing and health needs taken care of. At the same time, natural resources are scarce and the nation is considerably polluted. While it can be expected that reality-busting will have diminished the need for superfluous consumer goods, the necessity of planned production and distribution of resources, as well as cleaning up the environment will be important factors to contend with. Although all *social* institutions will have been destroyed, capital goods industries (factories and machinery) will still remain intact, as well as the know-how to operate such technology. In this context, supplying basic food, clothing, and shelter needs for the American populace will be considerably easier than might at first be apparent.

Finally, the 225 million of us will not exist in isolation. Rather, we will be surrounded by 3.5 billion people who desperately need both the capital goods and the technical skills which we have taken for granted. Thus, any society which we construct must take into account a five- or ten-year crash program in supplying other nations with the goods and services they need.

In this chapter, two models of a possible post-reality-busting America will be described, as well as three shorter illustrations of what America might come to be like without reality-busting or a similar transformation. These models obviously do not exhaust the possibilities, but are employed for purposes of visualizing the future so that steps may be taken toward arriving at alternative goals and ways of achieving them.

Model I: From Each According to His Ability, to Each According to His Needs—Computerized Communism

Model I divides American society into regional soviets, each of which is connected by computers and elaborate media of mass communication for purposes of broadcasting needs, ideas, products, carrying on debates and communicating with other soviets, as well as the world at large.[1] Each soviet is more or less independent, having the capability of manufacturing basic food, clothing and shelter needs, while sharing larger capital goods industries with other soviets. For example, the capacities of United States Steel are shared among three soviets to prevent any one from assuming complete control. Members of each soviet constantly travel to and from other soviets, exchanging information, undergoing new experiences, and participating in alternatives.

The Economy

Within each soviet, work is organized around the needs of the populace according to socialist principles. Factories which produce food, clothing, and shelter needs typically are automated, as are many of what we now consider the less desirable tasks—for example, garbage collection. Such plants are managed by administrators who are elected by the populace, after passing an exam which demonstrates that they are qualified. Each administrator is required to spend a certain amount of time in some other occupation so that he does not lose sight of the goals of production. The manufacturing of other goods is based on demand: Either those who want them produce them, or if they cannot undertake such production (because the task is beyond their means) they submit their needs to the soviet planning board which puts out a bulletin as to the exact tasks required. Each individual is required to put in a twenty-hour-per-week contribution to the Soviet in exchange for his food, clothing, shelter, and health benefits, as well as a credit card allowance for a certain number of other goods and services. If the needs of the populace are not taken care of on the basis of voluntary contributions, then the task required is more highly valued—that is, those who undertake it will have to put in less time (for example, 10 hours per week). The task increases in value until it is performed. If many persons come to undertake it, then it gradually diminishes in value till returning to the normal standard.[2] Many goods and services produced by individuals and collectives within the soviet can be distributed and exchanged at large co-op "market" places, which also serve as gathering points for concerts, dances, exhibits, and so forth. The planning board is composed of a group of administrators who oversee computers which automatically take in information from smaller collectives and publish lists of tasks still to be performed, thus regulating the economy. The planning board acts as a facilitating service, rather than as a decision-making body.

Soviets are connected in a similar manner. Regional computers transmit the needs of other soviets as well broadcasting their own needs and production capacities. If a given soviet does not wish to devote its time to producing a commodity when it has the capacity for such production, then arrangements are made for members of other soviets to visit and take over such production. In any case, the existence of multi-regional industries necessitates cooperation and coordination, with each soviet having to devote a certain amount of its energies to supplying the needs of other soviets. If a given task did not get taken care of, the same principle of labor credits which applied to economic relations within each soviet would apply on a national basis.

The contributions which individuals are "required" to make to the soviet are broadly defined. With scarce resources and little need for superfluous consumer goods, except perhaps those commodities required by other soviets and other nations, most contributions would probably be in the social service area, although it would be expected that a considerable number of persons would explore technological advancement to increase the capability of computers, automate the least desirable tasks, and find cures for disease. As such, there would be little distinction between work and leisure, and most persons would not be limited by the twenty-hour work week; rather, they would be doing what they wanted to do. Contributions could entail such things as finding new ways of relating to other persons, meditation, writing poetry, studying, travel, and so forth. No task would receive more pay than any other, because money as well as job status would cease to exist, nor would they be deemed necessary.

A crucial problem might arise as to whether or not a member of the soviet had to justify the usefulness of his contribution. This question might not be important as long as the major needs of the soviet were being taken care of, for with no higher status or profit attached to one task rather than another, no one would be jealous of what another individual did. The emphases would be on self-actualization, on creating one's own values, on one's own life in accordance with his own abilities (rather than with those of others). Only in situations of scarcity would those who were doing "nothing" become a problem. Yet it could be expected that the "social" attitude fostered through soviet education would make such an issue largely academic. Another problem might be that certain skills will disappear completely because of lack of practice by anyone. For example, it would not be necessary for everyone to construct a house, since machines would carry out this function. It could be held necessary then for persons to have a smattering of knowledge and experience with even "outmoded" tasks and machines in order to be able to control the machines so that someone could assume responsibility for their operation.

Education

Education will carry through constant reality-busting—that is, inculcate a critical mentality—while at the same time teaching social responsibility. There is no contradiction between these two tasks, for a critical acumen helps the social order to constantly evaluate its values and institutions. Education would be expected to be a life-long process. There would be no separation between means and ends, between enrollment and graduation. Growing up in the soviet would mean taking apprenticeships in various types of *contributions,* learning how the computers operated, seeing how parts of the collective go together, traveling and living temporarily in other soviets. This is the way the student makes his contribution. Given that there is no graduation, apprenticeships gradually become lifelong occupations which can always be terminated when other tasks become more interesting and challenging. As education is not separated from "real life," the "student" comes to see that he is part of the problem and part of the solution, responsible for all that goes on around him and for his own life. Messages which travel from computer to computer, which are broadcast on radio and television frequencies have a direct impact on his own behavior; he cannot divorce himself from their influence, nor does he want to, for his life depends on his ability to respond in kind, in turn to create messages, to communicate. Part of the apprenticeship period could be expected to entail work in agricultural areas and in basic industries for reasons noted in the previous section.

It will be necessary for students and most members of the soviet continually to move around, in order to avoid "contamination" by a given value framework which might prevent development of the ability to critically evaluate one's own particular circumstance. This would be especially important for young children, who are highly susceptible to indoctrination. All students would be expected to have a course in computer programming and mass communication in the same sense as we now learn how to drive a car. In fact, since everyone would grow up within easy access of computers and two-way television and radio sets, it could be expected that such knowledge might become "common sense."

Everyone in the soviet thus becomes both teacher and student, for one is always showing another how to do things or is being shown, learning from questions or answering them. Again the method, the means of education, becomes the end; there is no separation between the way one learns and his lifestyle.

Relationships

Relationships would be highly fluid and flexible, and would not be bound by legal certificates such as marriage licenses. Many possibilities exist depending upon degree of commitment and dependence on another person, as well as the duration of the relationship, that is, whether it is temporary or permanent.[3] On the basis of these criteria alone, four types of dyadic (two-person) relationships exist:

1. *Partial Commitment–Temporary Involvement:* Here we find individuals interacting on a limited basis with no real dependency or commitment. The summer fling, in which one has several part-time relationships going at once, would fit this description.

2. *Total Commitment–Temporary Involvement:* Here persons become totally committed to and dependent on another person, but for a relatively short span of time. Serial monogamy today fits this model, in which we are with only one person at a time, but divorce is frequent.

3. *Partial Commitment–Permanent Involvement:* In this relationship, individuals are moderately committed to other persons for indefinite periods of time, while dependence and commitment are spread among several different people. This is similar to having lifelong friends, except that the relationship is not restricted by sexual taboos. The advantage of this model is that one's needs can be satisfied by several different people.

4. *Total Commitment–Total Involvement:* The best example here is the monogamous marital arrangement typified by the nuclear family, in which one restricts one's commitments and involvements to only one other person.

Beyond these categories lie extended families and group marital arrangements often taking place within the context of communes and other types of collectives.

Communes may in fact form the basic unit of the soviet, providing for an immediate sense of community, sharing, and brotherhood. Such communes might take a thousand different forms, either organized around shared occupational or philosophical interests, or based on some other criteria. Communes would constantly form and dissolve depending upon the interests and commitments of their memberships. Communication between communes would either rely on person-to-person messages or on two-way television and radio hookups. The advantages of having communes as the basic unit would be that the relationships which take place on communes would be similar in nature to those occurring in the soviet and in the nation at large. There would be little difference between day-to-day orientations and that which one held toward larger societal abstractions. Given a variety of communes, individuals would not be restricted in the nature of interactions and interests which might be developed, nor would they be living under the constant threat of loneliness. As education places emphasis on youth traveling from commune to commune, and to other soviets, many communes might be expected to perish with each generation. In any case, such an education would prevent collectives from becoming institutionalized.

Individuals could be expected to relate to the communes which they chose to reside in under the same two-part classification used to describe types of dyadic relationships. In fact, many communes could be expected to operate on the basis of one of the models. Thus, those individuals seeking total commitment and involvement in only one commune would live together. An occupational or religious commune might fit this description. Those seeking to spread their involvements among different communes for limited periods of time (partial commitment—temporary involvement) would organize into more transitional groups. For more abstract and larger units of organization, this description would begin to break down, because of the necessity of each commune and individual in the soviet to make his contribution, in exchange for basic food, clothing, shelter, and health services. Almost by definition, then, each individual would have to say that, regardless of what his contribution is, he is at least partially involved in and indefinitely committed to the soviet. While some individuals may put in only a minimal amount of time (twenty hours) and others perhaps as many as sixty hours, it would be difficult to ascertain what was and was not a useful contribution, thus making such categorization irrelevant at this level.

Ownership

Each soviet will control for a given number of years a parcel of land from which individuals can lease small units, depending on their needs and abilities. Agricultural communes would be expected to be able to show greater need than one built around religious principles. Most land would be public or rented for short periods of time. There would be no private property as there would be little to hold on to. In the same sense, the ownership of persons as possessions would disappear. A major problem would be the control under a rental or lease arrangement of land. If basic food, clothing, shelter, and health needs are vouched for, then no one group could demonstrate a need for any large parcel. Moreover, it might be expected that communes dwelling on specific pieces of land would be willing to take in new members whose desire for that piece of land would demonstrate similar values. This might mediate their having to give up the land to any new group. In any case, control would be limited by review every five years, at which time a group could petition for an extension. There would be no such thing as inheritance. Rental commodities could be handled on a first-come, first-serve basis.

Checks and Balances

Open radio and television channels would insure not only that each soviet and each collective could constantly broadcast information, demands, and calls for help, but it would also create a situation of on-going debate and analysis, thus making it difficult for one collective or soviet to seize control of the nation. Moreover, as the larger industrial concerns are mutually operated, no one soviet could force others to act in a certain manner through the economic control they exercised. In a situation of constant communication, there would be few secrets; individual soviets and collectives would be in constant touch with the latest technological developments in any other soviet and collective. On the individual level, persons would be constantly evaluating existing values, ways of doing things and technological developments. Even should one soviet seize control over another, subjugation of the population would be extremely difficult, and subjection of the nation even more so. Thus, decentralization in the form of soviets and communes would provide a viable defense against the threat of dictatorship. Perhaps the most important safeguard, however, would be the attitude which the soviet would inculcate, the feeling of trust and empathy, of sharing and working interdependently in a common circumstance in which each person has a voice and a responsibility for the direction that circumstance will take. While there are no elections in the strict sense of the word, computers preserve what might otherwise be tyranny of the majority, by processing all demands according to need.

Relation to the Outside World

For the first five to ten years of operation, some of the most needed tasks will be those which help supply goods and services for the developing nations. Thus, Ghana may urgently need the tractors which can only be produced in a specific American soviet. The interaction of soviets on a national basis will form a transitional stage toward international soviets, in which the world's goods and services are managed according to the dictum "From each according to his abilities, to each according to his needs." The concept of nation–state will disappear and a world federation, highly decentralized to meet divergencies of culture, will become a reality.

Model II: The Federated Commune—Decentralized Socialism

Our second model postulates the same givens as Model I. The core unit of this model is the commune which elects representatives to serve on a planning board. The planning board acts as administrators of food, clothing, shelter and health needs, but, as compared to Model I, makes most of the decisions itself with the aid of computers.

Those persons not residing on communes fit under the general heading of *the people at large*. It is expected that these persons are either in the process of moving from one commune to another, or, for the time being, do not wish to reside on a commune.

Economy and Polity

Food, clothing, and shelter plants are automated and such commodities are guaranteed, *regardless* of what individuals do. It is expected that enough persons will voluntarily take care of operating such installations without having to rely on labor credits or other means of conscripting persons for the completion of necessary tasks. Each individual receives a specified amount per week of the guaranteed production. If a commune does not want to receive its share, they notify the planning board and are allotted an equivalent amount of land and/or materials to handle such production themselves. Thus, there is maximum freedom of choice provided each individual and commune. Those communes which want to exchange goods and services beyond that which is guaranteed can do so in open market places or by sending out bulletins through the planning board specifying what they have to offer and what they need. Such information is then distributed in the form of bulletins and through representatives back to each commune or to the public at large. There is no private property. As in Model I, land, buildings, and equipment are leased from the planning board for a certain number of years, subject to periodic evaluation.

Each commune, as well as people at large, elects three types of representatives to the community, regional, and state planning boards: politicians, experts, and mediators. *Politicians* are elected to represent the people at large or communes' attitudes and opinions on the general value code, if such a code is necessary, as well as to articulate positions regarding intercommunal conflicts, and issues affecting the larger federated commune network—relationships with the outside world. In essence, they articulate what either a commune or the people at large want and need. *Experts* are those persons who represent the commune or people at large on what is possible to produce or consume given scarce natural resources, pollution, conditions in the outside world, technological proficiency and development, and population size. Thus, the experts would form one "house" of the planning board, and the politicians the other. *Mediators* are chosen to arbitrate conflicts and facilitate decision-making on the planning board, as well as to help resolve conflicts occurring between communes and between individuals. Mediators serve to facilitate an atmosphere of working things out, rather then letting situations deteriorate into open warfare between individuals, communes, and regions, or between experts and politicians.

The planning board rotates by a third each year, with individual members discouraged from seeking a second term in office. This prevents the board from becoming institutionalized and dominated by specific individuals. No representative can vote on a given issue unless he first passes a test designed to gauge whether or not he knows enough about the issue at hand to make an informed judgment. If a representative does not choose to vote, this would be a signal that he wishes to go along with whatever decision is arrived at. Emphasis on voting in the planning board is on working out a consensus decision, rather than a majority-minority report. Those groups which did not wish to go along would, as noted, have the option of receiving in kind materials to produce a given product. However, since it would be far more efficient to produce most commodities on a regional or federated commune basis, the undertaking of such options would not be frequent. It is expected that regarding the creation and implementation of various values, most communes would be left to their own devices; only in making economic decisions, or in areas where the undertaking of given projects or the carrying through of a given ideology trespassed on the rights of others outside the commune, would mediators and members of the planning board be called into session.

Sheriffs are elected from time to time, as necessary, by the members of communes and the people at large, to work with mediators in the event of a homicide or other violent grievance. When they are no longer needed, they return to their normal status.

No member of the federated commune system receives any greater status, salary, or privileges than any other, irrespective of the type of contribution they do or do not make. The task of members of the planning board is primarily administrative, serving as links of communication, between the people at large and communes, rather than one of pure decision-making. What is to prevent the planning board from seizing control?

Education

Each child at the age of six is required to leave the commune he is raised in and enroll in an educational institution which will give him experience on many different kinds of communes, as well as inculcate a critical mentality and the ability to create his own values. In practice this would mean that children would serve as apprentices on communes and in occupational experiences which differed substantially from those in which they were raised. Each commune, then, would have as part of its ongoing membership a resident group of students who, while learning and participating in a particular lifestyle, would also be questioning the activities of the commune and communicating information about it to the outside world. At the same time, students would be expected to return periodically to the school where they would discuss and evaluate their experiences and develop alternatives to those communes and occupations which already exist. As part of their education they would also be expected to experiment with alternative value frameworks and living arrangements. While ostensibly separate, most education would take place in the ongoing federated communal society, yet maintain its autonomy to prevent indoctrination into any one communal pattern or lifestyle.

One of the functions of the educational unit would be to create the information tests which are required for participation in the voting process. In fact, one of the projects students would be expected to get involved in, and thereby have some control over, would be the making up of questions relevant to deciding various issues. Again, this would prevent professors from seizing control of the political process by being able to regulate voter qualifying exams. The faculty of such institutions of learning would be chosen by the planning board and would only serve for specific periods of time (for example, three years). A constantly rotating faculty, derived from both the people at large and the various communes would help keep discussions relevant and stimulating, rather than having them bog down in stale ideas. At the age of eighteen, students would be expected to begin forming their own communes or join those already in existence.

Relationships

The same types of relationships as projected for Model I would be expected to occur in this society. However, not only would individuals be relating to each other along different degrees of involvement and duration, but communes would also relate to the planning board and the federated communal system along similar lines. Thus, a given commune might decide they wish to receive only partial services but remain full-time participants, that is, they wished to make their own food, clothing, and shelter, while having their health needs taken care of by the planning board. Or, they may be totally involved in decisions the planning board arrives at, but only for a limited period of time. Finally, they might be partially committed for only a short period of time. The type of relationships which developed would, in large measure, be determined by the nature of the commune and the particular circumstances it was into at a given moment. Maximum flexibility would thus be maintained as well as individual autonomy.

Relation to the Outside World

Communes and the people at large would be expected to help other communes in trouble or to aid developing nations, but there would be no necessity that they do so. The planning board would discuss at each of its meetings what percentage of its goods and services should be allotted for other regions or nations, depending upon the level at which the problem arose. Since efforts would have to be made to regulate consumption of natural resources, population, pollution, and consumption, some type of world-wide cooperation would be inevitable. Fuller's *World Game* might serve as an example of such planning, in which resources and needs are plotted on a world maps and distributed according to ability and necessity. If another nation attempted to subvert the federated communal network, it would run into much the same difficulties as postulated for the first model—having to seize control of a decentralized society which was in contact with each part of the whole, but which was strongly autonomous both in terms of ideology and values, and in many cases, economically.

Model III: Technocracy—The Scientific Society

A technocracy is a third alternative for American society. Such a society would develop without a reality-busting situation having taken place, yet within the context of the same environmental circumstances which are part of Models I and II. A technocracy is a society run by experts on the basis of scientific analysis. Tasks are performed and decisions rendered because of expertise and merit, rather than popular election and control.[4]

Economy and Polity

All material and psychological needs are satisfied on the basis of scientific analysis of each individual's personality make-up. Experts decide with the aid of whatever technological machines they have at their disposal who should work at what task, how many hours it would be desirable for him to put in, and how this balances with the needs of the state (equated here to mean the entire population). Thus it is expected that each individual will be working at the task he is best capable of working at; there will be no competition for jobs or for movement up the occupational hierarchy. Rather, individuals will be rotated to more complex tasks when they show evidence that they are capable of such performance. Goods and services are distributed equally for tasks performed, in much the same sense as Model I. Every month each individual is evaluated through psychological tests and interviews as to his present material needs and desires. Such information is then fed into a computer and a new allocation, if necessary, dictated. Material allocations only last for each month, but can be renewed if one's personality remains constant. There is no private property.

The technocracy is operated on the basis of rational principles, logic, and scientific measurement. The battery of tests which each individual must submit to each month is in effect his vote, the way he would like to see the state operated according to his needs and abilities. Experts, with the aid of computers, calculate and weigh each individual's personality matrix against available resources and the personality matrixes of the hundreds of millions of other individuals who compose the state. If a given individual refuses to go along with decisions rendered by other experts or computers—an unlikely occurrence because of the structure of the educational institution—such an individual could be considered dysfunctional for the state and eliminated.

Education

As with the other major institutions of the society, education is carried out under scientific guidelines. Each child is carefully trained to fulfill the potential he is born with or that which emerges in his early years. All other interfering stimuli are weeded out through elaborate behavior modification mechanisms. For the most part, educational training is handled by teaching machines which regulate frustrating experiences and "deviant" lines of reasoning. Experimentation is permitted but only under carefully controlled circumstances. Boredom does not exist, for each child is doing what he is capable of doing. A problem which is constantly encountered is that a child's potential may only develop after many years of free experimentation; yet the technocracy has developed mechanisms to speed up this process, so that error is hardly likely.

Under such training, it would be difficult for any individual to refuse to perform his designated task, for why should he, and even with such an idea in mind, there would be little in any person's background which might teach him how to carry on such a revolt. Moreover, part of the role of each expert is constantly to question the logic of his tasks (that is, to make sure they are scientifically correct), and to develop further scientific research and application. Accordingly, there may be, at some point in time, an individual who in carrying out his self-designated task arrives at a point in which the logic of the entire state is called into question. He has refuted one of its basic assumptions. At such a point the technocracy would be expected to either adapt a new logical system as a basis for allocating tasks and educating the populace, suppress the information as subversive and therefore dysfunctional for the system, or fall into a state of chaotic absurdity. Again, the likelihood of such a development would be rare.

Relationships

The technocracy makes computer dating come true. Hassling over whom one is going to fall in love with becomes an anachronism as you are provided with the name of the person or persons most capable of relating to you at each point in your career. Information for carrying out such matching is derived from a monthly interview. Children are raised by expert nurses and pregnancies nurtured in test-tubes to prevent inconveniencing the mother, and incapacitating her. At any given moment, then, we might expect to be living with either one or a number of other persons, depending upon our particular occupational and psychological needs.

Relation to the Outside World

The technocracy can only run on scientific principles if all variables are taken account of and controlled. This would necessitate a world technocracy, so that all the world's peoples could make the best use of their capabilities as well as having their needs fulfilled. If American society were the only technocratic state, all dealings with other nations would have to rely on the maximum amount of information available. Thus, experts would be trained to reside in every country, filing reports on that nation's needs and aspirations, the chances of revolt, exhaustion of natural resources, pollution, and over-population. Circumstances could be envisioned whereby the technocracy would have to intervene in the affairs of other nations in order to insure a functional world order according to the scientific dictates upon which such an order was based. The ability of another nation to question the scientific principles on which the technocracy was founded might create such a problem.

Model IV: Oligarchy—Rational and Not-So-Rational Self-Interest

An oligarchical American society is one in which a few persons make all political and economic decisions for the rest of the populace. All

givens would hold; reality-busting would not take place, though discrimination against any group on the basis of ethnic background, race,
or sex would not be practiced. In such a society, goods and services
are awarded for performing tasks the oligarchy deems necessary. Each
individual is required to work twenty hours per week in exchange for
his allotment. The remainder of his time is his own to do with as he
sees fit, providing he does not take such opportunity to challenge the
ruling clique. Since most persons are well fed, housed, clothed and
kept in good health, it could be expected that few would be willing
to try to overthrow the oligarchy. Why should they want to? Moreover,
any frustrations which might occur on the job could be more than
made up for in the free and open relationships which individuals
could participate in, and in the types of entertainment experiences
which are available. For example, the oligarchy would constantly
develop new drugs for increasing pleasure, sensation palaces, and new
natural wonders. The populace is thankful for the assumption of political and economic decision-making capacity by the oligarchy. Those
who were not thankful might soon find themselves either in detention
camps or in ceremonial burial grounds. With a relatively satiated and
indifferent populace, there would be little chance that many would
come to the aid of those so detained.

The oligarchy could be expected to perpetuate itself by co-opting
those with the "right" talent into its ranks, as well as through the
normal processes of reproduction. Education would be conceived
under the same general classification as most other work, individuals
choosing which course of study they would desire to spend twenty
hours a week involved with. Those subjects or classes which the
oligarchy deemed necessary, and subsequently those tasks which did
not get performed, would be offered under the same basis as occupational tasks in Model I—the fewer persons involved or volunteering
for the task, the fewer number of hours per week would be required
of those who did volunteer. As the number of volunteers increases,
so too does the number of hours the "scarce" task is good for until
it returns to the norm.

It is expected that the oligarchy will regulate the type and number
of consumer commodities available (though not the number of potentially satiating experiences) owing to the shortage of natural resources,
pollution, and the size of the population. Relations with other nations
might be limited to trade for necessary materials and aid designed to
keep the rest of the world satiated enough to prevent outbreaks of
war or revolution which might endanger the existence of the oligarchy.
Yet, the oligarchy would not attempt to exploit the labor or the raw

materials of other nations because of the frustrations such tactics would breed. Instead, the guiding philosophy might be expected to be: "A happy populace is a non-threatening populace." On the other hand, given the world's limited resources and expanding population, the oligarchy would attempt to apply both positive (in the types of experiences and commodities supplied) and negative (armed force and economic sanctions) pressures to prevent other nations from using up more than their share of the earth's abundance. If the populations of other nations are neither economically nor psychologically insecure, the application of negative pressure would be uncommon.

Model V: Anarchy

If each of the four models described above fails and no new models arise to replace them, or if America proceeds along its present course, then we might expect the earth to perish under the spread of pollution, over-population, or nuclear holocaust. Given that a sizeable percentage of the population is destroyed as well as almost all of the capital goods productive capacities, a state of anarchy might become a viable model. Anarchy, in this case, would mean the rebirth of small communes and settlements, highly flexible and transient in character, with few if any lasting values. Communes exist as isolated units with only chance communications with other settlements.

> *Economy.* Hunting and gathering; primitive agriculture; stealing; limited trade.
> *Polity.* Whatever is "right."
> *Education.* By experience.
> *Relationships.* Experimentation.
> *Relation to the Outside World.* None.
> *Checks and Balances.* Might makes right. Intelligence. Love. Commonality of experience. Survival.[5]

Summary

Each of these models has, depending on one's perspective, advantages and disadvantages. Some of us would find the prospect of living within a technocracy stimulating and self-actualizing. In such a society all our needs would be taken care of; there would be little threat of insecurity. However, others of us would no doubt find such an atmosphere stultifying, an impingement on our alleged freedom of choice and desire for adventure. It would be possible to combine aspects of each of these models, as well as creating myriads of others, just as it is possible to create many different value configurations and games to play. In constructing an alternative model for American society, the means of developing such a society cannot be separated from its inception. Accordingly, the concluding six chapters of this book will consider the tactics of social change and reality-busting: How we are going to get there. If change is to become the norm rather than the exception, the life styles developed in the course of transforming American society must become those of the new society; to do otherwise is to find that there is a difference between the way we live our lives and the societal norms and values whose prescriptions we would follow. It is this very dichotomy which has made American society into a social problem.

NOTES

[1] I am indebted to James O'Conner of the Economics Department of California State University, San José, for many of the ideas which make up this model. Others who aided in this conception are Pat Fagen, Bob Allen, and Dave Eakins.

[2] For discussions of this type of economic structure see Oskar Lange and Fred M. Taylor, On the Economic Theory of Socialism (New York: McGraw-Hill, Inc., 1964); B. F. Skinner, Walden Two (New York: The Macmillan Company, 1962).

[3] For development of this framework I am indebted to discussions with Robert Thamm who is currently writing a book on the new family.

[4] For discussions of possible technocracies see Michael Young, The Rise of the Meritocracy (New York: Random House, Inc., 1958); Issac Asimov, Nine Tomorrows (New York: Doubleday & Company, Inc., 1957); Issac Asimov, The Earth Is Room Enough (New York: Doubleday & Company, Inc., 1955); and Aldous Huxley, Brave New World (New York: Harper & Row, Inc., 1960).

[5] Anarchy is not necessarily chaos; rather it is existence without the demands of a state or society. For extensive discussions of anarchy see Robert Paul Wolff, In Defense of Anarchism (New York: Harper & Row, Inc., 1970); George Woodcock, Anarchism (New York: World Publishing Company, 1962); Irving L. Horowitz, The Anarchists (New York: Dell Publishing Co., Inc., 1964).

three

how are we going to get there?: the tactics of reconstruction

13

organizing: change America before America changes you

Social problems are by definition group problems. It follows, there-fore, that any attempt to deal with such issues, including the problem of American society, must involve numbers of people. One of the primary problems of organizing is relating personal identity crises and hassles to group actions. Another problem is bridging the gap between small-scale organizing (free schools, food conspiracies or cooperatives) and larger efforts. For example, it is relatively easy to start a food conspiracy or free school serving fifty families. But how does one go from there to a food conspiracy or free school dealing with fifty thous-and people? The political impact of the organizing effort is often directly proportionate to the numbers of people involved. In this chapter, I shall critically evaluate different methods of bringing about social change in American society. The goals of reality-busting and the models outlined in the previous chapter should be kept in mind throughout the course of this discussion, for tactics cannot be divorced from the ends they seek. Finally, I shall discuss the relationship of domestic tactics to the needs and demands of other nations.

273

Let the People Decide: Who Speaks for Whom?

There are many different types of organizing, yet certain general conclusions can be drawn from these diverse experiences and situations. First, any potential organizer must know himself—that is, have a good understanding of who he is and what he is trying to do—and the political connotations of his actions. Those who fail to acquire such knowledge will have difficulty convincing others that they are sincere and that they know what they are doing.[1] Some of the tactics discussed below, and more specifically in subsequent chapters, are techniques for getting one's head together. Organizers enter a given community or constituency in one of four ways: they are invited in by a local group or organization; they are sent in as representatives of a group outside the community; they enter the community on their own; or they are already residents of the community who want to bring about some type of social change.[2] The specific community or situation determines in large degree the types of organizing tactics one wishes to employ. Organizers often experience early failure by attempting to employ tactics which led to success in one situation, without attempting to see whether or not they are applicable in a second social context.

When an organizer enters a specific community or constituency (for example, a factory), the initial impression he creates is highly important, for, if he is a stranger, particularly one from a different social or ethnic background, his rhetoric and actions will be carefully watched.[3] As a result, being from a similar background as those one is trying to organize helps reduce initial tension and potential differences in perspective. For instance, attempts by white "radical" students to organize factory workers and ghetto blacks have often met with open cynicism and hostility in that the latter feel the former are playing at poverty and condescending to lend a helping hand. Moreover, differences in social background make empathizing with a particular community or constituency's problems all the more difficult. Such "elitism" is often revealed through attempts to channel organizing efforts into a particular ideological framework, which the community has little comprehension of and may lack interest in. Putting one's "own trip" on them ends in manipulating the very persons one would aid for the organizer's own purposes. Thus, when Weathermen and others employ the rhetoric of the Left—"pig, imperialist, chauvinist"— in the context of a working-class community, they often alienate those whom they would speak for.[4] As efforts to apply what worked in one social context to that of another often fail, so too efforts at applying ideologies which were effective in one type of national crisis (for example, China) to organizing in the suburbs and ghettos of America tend to have negative consequences.

Organizing should begin, then, with the community's or constituency's own definition of the situation, with how they see issues which impinge upon them, rather than with the organizer's interpretation. One of the first things an organizer must do then, is to listen to what is going on, particularly if he is new to the community. This may mean hanging out at local bars, gas stations, stores, or wherever many people in the community happen to congregate. At the same time, the organizer should familiarize himself with the enemy, the power structure, whether vested in local interests or national corporations or institutions.[5] It is important for the particular constituency or community one is trying to organize to develop its own group. The organizer should stay in the background. After finding out what the problems are, what people may be willing to get involved in, attempts should be made at finding out who the informal community leaders are. Many times the formal community or constituency's representatives have been bought off by the power structure and cannot be trusted to carry out projects aimed at fundamental change.[6]

Getting informal leaders to drop in at the same time for "discussions" can initiate a process whereby organizational meetings can be held. If the organizer is appealing to his own constituency he may want to canvass the neighborhood, leaflet, or use the mass media to announce more formalized gatherings.[7] Once a meeting has been called the organizer should stay in the background, letting the populace air their particular gripes and letting informal leaders emerge as official representatives. If the organizer himself wishes to play a power role he not only runs the risk of putting his trip on those who might not share or be willing to follow his particular interpretation of the situation, but he can also be branded as an outside agitator and "run out of town." Even more important, if the organizer sets himself up in the role of leader, his demise at the hands of the power structure will result in the collapse of the organization. On the other hand, if leaders come from the "grass roots," attempts to eliminate the organization by destroying its leadership will serve only to crystallize the community and generate still more leaders.[8]

After several initial meetings, teach-ins and various types of workshops can be held in order to educate the community or constituency. These can be anything from coffee klatches in the suburbs to large university seminars. Workshops typically center around three sets of issues: preparing for a given social action; education about the need for that action and its place in the context of larger issues of social change; and how to carry out the action.[9] Here, both the specific, concrete problem and the enemy—those who either cause or prevent resolution of the issue—must be clearly identified. In other words, in whose name is a given social action being taken, and what are the specific grievances the community or constituency wants redressed? [10] Discussions which center only on abstract philosophical or political questions soon lose their ability either to attract people to meetings or to get them concerned about actually doing something.[11] At the same time that the organizers are listing concrete demands, they should also meet the enemy or at least establish open lines of communication. All this becomes particularly difficult if, in the course of organizational discussions, the victim and enemy become one and the same.

As we have noted, there are many different constituencies and types of communities in which to organize. Each has its own special problems. For example, factories are difficult for outsiders to organize in, particularly students who come from social backgrounds which are different from the workers', speak a different language, and do not really need the money they go to work in factories to earn. Anyone who attempts to do this type of organizing must be especially careful that the job he performs has not put another person out of work. Companies with a long history of dealing with unions or those who have achieved some sort of detente with their union, are particularly wary about outside agitators who might wish to change the type of equilibrium they find comfortable. Union leadership often takes a similar position. Moreover, workers run the risk of losing their jobs if they openly side with issues unpopular among union or corporation hierarchy. If one cannot get a job in a factory, attempts can be made to organize in local bars, outside the gates, or through contacts on the inside. All of these are difficult tactics in that the establishment of rapport and the sharing of common interests are hard to communicate in the little time one has available. Also, as we noted in Chapters 1 and 9, many workers crystallize their problems along radically different dimensions than students who might wish to organize them. This is particularly the case on the question of racism where white workers feel their jobs are threatened by increases in a nonwhite work force. Some successful communication and rapport has been opened up by supporting strikes and other conflicts between union and management, primarily by joining picket lines.[12]

Those who would organize for woman's liberation must deal with two issues: woman's alienation from other women, and alienation from herself. While ostensibly it would appear that women have much in common, the status of women in American society has forced them to compete with one another for the attention and potential security of male companionship. Cast in a subservient role, women find their primary allegiance to men who in turn define who women are and what roles they are supposed to play. Woman's liberation spells independence, a threat to the security provided by male dominance. Since this is so, many women are reluctant to become involved, especially when encountering objections from their husbands or boyfriends. The press has also served to provide a sensationalistic view of what "Women's Lib" is attempting to do, making many women shy away from the stereotype rather than consider the issues raised by the movement. Some women also feel that "liberation" will destroy their identities as women, re-making them in the image of men. In general, "Women's Lib" organizers must attempt to focus on specific problems which women face in their day-to-day lives, attempting to re-educate women in the process to countering the general problem of male chauvinism.[13]

Organizing in minority communities should, if possible, be done only by representatives of that particular ethnic background. Thus, blacks should organize blacks, Chicanos organize Chicanos, and so forth. We have already noted many of the problems which result when whites attempt to organize in black or Chicano communities. It is also imperative that black and Chicano college students remain in contact with the communities they emigrate from, so they can find out what their community needs are and how they might contribute to the process of transforming that community.[14] For minority college students to attempt to bring about national social change without maintaining such contacts is to fall into the same trap as their white counterparts who would apply abstract ideologies in behalf of a populace they have never made contact with.

Organizing in the suburbs often means starting with one's own family and building outward through your friends and theirs. Even the country club can provide a viable setting for initiating discussions and staging events. Most of those who dwell in newer tract neighborhoods scarcely know the person who lives next door, let alone those who may live down the street. One of the first problems then is finding some sort of common ground for getting people together, either by attempting a block party, or holding a meeting concerning some issue which may specifically affect that particular housing tract. Once the suburb becomes interested in a specific, concrete issue, other problems can be brought in, and a general framework formulated for analyzing them. In many suburbs there are no informal leaders, in that these may be bedroom communities in the true sense of the word. All one's friends and associates may reside outside the housing tract, so that the only time you are home is to entertain, sleep, or watch television. Such a situation tends to breed a tremendous feeling of alienation and isolation. Of course, many persons living in such neighborhoods like it that way, want to be left alone, and view their home as a place to escape to—far from the day-to-day problems of business and politics. In large part, they don't want their indifference challenged unless they can see positive means of affecting problems which they feel directly affect them—such as two-session schools, traffic lights, and attempts at rezoning.

Means and Ends

The means employed to organize are in large measure determined by the ends being sought. Yet, in many cases the means are the ends, so that the way the organizing is carried out determines how the goal will be structured. For example, if the goal of a particular social change tactic is to alter the power structure in a given community from one of power-elite versus the masses to one of participatory democracy, then an armed insurrection will not necessarily guarantee that anything will have changed at all. If change is a constant, then the process by which change is undertaken becomes a critical problem in organizing. Issues such as whether to have a highly centralized or decentralized organization are crucial: Does one want efficiency and tight planning, with large numbers of persons being left out of the decision-making process, or the participation of everyone knowing that the same material must be gone over in hundreds of small meetings and everyone given a chance to have a say on this or that tactic or issue? [15] Ultimately, if one wants to bring about a socialist form of government, people have to begin to think and act as socialists. A magic transformation will not automatically occur after the revolution as has become evident by the form socialism has taken in many Eastern European nations.[16]

Equally important in any discussion of means and ends are two questions which most organizations designed for social change must at some point face: whether to work through legal or extra-legal channels and whether to employ supposedly "violent" or nonviolent tactics. The issue of working within the legal framework of American society often means deciding whether or not that framework is just— that is, which takes precedence: law or justice? In the same sense, if one wishes to decide whether to change or not to change American society by working within and accepting the premises of its various institutions, then one must also often weigh which takes precedence: individual conscience or the duty to obey [17] the ongoing legal and value structure of that society.

In practice this issue revolves around the right to dissent, through both legal and extra-legal channels. For example, if someone feels that American involvement in a war like the war in Vietnam would be immoral and not in the best interests either of himself or of the nation, what means are available to him to voice his protest? If he refuses to serve in the war, then he is eligible for a prison sentence; he has broken the law. But if the law, in his eyes, is not a legitimate one, how else may he keep from being drafted? How can he possibly work within the legal framework and still refuse to serve? Of course, he can attempt to change the law by attempting to get a court ruling on its legality. But what if the courts refuse to rule on the issue, as has been the case with the Vietnamese war? [18] He can also attempt to elect legislators who will change American foreign policy, but if his opinion is not in the majority, must not he still serve?

Once the organizer steps outside of legitimate or legal channels of dissent, what effect does such an effort have on the resolution of the issue? How must the political process be altered in order to bring about resolution? If one law is not recognized, how many others must also be de-legitimated before a more just system is worked out? If a given law is not legitimate, what authority can it have over our actions; is it our duty to refuse to obey it? If a given institution is outmoded, archaic, and dysfunctional for our lives and those of our friends, is it not our duty to refuse to acknowledge the sanctions that institution would impose, even if this means refusing to obey laws which follow from it? Refusing to follow institutional mandates may mean refusing to buy certain goods, refusing to work at traditional jobs, refusing to get married, refusing to accept traditional forms of education. While there may be no laws against such actions, there may exist, in fact, strong social or political sanctions against carrying out these refusals.

Breaking the law as an act of dissent often means that one's conscience takes precedence over the legitimacy of the state. It follows, then, that one must first know what that conscience is. *Who* is refusing to go into the army? *Who* is refusing to take his place on the assembly line or in front of long, streamlined, air-conditioned, plastic-coated supermarket counters? Sometimes it is only through the act of breaking a law or norm that we can find our conscience, but more often than not action in itself cannot maintain sustained effort against a strong opposition, nor can it aid in formulating alternatives to the way things are done now. Most actions of this nature are in response to actions the state has initiated, so that it is the other side which defines the terms of battle and resolution. Finally, it is difficult to organize, to know what concrete goals one wishes to bring about in the heat of mindless combat.

Often it is necessary to break laws which are not in themselves unjust in order to draw attention to problems which do not at present fall under direct legislation.[19] Fifty people blocked a busy street in Washington during the May Day demonstrations of 1971 in order to confront an apathetic populace with the fact that the war was still on. The effort was not to alter the law which states that streets should be open to car and bus traffic, but rather to draw attention to other grievances. On the other hand, appeals to conscience can be made by filling jails with those who intentionally break unjust laws—for example the draft—and, in so doing, arouse the empathy and sympathy of other Americans. In such cases where this tactic is employed, careful attention should be kept on the relationship of the tactic to the change desired.

The issue of law versus individual conscience can be extended to include the actions of nation states. For example, many have held that the actions of American forces in Vietnam are illegal, but who is to rule on American military operations, to which court of justice are military commanders and the men who direct them to be brought? [20] Yet, thousands are arrested for protesting these illegal actions in the face of a double standard which condemns violence at home (that supposedly committed by protesters), while condoning it abroad.[21]

The right to dissent, where individual conscience takes precedence over law and order, is a fundamental one for democracy, a word which of late has come to connote only those actions which stay within legal channels. Democracy also means the right to create one's own values and rules to live by and to change those values and rules when they are no longer applicable, to decide what is in fact legal or illegal. It is upon this basis that the issue of whether to employ legal or illegal tactics must be resolved, for employing legal means within a society based on many unwarranted and thereby illegitimate assumptions is to escape rather than deal with the issues at hand. In a similar sense, however, if one believes the legal framework of American society to be legitimate, with only certain laws unjust, then tactics which may serve to discredit the entire legal system should be carefully thought out.

Finally, whether or not an organization follows a legal or illegal course of action depends, in large measure, upon what their constituency is—that is, upon whether or not such a tactic will alienate rather than win the support of those persons and groups the organization would influence, and whether such alienation is worth the price of victory or, indeed, makes victory impossible.

Like the debate on whether to work within or outside traditional legal channels, the issue of whether to employ violent or nonviolent tactics, especially in terms of civil disobedience, has plagued and divided the protest movement, and consequently is of prime concern for the organizer—if not for himself, then for those he would organize. Some would hold that the issue is really a bogus one, that ends should take precedence over means, and, in any case, what is violent largely depends on one's definition. Thus, there is violence done to things through property destruction and to people through physical injury. Yet what of long-term violence—starvation due to poverty caused by neglect of the poor by the rich or by the government? What of the violence and damage done to the psyches of children who daily attend regimented classes?

What is considered violent depends not only upon which subculture within a given society is debating the issue, but also which generation within that subculture.[22] In fact, those who deny the "violence in man" may be themselves living an illusion.[23] One need only skim through such illuminating studies as those done by Ardrey (The Territorial Imperative) and Morris (The Naked Ape), which compare aggression in animals and man, to gain confirmation for such an hypothesis. Moreover, much depends on who is doing the violence to whom to say whether or not it is legitimate. For example, it is legitimate for police to kill members of the Black Panther party in a premeditated fashion, yet it is not legitimate for the Panthers to arm themselves in defense against such attacks. It is illegitimate and violent to burn down an ROTC building, or ghetto stores, but it is legitimate to napalm Vietnamese villages, defoliate Vietnamese forests, and prepare for nuclear war.[24]

Moreover, violence is not necessarily irrational behavior, even for those who would employ such labels as sanctions against domestic protest. Emotional states of anger, expressions of rage and rationality, are not opposites, for one must feel the necessity of responding in a given situation. Not to feel anything when viewing or living under conditions of poverty, not to feel anything when listening to the cries of napalmed children is irrational. To bomb villages from a height of 10,000 feet in carefully planned maneuvers is irrational because it ignores the plight of those who will become the recipients of the bombs. As Hannah Arendt notes, rage and violence are only irrational when they are directed against substitutes.[25]

Perhaps the main argument in favor of those who call for the use of violent tactics is that they can bring change (witness the Watts riots), and at the very least they bring recognition of the problem and the necessity of doing something about it. Therefore, can violent conflict be as functional for a given society as social conflict? [26] It is on this last point that the argument for nonviolence is centered. Given that violence brings about a recognition of the problem and *some* action, how long does the change last? Are lasting reforms carried out? Have fundamental divisions in the society been reconciled? Finally, it is often extremely difficult to prevent the means employed for bringing about change from becoming a prime factor in structuring the ends. In other words, the tactics of armed revolt or decimation of property do not necessarily engender attitudes necessary for bringing about a demo-cratic socialist form of government.

Thus, while violent protests attract large crowds, and in the process awaken large numbers of people to pressing issues (such as police brutality), these methods should be evaluated in terms of their long-range effects. There is also, however, a diminishing return from such tactics, for there is a thin line between confrontations with police—rocks versus tear-gas—and a happening in which large numbers of people are momentarily swayed by rhetoric, but, because they do not really know what issues they are protesting, their commitment lasts only a short while. While violence may help arouse concern within an apathetic populace by confronting it for the first time with a challenge of "where are you at," more than such a temporary arousal is necessary for long-term commitment and change. And, it is argued, it is this very commitment which is necessary for *American* society to be funda-mentally altered.

In essence, the use of violence, either to overthrow the government or to bring about social change, is playing the power structure's game. The government is well-armed and equipped to handle violent protest or armed rebellion and is quite used to dealing with such tactics. In such a confrontation, by definition someone wins and someone loses. Change takes place because the other side is suppressed, but only the symptoms have really been dealt with, for the inner turmoil of the defeated still remains a festering sore which can burst forth at any moment to renew the battle. The real issues have not been dealt with, merely hidden.[27] The aim of nonviolence, on the other hand, is not to play this game but to win the opposition over so that *both* we and they win.[28]

The use of nonviolent methods—passive resistance, refusing to fight back—becomes a kind of "moral jujitsu" which catches the other side off guard, opening them up to new ideas and alternative means of resolving conflict. Nonviolence challenges the opponents' reality structure, breaking it apart when our actions do not conform to their expectations.[29] There are other advantages, as Gregg comments:

> In this moral jiu-jitsu, the nonviolent person has superior position, poise and power for many reasons. First, he has taken the moral initiative. His conduct is new, unexpected, and unpredictable to the person habituated to violence. Second he is not surprised. He knows, by reasoning or by intuition and faith, what is really taking place in such a struggle, and how to control the process. Third, his self-control and lack of anger conserve his energy. Moreover, he is not in as suggestible a condition as his assailant.
>
> He has still another element of superior power: he has demonstrated his sincerity and deep conviction. To be willing to suffer and die for a cause is an incontestable proof of sincere belief, and perhaps in most cases the only incontestable proof.[30]

Nonviolent tactics, since they require a great deal of "inner strength," perseverance, and fortitude, require that we know what we believe in, what our values are, what our lives stand for, who we are. In this sense, violence is often used as a cover for a lack of such knowledge. Oftentimes individuals are forced out of their apathetic state only through some sort of jarring action, but such action does not have to be physically violent, for nonviolent action can lead to an equal test of values, if not more so. In fact, as Gregg notes, nonviolent action resembles the values men use in traditional warfare in numerous ways:

1. It has a psychological and moral aim and effect
2. It is a discipline of parallel emotion and instinct
3. It operates against the morale of the opponents
4. It is similar in principles of strategy
5. It is a method of settling great disputes and conflicts
6. It requires courage, dynamic energy, capacity to endure fatigue and suffering, self-sacrifice, self-control, chivalry, action
7. It is positive and powerful
8. It affords an opportunity of service for a large idea, and for glory [31]

Think of how frustrating it must be to fight someone who does not fight back, at least in the traditional manner, yet who is not a coward, who refuses to give in.[32] The nonviolent person does not necessarily fight over a physical boundary, as in the case of invasion; rather the boundary which is defended is a state of mind, and nonviolent tactics are adjusted accordingly.[33]

The essense of nonviolence is self-governance, and self-governance leads, on the state level, to self government.[34] There then becomes little difference between life style and defending one's given point of view, one's conscience. Nonviolence does not avoid suffering, but helps to minimize it. Men come to be treated as men, not machines or agents of technologically efficient weapons.[35] Because of the success of nonviolence, the government often sends agent provocateurs into crowds to stir them on to violence which then justifies the use of violent tactics on the part of the police or national guard.

Nonviolence is not a synonym for passivity, as will be noted below. Rather, it is an attempt to have means and ends unite in the process of bringing about social change.

Confronting the Power Structure

After a group has become organized, the question of how to make the organization's power felt can be dealt with. In this section, we will survey various types of tactics for dealing with recalcitrant power structures, from working within the system to change it, to total revolution. Regardless of the tactic employed, one problem which no organization can escape is the problem of being co-opted by the very power structure one would try to change. Traditionally, co-optation takes the form of buying off the leader of the dissident group either by providing him with a higher-paying job, or through token support of his efforts, thereby neutralizing the sting of his anger and his ability to attract followers. Co-optation, however, can take another form: The very act of solving certain social problems may in fact perpetuate the very system one would alter. As Herbert Marcuse pointed out some time ago,[36] and as we have noted in previous chapters, there appears to be no way to set up a dialectic between those who are part of the problem and those who would solve it. The social reality expands to encompass all forms of deviant social and political behavior, and to co-opt and use these very attempts at criticism to perpetuate its own legitimacy as well as to sell its products. One example springs to mind. In 1971, at California State University, San Jose, the budget for the EOP (Educational Opportunity Program), already insufficient, was sliced from $250,000 to $50,000 dollars per year. A group of middle-class white students enrolled in one of my classes became interested in doing something about this cutback, yet, on closer examination were faced with the following quandary: EOP funds enable essentially nonwhite minority students to get a college education and for all practical purposes a larger share of the pie. With their college diplomas, they can buy more of the goodies American society has to offer and can seek employment in any of the giant concerns which help perpetuate the problem of American society. At the same time, however, the enrollment of nonwhite students in college as presently constituted effectively destroys their distinct identities and co-opts them into the mainstream, where they can no longer provide an effective alternative to the direction American society is presently taking. All the while, the middle-class white students who seek to resurrect these EOP funds are attempting to fight the alienation this very mainstream creates by helping nonwhite minorities become like them. Finally, of course, if they do not help the EOP program survive, they may be called racists.

But the dilemma is not only for the middle-class white student, for his youthful ghetto counterpart must choose between slow starvation and middle-class alienation, between unemployment and becoming and organization man. This assumes that Chicanos and blacks have distinctive cultures—that they have resisted the ideological lures of television commercials, new cars, deodorants, tract homes. If they have not, then we are not speaking of cultural pluralism at all, but rather an attempt to market one's culture as distinctive in the same way as one would attempt to sell a new car. In this sense, black- and brown-studies departments become means of gaining a larger piece of the pie, rather than alternatives to what is and what can be. And why not? If any form of potentially revolutionary action can be used to perpetuate the very institutions one is attempting to transform, then activists become tragic figures indeed: Let's get it all together—buy a Kent!

Perhaps one of the primary ways of preventing co-optation is to know the ramifications of both the problem being dealt with and the actions taken to alleviate it. This means that the organization needs a certain amount of education as to how various social problems they are concerned with relate to each other. It also may mean, as we have attempted to point out in this book, that a given organization will discover that American society itself is a social problem and that the only way to prevent co-optation is to transform the entire society or all institutions at once. Another means of preventing co-optation is to be aware that it is a possibility—don't enter negotiations naively, thinking that all your demands are going to be met. Finally, if a group is diligent in seeking redress for its grievances, then no matter how many efforts are made at co-optation, as long as the problem is not resolved, the group can remain effective in its efforts.

Political Parties

The most traditional means of confronting those in the power structure, if they refuse to grant our demands, is to attempt to get persons elected to public office who represent our point of view. For example, in the spring of 1971, in the Berkeley City Council elections, a radical caucus was organized which elected enough persons to be able to have considerable influence on the council, as well as electing a sympathetic mayor. Yet, equal efforts have often taken place within the Democratic and Republican parties, where co-optation has been rather easy, and the grievances absorbed or neutralized by the broad party banner of compromise. There are currently several attempts at organizing nonwhite minority group members—namely, Chicanos and blacks—into national political parties specifically designed to represent their interests. In the past these minority groups attempted to make their numbers felt in both of the major political parties, but, lacking sufficient organization, their leaders were often bought off, and the general populace voted for whoever made the grander promises. Thus, attempting to force change through being able to deliver a substantial number of black or brown votes has not proved effective.

Empty pledges do not resolve long-standing problems, and the Chicanos have organized (in the southwestern United States) the La Raza Unida party, which does not support either major party but rather lobbies and otherwise directs its efforts toward establishing economic, social, and political power among Chicanos. La Raza Unida operates all year, rather than strictly around election time, and considers issues on a broad spectrum from the unionization of farm workers to establishing day care centers and women's rights. In addition, it attempts to set up democratic councils which will run their own communities, give support to all Third World peoples, and work for prison reform including the right of prisoners to vote, to get paid for their labor, to organize and bargain collectively, to enjoy familial and conjugal visits, and to undergo rehabilitation. When laws are broken, Chicanos are tried by a jury of their peers (other Chicanos) rather than by whites.[37]

There have been several efforts to organize a national black political party. Such a party would not only serve to rally black people around projects of mass action and the achievement of black economic and political power. In addition, a black political party would set an example for other parties and persons in the type of progressive programs it proposed,[38] including the implementation of socialist forms of government in the United States. In attempting to initiate such policies, a national black political party would not align itself with either the Democrats or Republicans but would instead work for black control over black communities, including economic organizations, education, police, and the courts. Being in the minority, a black political party would have to take advantage of divisions among whites, thereby attracting those sympathetic with the goals of the black community.[39] It would also acknowledge the fact that the transition to socialism is a long and slow process, requiring constant education heightening the contradictions of corporate capitalist America. To be effective, however, education cannot only take place in the classroom, but must be gained by experience in organizing black self-interest groups. A national black political party would serve as a focus for bringing about the transition to socialism through its organizational efforts on local and national issues.

Other writers have urged that a national coalition be formed among blacks, Chicanos, intellectuals, students, and youth—particularly since the advent of the 18-year-old vote—to challenge the existing two-party structure.[40] Such a party of the Left would not, however, organize itself along the lines of the other two parties, but rather would develop new ways of gaining political power, especially working to organize grass-roots economic and political groups which could gradually challenge local and ultimately national power structures. To engage in similar tactics as its opponents would leave it open to both co-optation and the same types of bureaucratic alienation and compromise which sap the energies and political idealism of many of those who would try and transform the Democratic and Republican parties from the inside. Though the Democratic party was transformed to some degree at the 1972 National Convention, the overwhelming defeat of George McGovern by Richard Nixon shattered the myth that the Democratic party was united behind new, progressive leadership. Similarly, the fact that almost half of the 18–21-year-old vote went for Nixon dealt a severe blow to the idea that the new youth vote would radically transform American society.

Efforts at local political organizing encounter attempts by the power structure to deny voter registration through questioning all those registered by the dissident party; the threat of economic sanctions including loss of jobs or evictions if a certain individual is elected; and often acts of violence designed to intimidate voters. Still other tactics of repression include attempts to frame those running on a "people's" platform. The most effective means of countering such

attacks is to be politically *and* economically together, to know why
you entered into political confrontation, to be united in your resolve.
Organizations which are fragmented, the products of constant power
struggles within their ranks, often collapse under the weight of outside
pressure and influence. Moreover, an organization which hopes for
victory cannot fold up at the first sign of success at the polls. Short-
term victories by one's own organization are often turned into long
run gains by an opposition which is patient and willing to wait for its
adversary to break ranks after the first flush of success. Countering this
threat means having a tight and well-educated group. Indeed, education and gaining publicity for one's ideas, not immediate victory, may
be the prime goal of initially entering a political campaign.[41]

Boycotts

Organizing a political party, placing a referendum on the ballot, or
attempting to bring test cases before the courts is often either not
possible, has been tried and failed, or is not germane to the types of
immediate issues a group is fighting for. In this situation, an effort
which can be employed is the boycott, the withdrawal of support for
some aspect of the political and economic system. Boycotts have been
used in a wide variety of areas with varying degrees of success. For
example, a strike is a type of boycott used by labor unions to force
management to recognize their grievances. Other strikes have been
used against bus lines to force integration; against retail markets to
force the selling of union grapes; against construction companies to
force the hiring of more minority workers; and against the army to
force an end to the war in Vietnam. Boycotts often take a long time
to bring results—depending, of course, on the size and power of the
group that one is boycotting. The grape strike lasted five years; the
war in Vietnam has not been fully halted. However, efforts against
businesses with local ownership who are highly dependent on their
own communities and who have no ready access to another source of
potential "customers" take much less time to prove their effectiveness.

A boycott is a negative action: One is refusing to purchase in, enlist
in, ride on, or work in a given operation. In terms of long-term organizing, then, when a boycott is being undertaken, survival becomes a
prime consideration. Thus, attempts should be made to start consumer
and worker cooperatives, food conspiracies (where each person puts
in a certain amount of money and someone representing the group
buys wholesale), and cooperative living arrangements. During a rent
strike initiated by a tenants' union, cooperative living may become a
necessity.

In conducting positive and negative actions at the same time, the power structure is being confronted with regard to its repression, while the protest organization is becoming self-sufficient, its members learning to work with each other, creating their own forms of organization, their own values, and moving toward a socialist America. Another advantage is that the power structure does not strictly determine the terms of the action, on what battleground it will be fought, and the rules under which combat will take place. In this sense, the "entertain me" syndrome which has dominated both mass society and protest movements alike is broken.

If the boycott is the first action a given group decides to employ, then the target should be one which brings immediate results. Particularly in a new organization or among constituents who have never been organized before, some type of initial success is necessary in order to keep up the morale of the group, and solidify it for future actions of a longer and more difficult duration. In the face of even temporary defeat, the organizer should attempt to maintain a positive attitude, for any sign of negativism on his part will soon be picked up by the general membership and rapidly become a self-fulfilling prophecy.

A boycott involves many of the same types of actions as those used in organizing in the first place. Mass leafleting and block meetings to disseminate information and attempt to gain further support are a necessity. Guerilla theater can dramatize the issues at hand. Informational picketing can be used to "stop" would-be shoppers from entering a given store. If the store has branches in other towns, attempts can be made to initiate sympathy strikes in those areas.

Massive consumer and worker boycotts or strikes can transform the American economy by de-legitimating American society. If people refuse to buy many of the superfluous commodities produced and, at the same time, if they refuse to work in plants which produce such commodities, a national economic crisis will be provoked. Needless to say, such an effort would require national organizing of a highly planned and effective nature. Yet, local boycotts designed to bring about the same effect, become testing grounds and ultimately the starting point of any national effort.

Interfering with Others

At the next level of intensity or militancy are tactics designed to force others to confront the issues one's organization is raising, to interfere directly in the day-to-day lives of those whom one would influence. While boycotts indirectly attempt to achieve the same purpose, they are usually not designed to refuse to let anyone else buy or rent. Typical of this set of tactics is the militant picket line, usually employed by unions to keep scabs from taking jobs in the factory, but increasingly used by those who block draft board entrances and school administration buildings, to prevent business as usual. Another such tactic is to jam or block traffic arteries of a busy city in order to force people out of their apathy. Still other forms include sit-ins, lie-ins, wade-ins, and even "reverse strikes." A reverse strike is the carrying out of the dictates of the bureaucracy to such an extent that the organization becomes paralyzed by one's demands, and the red tape involved.[42]

Interfering with the rights of others when used by the Left is most often employed under the philosophy of nonviolent resistance. In blocking a draft board, for example, a group of persons will link arms preventing anyone from entering, yet they will not beat up those persons who attempt to force their way into an establishment. In a similar sense, sit-ins paralyze an organization or business by making it impossible for work to continue, rather than by destroying the materials managers and secretaries need to do their jobs. Such tactics, then, typically necessitate large numbers of people, particularly since they are illegal; the arrest rate goes up accordingly. They also require a great deal of self-discipline, entailing refusals to fight back if assaulted, not playing the other side's game. The reasons for this have been noted above. Suffice it to say here that this tactic is employed to get others to join in the action, destroy the adversary, gain his sympathy, and have him come over to our side. In practice, of course, conversion must await later efforts.

Those who oppose these tactics often claim that they are undemocratic, and mean resorting to the very style of living the protesting group claims they are opposing. While ostensibly the case, the counter argument can be made that there is no such thing as pure freedom, that the American establishment constantly interferes with the rights of others, whether through molding the educational process or drafting those who do not choose to commit genocide in Southeast Asia. Furthermore, our refusals to do anything only support the ongoing "definitions of the situation," so we cannot claim neutrality. Thus, efforts to force confrontations with problems one is responsible for are legitimate in the context of American society.

Guerilla Warfare

Guerilla warfare has usually been associated with the efforts of a captive population to free itself, but one which lacks sufficient military power to do so. Guerilla warfare, if carried out for a long period of time, signifies the beginning of a general revolt, though this has not always been the case. We tend to think of the guerilla warrior in the context of underdeveloped nations in Asia, Africa, or Latin America, though the concept fits specific protest actions occurring in the United States. For example, ghettos can be seen from a police perspective as enemy territory, in which it is difficult to distinguish between the criminal and the rest of the population. In such a situation, the criminal becomes a political agent, representing the oppressed populace.[43] Guerilla warfare can take many forms. It might entail burning down or blowing up buildings or other centers of "capitalist" and "imperialist" activities; still others may see guerilla warfare as cutting power lines, selective assassinations, kidnappings, mass thievery, or dropping "acid" in the water supply.

In a large urban population, guerilla warfare has the advantage of enabling the guerilla to disappear among the people "as a fish swims in water." Not knowing where attacks come from, or when and in what form they will take place, those in the power structure are thrown into a panic. If they attack all those who look like the guerillas, meaning the general populace, they risk the chance of a full-scale rebellion; if they do not attack or force this populace to give up its "heroes," they risk an eradication or at best a gradual weaning away of their (the power structure's) power. It is for this reason that such tactics work best among a sympathetic populace in whose homes one can hide and gain camouflage for his activities. Guerilla tactics can bring increasing repression, so should be used only when there are no other effective strategies at hand or all else has failed. Even then, to convince someone who has little hope that your efforts might help them win may prove extremely difficult.

While terrorism and sabotage help publicize the issue and perhaps result in some change, there are other, less violent, means which can prove more effective. Power rests on respect for authority; it demands allegiance. If the government is not respected, it has a difficult time legitimating itself.[44] When one attacks the government through armed insurrection or traditional guerilla tactics, he is acknowledging that government's existence, and, in a sense, legitimating it. Therefore, another effective means of bringing about change is to de-legitimate that government by refusing to recognize its existence—by laughing at it. For example, loudspeakers can be used at rallies where government representatives are to speak with tape-recorded laughter or sounds of trains or the ocean. In such a situation, the government often resorts to violence in order to attempt to restore the power it has lost—for it must have power over someone in order to claim power in the first

place—but the use of violence only points out how impotent that government really is. In the spring of 1970, the use of violence by national guardsmen to quell campus uprisings could be held as evidence of such a breakdown on the national level. And, predictably, the implementation of force weakened rather than strengthened the government's position. It is out of this perspective that Hannah Arendt contends that power and violence are opposites: Where the latter prevails, the former is absent.[45]

Revolution

Thomas Jefferson said:

> When government violates the rights of the people, insurrection is for the people, and for every portion of the people, that most sacred of rights and the most indispensable of duties.[46]

And, many years later, Abraham Lincoln wrote:

> This country, with its institutions, belongs to the people who inhabit it. Whenever they shall grow weary of the existing government, they can exercise their constitutional right to amend it, or their revolutionary right to dismember or overthrow it.[47]

Revolutions are built on rising expectations. They do not occur when one does not expect change to take place, when one has little hope; rather, occur when change is beginning to take place, but too slowly—when there is hope without immediate fulfillment. Such a situation exists today among two groups in American society— nonwhite minorities and youth. Because of the passage of much legislation, however token, nonwhites are expecting significant social improvements. In a different sense, a generation of relatively affluent middle-class youth, brought up to believe in values their parents never practiced, also expect change to take place.

There are many questions which must be considered when one speaks of the possibility of a revolution in American society. Who is it that will lead the revolution, and whom do these leaders speak for? If there are to be no leaders, if American society is to be transformed through mass reality-busting and de-legitimation, still, who is to define the greatest good? Richard Neuhaus puts the problem this way:

> How can it be reasonably assured that the revolutionary elite, which by definition is not of and by the people, will remain for the people in a way that does not betray the authority it claims from the people? [48]

If a revolution is mass- rather than elite-oriented, who is to set the goals? Is a democratic revolution possible?

While it may be difficult, as we have noted, for the police to distinguish between the criminal (guerilla) and the people who reside in the ghetto, it is even more difficult for the middle-class youth, bent on rebelling, to distinguish the enemy (his parents?) from the victims (the people). Whom is he to attack, where should he focus his revolt? Even if the goals of the revolution, as many on the New Left have pointed out, can only be defined out of the action of revolt, at some point this action must be pointed toward a concrete end. But that end may not be a positive one—need it be?

> The master seems to have solicited the rebel's views on the revolutionized, good society. The rebel would be embarrassed to confess the truth: that he has no such views. Industry? Agriculture? Foreign trade? It is

not such matters that drive and preoccupy him. The victorious future is at the moment any society in which certain individuals no longer have power, no longer exist. The rebel fights for something that will not be like *this*. He cannot answer the question about the future because that is not his question. It is not the future that is victimizing him. It is the present. It is not an anticipated Utopia which moves him to risk his life. It is pain. "Turn it over!" he cries, because he can no longer bear it as it is. . . . His motivating vision of change is at root a vision of something absent—not of something that *will* be there, but of something that will be there *no longer*. His good future world is elementally described by its empty spaces: a missing landlord, a missing mine owner, a missing sheriff. . . . The fundamental revolutionary motive is not to construct a Paradise but to destroy an Inferno.[49]

Yet, ironically, as Oppenheimer shows, action and sentiment often lead to both humanistic and fascistic values, for action for its own sake can also lead to violence for its own sake. In this instance, the means/ends dichotomy disappears, and as the means (violence and action) become the ends, so too do the goals of the revolution disappear, unless, of course, there were no goals to begin with.[50] The old Left of the thirties planned and *then* acted, but they did not build the revolution either. Some youth argue for blowing it up now and worrying about the goals later.[51] Jerry Rubin, among the spokesmen for this position, points out that "A society which suppresses adventure makes the only adventure the suppression of that society." [52] He also has said that "Only by breaking rules do we discover who we are." [53]

If ends disappear, if revolution becomes "permanent"—a conclusion which is possible, as we saw in previous chapters—then the means which one employs become particularly important. In a violent revolution one is engaged in a war in which there are winners and losers, therefore the appropriate revolutionary organization is military in nature. Such a revolution is not a happening, despite the rhetoric of many would-be American liberators. It is not the product of being temporarily overwhelmed by passionate language. It entails a long-term commitment, an understanding of what the goals of the revolution are and how one relates to those goals. The revolution and the individual should become one and the same. It is not a two-hour demonstration after which one goes out for pizza and beer.[54]

Can a revolution be democratic? Once the goals are chosen, is there any room for voting or debate? Adherence to a strong ideology is antidemocratic, for such adherence restricts one's options, limiting argument to tactics rather than goals. Moreover, in an armed struggle, humanitarian values are unlikely to be preserved, especially by those most caught up in the fight. If the end justifies the means, then nothing must stand between us and that end—neither mates, lovers, nor friends. People come to be used and manipulated for these ends. When the revolution is over, how is a switch in values possible—for example, from using people to treating them as human beings, from adherence to a strict ideology and organization to open democratic debate? After such a struggle, what is to prevent a new elite from being as ruthless as the previous one? Finally, in a violent revolution each side has its own legitimacy: The fight is to the death, there are no prisoners. By this is meant that revolution is treason to all the laws which govern the existing state, and for the revolutionist, to not be for him is to be against all that he believes in.[55] The goals of this type of revolution then must constantly be evaluated, lest they be lost—that is, lest the revolution become too dehumanizing and in practice offer no alternative at all to the present regime.[56]

But what if the goal is not an armed revolution, but rather a nonviolent one? Is a military organization then necessary? If the goal is a changed society, rather than a revolution per se, there are a variety of means which might bring such change about.[57] Are the poor, the non-white, and youth willing to stake all in a revolution in the traditional sense, and for what? Are the present goals of white and black radicals so impracticable that they cannot be met under present governmental and economic forms? [58] If the government is "tolerant," and gives in just enough, then the spirit of the revolution is silenced. For:

> Despite strong arguments that paramilitary and nonviolent struggle can undermine a system and create a revolutionary climate (that is, so that the outposts of reform fall), this has never really happened. Nowhere has significant revolutionary warfare begun except where the regime had already refused (hence, for whatever reason, was unable) to make re-forms. Every guerilla outbreak has begun only after some colossal break in the system—for example, refusal to hold elections, large-scale purges, arrests and shootings, the alienation of some significant group by refusing to permit it any access to some (even limited) power, massive repression of some potentially revolutionary minority group, and so forth.[59]

Revolution, as a tactic, if it is played according to the same rules as those of the power structure, must probably fail, for few among the Left or nonwhite want to die. And even then, there is little chance they can match the weaponry, or gain sufficient support to topple the state. If revolution is to occur, it may only come through the long-term efforts of small-scale organizing, communes, and caucuses which gradually undermine the fabric of American society, replacing it with a new form and content.

Survival as a Tactic

During the fight to transform American society, one must survive. There are many different ways to survive, some which entail a sep-aration of political action from life style, others which force no such distinction. For the committed organizer, it is obviously best that no such distinction be made. In fact, all actions can be seen as having political connotations.

Communal living seems to offer many advantages both for employ-ing many of the tactics discussed above, as well as for defense and pure survival. Communes that take on political actions are often labeled affinity groups. Such groups are tightly knit, independent, highly flexi-ble, and supportive. If a given commune gets "busted" there is a good chance that many others will not know of the action, and the move-ment is not destroyed. Rural communes can survive by growing their own food, but are often isolated from the issues they would become involved with. Urban communes are more susceptible to political pressures, but are also located among the communities they would organize. In an urban setting one person can work at a "straight" job, supporting many others who are full-time political activists.

Individuals and communes can sell various services and commodities to mass society (leather goods, jewelry), but there is often the risk of co-optation—that one is so much into making a living that he forgets the political connotations of his activities. Experiences can also be sold—rock music, encounter groups, meditation sessions—which, while profitable, can be used as a political tactic, subverting many of the values of American society. Here too, co-optation is possible, as these experiences come to be treated as new consumer goods rather than as ways of changing one's life style.

Recently there has been a series of publications discussing new life vocational interests or vocations for social change [60] where one can go to work at changing America while being paid for it. Such occupations include setting up free schools, drug clinics, research and action on ecological problems, social service organizations, and others. One can also make a living by organizing and running food co-ops, storefront learning centers which are paid for by the community, and by selling the community a necessary service which they are not currently paying for—for example, something to eradicate pollution problems.

If all else fails, there is always welfare, stealing, borrowing and generally "ripping off the system," which can serve both political as well as survival needs. Learning to survive free of charge in America need not be illegal, but often requires high creativity, guts, and savoir faire.[61]

In the final analysis, as Carl Oglesby has commented:

> It is neither in the nature of the state that it can give political freedom nor in the nature of political freedom that it can be given. Political freedom is not a license to be purchased or petitioned from a higher power. It is not a gift. It does not exist as a fund under the superintendency of privileged offices. Political freedom is in political man, in his life, and it exists when he claims it.[62]

The Whole World Is Watching: National Tactic I

The goals and tactics of changing American society do not exist in a vacuum. All nations, and particularly the underdeveloped countries, are watching the transformation or lack of transformation of our society. For some years now it has been apparent that once a country begins to industrialize, the demand for more consumer goods inevitably follows the demand for the satisfaction of basic physical needs—food, clothing, and shelter. Regardless of the type of society which previously existed, or the strength of its cultural tradition, industrialization and technology seem to have their sway. In this sense then, the United States, as the prime industrial and consumer society represents a model for the future of the world. How we handle the dilemmas wrought by these consumer products and the types of cultural values which have grown up around them is of utmost importance to those who will find themselves in a similar position in the future.

The question can be put this way: Can current underdeveloped or developing nations change the course of their industrial revolution away from material affluence and toward other types of goals and cultural values, or is such affluence inevitable? The relationship in America of poor and nonwhite persons to the larger white, middle-class society provides a microcosm of this very problem and conflict. While poor and nonwhite groups could benefit from a change in the social structure which gave them a more significant place in the political and economic future of American society, for the most part the type of structural change desired by these groups does not represent a fundamental shift away from a materialistic culture. Logically, then, when poor, nonwhite members of our society occupy the same types of jobs which middle-class Americans now find alienating, they too will become alienated. When the populations of underdeveloped nations occupy this same position, they will undergo this same experience.

Given that some type of industrialization process is necessary to feed large populations, what alternatives exist to prevent overdevelopment? Once rising expectations toward material well-being have been created, can a ceiling be reached after which such expectations may be channeled in another direction? Are there enough raw materials to provide for such overproduction, or must nations go to war over them?

Who will finance industrialization? What will prevent the West from continuing to use up raw materials from the new underdeveloped nations? If money is given by Americans for such an industrialization process, can they expect to have some say or control in how such monies are allocated, in the type of government which comes to exist, in how that nation votes at the UN? Should the West begin paying reparations in the form of foreign aid for the hundreds of years it exploited and took raw materials from the underdeveloped nations? How will changes in our orientation toward material production and consumption on the domestic scene affect the national marketplace?

How will our actions affect how raw materials are used and what type of culture develops in other countries?

The ideological clash between capitalism and communism has been waged over the underdeveloped nataions which are seeking to industrialize as rapidly as possible and are more oriented toward nationalistic rather than ideological perspectives. For the United States, this means supporting the status quo, equating law and order with democracy and stability, instead of meeting the urgent needs of local populations. That this type of equation has proved unstable in the long run is quite evident. Communist ideology, on the other hand, has gained much from supporting internal movements within underdeveloped nations which sought rapid social change in order to meet at least their basic needs. What must then be altered is our attitude toward revolution, not only in underdeveloped nations, but domestically as well. This may mean either adopting an isolationist position in which we let underdeveloped nations work out internal disputes for themselves, or providing outright support for those who would revolutionize a given society. Future stability and security must come to rest on a world population whose basic survival needs have been met, not stifled by archaic dictatorships or American foreign policy and its ideological and economic "prerogatives."

Given the population and ecological crises, there is a certain limit to the amount of raw materials available, and the way these raw materials can be used. Ehrlich and Harriman have proposed that a tax be levied on the overdeveloped nations so that these nations can be *de-developed,* and underdeveloped nations financed for their own development. At the same time, there must come into existence a world planning board which can assess the world's resources and how they should be distributed—from the "have" to the "have-not" nations. Population must be controlled in a similar fashion. In the United States this would mean that those having more than two children would be heavily taxed, or even put in prison, while those who abstained or had themselves sterilized would be rewarded for their abstinence. Other nations would of course have to adopt similar measures, free abortions, and other birth-control devices in order to limit their own population growth and make economic development a possibility. A decline in the population of the overdeveloped nations would free much of our resources for use in aiding the developing nations, both in terms of material as well as technical assistance.[63] Ultimately, some type of world federalism, world government, and socialism would becomes a necessity.

World-wide economic planning, however, would probably spell the end of cultural pluralism as more and more cultures were forced to adjust to a world economic and engineering norm in order to get their share of the available raw materials in the most efficient way possible. The United States is a microcosm of this problem, as black and Chicano cultures, in the process of getting a larger piece of the pie, become co-opted into the mainstream. The equitable division of resources must also conflict with capitalism; thus, ultimately, any fundamental change in foreign policy must entail domestic economic transformation—namely the elimination of the *need* for expanding markets and ever-increasing profits.

Disarmament and the Quest for a Lasting Peace: National Tactic II

Not only must planning and arriving at an equitable division of the world's natural resources become a necessity, but resolving the nuclear arms race has become equally important. Preparation for war and economic development are intimately related, one cannot be resolved without resolution of the other. With economic development, there would be considerable lack of incentive to invade the United States, a possibility many politicians feel would result if we were to take off our guns. Frank points out:

> An occupation by an enemy possessing superior arms seems to be what American political leaders fear most—as one expressed it: "In the face of Communist ideology any nation that lays down its arms can expect immediate occupation." Sometimes the fear of occupation takes the form of a nightmare of hungry, armed Asians and Africans swarming over us, a fear I find hard to take seriously. Most people do not leave home that easily, and if life were getting steadily better at home and they were no longer hungry, the major incentive for such a mass migration halfway around the world would be gone. The chief safeguard against such a possibility would be the raising of the impoverished nations' living standards which would progress rapidly once the preposterous burden of armaments was lifted.[64]

In light of the above discussion, how might the threat of nuclear war be eliminated? To view the stockpiling of nuclear arms as a deterrent to war is in a sense to see capital punishment as an effective deterrent to murder. Such stockpiling of weapons does little to stifle the outbreak of small, conventional wars, ones in which the rebels cannot be easily distinguished from the people, thus preventing large scale use of nuclear weapons. And, the policy of mutual deterrence "includes no provisions for its own resolution." [65]

Critics of the nuclear deterrence system have come up with many different stages and plans for easing world tensions by reducing world armaments. One of the most general of such plans is proposed by Oglesby. There are four stages:

> First, each side must commit itself to the view that global war is an un-satisfactory means of securing global objectives, since what such a war might win is under all conditions drastically less than what it will most certainly lose.
>
> Second, a global truce line must be unambiguously drawn.
>
> Third, it is through the process of defining and securing the truce line that the rival powers build up a store of information about each other, develop and habituate themselves to a modus vivendi, and begin to create a communication system. . . .
>
> Finally, the dividend of this patience is that the common interests so necessary to a more productive relationship will have had time to incubate. . . .[66]

These rather general suggestions assume that understanding of the other side's position will lead to an increasing agreement as to what each side shares with the other, and how peace is in the interest of both sides. What this position also assumes—and not illogically—is that if we alter our language, if we attempt to see the "enemy" as he is, not as how we would like him to be (the personification of evil), then this will alter our attitudes toward making peace.[67]

Perhaps the "safest" attempt at reducing the arms race and the impending threat of nuclear annihilation is "arms control." This plan envisions stabilizing both Russia and the United States at the present degree of armament which would be controlled by inspection teams. There are several drawbacks to this plan, however. First, leaving both sides armed to the teeth does not limit the possibility either of accidental use or of premeditated implementation of such arms. Moreover, in the absence of a trusting relationship between both sides, there would develop an atmosphere of constant frustration and anxiety about whether either side had broken through in the arms race, thereby violating the treaty.[68]

Another proposal, known as "gradualism," is defined by Etzioni:

1. First, the United States *unilaterally* takes some symbolic steps to reduce international tensions.
2. After a number of these, it makes some *concessions*, expecting the Russians to *reciprocate*. . . .

3. Finally, when unilateral symbolic moves and reciprocated concessions have markedly reduced international tension, the United States suggests *multilateral negotiations*. . . .[69]

Gradualism is designed to assure minimum risk for both sides, while at the same time reducing the nuclear arms race. A variant of such a plan holds that, instead of dismantling nuclear disarmaments first, conventional weapons will go first—including the selling of such weapons to other nations. Thus, not until a state of trust is built up will each side disband its ultimate weapon.[70] The use of gradualism, as other authors suggest, should also entail the following:

> Our unilateral acts must be perceived by an opponent as reducing his external threat . . . accompanied by explicit invitations to reciprocation . . . executed regardless of prior commitment by the opponent to reciprocate . . . planned in sequences and continued over considerable periods regardless of reciprocation by an opponent . . . (and) announced in advance of execution and widely publicized to ally, neutral, and enemy countries as part of a consistent policy.[71]

Since the preparation for nuclear war has not brought political stability, has not insured against the destruction of the political state, and has only brought an increasing reliance on technological solutions, what must again be emphasized is that trust only develops as people's attitudes toward each other change.[72] Sibley has called for a kind of breakthrough in such attitudes by using the analogy provided by Hans Christian Andersen's tale, *The Emperor's New Clothes*:

> At the outset, we might ask ourselves what the naive child in [this tale] . . . might think of contemporary military policy; for Scripture tells us that God often grants wisdom to babes and sucklings and denies it to the old and experienced. The child would in its innocence wonder how grown men could expect to advance morality through threats of mass annihilation; how disarmament could be brought about by building up armaments; how security could be promoted through accentuation of fear; and how democracy could be upheld through development of "over-kill." One can conceive the child shouting out: "But all this doesn't make sense. How can morality be advanced by threats to kill? How can building large quantities of missiles prepare the way for disarmament? How can inculcation of fear lead to security? How can democratic government be protected by stating that under certain circumstances we are prepared to reduce a hundred million living human beings to lifeless things?" [73]

The child calls the system's bluff, and says, "Let's just unilaterally disarm ourselves, for what good have our weapons been?" This might, according to Sibley, result in the following dividends:

> The over-all objective of such a policy would be to prevent war and to assist in the establishment of machinery for peaceful change. Hopefully, it would do this in a number of ways. First, it might evoke reciprocal responses from the remainder of the world. Second, even if the response were not immediately forthcoming, it would stop the arms race; for while other states might continue their military establishments, it is difficult to imagine their continuing to increase their expenditures on arms. Third, a consistent policy of unilateralism would make it possible for the United States to devote its energies to the discovery and development of an effective defense scheme. Once central reliance on the military had been renounced, there would be a real incentive for the working out of non-military methods. Fourth, it would be designed to strengthen international organization; for a nation no longer using obsolete military methods would necessarily have to think of international organization as a vital substitute. Finally, it would contribute to the establishment of an international atmosphere within which alleviation of tensions could more likely take place. It would not itself eliminate all sources of conflict; but it could assist in making them far less dangerous for the survival and welfare of the human race.[74]

Such a disarmament plan, as envisioned by Sibley, would take three stages, lasting a period of six years. The first stage would entail a six-month preparation of the public for what is to come, including advocacy via newspapers, educational sessions, and so on. The second stage, lasting eighteen months, would involve the destruction of all nuclear weapons. The third stage, lasting the final four years, would include the destruction of all conventional weapons.[75] This plan also has the advantage of giving the United States the initiative; no longer would we be merely *reacting* on the basis of the presumed actions of other nations. Moreover, a nonviolent resistance administration could be developed to defend against an unlikely attempted takeover of the United States by hostile forces. Yet, what would such force have to gain from such a takeover? And why should we assume that such a takeover would be imminent?

> Suppose, says Socrates, that Russian Man were to decide that war under present conditions is intolerable and were publicly to destroy all of his weapons—would you, American Man, leap to destroy him in a nuclear holocaust? Of course not, replies American Man—we are only concerned

with protecting ourselves, not destroying others. Would you overrun the Soviet Union, asks Socrates, and enslave the Russian people? For goodness sake, American Man replies with a grin, we have no imperialist ambitions—in any case, a world unified under our way of life would be as good for them as for us. To tell the truth, he adds, we'd welcome the chance to get rid of our weapons and live in peace. Very well, then, says the wise Socrates, do you think that Russian Man would leap to destroy you with his nuclear missiles if you were to lay down your weapons and render yourself defenseless? [76]

Moreover, such a unilateral disarmament would catch both the Russians and Chinese off-guard, we would be violating their expectations, because we were no longer playing their game. Finally, this position would tend to weaken the stance of hard-liners both here at home, and in Russia and China, who would have difficulty in making a strong case for continued use of arms and the maintenance of large defense establishments.[77] Ideological disputes then, would have to be fought out in terms of which was more viable, rather than which possessed the strongest military.

The case against unilateral disarmament is that the communists would then go on to annex the rest of Asia, Africa, and Latin America. But, again, this could occur only if the population is *susceptible* to such annexation. And, if they did—would the way of life now led by persons in these societies be worse than it now is, or better? Do more Cubans go hungry, diseased, ill-clothed, and poorly housed now than they did under Batista? Do more Chinese now than under Chiang Kai-shek? Gradual disarmament based on reciprocation and inspection systems leave open the question of how such inspection is to be enforced: What happens if a nation violates the treaty, and begins the arms race again? Who is to punish that nation? Who can? Complete disarmament leaves open no such possibility.

NOTES

[1] O. M. Collective, *The Organizer's Manual* (New York: Bantam Books, Inc., 1971), pp. 3, 26.

[2] *Ibid.*, pp. 13–14.

[3] Si Kahn, *How People Get Power* (New York: McGraw-Hill, Inc., 1970), p. 2.

[4] Michael P. Lerner, "Weatherman: The Politics of Despair," in Harold Jacobs

(ed.), *Weatherman* (San Francisco: Ramparts Press, 1970), p. 402; O. M. Collective, *op. cit.,* p. 18.

[5] Kahn, *op. cit.,* pp. 11–12; O. M. Collective, *op. cit.,* pp. 33–37. See also W. Ron Jones, *Finding Community* (Palo Alto: James E. Freel and Associates, 1971).

[6] Kahn, *op. cit.,* pp. 39–45.

[7] O. M. Collective, *op. cit.,* p. 162.

[8] Kahn, *op. cit.,* pp. 39–45.

[9] O. M. Collective, *op. cit.,* pp. 38–40.

[10] *Ibid.,* p. 39.

[11] *Ibid.,* p. 108.

[12] *Ibid.,* pp. 275–280.

[13] *Ibid.,* p. 240.

[14] *Ibid.,* p. 214.

[15] Paul Sweezy, "The Transition to Socialism," *Monthly Review,* May, 1971, p. 10; also Charles Bettelheim, "More on the Society of Transition," *Monthly Review,* December, 1970.

[16] O. M. Collective, *op. cit.,* p. 13.

[17] Howard Zinn, *Disobedience and Democracy* (New York: Random House, Inc., 1968), p. 8.

[18] *Ibid.,* p. 72.

[19] *Ibid.,* p. 32.

[20] *Ibid.,* p. 88.

[21] *Ibid.,* p. 95.

[22] Henry Bienen, *Violence and Social Change* (Chicago: University of Chicago Press, 1968), p. 106.

[23] *Ibid.,* p. 11.

[24] Zinn, *op. cit.,* p. 50.

[25] Hannah Arendt, *On Terror* (New York: Harcourt, Brace & World, Inc., 1970), pp. 63–64.

[26] Louis Coser, *The Functions of Social Conflict* (New York: The Free Press, 1956).

[27] Richard B. Gregg, *The Power of Nonviolence* (New York: Schocken Books, Inc., 1969), p. 62.

[28] *Ibid.,* p. 50.

[29] *Ibid.,* p. 45.

[30] *Ibid.,* p. 47.

[31] *Ibid.,* p. 100.

[32] *Ibid.,* p. 128.

[33] American Friends Service Committee, *In Place of War* (New York: Grossman Publishers, 1967), p. 51.

[34] Satish Kumar, *Non-Violence or Non-Existence* (London: Christian Action), p. 19.

[35] Barbara Deming, "On Revolution and Equilibrium," *Liberation,* February, 1968, p. 11.

[36] Herbert Marcuse, *One-Dimensional Man* (Boston: Beacon Press).

[37] "La Raza Unida Party," *Rasca Tripas,* December, 1970.

[38] "A Transitional Program for Black Liberation" (New York: Merit Publishers, 1969), p. 7.

[39] *Ibid.,* p. 10.

[40] Franz Schurmann, "System, Contradictions, and Revolution in America," in Roderick Aya and Norman Miller, *The New American Revolution* (New York: The Free Press, 1971), p. 91.

[41] O. M. Collective, *op. cit.,* p. 168.

[42] *Ibid.,* p. 133.

[43] Martin Oppenheimer, *The Urban Guerilla* (Chicago: Quadrangle Books, 1969), p. 38.

[44] Arendt, *op. cit.,* p. 45.

[45] *Ibid.,* p. 56.

[46] Quoted in Peter L. Berger and Richard J. Neuhaus, *Movement and Revolution* (Garden City: Doubleday & Company, Inc., 1970), p. 145.

[47] *Ibid.*

[48] *Ibid.,* p. 177.

[49] Carl Oglesby and Richard Shaull, *Containment and Change* (New York: The Macmillan Company, 1967), pp. 146–147.

[50] Oppenheimer, *op. cit.,* p. 64.

[51] Jerry Rubin, *Do It!* (New York: Simon and Schuster, Inc., 1970), p. 125.

[52] *Ibid.,* p. 88.

[53] *Ibid.,* p. 103.

[54] Berger and Neuhaus, *op. cit.,* p. 152.

[55] *Ibid.,* p. 154.

[56] *Ibid.,* p. 168. For a discussion of revolutionary movements on an international scale see Barbara and John Ehreneich, *Long March, Short Spring* (New York: *Monthly Review Press, 1969);* Tariq Ali, *The New Revolutionaries* (New York: William Morrow and Co., Inc., 1969); and James Chowning Davies, *When Men Revolt and Why* (New York: The Free Press, 1971).

[57] *Ibid.,* p. 190.

[58] *Ibid.,* p. 181.

[59] Oppenheimer, *op. cit.,* p. 165.

[60] For example see *New Life Vocations.* Career Planning and Placement Center. California State University, San José; and Vocations for Social Change, Canyon, Calif.

[61] Abbie Hoffman. *Steal This Book.* New York: Pirate Publications, 1971.

[62] Oglesby and Shaull, p. 163.

[63] Paul Ehrlich and Richard Harriman. *How To Be A Survivor.* New York: Ballantine Books, 1971, pp. 166–202.

[64] Jerome D. Frank. *Sanity and Survival.* New York: Vintage, 1968, p. 277.

[65] Charles Osgood. "Reciprocal Initiative." In Richard A. Falk and Saul H. Mendlovitz. *Disarmament and Economic Development.* New York: World Law Fund, 1966, p. 158.

[66] Oglesby and Shaull, pp. 19–21.

[67] Thomas Merton. "War and the Crisis of Language." in Robert Ginsberg ed., *The Critique of War*. Chicago: Henry Regnery Co., 1969, pp. 113–114.

[68] Amitai Etzioni. *The Hard Way to Peace*. New York: Collier, 1962, p. 127.

[69] *Ibid.,* p. 95.

[70] *Ibid.,* p. 144.

[71] Osgood, pp. 181–183.

[72] Mulford Z. Sibley. "The Case for Unilateral Disarmament." in Robert A. Goldwin. *America Armed*. Chicago: Rand McNally, 1969, pp. 114–118.

[73] *Ibid.,* p. 121; 113–114.

[74] *Ibid.,* p. 121.

[75] *Ibid.,* p. 122.

[76] Osgood., p. 174.

[77] Sibley, pp. 134–135.

14

we are the new society: education for change

One primary tactic for changing American society is education. Not the education of most public schools and colleges in which students now lead half-lives—being neither scholars, nor fully involved in extracurricular pursuits—but an education that has students confront options which are particularly relevant to their situation and has them act on the basis of these options. As long as students continue to sit passively in their seats, be receptors rather than initiators, their minds wandering to far-off lands, bedrooms, football stadiums, and sunny beaches, they will continue to legitimate present educational institutions and the larger society. If students are to become aware of the possibilities open to them, and if American society is to be transformed, then education as we have come to know it will have to be changed radically.

What should the new purpose of education be? As we noted in Chapter 8, education has traditionally served the society of which it is a part. In large measure, it produces conformists, uncritical citizens prepared to participate in corporations and in political life much in the same way as they did in the college classrooms. This form of edu-

cation legitimates the existing system for it reflects rather than challenges the values of the community. Such an education provides little
sense of self-actualization, independence, or responsibility. Yet education, almost by definition, should be subversive; it calls into question
all that presently exists if that present order cannot stand the test of
critical judgment. In a rapidly changing society and world, education
which does not serve a critical function, which is not in the forefront
of such change, is not education at all, for it does not expand an individual's consciousness beyond the boundaries he establishes with the
help of radio, television, and newspapers.

It will be the purpose of this chapter to examine various types of
educational reform and revolt, from student power to radical classroom
transformation, the elimination of schools, and other alternatives.
What type of education is possible; how can it come about? How
does such change reflect more comprehensive alterations in the society
at large? How do the types of conflict and change now happening and
which will continue to happen on college and high school campuses
act as a beacon for such change in America? Can colleges themselves
become the communiites of the future, where learning, relating, and
creativity form the basis around which we order our lives?

Education for Justice

The faculty on most high school and college campuses has, in large
measure, been reluctant to institute reforms, for they would have to
reform themselves. It is the students who have provided the main
impetus for educational change in recent years. For the most part,
such revolts have centered around the relation between the campus
and the community—permitting politically active groups to hold rallies
and set up tables to distribute literature on campus; severing university
ties to business, especially in defense employment and research; ad-
mitting more minority students to college campuses under scholarships
funded by EOP (Educational Opportunities Programs); and recognition
that students should have a say in campus governance. Shouting
"Power to the people," campus revolutionaries have sought to take
over the decision-making processes of many colleges and universities,
seeking to have a say on who is admitted, which teachers are hired
or fired, use of university land, and, to some degree, on what goes on
within the classroom. This attempt to shift power from one group—
the college administration—to another, a student power group which
will determine what type of education it wants, has largely relied on
getting rid of what students don't like, rather than asserting what they

Courtesy of Gyula Szabo

do like. That is, students claim that if given power they will abolish tuition, get rid of ROTC, sever university links to defense research. Yet, the question is rarely raised as to what "positive" quantitative and qualitative differences will ensue if students do take control of the campus community. Will the type of administration substantially change? In other words, what alternative means of administering the campus are available to handle large numbers of students, each one seeking a meaningful and relevant education? Moreover, will only a small clique take control and run the campus as its fiefdom in much the same way as present administrations now govern the campus community? Given that most college students are conformist and apathetic, what is to insure that students and faculty will have any greater interest in governing themselves and handling day-to-day decisions than now?

It is quite often easier to become a campus revolutionary than a societal one because most students do not have jobs, marriage partners, families, or private property (houses and cars). Also, the physical characteristics of the campus community make it easier to mobilize large numbers of students on fairly short notice, creating a feeling of solidarity and a sense of power.[1] Yet, much of this revolution becomes highly academic if for no other reason than because of lack of commitment and responsibility; and this is not just due to the high attrition rate among college students because of graduation. Rather, it is because many campus actions become just another happening—one revolts for a couple of hours, or at best a couple of days. This is not to say that some students are not well-informed on particular issues and are ready to see a revolutionary commitment through to the end. It is just that their numbers are few, and the intensity of their commitment little understood by fellow "activists" or "fellow travelers." And this is again because we are not teaching responsibility, commitment, or creative decision-making. So much easier to come upon a group of people with picket signs on campus and ask "What's happening?"—often meaning, "Can you entertain me for an hour or two between classes?" or "I've got nothing better to do."

It is true that the issues which students raise are serious and involve substantial political and educational questions, but most campus revolutionaries do not go far enough, do not see what is happening within their own ranks, and do not know what they would do should they win. And this is primarily because they have limited their revolt to questions of whether ROTC should be permitted on campus, or if we should have a black studies program—rather than questions about the type of education they want. Of course, it is much easier to seize a building or shoot squirt guns at the ROTC than to create one's own values and undertake a personal commitment toward them; to bear allegiance to yourself rather than the local head of SDS as a source of these values. While the seizure of buildings gains publicity and draws large numbers of students, it does little to alter the daily educational experience most students undergo. This alteration must take place if social change both on campus and in American society is to be more than a coup d'état, a change in who governs rather than an alteration of the type of government which is then to ensue. There is little publicity in self-education, in trying to find out what we want, what we are responsible for. It is quite difficult, for we must entertain ourselves—initiate actions, rather than react to events around us.

In terms of educational reform *the means are the end*. If we are quiet, acquiescent followers during the revolution, going along because it feels comfortable and helps alleviate the boredom, then should the group we have affiliated with seize power, our relationship to them will continue to be much the same as it is to the present administration. What incentive, then, is there for us to change? If, on the other hand, we participate in such a revolution because we know what the issues are, we know what we want to try to do once we have the power— because we have some measure of control over decisions which concern us—then means and ends become consistent, and real change takes place. At the same time, student and campus revolt and reform cannot be divorced from the larger society; the school provides a microcosm for more profound changes in society as a whole. The schools, like citizens, are not neutral: They either work toward changing existing institutions and problems, or they support them. Yet, the university can also provide a ready scapegoat for one to throw himself against when unable to reach those who are a more direct cause of his frustrations. And when such attacks fail, one has little to lose. Prison sentences are rarely handed out for most types of university protest, although they are becoming more frequent.

If most campuses were underdeveloped countries, in which the prime source of alienation was lack of suitable jobs, food, and political representation, what would first have to be altered would be the social system—the way economic goods and jobs are distributed. This might necessitate a dictatorial type of revolution, in which means and ends can be split, the latter justifying the former. However, in so-called developed or overdeveloped societies—Western Europe and the United States—revolution takes on a much different meaning, for here the enemy is of a much different nature.

What if the way of life is the enemy? If such is the case, then to seize college buildings will not necessarily guarantee the fruits of the revolution, even if the administration should give in. If the enemy is a conformist, apathetic student body and populace, then there is little that this type of action can do to alleviate the problem, for the means make the ends impossible to achieve. In fact, by coming to view the problem in terms of *quantitative* solutions, a type of co-optation may result in which would-be revolutionaries come to play the administration's game and are brought off with more positions in departmental meetings, places on university committees, freedom of the press, and so forth. And the average students go their own way, having nothing to say anyhow. Freedom of speech and the press mean very little to them nor do places on committees. In such campus revolts, the issue is no longer who sits at the top of the hierarchy, but what attitude is taken towards self-governance and what do proclaimed values actually mean to those who would preach them—what do they mean in practice? While shouting "Power to the people," in a sense, the enemy may well be the people themselves. In sum, while campus revolts purport to deal with existing problems, they often immerse themselves in lesser issues, and are brought off and co-opted into thinking that they have, in fact, solved the problem, when they really haven't solved anything at all.

Existential Education: Commitment in the Face of Absurdity

Once a class at California State University developed a project, known as "Rap City," in which fifteen tents were set up in the middle of the campus in an attempt to develop an alternative life style. Students slept in the tents for several nights attempting to develop the type of community missing at large state universities and colleges. For the most part, the project was a failure, for other members of the student body and faculty would come by and view the tents as a kind of happening instead of "rapping" about various issues—an alternative to work, material consumption, and empty relationships. They expected to be entertained, and when they were not, they wandered away, no doubt bored, wondering what they had missed. The purpose of "Rap City" had been to get students and faculty to question their values, life styles, laws they lived by, rules they followed, to get them to see that they could create their own life styles. Unfortunately, the main question became "What am I supposed to do at Rap City?" For many members of the class, this was a telling experience, for it demonstrated to them—especially when the instructor refused to create any action— that the project was indeed in their hands, to make of it what they would. They were free to choose, but such freedom wasn't always as much fun as they had envisioned. They found that they did not necessarily want to create their own values, for it was so much easier to remain half-satisfied, and have others tell them either directly or indirectly what to do. This project raised many serious questions in both the students' and the instructor's mind concerning the ability of college students to overcome the conditioning which they have received since kindergarten.[2]

The first step that may be necessary to change this mode is to initiate a type of existential education. Philosophically, existentialism refers to an attitude toward life which posits the individual as living in a basically absurd condition—he is born into a meaningless world in which he is condemned to be free, to choose his own meaning, to live but sixty or seventy years in the face of imminent death. Humans are not immortal: whatever things they accumulate, whatever decisions they make, are temporary at best. The major tenet of existential philosophy is that existence precedes essence. Sartre explains:

> What is meant here by saying that existence precedes essence? It means that, first of all, man exists, turns up, appears on the scene, and, only afterwards defines himself. If man, as the existentialist sees him, is indefinable, it is because at first he is nothing. Only afterwards will he be something, and *he himself will have made what he will be.* . . . Not only is man what he conceives himself to be, but he is also what he *wills* himself to be after this thrust toward existence. Man is nothing other than what he makes himself.[3]

The world, however, does not have to be absurd only because man must ultimately die; and man is not born nothing merely because of philosophic definition. The world can be considered absurd and man free because the society and institutions which he lives within are largely irrelevant to his existence. He is free because these institutions, traditions, and values mean little to him. He is free to create new ones. It can be contended that this is the case today for many persons now living in American society. In recognizing the irrelevance of American institutions and values, one becomes condemned to freedom, to choosing his own life. According to this school of thought, it is the first purpose of education to make the student aware of his existential condition. Students must come to see that there is no certainty in this world, either in terms of educational content or method—everything is a possibility, open to constant and often agonizing change, and criticism and society must come to be viewed in the same light.[4] Both negative as well as positive aspects of life must be exemplified.

Kneeler comments:

> Education itself has a moral duty. It is to lead man through *every* experience that constitutes his life, not veiling or adumbrating the ugly and enhancing the beautiful, not hiding from latent evil and focusing on all-pervading good, but facing squarely what Harper calls all the "wastes of shock, confusion, struggle, failure," and the rest, so that the individual knows them to be a part of life and is . . . ready to meet disaster as well as success. . . . "Education for happiness" is a dangerous doctrine. Why teach such delusion? There is no happiness without pain, no ecstasy without suffering.[5]

In the same sense, education for security is nonsense, for life is founded on insecurity which must be faced and dealt with accordingly. There is no longer any place to escape to, nowhere to hide—freedom can no longer be seen in the negative—*freedom from*. It now becomes *freedom to*—freedom to choose life over death, to make one's own values, to be responsible for one's own life:

> Let education be the process by which we awaken in each learner the truth that *he is responsible for his very desire to flee* responsibility; ". . . the peculiar character of human reality is that it is without excuse." [6]

In the classroom, the student must not become the unwitting victim of a type of self-fulfilling prophecy. He must not be treated with unwarranted expectations: "You are black, therefore you will be a poor student and I will treat you accordingly" or "others have told me of your brightness, therefore I will treat you as if you are an exceptional student." [7] The student must exist on his own standards and merits. The existential teacher's role can be depicted in the following way:

> The teacher is not an actor on a stage in front of an audience, performing so as to elicit applause and acclaim. He does not want imitators. Constructively, he seeks three goals: (1) the treatment of subject matter in such a way as to discover its truth in free association; (2) the achievement of what Harper calls the "autonomous functioning of the mind," in such a way as to produce in his charges a type of character that is "free, charitable, and self-moving"; ("When one sees one's own ideas quoted verbatim, one's heart should sink"); and (3) evidence that his students hold something to be true because they have *convinced themselves* that it is true. This last ideal does not mean that truth is revealed, or instrumental, or discovered, but rather that it has been thought out afresh by every individual student, as if it had never before been conceived.[8]

In other words, if traditional values are indeed worthwhile, if traditional societal institutions are to survive, they must be re-created by each generation. Nothing can or should be accepted *a priori*.

Much of existential educational philosophy contains elements of pragmatism within it—that is, learning is through action, through problem-solving, through engaging in constant confrontations and crises. Students must begin with *their* problems, stated in their language as seen through their eyes.[9] It is up to the teacher to aid them in their quest, to point out other relevant questions, and other social issues which may impinge both on solutions to their problems and lead them to related areas of crisis.[10] Part One of this book was, in part, just such an effort because it attempted to show how many problems relate to each other, and to us, and how solutions to one encompass solutions to others. Teaching comes to be based on questions rather than answers, for answers seem to prestructure the world, to limit inquiry. Questions pose problems.[11] Yet it is important that the teacher demonstrate a commitment and responsibility to his *own search* while at the same time discouraging imitations of his life style. He should not act with certainty and should be open to change. Teaching, in the long run, becomes a contradiction of sorts, for the teacher is teaching students to no longer need him, to rebel against his existence, to challenge everything he says and the society he may inadvertently represent.

The existential challenge for education, then, is to get students and faculty to live active lives. The status quo destroys brain cells and inhibits growth.[12] One must constantly choose, however painful such a choice may be, and one must assume responsibility for such choices, for there is no one else who will make these choices for us.[13] Teachers' ideas come to be submitted to the same criteria as students—*what* is right, rather than *who* is right (not to be confused with the "who we are" and the "what we are").[14] This prevents indoctrination. The goal is to involve students in an existential frame of reference, so that they play a greater part not only in determining their own educations, but in expanding their awareness or consciousness. Education becomes confrontation with other realities, producing growth and creating an awareness of different ways of perceiving the world and of specific problems in that world.

One such program would have students answer each of these questions in turn: Who am I? What problems concern me? Who do I want to be? What is my relationship to others? What is their relationship to me? How might I want to change this relationship? What is the relationship of the group to its individual members? How does personal commitment relate to group commitment? And, what is my relationship to the problems faced by the larger community and society as these problems are mediated by various groups I belong to? Thus, incoming freshmen would undergo a series of reality exploration seminars. In order to find out who they are, they would be asked to view themselves through different mediums—films, books, painting, poetry, sculpture, and so forth. They might sit for hours in a totally dark room with other persons, then grope around such a room, touching, attempting to communicate without words. Similar experiences could take place in woods, at the beach, anywhere.

These seminars might also engage in body painting, sensitivity sessions, verbal encounters, philosophical discussions about the meaning of life, of communication. Video tapes could be employed in filming group interaction, watching ourselves listening to ourselves. Who are we; who do *all* our senses tell us we are? Gradually, we might get a sense of ourselves, what problems we face, and how these problems are related to our interactions with other persons and with the larger society. We might get a sense of our freedom, as well as how this freedom is related to our interdependence with other people. We would find out why we are, in fact, interdependent creatures. As such, we would become *personally* motivated to learn more about society, to change those aspects of society which we find offensive, and what possibilities are open to us. We would learn that we are responsible for our own lives, for the creation of our own values. The freshman year would end with students deciding either to continue or to leave school, to find options for resolving issues they are concerned with.

In this program, individual activities (finding out who we are) give way to group activities and group projects (personal commitment becomes social commitment). Ultimately, the social activities the group, or seminar, creates are related to changing the larger social problems which encompass American society. While beginning with reality exploration in the freshman year, the sophomore program is concerned with the tools necessary to reconstruct society, to bridge the gap between where we are and where we want to be. This might consist either in seminars dealing with tactics or basic courses in sociology, psychology and biology. The upper-division program could revolve around individual or group tutorial programs in which students either remained at college further exploring reality or ways of changing America, or of leaving the campus entirely to work in the community on much the same types of projects. Throughout this program, students as well as teachers would be responsible for setting the curriculum, what they wanted to do and how they wanted to do it—even if this meant destroying the format initially set down above. Does that sound contradictory? Perhaps. But it might be a means to break out of the cycle established by twelve years of regimentation.[15]

Another means of getting students to create their own values is to set them free. One such program is that developed by A. S. Neill:

> My view is that a child is innately wise and realistic. If left to himself without adult suggestion of any kind he will develop as far as he is capable of developing.[16]

This statement is the philosophical base of one of the most "radical" attempts to alter education developed in the twentieth century. Forming a school in England called Summerhill, Neill set out to show that the main restriction to youthful educational growth was adult interference. Neill reversed the traditional dictum: Instead of the child adapting his needs to those of the society through large impersonal educational institutions, the school adapted itself to the needs of the student.[17] Such a proposal is particularly relevant in considering the education of ghetto students who must adapt their values to those of middle-class white society as well as a general alien school framework—only to return home in the late afternoon and early evening to an entirely different cultural orientation. Neill feels that Summerhill creates a type of education for happiness. If the child is free to grow on his own, then he will be happy—and a happy child is a growing child.

The Summerhill approach begs many questions, especially about its adaptability to educational reform in the United States. The main issue raised by critics is whether or not children can grow and regulate their behavior on their own, and if, through such freedom, they can learn responsibility and commitment. This school, like many others, has a "town meeting" to set up rules and regulations and to settle differences. As Neill has pointed out, in a sequel to his Summerhill book, this results in "freedom—not license."

> I define license as interfering with another's freedom. For example, in my school a child is free to go to lessons or stay away from lessons because that is his own affair, but he is not free to play a trumpet when others want to study or sleep.[18]

There is something in the attitude at Summerhill which conveys a responsibility for one's actions vis-à-vis others, and probably a sense of commitment toward the school itself which grows from the development of any small community—at least at its founding. Holt believes that sensitivity to the feelings of others at Summerhill is derived from free and open interaction:

> Because Neill's reaction is immediate, personal, and authentic, not impersonal, bureaucratic, and assumed, it is instructive. Now and then, as when a child swipes one of his garden tools just when he needs to use it, he may get angry. His anger conveys to children what really is wrong about stealing—that it hurts the person you steal from. It has nothing

to do with anything so abstract and foolish, not to say mistaken, as the notion that property and property rights are sacred. What counts is that when you take something from someone you inflict on him a time and energy wasting, anxious, painful experience. He hunts frantically for the missing object, can't find it, tries to think where he might have put it, wonders whether he might have left or lost it somewhere else, wonders whether someone else might have borrowed it and forgot to tell him, wonders later whether whoever took it will remember to return it, or even means to return it, wonders if it was taken on purpose, which of his enemies or even friends might have done it, wonders perhaps whether his friends really are his friends. All this hurts. Moreover, whatever it was he wanted to do, he can't do, because of what is missing. When we steal from people, this is what we do to them. They hate it, and we shouldn't do it. This is what children learn from the quick and natural of people from whom they steal.[19]

But the primary question is that education involves almost constant growth and change, growth and change which is often painful for it forces us to give up old and comfortable ways of viewing the world. Such educational growth does not always arise automatically from leaving the child alone as in the Summerhill approach. Often it is necessary to have others question our values and ideas, to challenge our complacency, to confront us with certain issues and questions relevant to our existence and to our interaction with others. "Doing your own thing" has often been used as a justification for the worst form of copping out—watching others being beaten or killed. Nor do "free schools" necessarily prepare one for living in and transforming a regimented society. There is no automatic transition. Moreover, if education means growth, such growth cannot always be judged by happy educational experiences, by contented faces and smiles. Happiness and education are not necessarily compatible; in fact, a good case can be made for the idea that man's emotional make-up is created through a conflict of opposites. What one does educate for is knowledge—either for its own sake or as a means to action, to prepare oneself for action, for handling painful and anxiety-producing questions.

Summerhill is a small isolated rural English experimental school which in the past has attracted the parents of many youths who were considered delinquent by the surrounding society. Neill attempted to show that if the negatives of the larger society were removed, the positive would develop of its own. But one does not have to leave the child completely alone to avoid impinging on his freedom; one can attempt to bring out what is already in the child. Since a new society cannot develop simply by dropping out of the old one, we must encourage and challenge each other to create such a society.

> We can think of ourselves not as teachers but as gardeners. A gardener does not "grow" flowers; he tries to give them what he thinks will help them grow, and they grow by themselves. A child's mind, like a flower, is a living thing. We can't make it grow by sticking things onto it any more than we can make a flower grow by gluing on leaves and petals. All we can do is surround the growing mind with what it needs for growing, and have faith that it will take what it needs and grow.[20]

Can such principles as Neill developed apply to large public schools and colleges in the United States? Or can some modification of Neill's philosophy come to take form here? One such proposal is the University Without Walls in the Midwest. The following statement gives a brief indication of the form of the university:

1. Admission: Persons 16–60 years of age, interested to learn [sic].
2. Program for each student worked out individually to meet his needs and interests.
3. An Inventory of Learning Resources, well-indexed [computer memory-bank?], will direct the learner to sources (print, tape, persons, laboratories, etc.) of knowledge he seeks.
4. Courses, laboratories, studios, etc. in all the participating colleges will be open to qualified U.W.W. students, but most of the learning will be independent and self-directed, carried out by the student alone or with a small group of peers.
5. A student begins his work by attending for one quarter [10 weeks?] a center on or near the campus of one of the participating colleges. Here he meets his fellow students, a team of faculty representing different specialties, and with his advisor works out his personal learning program. He attends two groups during the first quarter—one directed to understanding self and others (L-group), the other toward improving basic learning skills.
6. From time to time, a student will again join a group of peers [with homogeneous or heterogeneous interests] at one of the campus centers.
7. At least one term will be spent in an off-campus field center; some students may live for a time in each of several different subcultures in the U.S.A. and abroad.
8. A dialogue is continuously maintained between each student and

his advisor. This may be done face-to-face, or by letters, or telephone, or tapes, or records, or papers read and returned with comments. Communication between a student and other faculty, and a student with his peers is also expected.

9. "Faculty" for the U.W.W. may include, in addition to persons teaching in one of the participating colleges, experts from any walk of life: agriculture, business, science, the arts, politics, etc.

10. Each student will complete at least one major project of excellent quality in his chosen field of work.

11. Each student keeps a cumulative record of his activities and learning. He may use standardized tests for his own guidance.

12. If a student wants a Bachelor of Arts degree he applies when he believes he is ready for it. No fixed Commencement dates. His achievements are reviewed by a committee of faculty and students, who recommend a degree or further study.[21]

There are other types of experimental programs which view the student as the locus of creating his own values and his own educational experience, indeed, his own life. There is a college which grants a degree after four years no matter what you have done. Perhaps the most popular of such programs have been the "free universities" which have developed to sponsor activities and curricula unavailable under more so-called "legitimate" forms of education. Some of these universities have grown up within the walls of academia, while many others have chosen, for one reason or another, to stay outside campus walls. The following statement of purposes is from the catalogue of the Midpeninsula Free University, at one time one of the largest in the country.

PREAMBLE

What an organization does is the best indication of what it is. And the various activities described in this catalog give, perhaps, the clearest picture of what the Midpeninsula Free University is all about. Yet since what we are doing falls short of what we hope to do it has been felt that some statement of our intentions is necessary. We feel that the American educational establishment has proven incapable of meeting the needs of our society. It often discourages students from thinking critically, and does not afford them meaningful training to help them understand the crucial issues confronting mankind today. Bound to the existing power structure, and handicapped by modes of thought fostered by big business, by the military establishment, by consensus politics, and by the mass media, it is unable to consider freely and objectively the cultural, economic and political forces so rapidly transforming the modern world. The present educational system in fact defends the status quo, perpetuating its evils and perils. The system has become rigid; it is no longer receptive to meaningful change. A revolution in American education is required to meet today's needs, and a new type of education—a free university—must provide the impetus for change.

therefore we affirm:

That freedom of inquiry is the cornerstone of education.

That each individual must generate his own vital questions and program his own education, free from central control by administrative bureaucracies and disciplinary oligarchies.

That the class character of age in our society subverts education, and that the young are not too young to teach, nor the old too old to learn.

That education is not a commodity, and should not be measured in units, grade points and degrees.

That education aims at generality rather than specialization, and should supply the glue which cements together our fragmented lives.

That education is a process involving the total environment, which can only occur in a total community, in which each individual participates equally in making the decisions which importantly affect his life.

That education which has no consequences for social action or personal growth is empty.

That action which does not raise our level of consciousness is futile.

That the ultimate politics will be based on knowledge, liberty, and community, rather than on hate, fear, or guilt.

That the most revolutionary thing we can do is think for ourselves, and regain contact with our vital centers.

That the most important questions which confront us must be asked again and again and answered again and again, until the millennium comes.

That the natural state of man is ecstatic wonder.[22]

An example of some of the courses which can be taken at this particular Free University are the following:

EN-22 IMAGINATIVE REALISM:

Reality can be a good trip, and imagination can help energy go in the right directions. We will develop trust and awareness by means of encounter, yoga, psychodrama, dance, music and hypnotism. We will try to stay at the growing tip of your awareness. No rough stuff, but we hope much excitement. Dress comfortably.

Thursdays, 7:30 Los Altos.

EN-38 LET'S GET FUCKED UP AGAIN

I'm getting so tired of being straightened out by encounter classes that I don't know what to do with the rest of my life. I think it's time to get fucked up again and start over. In this class, we'll go out to topless joints, move to the suburbs, throw cocktail parties, bitch about our mates, buy suits, bras, makeup, and the *Ladies Home Journal,* take diet pills, and get into alcoholism, insensitivity training, and how to be uptight, bourgeois, fascistic, frigid, and uninvolved. Before coming to class, tell a hippie to get a haircut, and buy Savings Bonds or Freedom Shares. European descent only, please.

Friday: 8:00 P.M. Chuck's Steak House, Los Altos.

Fee: $19.95. Charge for expenses: $4.85 a fifth.

PL-15 HIKING

We will take some one-day hikes, nearby, usually on weekends but possibly during the week. We will also take some weekend trips farther away. We choose our own route when that seems more interesting than the trails.[23]

Other classes include "Graffiti on the Wall," "Anarchy," "Counter-insurgency in Thailand," and "Paper Airplanes."

In general, experimental colleges and free universities may offer the following advantages over traditional liberal arts colleges and universities:

1. They close the gap between "academic" and "real" life. Students in most experimental colleges ostensibly make no separation between the way they live their lives and the types of college activities they engage in: Whatever they are doing is always "relevant," for education is not limited to the classroom experience.

2. They make it possible for students to plan their own curricula, select classmates, hire and fire faculty, in essence, to create their own lives. They enable students to assume responsibility for their actions.

3. They are flexible; programs can immediately be scrapped if they are not working out. In this sense, they are educating for a society in which change is a constant.

4. They build a sense of community. Most experimental college programs are small, have frequent planning sessions and social get-togethers which throw members in constant contact with each other. Moreover, living arrangements among students and faculty are often of a communal nature, which cuts out formality and phoniness.

5. Lines between faculty and students are often not clearly drawn, thus enabling almost anyone to be able to teach a class or become a student in one. Most seminars are run as research teams exploring different types of questions, rather than as formal lecture situations. Status is quickly dispensed with. Teachers are called by their first names and subject to the same type of criticism as any student. Flexibility in teaching enables members of the surrounding community to offer courses which might otherwise have little chance of appearing on most college campuses.

6. Experimental colleges not only bridge the gap between "academic" and "real," but they also tend to provide opportunities for

students and faculty to apply the results of their research, encouraging community involvement in pressing social problems. Having "value-free" education is not usually a crucial issue.

7. There are typically no grading pressures, with most classes being offered under systems of pass-fail, or pass-incomplete. Evaluations are not strictly left to the instructor, but may be based on the concurrence of peers or one's own judgment.

While experimental colleges have many advantages, particularly when their programs are more "paper" than reality, they also suffer from numerous difficulties which make their operation sometimes arduous.

1. Many students enrolled in experimental college programs find great difficulty in breaking the "entertain-me" cycle engendered by attending twelve years of public school. As such, they are not used to running their own lives or being committed to self-education. They don't know how to use the freedom they are suddenly faced with. Consequently, they have trouble following through on programs and curricula which they initiate.

2. Being unable to assume responsibility for their own actions, students often do not show up for seminars they have created. Yet, they become frustrated when they realize they have no one to blame but themselves.

3. Freedom in experimental college programs often comes to mean freedom to escape, to avoid confrontations either with oneself or with material that is juxtaposed to one's reality framework. Many times students expect to be rewarded for "doing their own thing," meaning being left alone. If education does not expand awareness, however, then it is not education at all but a maintenance of the status quo. As such, many students end up taking all guitar classes or courses in cooking, enterprises they could very well undertake outside the college.

4. In relation to the avoidance of confrontations, experimental colleges are often beset by problems of defining what is and is not a relevant curriculum, particularly in those programs administered by state-supported institutions. There are usually three types of students that can be found in an experimental program: those who desire traditional academic training but under a more flexible rubric than regular college; those who want to "get their heads together"; and those who need college as a place to avoid making decisions, as an excuse for not working, or as a means of escaping the burdens of

living in American society in general. Frequent discussion over what a given college should emphasize often creates factions among both faculty and students, turning planning sessions into sham debates where the vote has already been predetermined by yesterday's meeting. This is not to say that debate about such issues is not relevant and stimulating; rather, many programs never get beyond this point.

5. Many experimental college programs are financed directly by state-supported institutions or are an adjunct of those institutions. As such, these programs are not really free of such things as filling general education requirements as defined by state boards of trustees or regents. Freedom to create a different type of curriculum exists more in name then in fact when those who are creating that program must submit their results to an evaluation team outside the experimental college. At the same time, however, links with established institutions are often necessary in order to achieve accreditation, as many students want to go on to graduate or professional schools. Some students request grades rather than pass-fail, and many of the same problems that exist in regular colleges also come to exist in those of a more experimental nature. Experimental colleges, thus, do not exist in a vacuum, and problems of financing and accreditation, even for those which call themselves "private," are unavoidable issues.

6. Many experimental colleges, while claiming greater flexibility, are often of narrower teaching scope then more established and traditional institutions. This is because they have a small number of faculty, who are usually generalists rather than specialists. Therefore, someone who wants to become an artist, for example, can often do better in more specialized programs.

In large part, the type of criticism one levels at experimental college programs depends on who one is and from what vantage point he is speaking. Changing our multiversities into experimental colleges is one of the primary means of organizing for social change in America.[24]

Most freshmen entering college have little idea of what they want to study or even what questions they want to ask. In fact, most freshmen don't want to be freshmen at all, it's just that there's nothing else to do, no place else to go. Perhaps a couple of years' break between high school and college would provide a means of maturing, of finding out about life on one's own while not under parental or college guidance, and would prove a far better form of education than being forced into some type of school program, no matter how experimental. After such a "sabbatical," if they do desire to return to school, they will have a better idea of the questions they want to ask, and the problems they want to solve; they might be more personally motivated to undergo the rigors of a disciplined confrontation and challenge, or to make a commitment necessary to bring about educational reform and change. Having thousands of youth wandering through the streets and country side would, of course, pose a problem in a society used to law-and-order and regimentation.

Schools as New Environments

As our society changes more and more rapidly, the creation and acceptance of alternative life styles and forms of consciousness will become a primary goal of education. In this enterprise, technology can prove of vital assistance, not only by providing teaching machines, computers and closed-circuit television, but also in the stimulation and creation of new environments which challenge students' minds and ways of viewing the world. Again, such machines and technologies are only auxiliary aids in the education process and should be thought of as such. Students should not be taught according to the needs of machines they would learn from. One example of how technology can create a new learning environment is provided by Leonard in his book *Education and Ecstasy*. He describes children sitting in large domes which house individual learning centers which provide that, at the touch of a finger, questions and answers may be pictorially projected onto a screen, or translated into other symbolic representations. Similarly, the child can have a dialogue with a computer which constantly challenges him not only to consider different possibilities, but also to think of them in other logical forms, or through the use of other senses.[25] In other parts of this same school, children learn to re-create and role-play different cultures and different historical situations; to "bust their realities" and expand their consciousness. In such a way history becomes real, and different cultures come alive in the possibilities they hold for American society in the incorporation of different ideas and values as alternatives to contemporary dialogue.[26]

Teach-Out

Educational reform and innovation does not take place in a vacuum, nor can what goes on in high schools, colleges, and universities be divorced from the society of which it is a part. Students at all educational levels must be exposed to learning more than "old things" in new ways (the practice of many experimental schools and "open" classrooms). Rather, social problems, the tactics of social change, and doing social change must become a part of every curriculum. Many colleges and universities, as a result of the Cambodian crisis of 1970, have been talking about reconstituting themselves: All departments would direct their efforts to the resolution of contemporary social issues. Thus, art departments might graphically depict a given issue, drama departments play out its consequences, engineering units delve into its technical aspects, and social scientists find out ways of solving the human conflicts involved. The community would also participate, since it would be this community which would feel the primary brunt of reconstitution efforts. The gap between the university and the surrounding society would be broken down as white- and blue-collar workers met with college students and faculty in attempts to find out how American society can be changed and many of its problems resolved. Classes could be held in the suburbs, in storefronts, in downtown areas, and on farms. Ideas would not be divorced from action. The community comes to have its values directly challenged and, in turn, it could challenge the programs put forth by former members of ivory towers and "summer camps." No longer does the campus merely *react* to legislative investigation and witch hunts; rather, it acts in concert with the community to change the status quo. In this way, one does not go to school for four years: There is no graduation; education is for keeps.

We Are the New Society

There is another means of reconstituting American society. While teach-outs may make piecemeal attempts at reviving the system and altering it, this tactic may be unable to change the entire society at once. Why not make existing colleges and universities into the new society: *refuse to graduate,* to become a part of the consumer–military–industrial complex; refuse to go to work; to go into the army; to shop at Macy's; stay where we are and, in so doing, destroy the outmoded and alienating institutions of America. This is not as outlandish as it may first appear. Most students do not want to graduate. They find comfort, companionship, and solace in the campus community. They don't want to go to work, but few other alternatives have been proposed to them. Being caught up in the same "entertain me" philosophy as their parents, they are waiting for something to happen, rather than making it happen themselves. This is only one side of the coin, however, for most industries cannot presently employ those who will graduate: They would just as soon see their sons and daughters remain in school.

Given that a change in values would make most existing work unnecessary, that technology would easily satisfy basic food, clothing, and shelter needs, the time has come to create a society based on other values, such as relating to people, learning, creativity, and political participation. What better place to start such a society than in campus communities already oriented to a large degree toward these very values?

The first step would be to prevent all students from graduating, by eliminating the bachelor's degree and making the Ph.D. the only certificate of educational achievement awarded. This would be only the first step. The Ph.D. would soon vanish, however, as soon as it became apparent that there was no longer any place to graduate to. The change-over could be facilitated in reality by keeping the bachelor's degree but making it impossible for anyone to receive it. Thus, sociology majors would be required to take courses in sociological theory and methods, but such courses would never be offered, because the faculty would only teach electives. The state legislature and anxious parents, at least for the first couple of years, would continue to finance such educational institutions, in that they would either not realize what was taking place, or would rationalize it.

The campus, no longer having to grant degrees, would expand its curriculum. Engineering and physical-science schools would develop machines for taking care of basic physical wants. The social sciences and humanities would create seminars in political participation; the gap between administrators, faculty, and students would break down; and "citizens" would reconstitute themselves on the basis of a new electorate and governing body which would consist of *all members* of the new society. In such an atmosphere, there would be little reason for students to stall around: This community would be whatever they would make of it, there would be nothing left to wait for.

After a few years, the larger society might begin to need college graduates both to work in its industries, to buy its commodities, and to serve in its wars. But by then it would be too late, for the colleges would have done their job and students would have little need for leaving a society they have themselves constructed. In this way, the argument presented in Chapter 12 is carried to its logical conclusion: The old order is destroyed—not violently, but by refusing to participate in and acknowledge its values. Gradually, these new societies would link with one another and set up outposts in the surrounding community, attracting disenchanted engineers, politicians, white- and blue-collar workers, and the poor. The larger society could not very well destroy these communities, for they would need those who inhabited them, the youth of America, and would soon become dependent on these youth as the key to America's future. Instead of attacking the old society, then, colleges form their own positive affirmation of a new community, one not only inhabited by college students, but by all age levels who want an alternative to what is. It would be in the crises that such a move created that America might be fundamentally altered.

Recreation as a Subversive Activity: Make Up Your Own Games

Recreation, viewed typically as an extracurricular activity on most campuses, reflects the dominant values, institutions, and images of American society. It cannot be ignored in our search for solutions. With the current and projected increases in leisure time made available by shorter work weeks, longer vacation periods and rising salaries, recreation will come to provide a means by which most Americans attempt to act out frustrations stemming from their inability to find a meaningful and worthwhile identity in other aspects of their lives. However, if recreation is but "more of the same," then it can do no more then reinforce and give legitimacy to an America which is rapidly destroying itself. Recreation, however, can become a vehicle for social change.

What values and images does recreation in America create and reinforce? One of the first things a child learns on the playgrounds of his elementary school is that he must play the games the teacher selects. He cannot make up his own games as he does with his friends, nor can he change the rules anymore. Once outside the schools, the same attitude prevails: American society is a given; its values and rules are sacred, they cannot be tampered with; one either learns to play *the* game or is denied recognition and legitimacy, and ultimately is ostracized.

In a similar sense, the blind acceptance of games as givens, also breeds a good deal of passivity into the heads of young children, for while they are *active* in playing basketball or football, they learn to be on the receiving end of a set of directions, not to question the way games are played, only, if ever, who wins and loses. Communications are mostly one-way, from the rule book, the coach and the playground director to the child; never from the child to the playground director to the rule book. This process of communication is also found in the relationships of teacher to pupil in the classroom, in the relationship of commercials on television to the passive viewer, in the relationship of politicians to the public they serve, and in the relationship of professional sports to spectators. Needlees to say, recreation preserves the status quo.

Recreation is perhaps the last bastion of competition in an America where the economy is planned by the five hundred largest corporations, and where the average middle-management employee cares more about his retirement, health and medical benefits, job security and accumulated vacation (the fringe benefits) than rising to the top of the corporation. Much the same attitude, as we have noted, holds true for life in the suburbs. Why then does recreation still preserve the competitive state of mind? What is one competing for? In a sense, recreation serves the function of substitute gratification; if competition is taken out of the job and marketplace, then one can take out his frustrations in the form of make-believe games. We make believe that winning or losing is significant, both when we are the players of the games in school and then later as spectators vicariously identifying with and living through the feats of professional athletes.

In part, the existence of competition in recreation confuses us, for it is valued on the playing field but may be considered even subversive when transferred to our *real* roles. Most competitive games or sports have a reward system where there are "winners" and "losers." This bolsters the identities of those who cannot seem to find any innate rewards from their regular activities. Thus, the student who must memorize large amounts of data, rather than work on solving a problem which is immediate, personal and relevant for his continued existence and survival, is rewarded by making the honor society or the dean's list. In the same way, the basketball team gets a trophy for winning the tournament. But what does such a victory symbolize? So one makes honor roll, so we win the basketball tournament. Have either of these enabled us to deal with and solve the problems stemming from values and institutions which frustrate and endanger our lives at every turn? We can make a hundred dean's lists, but education will continue to be just as boring and irrelevant. And what of those who don't win? What then of the hundreds of losers who make the winners' victory possible, and the thousands of spectators who are not even allowed to compete in the tourney because they lack the skill and competence and can never attain it—the permanent losers? What kind of society is it that builds up and plays upon such a dichotomy, making false victories the only ones possible? There are heroes, but only in the eyes of others. There is little self-satisfaction when nothing has been achieved, no real problems dealt with—when the applause has died down and we are alone.

It has been said that sports and recreation as currently practiced build discipline and stamina; yet they also build conformity, passivity, and the desire to win. With increasing technological mechanization it is doubtful, though, that recreation will continue to build stamina: One will simply lie down in the gym and different machines will do things *to* him; the same for hunting, fishing, golf, just as American society does things to us. But it *is* fun and comfortable, just as it is fun and comfortable to shop at Macy's, buying superfluous commodities which use up raw materials from parts of the world which desperately need such materials, and then dispose of these items and create pollution. But shopping is fun. In the same sense, just because we feel comfortable and secure playing football, baseball, and basketball does not mean that the consequences of participating in these activities are not damaging in the types of people they produce. The Romans no doubt enjoyed watching the Christians being fed to the lions.

In order to change recreation, to break the cycle caused by the acceptance of a *priori* rules and values, and the "entertain-me," "win-lose" ramifications which inevitably result, "recreation" must be taken at its word meaning: to *re-create*. Children on playgrounds would be permitted, or situations set up whereby they could *create their own games and rules*, where games and rules could constantly be brought under fresh examination and altered, where the process of creating games and rules would take precedence over preserving outmoded forms of recreation. Emphasis would be on flexibility, on constant change, rather than bolstering up an already shaky status quo.

As the creation of one's own games and rules can only grow out of personal experience, so too, success in these games can only be based on self-evaluation. As the scientist attempting to find a cure for leukemia is not worried about who else finds a cure first, but rather desires to cooperate with them in the pursuit of finding such a cure, so too, cooperation comes to pervade these new games. Success comes to be measured by the types of relationships that evolve in the course of the game, in the types of insights one gets, in the types of values developed: Recreation is no longer "extracurricular"; rather, it is the way you live your life. Similarly, no game would have a higher status than any other, because playing a game such as baseball, when you really wanted to play "zenobogan," a game you had created, would not make any sense. The false reward system would come, on elementary-school playgrounds and gradually in the society at large, to be seen for what it is

The initiation of the "creating your own games program" would no doubt raise havoc among parents who want to see their child be the starting pitcher on the local little league team, and so efforts would have to be made to invite parents to also participate in creating their own games, or a least to give them an understanding of what you are trying to do. Ultimately, the creation of one's own games leads to the creation of one's own life styles, to a participatory democracy. In a society with an increasing amount of leisure time, recreation will become a key to the future, either subverting what is or maintaining the last dregs of a tradition still trying to sell itself on its own worth.

NOTES

[1] Seymour M. Lipset, "American Student Activism," in Gary R. and James H. Weaver, The University and Revolution (Englewood Cliffs, N.J.: Spectrum, 1969), p. 33.

[2] Neil Postman and Charles Weingartner, Teaching as a Subversive Activity (New York: The Delacorte Press, 1970), p. 14.

[3] Cited in George F. Kneller, Existentialism and Education (New York: John Wiley & Sons, Inc., 1964), p. 3.

[4] Van Cleve Morris, Existentialism in Education (New York: Harper & Row, Publishers, 1966), p. 119.

[5] Kneller, op. cit., p. 84.

[6] Ibid.

[7] Herbert R. Kohl, The Open Classroom (New York: Random House, Inc., 1969), p. 19.

[8] Kneller, op. cit., p. 116.

[9] Postman and Weingartner, op. cit.

[10] Kneller, op. cit., p. 136.

[11] Postman and Weingartner, op. cit.

[12] George B. Leonard, Education and Ecstasy (New York: Dell, 1968), p. 217.

[13] Kneller, p. 156.

[14] Ernest E. Bayles, Pragmatism in Education (New York: Harper & Row, Publishers, 1966), p. 87.

[15] For a similar proposal see, Robert Theobald, "Freedom in Education: The Internal and the External Crisis," Weaver and Weaver, pp. 96–98.

[16] Cited in Fred M. Hechinger's article in Summerhill: For and Against (New York: Hart Publishing Co., Inc., 1970), p. 35.

[17] Ashley Montagu, in Summerhill: For and Against, op. cit., p. 49.

[18] Cited in Bruno Bettelheim, in *Summerhill: For and Against, op. cit.,* p. 106.

[19] John Holt, in *Summerhill: For and Against, op. cit.* p. 91.

[20] Eda J. Leshan, in *Summerhill: For and Against, op. cit.,* p. 134.

[21] Goodwin Watson, in *Ibid.,* pp. 187–189.

[22] From the Midpeninsula Free University Catalogue, Palo Alto, California.

[23] *Ibid.*

[24] For discussions of experimental college programs see, Jerry Gaff (ed.), *The Cluster College* (San Francisco: Jossey-Bass, 1970); Judson Jerome, *Culture Out of Anarchy* (New York: Herder and Herder, Inc., 1970); Harold Taylor, *How to Change the College* (New York: Holt, Rinehart & Winston, Inc., 1971). See also William Caspery, "Experimental Colleges: Some Problems and Solutions," October, 1970 (unpublished); Conrad A. Balliet, "Impressions of Changes," 1971 (unpublished); Kenneth Freeman, "Bensalem, the Experimental College at Fordham University: A Personal Report," 1970 (unpublished).

[25] Leonard, *op. cit.,* pp. 147–150.

[26] *Ibid.,* pp. 166–172.

15

will the real self please stand up: encounter groups and sensitivity sessions

I do my thing, and you do your thing.
I am not in this world to live up to your expectations
And you are not in this world to live up to mine.
You are you and I am I,
And if by chance we find each other, it's beautiful.
    If not, it can't be helped.[1]

—Fritz Perls

You are invited to the mountains on a retreat. You know very few people, but then, someone has said it may be interesting and there is nothing else to do. You arrive at a lodge nestled among large pine trees, people drinking early morning coffee to wake up. There are seventy-five of you, more or less, standing around. Someone comes in and tells everyone to take off their shoes and lie down on the floor. You are to participate in a sensitivity session. You lie on your back, close your eyes, and the leader tells you to breathe deeply, and you can hear seventy-five people inhale, hold their breath and slowly exhale. And again. And again. The silence, except for the breathing, is almost deafening. You feel the breath coming in and going out. You are asked to tense your leg muscles and then release. And your abdominal muscles. And your stomach muscles, your breast muscles, your neck muscles, your facial muscles. You gradually begin to become aware of your body. Your thoughts begin to slowly slip away. This is you, but you've never quite thought about YOU in this way before. You begin to relax, and think less about those you are going to meet, about those you already know, about past and future.

Everyone stands up and with their eyes closed and hands at their sides slowly begin to move about the room, exploring the space around them, bumping into other bodies, a giggle here and there, moving about the room. You are asked to stop and reach out and pick out one other person with your eyes closed and, when you have, to separate yourself from the group and to sit down facing each other. You take the other person's hands and try to tell what kind of person they are by the touch of their fingers; you try to send a message through your hands to their hands. You reach out and feel their face with your eyes eyes closed—their hair, the shape of their nose and chin. What kind of person are they? How do they feel to you—callous, aggressive, gentle, kind? You open your eyes and stare into the eyes of the person opposite you, and they into yours. What do their eyes say to you? Who are they? What separates the two of you? You are told to show the other person how you feel. You hug them. You close your eyes again and find another partner—this time, you hope, someone of the opposite sex. You fight the temptation to peek to half open your eyes. You know you're not supposed to hustle, but it's hard to fight the "system," to treat everyone as a human being, to find out what you have in common with everyone.

You (a male) are with a girl this time. You are told to find out who she is by exploring her form, her face. They've got to be kidding. You are being lifted up into the air by a group of eight people whom you have been told to trust; you are being swung back and forth by these people–strangers before today. You are floating free but warm and close to those who hold you above them. You are rolling over and over bodies stretched out on the floor. Everyone is laughing, and they are rolling over you. You are in a tight circle together, feeling the group together, rocking slowly back and forth together, chanting "Om" together, hugging each other together, crying together (the wine of communion—a shared tear).

You're stoned, but have smoked nothing. You're stoned on the people you've met today in the woods—their shapes, their smells, their laughter, their eyes and hands. Now you are talking to them, listening to them, feeling with them; the past and future have disappeared, the clock has stopped—you are holding hands with a present which lasts forever.

Such is your first non-verbal encounter. Sensitivity sessions and encounter groups are tactics used to get our heads together, to better our relationships with other people, and to acquaint us with human potentials and possibilities. As such, they become part of the arsenal of strategies which can be employed to change American society and to bust reality.

In the Beginning: The Underpinnings of the Encounter Movement

The encounter group movement traces its history to early experiments in psychodrama conducted by Moreno in the late thirties. From these early role-playing groups, The National Training Laboratory was formed in 1947 to develop human relations skills. Called "T-Groups" these sessions were designed to aid management personnel in their communication with one another. It was felt that these groups would provide primary links between the individual and the larger social structure, thus acting as an aid to both learning and rehabilitation.[2]

More recently, encounter groups have taken a variety of different forms, perhaps the most popular of which draws its perspective from Gestalt psychology. Gestalt psychology holds, in brief, that an individual must be experienced in terms of his "field" or surroundings, and that individuals themselves are fields; consequently, a person must be able to experience his whole self, not just a part of it. Gestalt therapy attempts to get us to become aware of our Gestalt, or totality, to fill in the holes in our personality, to find out who we are. One means of doing this is by telling given individuals how we really experience them, without put-on smiles and phony handshakes. This aids them by shattering illusions they may have been living under.[3] By learning to accept who we are, we learn to live in the present, without unwarranted expectations; otherwise, we are never aware of ourselves, we are always somewhere else and, indeed, someone else,[4] in the past or future. Gunther puts it this way:

> If you carefully observe your behavior, you will find yourself seldom making direct contact with reality, and much of the time conceptualizing your existence. By verbalizing, analyzing, and imagining, you filter the unique, evolving differences of each event. Most people react to new situations in established patterns, allowing past experience to dictate or color the actual. Rather than being in contact with what is, they con-

tinually operate from a frame of reference of how things were, how things should be, how they would like them to be.[5]

As we become aware of who we are, of our body and our mind and of those persons and events around us, of our entire Gestalt, we come to accept responsibility for our own actions, because we know, for the most part, "who did it." At the same time, we come to have some control over our lives.[6]

From its early beginnings the encounter method has spread both to those who want to adjust to the norm of American society (get over their "mental illness"), and those who want to break beyond this norm, to become acquainted with aspects of themselves they never thought they had. As one becomes sensitive to himself, he becomes sensitive to others, and to a society which is a part of him, his self, and his potentialities. It is a both-win type of situation. In developing oneself, one must change American society. To change oneself without realizing and working for change in the larger arena is not to change oneself at all, but rather to live in a vacuum, in which one's "new self" becomes as phony as the old.[7]

The basic task of changing or opening a person up can be seen in a number of ways depending on the particular author one is referring to. For example, William Schutz sees it as a threefold approach:

(1) removal of emotional blocks; (2) development of an awareness of himself and his feelings; and (3) development of a sensitivity and perceptiveness about other people and the world around him.[8]

Regardless of the way personal change is conceptualized, one finds that interpersonal relationships can become an art form, and relating to others becomes a creative act.[9] Guided by experimentation and sensitivity, we let whatever happens happen and see how we feel,[10] not out of moral abstention, but out of a sensitivity to ourselves and others. Many changes which come about through encountering may not be perceived immediately, yet it prepares us for future change by showing us the possibilities of a self we never knew we had. The process, however, is not particularly comfortable or always beautiful, hence the "encountering."

Who Are We?: Finding Out About Ourselves

Since the mind and the body are both related, a tense body will make for a tense mind, and vice versa. Thus, we must first set about finding out how to relieve these tensions in order to relax our minds. Once relaxed, we will be able to find out about our "lost" senses, those aspects of our body which have been dulled, repressed, or forgotten about in the artificial, hurried atmosphere of American society. As we begin to develop these senses, we will come to realize how much we have been missing, and what effect this absence has had on our interpersonal relationships, and on problems which these relationships call to mind.

Numerous exercises are available to help you relax your body. For example, lie down, close your eyes, and try to empty your mind of all thoughts. Try breathing in and out and concentrate on how the air feels when inside your lungs and when entering and leaving your lungs. Tense various muscles in your body; concentrate on these muscles, see how they work, come to feel their working within you. You might try screaming as loud as you can to release the tensions you feel, or smashing a pillow aganist the bed or wall until you have drained off excess pressure.[11]

After you have relaxed you can begin to sensitize yourself not only to your environment, but also to your five senses, to re-experience these within yourself. One of the exercises which may help in this effort is to put different smelling articles and organic substances (food) in a paper bag, then pass the bag around a room of friends who can only smell, not touch or look at the contents. Still another variation of this is to put differently shaped and textured substances in a bag and have each person reach in and touch whatever happens to be in it. You can also try eating silently by yourself or with a group, listening to the sounds of munching, concentrating on the taste of what you are eating, and the digestive process. Feel a glass of wine running down your throat; what does horseradish do to your tongue? [12]

Another way of becoming acquainted with your body, and the environment immediately surrounding it, is to sit silently, either in the woods, on campus someplace, anywhere. Listen to yourself, and to your environment, to the noise around you, the sounds. One sociology class sat silently in a bank listening to the sounds of rustling money, tickertapes, computers, and the voices of bureaucratized tellers. Try to see what the relationship between yourself and your environment is, not by analyzing it, but by *feeling* it, by sensing it, the relationship between your hand and your eye, your eye and your mind, between your eye and the leaves lying on the ground, and the voices around you.

Finally, you might try fingerpainting again. What types of sensations does such an experience leave in your fingers? Put a record on—first acid rock, then jazz, then classical. Do these differences in environmental sounds make a difference in your fingerpainting, in what you draw, in your relationship to the fingerpaints and canvas before you? Why?

Becoming aware of ourselves can of course go much further than this. Zen Buddhists employ a wide variety of techniques and rituals to find out who it is that is doing the action. Who is it that is thinking when we are thinking? Who is it that is touching the objects in the bag? Have you ever been able to see yourself—see yourself walking? Becoming aware of ourselves also means becoming aware of others in our environment (Gestalt), and seeing how these others relate to us.

Let It All Hang Out: Nonverbal Encountering

Sidney Jourard has commented:

> If it is true that modern man lives out of his body, in a state of relative "unembodiment" . . . then I can surely awaken your experience of your body by touching you. And if Being discloses itself to our consciousness via our sensory channels, then I can inquire into the means by which you disclose your being to me. How do you let me perceive you? Via my eyes? Ears? My touch receptors? . . . For you to let me know you by touching you, you have to let me get "closer" to you than if you limit yourself to verbal disclosure. When you let me touch you, you are disclosing your embodied being to my consciousness, by means of my tactual sense.[13]

Nonverbal communication is a means of awakening people and communicating where words are often lacking. In fact, in many instances it is best to begin with nonverbal communication even before attempting a verbal encounter, for through nonverbal means a closeness and empathy may be established which will aid the verbal communication process. Moreover, if we begin by touching, this prevents others from using words as defense mechanisms, to hide behind, to escape.

There are many different ways to touch another person, and to let yourself be touched. Perhaps one of the most general ways is to just let it happen and to let yourself feel the experience, for the way you touch someone and the way you let yourself be touched directly reflect aspects of yourself, your personality, and how you orient toward the world. What does the other person's touch do to you, how do their finger's feel on your skin, on different parts of your body? What does the way they touch you tell you about them? If members of the same sex are together, this helps break down one of the most profound taboos in our society: two persons of the same sex embracing or

touching. The attempt is to get to know people as people, not people
as sex objects.

In some instances, we may attempt to communicate nonverbally
with another person for one hour, or an hour per day for a week—
not necessarily with our eyes closed, or not necessarily at a total non-
verbal level. The aim is to prevent easy escape or retreat from one

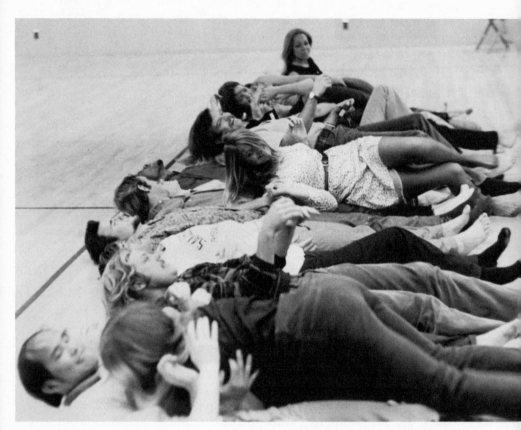

Courtesy of American International News Service

another, to continue to try and communicate. There are often long
silences when people have little in common and they have nothing
"verbally" to say to each other. While this may be true on the verbal
level, nonverbally we may have a tremendous amount to communicate, it is just that we do not realize it yet, for we have never really
been forced to use our other senses in this manner.[14]

There are several ways to break down alienation through non-verbal encountering. One such mechanism is to have a given estranged person attempt either to break into or out of a group which forms a closed circle and tries to prevent such an attempt. If the individual is trying to break in, the group members may either be facing him in a circle or have their backs to him. This exercise helps bring to the fore many latent feelings of alienation as well as crystallizing those already on the surface, and provides a good means of not only discussing but of feeling the problem.[15]

Another exercise adopts the reverse attitude by attempting to build trust between people in a group. Through the building of such trust, individuals begin to feel less alienated and become more open and honest with those they come in contact with. There are two forms of trust games. In the first one, a group of seven or eight people form a circle. One member of the circle stands in the center, closes his eyes, puts his hands at his sides and then is either spun around until he loses his balance, or is passed around the circle until he loses his balance and then must trust the other members of his group to keep him from falling. This usually ends by the person being gently rocked back and forth, getting used to trusting others. Another variation of this trust game is to have one member of the group lie down in the center of the circle, either face up or face down, close his eyes, and have the rest of the members of the group pat him all over, sensitizing him to their touch. After a few minutes he is then hoisted by his fellow group members, who then carry him around the room, or rock him back and forth, so that he comes to have confidence that they will not drop him. Each member of the group gets a chance at each of these exercises, and a sense of group togetherness, spirit, and empathy is conveyed in the process.

Several other group techniques can also be used to enhance communication between people, and to gain an awareness of our senses. A group can sit closely together, holding hands, silently, and attempt to get a sense of the group, to establish a group-mind (symbo), to feel with one heart, to breathe with one breath—that humanity has certain basic things in common, and that these take precedence over the relatively superficial differences between people.[16] Another variation of this is to have a group chant or hum, until the sound reverberates through all members of the group, as though the sound is coming from one body with one breath. The usual chant employed is "Om," taken from the East, but many others can also be used.[17]

There is also what is known as the "Gunther Sandwich." In this, members of the group lie down side by side, each with arms around a person to the front. Lying still like this builds up a sense of group unity and closeness.[18] A variation of the Gunther Sandwich is to have everyone lie on their backs, side by side, with their eyes closed, and to have the last person in the group roll over everyone until they are first; and then the next to the last person does the same, and so on until everyone in the group has rolled over everyone else. (As you might predict, this usually produces much laughter.)

Finally, the group may engage in a nude bath or swim, or a nude massage. When clothes are dispensed with as needless barriers to communication, when fat can no longer be hidden, when sagging bodies do not matter, then everyone is together in being open and revealed.[19] Body painting can also enable us to notice aspects of our body and of other bodies which we probably never thought about before. We begin to really *see* pores in the skin, contours, shapes.

Tell It Like It Is: The Verbal Encounter

Verbal encountering is a direct response to other-directed and superficial types of relationships in which one always has to play games with those he associates with, holding back things he would like to say, smiling even when he does not feel like doing so. The verbal encounter is an attempt to develop not only closeness in interpersonal relationships, but also a new sense of honesty and trust between people.

There are several variants of ground rules which should be employed in an encounter group. Among these can be included:

1. Nothing which takes place should go beyond the encounter group; people should be able to say what they feel without having it used against them at a later time, or by someone they do not know. They should be able to trust group members.

2. All discussions should be related to the here and now; discussions of past actions should be tied to the present. At the same time, gossip should be avoided, talk only to and about those persons who are there in the room with you.

3. Persons in encounter groups . . . should discuss immediate personal feelings, rather than abstractions. They shouldn't be afraid to say what they feel; no holding back.

4. Each person in the group has a responsibility to speak for himself, not for others; neither should he give advice.

5. If one joins an encounter group, he should make a commitment to go more than one time. Some sessions are painful or boring, but these are often because of the very problems that must be encountered.

6. Some encounter groups request that persons only make statements about what they feel, rather than [ask] questions. At the same time, moral imperatives (oughts) should be avoided.[20]

Encounter groups typically go through the following process, depending on the facilitator (group leader). First, most persons will mill around wondering what they are doing in the group, making small talk, feeling uncomfortable, waiting for someone to give them directions. During this time there is resistance to the expression of personal feelings about the immediate situation; some past actions or feelings may be discussed. Gradually, there develops a feeling of frustration and the articulation of negative feelings about where the group is going or toward the facilitator. Sometimes facilitators manipulate the group through different types of sensory awareness exercises in order to break down barriers in communication. Other facilitators, however, feel this is artificial. Ultimately, maybe after several hours or sessions, one person takes the risk of talking about something that is deeply personal and relevant to his situation. Others may soon follow. Sympathy and empathy begin to develop among group members and trust begins to form. Persons in the group begin to express positive and negative feelings toward each other. Gradually an atmosphere of self-acceptance comes to pervade the group and façades begin to crack. Individuals receive feedback from others in the group; confrontations develop and stronger feedback results. Members of the group become friends; the group feels warm and close, relationships established in the group entering into group members' regular lives. By the time the series of encounter sessions ends, group members have become more open and honest, more flexible and confident.[21]

Becoming a facilitator involves going through many encounter group sessions to develop a willingness to talk about one's own feelings. Facilitators are not in teacher–student relationships with others in the encounter group.[22] Some facilitators, as we have noted, use different types of techniques to get encounter groups going. One of the primary techniques which can be employed to gain greater empathy with oneself and with others in the group is called "doubling." In doubling, individuals imitate others both bodily and verbally, providing a mirror image of their actions and words. This has also been called the alter ego technique—individuals do exact opposite imitations of those they are supposed to be mimicking. One can also imitate people he would like to be, his day-dreams, or childhood experiences.[23] In all these instances, the attempt is to bring these experiences or fantasies into the present. Role-playing and psychodrama also produce insights in enabling us to see how we "would have" reacted had the situation been "real."

One way to begin an encounter session is to give first impressions based merely on physical impression or the limited exposure which we have received from a few brief moments of waiting for all the group members to arrive. Each individual might take a turn standing in front of the group.[24] Another technique which may be employed to open people up is to use free association with various types of word games. People learn by analogy; we could go around the group and ask: "If he were a color, what color would he be? A food? A plant? A type of animal? This technique provides many avenues for discussion and insight into self-conception and empathy with other persons.[25] A variation of this exercise is to carry on a conversation by free-associating words. If you were to say the first word which came into your mind, I would then repeat the first word which came into my mind: cloud-white, limp-flat, I-you. Another means of doing this is to have a group story or fantasy in which members of the group all put their heads together in the form of a wheel with spokes and spontaneously create a tale.[26] We can also slightly alter our everyday interactions with others by lowering our voices, by standing extra close to someone, or by refusing to look at the person we are talking to. These slight variations aid in bringing out certain "unconscious" rules which we may practice in interaction situations which are a part of our self-image, an image which may be outmoded.

Not perhaps since thousand-hour marathon dance concerts during the thirties have marathons been viewed in such a positive light as they are in the encounter group movement today. As the marathon dance concert exhausted participants to the delight of the audience who would pay to see them, the participants in a marathon encounter group session use the same sense of exhaustion to open themselves up for their own benefit. Locked in a room for twenty-four to thirty-six hours, participants get down to the "basics" and are usually unable to maintain their defense mechanisms. The marathon is:

> . . . not unlike a "pressure cooker" in which phoney steam boils away and genuine emotions (including negative ones) emerge. The group atmosphere is kept and focused every moment on the objectives at hand: to produce *change in orientation* and new ways of dealing with crucial problems.[27]

As an extended encounter group session, the marathon serves similar purposes but attempts far more radical shifts in orientation as sessions are usually more intense than the average encounter group. Individuals get physically and psychologically tired of playing games, they become transparent, and a new sense of intimacy develops, for one is no longer able to hide behind anything, as the thin veneer of self is peeled away.

I've Got a Truer Self than You: Problems of Encountering

Encounter groups do not take place in a vacuum: problems brought to the encounter group situation, while quite personal, may be due to the social situation one exists in. If one returns home from his encounter group session with a feeling of self-confidence and good will, only to turn on the evening news or read about American troops annihilating women and children at My Lai 4 in Vietnam, one can become very depressed and alienated again. The social situation has to be altered concurrently with exploring the possibilities of inter-personal and personal relationships in encounter group situations. An encounter group can, however, sensitize us to the need of empa-thizing with the problems of others, and may in fact cause us to become involved in various critical issues affecting American society.

Frequently, changes of behavior that occur in encounter sessions do not last unless these encounter sessions are repeated. They are instead vacations from the "real world" when the very thing such encounters were intended to do was to re-establish the individual in the "real world." For some people they are more a form of escape than confrontation.

If encounter sessions are not repeated, individuals can be left hanging, that is, a given individual can become deeply involved with working through problems and with revealing his self, only to be left up in the air when the session ends. This is especially dangerous for potential suicide cases who have had all their defense mechanisms destroyed, but have been left with nothing to replace them. The old self has been taken away, but there is, as yet, no new self. Many encounter group sessions and marathons are run by amateurs who do not know how to handle such problems when they arise, or who do not know how to cope with serious psychological maladies which may be uncovered.

There are still other problems. Encounter groups may become just another form of gamemanship, or one-upmanship. "I've got a better self than you because I've been through a whole year of encountering while you've gone only one week." Or, "you haven't been through anything 'til you've been through a forty-eight-hour marathon." This "old pro" phenomenon is detrimental to the encounter group situation, for encountering is relating to people as they are now; it is not a status or competition game with prescribed roles and power positions in which individual participants manipulate others for control. But it can become this, and often sadistic and frustrated energies emerge from people who enjoy putting others down, not in the spirit of encountering them and coming to understand and love them, but merely as a game. In a similar sense, the problem of other-directed types of relationships may not really be solved by many encounter group sessions, for encounter groups may develop norms and values of their own, with specific expectations which group members must conform to or else risk being ostracized, if not during the immediate encounter session, then after it is over.[28] Relationships frequently develop out of encounter group sessions, but they may be as jaundiced as those which one is into on the "outside." They may be built around one's "encounter group personality" leaving out many other roles and situations one's friend is involved in. While appearing more honest, such "honesty" may make for early break-ups after the encounter sessions are over.

Moreover, individuals may approach the encounter group situation with certain expectations, which, if not met, can lead to apathy rather than real involvement. Much depends on the group leaders; not so much on training, but on their unique personality, what they bring to the situation, and on how they respond to cues within that situation. The problem of authority, who is to be the leader, and how he or she is to lead, is an important one for encounter groups to face.

Some psychological defenses *are* legitimate; paranoid persons indeed may have people out to get them. If these defenses are ridiculed or taken away, the individual may become shattered, for he may no longer be able to orient to the objective situation in which he finds himself on leaving the encounter group session. But, the real tragedy is that once the shell is cracked, there may be no yoke or real self inside—there may be nothing at all. The likelihood of this is high in a society such as ours, in which values are memorized and clothes adorn credit-card scarecrows. Taking away these superficial selves, then, can result in individuals adapting the role of "liberated person" much as they adapted their old selves, through memorizing its prerogatives, rather than creating their own values and lives. Anything to fill the empty shell they have been left with.

Sensitivity sessions can lead quite naturally to sexual relationships, sometimes on the spot. Most psychologists in running sensitivity sessions counsel against feeling sexual urges, thus making it taboo to touch certain parts of another person's body. This makes participants hold back. Of course, the idea is to sensitize yourself to treating people as people, rather than make sexual conquests. To deny the existence of sex in encounter sensitivity groups is perhaps to become as hypocritical as pretending that we do not ever like to think, which, is also taboo in many sessions. Feeling is what counts. Without intellectuality and sexuality, then, encounter groups limit themselves to only certain aspects of the human personality: How then can alienated persons become *whole?*

Finally, it may be that encounter groups will only work for those already predisposed toward change. If this is the case, then such a technique is severely restrictive in its possibilities for rapid and fundamental social change in American society. If we are not predisposed to such change, then this experience may prove negative rather than positive. Although the encounter group movement is growing—and it does entail risks—it is up to us to decide whether these risks are worth taking or not.

NOTES

[1] Fritz Perls, *Gestalt Therapy Verbatim* (Lafayette: Real People Press, 1969), p. 4.
[2] Leland P. Bradford, Jack R. Gibb and Kenneth D. Benne, *T-Group Theory and Laboratory Method* (New York: John Wiley & Sons, 1969). See also Carl Rogers, *Encounter Groups* (New York: Harper & Row, Publishers, 1970), pp. 2–3.
[3] Sidney M. Jourard, "Growing Awareness and the Awareness of Growth," in Herbert A. Otto and John Mann, *Ways of Growth* (New York: Viking Press, Inc., 1969), p. 11.
[4] Rasa Gustaitis, *Turning On* (New York: Signet, 1969), p. 49.
[5] Bernard Gunther, "Sensory Awakening and Relaxation," in Otto, *op. cit.*, pp. 60–61.
[6] Claudio Naranjo, "Contributions of Gesalt Therapy," in Otto, *op. cit.*, p. 130.
[7] William C. Schutz, *Joy* (New York: Grove Press, Inc., 1967), p. 20.
[8] *Ibid.*, p. 57.
[9] Herbert A. Otto, "Developing Family Strength and Potential," in Otto, *op. cit.*, p. 85.
[10] Gunther, *op. cit.*, p. 174.
[11] Schutz, *op. cit.*, pp. 36–45.

[12] Herbert A. Otto, "Sensory Awakening Through Smell, Touch and Taste," in Otto, *op. cit.*, p. 55.

[13] Sidney M. Jourard and Jane E. Rubin, "Self Disclosure and Touching: A Study of Two Modes of Interpersonal Encounter and Their Inter-Relation," *Journal of Humanistic Psychology,* Spring, 1968, p. 39.

[14] Schutz, *op. cit.*, p. 78.

[15] *Ibid.*, p. 131.

[16] Gustaitis, *op. cit.*, p. 122.

[17] Gunther, *op. cit.*, p. 170.

[18] *Ibid.*, p. 190.

[19] Gustaitis, *op. cit.*, p. 123.

[20] Keith Johnsgaard, "Group Therapy: Some Comments and Ground Rules" (Unpublished, California State University, San José).

[21] Rogers, *op. cit.*, pp. 15–37. For research findings on encounter groups see J. R. Gibb, "The Effects of Human Relations Training," in A. E. Bergen and S. L. Garfield (eds.), *Handbook of Psychotherapy & Behavior Change* (New York: John Wiley & Sons, Inc., 1970), pp. 2114–2176.

[22] *Ibid.*, pp. 65–68.

[23] Schutz, *op. cit.*, p. 60.

[24] *Ibid.*, p. 127.

[25] *Ibid.*, p. 66.

[26] *Ibid.*, p. 143.

[27] George R. Bach, "The Marathon Group: Intensive Practice of Intimate Interaction," in Hendrik M. Ruitenbeek, *Group Therapy Today* (New York: Atherton, 1969), p. 304.

[28] Rogers, *op. cit.*, p. 60; see also, Ruitenbeek, *op. cit.*

16

have a good trip:
psychedelic drugs

In many of the images that came to me I saw myself, sometimes with my wife, more often alone. I was a fur-capped Mongol huntsman, cold-eyed and cruel, bow in hand, striking down a running rabbit from the back of a racing, gaunt half-wild stallion. . . . So extended was time that once it seemed to me I lighted a cigarette, smoked it for hours, looked down and noticed that the cigarette still had its first ash. . . . I became aware of the body that encased me as being very heavy and amorphous. Inside it, everything was stirring and seemed to be drawing me inward. I felt that I could count the beats, the throbbing of my heart, feel the blood moving through my veins, feel the passage of the breath as it entered and left the body, the nerves as they hummed with their myriad messages. Above all, I was conscious of my brain as teemingly alive, cells incredibly active, and my mental processes as possessing the unity of perfect precision. . . . Later, we walked in the woods and by the river and it seemed that my love was so great it evoked a response from animals, birds and plants, and even from inanimate things. . . . The streets bounce, of course. The world is experienced as a physical extension of oneself, of one's own nervous system. Consequently, I felt the blows of pick axes wielded by construction men tearing up the street.[1]

Psychedelic drugs—acid, grass, mescaline, psilocybin, among others—have come to play a role in the youth culture. Yet, descriptions provided of their experience by youth have in large part been superficial in the sense that many never delved deeply into what they were experiencing. Some would reply that this was just the point—when you describe it, you lose it. You don't know what a trip is like unless you've been on one. This does not have to be the case. The purpose of this chapter is to present various analyses of what psychedelic drugs do to human beings and whether they are of use in helping us transform American society.

Let Me Lay a Joint on You

Marijuana, or grass, is perhaps the most commonly used psychedelic. It also has the mildest effects. As one drug study put it:

> There are no apparent reasons for cannabis' status as a Dangerous Drug. It is not addictive, its use does not in Western society cause crime or unacceptable sexuality, and it does not lead to addiction to the hard drugs. The major problem with this drug is that it is illegal.[2]

While millions of persons smoke grass, only a very small percentage of these turn to the hard drugs (such as heroin). Those who fit into this latter category do so because of urgent unresolved social and psychological needs, *not* because they have smoked grass. This may particularly have been the case with the rise of heroin addiction among GIs serving in Vietnam.

An important variable to consider in smoking pot or in turning on with acid or other drugs is the individual himself—what *he* brings to the situation. Our particular personality make-up and our on-going problems will have a profound effect, particularly with the stronger psychedelics, on what type of "experience" we have (that is, whether we have a good or bad trip).[3] Another variable is the situation in which the drug is taken—whether we are with friends, in the woods, with strangers, in a large crowd. A congenial environment is, of course, the most beneficial to the smoking of grass, particularly for the novice who does not know what to expect when he gets stoned. The culture itself—the particular society or subculture within which the drug is taken—will also matter, in that one subculture or society may define its use in one way while another may define its use in another. For example, if we are raised in a highly restrictive society our experience may be expected to be quite different than if we are raised in a highly permissive type of subculture. In the former case we may be expected to be plagued by guilt feelings and have difficulty "letting go"; in the latter case we may be far more open to the experience and to insights we might gain from it.[4]

For the neophyte, the effects of grass during the first experiences have to be learned—that is, perceptual distortions and other shifts in reality have to be pointed out. Thus, alterations take place or are perceived sequentially, rather than all at once. At first we see color changes, or find an increased appetite; then perhaps time distortions —time slowing up; then concentration on a fixed point or topic of discussion; and so forth. After one gets stoned a few times, no one needs to point these changes out to him, and moreover, they occur simultaneously.[5]

The primary difference between the stoned and the "straight" person is that the former employs "pure" or nonreflective awareness, whereas the latter maintains conscious awareness. What this means is that when we are stoned we experience the world without choice or association or thinking about it—it just happens. When we're straight, we tend to think or analyze given events, objects, and relationships—they don't just happen.[6] Perhaps the best way to point out the distinction is to consider the time distortion which occurs when smoking grass, and also on acid or mescaline. Watts gives the following description of what this time distortion entails:

> To begin with, this world has a different kind of time. It is the time of biological rhythm, not of the clock and all that goes with the clock. There is no hurry. Our sense of time is notoriously subjective and thus dependent upon the quality of our attention, whether of interest or boredom, and upon the alignment of our behavior in terms of routines, goals, and deadlines. Here the present is self-sufficient, but it is not a static present. It is a dancing present—the unfolding of a pattern which has no specific destination in the future but is simply its own point. It leaves and arrives simultaneously, and the seed is as much the goal as the flower. There is therefore time to perceive every detail of the movement with infinitely greater richness of articulation. Normally, we do not so much look at things as overlook them. The eye sees types and classes—flower, leaf, rock, bird, fire—mental pictures of things rather than things, rough outlines filled with flat color, always a little dusty and dim.[7]

But what transpires within us? We no longer function automatically. Whereas we normally walk along the sidewalk taking each step for granted, not thinking about each step, now we watch where each step is going, where our foot is being set down; in fact, we are fascinated by the process. Once conscious processes are delimited—everything is slowed down. Normally, we take certain things for granted so that we can concern ourselves with more important events and situations. When one is stoned, there is nothing to move to, past and future are no longer relevant—there is only the present, only *now*. Time lasts longer, because there is nothing to compare the present to; actions are not measured in terms of consequences, but rather in terms of what is. *It is timeless.* When the past and future are experienced, they are lived through the present, as though they were in the present (either through myths or daydreams). They are re-lived.[8]

Nonreflective consciousness or awareness means that everything is experienced afresh. This also means that we cannot apply conceptual categories we have learned from the past, so we become childlike and return to that world of innocence. Functional associations decrease. Objects come to be seen in themselves, not in terms of the function they might normally serve. A bridge is seen as a bridge, rather than as a connective unit wihch links both banks of a river; a blade of grass is seen as a blade of grass, a thin green object which waves gently in the breeze, rather than as part of a lawn which must be cut.[9] Again, there are no goals or consequences, nothing is assumed or taken for granted—a new world opens up, though "objectively" speaking this world is essentially the same as the old. One of the first things we come to notice is that our sensory awareness is greater—we smell, taste, and touch things in a new way, slower, with more concentration, then we did before (the blade of grass, for example).

As we are no longer bound by the past or the future, we are also not bound by old rules and ways of seeing the world, by "outmoded" conceptualizations. This permits our fantasy to play and creative free association to take place—the same objects are seen in new ways.[10] Since nothing is taken automatically, everything is permitted: a door becomes a skyscraper; thousands of faces are seen within the portrait of one face; round mountains become breasts, a bowl of jello a scoop of ice cream; stairs become escalators, winding through the house, through your body, down your bloodstream, to the sea, growing larger and smaller to infinity. At the same time, one experiences fewer inhibitions, since we are not bound by society's rules and values—since we must "start over" experiencing each object, each feeling, each sense, afresh. But why does the release of inhibitions not lead to violence and aggression? Primarily, it appears that violence and aggression in American society are largely tied to expectations and to specific conflict-laden situations. As the past and future no longer appear relevant, conflicts no longer seem to matter, we do not expect

them to develop—there is nothing to fight about. Moreover, grass usually seems to produce a sense of euphoria,[11] or exhilaration, probably because one comes to experience so many new and fascinating thoughts and feelings.

Finally, there is a fixating of attention because automatic responses to the environment are decreased. One becomes absorbed in an object or process, and thinks or feels nothing else. There is less side- or peripheral attention manifested—we do not do thousands of things at once. Memories can also be fixated upon, as can salient emotional experiences which one brings to the situation. It is these emotional states which can be accelerated under grass, resulting in feelings of paranoia, fear, and grief.[12] Laughter and tears are also much more easily produced, for there is nothing to hold them back, to keep us from feeling them. Since grass is most often smoked in social situations, we can also focus our attention on various interpersonal relationships. We can begin to see various "levels" of interaction which we "skipped over" before. On one level we notice everyone laughing, then we begin to see that some people are laughing because they are expected to laugh, then we begin to see that some people are trying to be the center of attention while others fit comfortably into the group, or the sounds on a record become clearer than the discussion, and then only certain sounds within a given record, and we go deeper and deeper, or we go down within ourselves either into fantasies or inside our physical frame seeing our teeth, and cranial cavity and. . . .

To Die and Be Reborn: LSD and Other Additives

In comparison to grass, acid is a much "heavier" trip and lasts for a longer period of time—usually from eight to ten hours as compared with from two to three hours for grass. Perhaps one of the primary differences and distinctions about an acid trip is its relationship to or similarity with religious mysticism. One of the characteristics about such a mystical trip is that we feel a sense of unity. Not only are our automatic responses broken down, as when stoned on grass, but the relationship between subject and object is also diminished, and even eliminated. There is a sense of unity with everything. When one is sitting on a chair the boundary between self and chair disintegrates; one's outer boundaries expand to encompass everything. Similarly, when going inside one's frame there is a sense of psychological unity —everything is "together." There is thus a distinct loss of self—we are the world and the world is us. We become a set of molecules flowing in and out as though we were reduced to another level, a level beneath our skin, so that the entire world is made up of molecules—when we die, we are only changing form (from human being to fertilizer), but the molecules continue to stream, organic and inorganic merge.

At this level, not only do questions of death seem irrelevant or "solved," but so too do questions of life, of meaning and purpose. American society is only so many empty games which one has been playing and taking far too seriously. We have stepped out of these games, dropped our skin, and become one with a universe in which all questions of purpose appear grossly beside the point. As Watts comments:

Life is basically a gesture, but no one, no thing, is *making* it. There is no necessity for it to happen, and none for it to go on happening. For it isn't being driven by anything; it just happens freely of itelf. It's a gesture of motion, of sound, of color, and just as no one is making it, it isn't *happening* to anyone. There is simply no problem of life; it is completely purposeless play—exuberance which is its own end. Basically there is the gesture. Time, space, and multiplicity are complications of it. There is no reason whatever to explain it, for explanations are just another form of complexity, a new manifestation of life on top of life, of play, and there isn't anything in the whole universe to be afraid of because it doesn't happen to anyone! There isn't any substantial ego at all. The ego is a kind of flip, a knowing of knowing, a fearing of fearing. It's a curlicue, an extra jazz to experience, a sort of double-take or reverberation, a dithering of consciousness which is the same as anxiety.[13]

Not only is the world experienced without question, as a sense of unity,[14] but one comes to feel more sure of his experience of the world in this manner than he has of anything in his life—there is no reason to doubt what he feels. Similarly, there is a collapse in concepts of space and time, there is no way to orient oneself to one's environment because one is his environment. Space and time are irrelevant as is the self out of which such concepts develop. Questions of logic are lost in a deeply felt positive mood, a sense of sacredness, or awe, of something beyond the self. While the experience appears "really real," it is also typically ineffable: It cannot be communicated or expressed in ordinary language. Finally, the experience is temporary, only lasting a relatively short period of time, but can lead to lasting change in one's attitudes or behavior.[15]

Many critics of the use of psychedelic drugs claim that this experience is essentially "counterfeit," that one cannot become an instant mystic. There is truth in the claim that when one "comes down" he cannot readily integrate this experience into his life—it is artificial in the sense that it has taken him out of his everyday situation. But so does much religious mysticism which causes people to sit on mountain tops contemplating the infinite, quite away from the commonplace world; or to starve themselves into seeing visions; and other forms of "spiritual enlightenment." This too is artificial. Through meditation, many of the same effects as those achieved in using psychedelics can be realized, and, once realized, can perhaps last longer. Of course, such a process takes considerable work and discipline.

Acid has many more effects on the individual than those manifested in similarities to religious mysticism. As in smoking pot, spatial perceptions and sensory awareness are greatly enhanced and distorted.[16]

Acid produces a type of synesthesia in which the individual becomes a part of the music he is listening to, dissolving into different light patterns which form according to the sounds he hears. Bodily feelings are also greatly enhanced, such as laughing, crying, melting, dissipating,[17] flowing across the floor as when one spills water continuing to spread thinner and thinner until we disappear. One's body cannot only be experienced in different ways, but the bodily image alters —that is, in terms of its size, the way it looks in a mirror. It can become the size of an atom, or of the universe.[18] It can also take on characteristics of an inanimate or animate object—a tiger for example:

> I have no idea how much time elapsed—surely not more than ten or twenty minutes as the clock would measure it—before I became conscious of myself moving across the floor of the apartment, moving as best I can recall by propelling myself along on my knees with my flattened palms also pressed against the floor. At about this same instant I found myself before a full length mirror and, looking into it, was confronted by a huge, magnificent specimen of a tiger! Simultaneous, I think, with my perception of this image I became aware of my tiger's body, of emotions that seemed to saturate my being, and of a narrow or compressed kind of consciousness that focused only upon what was being perceived and upon the emotional state on the one hand and basic physical sensations on the other. I was *in* this body, and *felt* this body, as I never have been in or felt my own. . . . Still later, how I got there I haven't the slightest notion, I was locked up in a cage in some zoo. It seems that I paced interminably up and down within the barred enclosure, looking out with a kind of flattened vision at people like paper cutouts who stood peering into my cage.[19]

One's body may also feel like another substance; blood becomes like cement or jello.[20]

Interpersonal relationships are also altered. Visually, other persons take on friendly images if one is in a congenial friendly atmosphere, and vice versa if not.[21] Communication undergoes considerable transformation. One study concluded by stating:

> Factors of especial importance in producing the peculiarly "psychedelic" varieties of communication include the following: the much-increased tempo of thought; feelings of empathy; heightened sensitivity to nuances of language and to nonverbal cues; greater use of gestures and shifts of posture and facial expression as means of communicating; the sense that communication is multileveled and much more meaningful than at other times; the sense that words are useless because the experience is "ineffable"; the feeling that communication by telepathic and other "extrasensory" means is possible; and the illusion that one is communicating

when one is not—particularly, that one has given voice to a message when actually nothing was said.[22]

During a "good trip," a kind of instant love or "galloping *agape*" of all persons, places, and things is experienced. One becomes a true humanist—all mankind is our family. We feel as though we could love everyone, that the hands of humanity are locked in an embrace which can never be broken.[23]

Some people insure themselves against bad trips by using a guide —someone to lead us through the experience. This is someone who has been through the experience previously, who can be trusted. This is because the situation in which the acid is dropped is so important.

Not all persons have good trips. Many people have difficulty letting go of their egos or identities and, as such, the ensuing conflict may tear them apart. Moreover, acid is a very powerful drug which can expose painful aspects of the self long repressed by strong defense mechanisms. As these defenses are stripped away, many individuals have difficulty in coping with their trip, and consequently "freak out" into excessive states of paranoia or other psychological maladies, some of which become more or less "permanent" attributes of the self. Since acid affects each person in a different way (that is, distorts or plays upon our personality in a unique manner), it is especially important that the conditions for a potentially good trip be followed. Dropping acid without some idea of what one is getting into can be highly dangerous, as is taking the drug to solve pressing social problems such as estrangement from one's parents. Finally, the type of acid one gets can become a significant variable. "Street acid" often contains speed and other additives which create "unwanted" reactions. Pure acid in a "controlled" situation is the safest.[24]

How lasting is a change in values and what type of change takes place as a result of the acid experience? Some experiments in "controlled" situations have reached the following conclusions:

Three days following the LSD session, a consistent and reliable increase was found in the extent to which an individual agrees with test items reflecting a deep sense of meaning and purpose in life, open-mindedness, greater aesthetic sensitivity, and sense of unity of oneself with nature and humanity. Decreases were found on values pertaining to material possessions, social status, and dogmatism. Also significant was the finding that changes in personal beliefs either remained constant or became still more prominent at later follow-ups. These were consistent results cutting across such factors as age, sex, religious orientation, or personality type. . . . [The individual also] tends to be less distrustful and guarded with others, warmer and more spontaneous in expressing emotion, and less prone to feelings of personal inadequacy.[25]

Moreover, these results apply despite pre-LSD differences between subjects in terms of openness toward the experience and other relevant values.[26]

Experiments have been done also in relating LSD to increases in creativity. The following subjective results have been reported in terms of viewing LSD as a creative agent or catalyst:

Some Reported Characteristics of the Psychedelic Experience [27]

Those Supporting Creativity	Those Hindering Creativity
1. Increased access to unconscious data.	1. Capacity for logical thought processes may be diminished.
2. More fluent free assocation; increased ability to play spontaneously with hypotheses, metaphors, paradox, transformations, relationships, etc.	2. Ability to consciously direct concentration may be reduced.
3. Heightened ability for visual imagery and fantasy.	3. Inability to control imaginary and conceptual sequences.
4. Relaxation and openness.	4. Anxiety and agitation.
5. Sensory inputs more acutely perceived.	5. Outputs (verbal and visual communication abilities may be constricted).
6. Heightened empathy with external processes, objects, and people.	6. Tendency to focus upon "inner problems" of a personal nature.
7. Aesthetic sensibility heightened.	7. Experienced beauty may lessen tension to obtain aesthetic experience in the act of creation.
8. Enhanced "sense of truth," ability to "see through" false solutions and phony data.	8. Tendency to become absorbed in hallucinations and illusions.
9. Lessened inhibition, reduced tendency to censor own by premature negative judgment.	9. Finding the best solution may seem unimportant.
10. Motivation may be heightened by suggestion and providing the right set.	10. "This-worldly" tasks may seem trivial, and hence motivation may be decreased.

The Social Impact of Psychedelic Drugs: A Critique

Perhaps one of the major shortcomings of psychedelic drugs is that they tend to lead people away from social concerns and societal responsibilities.[28] The drugs make such responsibilities, and indeed, many of the problems treated in this book appear phony and empty, games not worth becoming involved in.[29] For those deeply concerned about protesting the war in Vietnam, in doing something about, or suffering from, conditions of poverty and discrimination, such drug taking becomes escapism. Nothing is immoral, because problems of good and evil exist on another "level," they are "human" hang-ups. One critic comments:

> LSD enthusiasts talk of religious conversions, the awakening of artistic creativity, the reconciliation of opposites. The main change to be observed in such individuals, however, is that they have stopped doing anything. The aspiring painter talks of the heightening of his aesthetic sensibilities and skills, but he has stopped painting. The graduate student who withdrew from writing his dissertation in philosophy talks of the wondrous philosophical theories he has evolved. But nothing is written. It seems that the world of fantasy has become far more compelling than external things. Indeed, fantasy is substituted for reality.[30]

This is not always the case, as we have noted in discussing creativity experiments, but it happens.

Perhaps even more devastating is that an individual can become dependent on the drug rather than on himself for solutions to problems he may have. The drug replaces self-insight, other persons, or social action, as the answer to salvation and meaning.[31] In this sense, psychedelic drugs become a technological solution to a nontechnological problem. They often come to rival other pills for the social function they tend to serve, rather than affording a means of confronting existence and then doing something about that existence. Of course, those who rely on psychedelics will reply that there is nothing *to do;* that in fact doing is just another hang-up, another illusion. Perhaps— but is poverty, war, racism? Perhaps, again, if everyone dropped acid no one would fight wars, or treat people on the basis of their skin color. But not everyone has achieved a mystical union, and does not want to. So, who is to deal with those problems which remain, which plague American society today—the "enlightened ones" or the unenlightened?

Many people using psychedelic drugs treat the experience as a game. They put some on potato chips at a gathering, catching partygoers unaware. They drop some in a punch bowl to spice up a cocktail hour, even if others are not ready to be spiced up. Under such conditions acid becomes a new form of getting high, and serves the same essential function as getting drunk does for imbibers of alcohol. There is little attempt to gain insight—the effort is to have a good time, to escape. Acid is *socially* no more, no less, than any other pharmacological product, and is treated in the same way. People drop acid because it is the thing to do; it improves one's status among his peers: "Man, if you haven't dropped a thousand mics [micrograms] you haven't been anywhere." In a similar sense, dropping acid proves you're a "man" much as the game of "chicken" did for a previous generation. However, many of these "men" are now housed in psychotic wards, free clinics, or half-way houses, because the insecurities which made them play also "blew their minds."

In the larger social sense, acid can make one disinterested in the values which dominate American society—values of work, material consumption, other-directed types of relationships.[32] Of course, dropping acid can be just as much a function of other-directedness, of peer pressure—at least for the novice. But they do appear to alter values away from those of the technocratic society and so become "subversive" of that society. And it is on the question of "subversion" which much of the hassle over psychedelic drugs has come to rest, for not only has marijuana been associated with so-called "criminal" elements in American society, but it was also viewed as a stepping-stone to harder drugs—for example, heroin. This is rarely the case today, and when such a progression results, as we have noted, there are many more important sociological and psychological variables involved which create the progression. Marijuana and LSD are illegal, not for pharmacological reasons but because of the alleged clash between youth and "American" values.[33] Because the drugs help subvert these values, they are one tangible element of the youth counter-culture which can be changed and prohibited among so many that are "abhorrent"—sexual freedom, nudity, long hair, anti-war protest, honesty.

Psychedelic drugs add a new dimension to thought and feeling processes, as well as providing insights into personal and social situations. They enable us to relate to the world as a part of that world rather than as a separate entity. They demonstrate the necessity of victory by both sides in the sense that both are part of the larger whole. From this standpoint, psychedelic drugs can crystallize the necessity of participating in the solving of pressing social problems, because these problems are a part of us and we of them. Out of this perspective one can again start out—with the knowledge of why he is becoming involved, seeing through empty values and games, free to create his own values and rules to live by, free from his inhibitions. Acid and grass, *used correctly*, need not be conceived of as detached from the society within which they are employed; rather, they can become another means of raising consciousness about the problem of American society—not in terms of solution, but in terms of enabling us to see other possibilities in the types of roles and institutions which we can create. Again, this is only a first step; the next is to bring about this alternative society.

NOTES

[1] R. E. L. Masters and Jean Houston, *The Varieties of Psychedelic Experience* (New York: Dell Publishing Co., Inc., 1966), pp. 9–15.

[2] Bruin Humanist Forum, "Marijuana (Cannabis) Fact Sheet," in Charles Tart, *Altered States of Consciousness* (New York: John Wiley & Sons, Inc., 1969), p. 332; see also Michael A. Town, "Privacy and the Marijuana Laws," in David E. Smith, *The New Social Drug* (Englewood Cliffs, N. J.: Prentice-Hall, Inc., 1970), p. 122; Troy Duster, *The Legislation of Morality* (New York: The Free Press, 1970); Allen Geller and Maxwell Boas, *The Drug Beat* (New York: McGraw-Hill, Inc., 1969), pp. 79–95.

[3] Anonymous, "The Effects of Marijuana on Consciousness," in Tart, *op. cit.,* p. 336; see also David E. Smith, "An Analysis of Marijuana Toxicity," in Smith, *op. cit.,* p. 69.

[4] Mark Messer, "Running out of Era: Some Nonpharmacological Notes on the Psychedelic Revolution," in Smith, *op. cit.,* p. 163.

[5] Anonymous, *op. cit.,* p. 336; see also Andrew T. Weil, Norman E. Zinberg, and Judith M. Nelson, "Clinical and Psychological Effects of Marijuana in Man," in Smith, *op. cit.,* p. 29.

[6] Anonymous, *op. cit.,* p. 337.

[7] Alan Watts, *The Joyous Cosmology* (New York: Random House, Inc., 1962), p. 27.

[8] Anonymous, *op. cit.,* p. 341.

[9] *Ibid.,* p. 345.

[10] *Ibid.,* p. 347.

[11] *Ibid.,* p. 349.

[12] *Ibid.,* p. 354.

[13] Watts, *op. cit.,* p. 72.

[14] Walter N. Pahnke and William A. Richards, "Implications of LSD and Experimental Mysticism," in Tart, *op. cit.,* p. 401.

[15] *Ibid.*, p. 403.
[16] Aldous Huxley, *The Doors of Perception* (New York: Harper & Row, Publishers, 1954), p. 21.
[17] Pahnke et al., *op. cit.*, p. 409.
[18] Masters and Houston, *op. cit.*, pp. 68–69.
[19] *Ibid.*, pp. 76–78.
[20] *Ibid.*, p.79.
[21] *Ibid.*, p. 91.
[22] *Ibid.*, p. 100.
[23] *Ibid.*, p. 122.
[24] *Ibid.*, p. 131.
[25] Robert E. Mogar, "Current Status and Future Trends in Psychedelic (LSD) Research," in Tart, *op. cit.*, p. 394. See also Joseph Downing, "Attitude and Behavior Change Through Psychedelic Drug Use," in Tart, *op. cit.*, p. 430; Gunther M. Weil, Ralph Metzner and Timothy Leary, "The Subjective After-Effects of Psychedelic Experiences: A Summary of Four Recent Questionnaire Studies"; Weil, Metzner, and Leary, *The Psychedelic Reader* (New Hyde Park: University Books), p. 20.
[26] Ibid., 396.
[27] Willis Harman, Robert McKim, Robert Mogar, James Fadiman and Myron J. Stolaroff, "Psychedelic Agents in Creative Problem Solving," in Tart, *op. cit.*, p. 447. See also Beatrice G. Lipinski and Edwin Lipinski, "Motivational Factors in Psychedelic Drug Use by Male College Students," in Richard E. Horman and Allan M. Fox, *Drug Awareness* (New York: Avon Books, 1970), p. 13.
[28] Masters and Houston, *op. cit.*, p. 59.
[29] Watts, *op. cit.*, p. 58.
[30] Dana L. Farnsworth and Curtis Prout, "Harvard University Health Services Statement," in Horman and Fox, *op. cit.*, pp. 197–198.
[31] Robert S. De Ropp, *Drugs and the Mind* (New York: Grove Press, Inc., 1957), p. 4.
[32] Caldwell, *op. cit.*, p. 53.
[33] Frederick H. Meyers, "Pharmacologic Effects of Marijuana," in Smith, *op. cit.*, p. 39.

17

communes: cities of
the future or
villages of the past?

Communal living is becoming a new form of social organization for many Americans.[1] Returning, as they have been, to the pastoral ideal of the simple community freed from the complexities of urban civilization and technological imperatives, communes have been organized in an attempt to overcome the mistakes made by an America which suffocates the intellect and feelings and makes a mockery of moral sensibilities. Idealistically, commune members are looking for a challenge, for a chance to see what they can do, for freedom to create not only their own values and rules to live by but, if necessary, their own government and economic structure. They want to see what happens if you're permitted to do exactly what you want to do, to bridge the gap between work and leisure, to relate to people honestly, to change rules and structures when they are no longer applicable, to eliminate status-based interactions, to flow with rather than conquer the land on which you dwell, to educate yourself by living and doing, to try alternative familial arrangements, and to bring up your children in an atmosphere of freedom rather than in one of ill-disguised oppression.

More pragmatically, communes have formed as a means of providing economic solvency to a group of people. They are an effective way of organizing people along occupational, religious, and political lines. Pessimistically, communes provide an escape from American society and often from a self deeply tied to that society. Most communes probably combine aspects of all three of these attitudes. These small communities bring together much that has been discussed within the pages of this book and provide an example of an interdependently based alternative to a much fragmented America. As such, they can be conceived as a prime tactic in transforming our society, especially as a point of transition from where we are to where we would like to be.

Do Your Own Thing—But Inside the Community: A Contradiction?

It would appear that any effort to build a sense of community might fail if we each "did our own thing." This philosophy, centered around the youth counter-culture, has largely grown out of a repressive society in which many individual liberties have been denied—growing one's hair long, smoking grass, freedom to have a say in one's own education, freedom from serving in immoral wars, and so forth. "Do your own thing" comes to mean leave everyone alone to do what they want to do so long as they are not hassling you. This code also has its more positive side in that youth are now free to create their own values, their own types of relationships, their own education, their own artistic achievements which will be judged by them, rather than by their parents. On the other hand, it can become a cop-out for refusing to accept responsibility for the actions of those around you, or even your own actions; for refusing to become involved in pressing social issues which either directly or indirectly affect you, escaping when any type of confrontation appears likely. Taken in the extreme, this often means an inability to work together with anyone else, to compromise, and can lead to superficial, often highly transient relationships. Many communes have been destroyed because individual members refused to do necessary tasks—cook, clean up, take care of children, and respect the rights of others, however these rights had been defined and agreed upon.

"Do your own thing" can also help build the commune, and in fact is perhaps the only way a communal movement can develop and work in contemporary American society. One of the first tenets of starting any serious commune for those who are going to participate is to become close friends before embarking on the project. Inter-

personal relationships will prove to be the major problem. If a small group of people are congenial, if they can agree that doing their own thing means being with these people in a cooperative arrangement, then the project has a reasonably good chance of "success." In this case, there is little or no division between doing your own thing and attempting to make the commune work, because they are defined by group members as being one and the same. On a commune, subjective and objective worlds merge, the double bind is eliminated—we are doing what we want to do in an atmosphere which is commensurate with that idea.

Communes carry out the reality-busting argument made in Chapter 12. Members of these communities have dropped the "what" they are—traditional American society—and have begun to live as "who" they are. They have not only changed mental frames of reference, but physical ones as well. While some communes do adopt institutional ways of approaching the world and handling problems (that is, communes based on a certain function—for example, religious communes), many others attempt to live day-by-day, adapting their values and rules accordingly. They are flexible. Rules and values are treated as means, as are codes of morality—the ends become actualization and human fulfillment. For these commune dwellers people are seen as possibilities, life as an experiment: If the commune fails because of lack of discipline, another may be started. The categories of win and lose are thrown out—there is only growth and experience and *living*. If a specific commune collapses, then perhaps it should fold, for time and permanence are not the criteria by which such attempts should be judged.

We Are All Different: We Are All the Same

There are many different types of communes, but they all have basically the same purpose in mind—to construct alternatives to American society, to see if there is an alternative. As such, most communes respect each other's attempts, though their philosophical bases may differ quite radically. In many ways it is difficult to describe a commune, or compare communes—not because of the lack of "data," but because we must be on one to really know what is going on, to feel the mood. A commune is more than the sum of its parts, and it is perhaps this summation which is far more important than any possible analytic description. This should be kept in mind. (There is also a reluctance to bastardize the commune movement through mass publicity and over-study. Some communes have already been ruined through such "innocent" efforts. Primarily, however, descriptions create self-fulfilling prophecies often to the detriment of the subject they are used describe.)

Although descriptions of communes help those who would try to start them to have a better understanding of what they are getting into, such descriptions also serve to limit the alternatives available. If the function of communes is to develop a community based on the particular needs of their individual members, then it is these needs which must come first, which must form the basis of the community, rather than a description or ideology which one sets out to follow *a priori*. Any such description must take these factors into consideration. As such, no one commune will be described here; rather, a composite of problems facing typical communes will be undertaken.

There are many different types of communes. These tend to fall into two general classification schemes: rural–urban, and function–lack of function. In the first classification the urban commune is often used as a stepping stone to a rural one. Here persons rent or buy an old house which they employ as a kind of half-way house toward completely severing their ties with "American society." There are several prime advantages of the urban commune over its rural counterpart. For one thing, it is not artificial in the sense that technology is ignored, or that the socialization process is not accounted for. That is, most commune members are raised in the city and are equipped to deal with city life, so why not do so. Moreover, responsibilities vis-à-vis the larger society are not generally—according to most New Left political definitions—being ignored. One can live in the commune and work in a ghetto, teach school, campaign against the war, and so forth. The urban commune can provide a fortress out of which confrontations are engineered daily against "Amerika."

The urban commune, through its very presence, "keeps the heat on the community." Sometimes, however, commune members may become so immersed in the society they would change that they create no alternative at all, but work at piecemeal reform. While they are confronting the city the city corrupts their idealism, their community, with its ever-conscious presence. They are constantly subject to police raids, to harassment from local citizens, to pollution, to noise, and to other people. They are not free to develop their own community within the larger society, because that larger society never leaves them alone.

Another advantage of the urban commune is that it is easier to survive economically in the city. One or two members of the commune may hold down city jobs supporting others who either do no work or campaign for social issues. It is also easier to recruit additional members in that the urban commune is closer to "hip" population pockets. Again, however, this can become a disadvantage in that as more people drop in, community feeling and solidarity are disrupted. These drop-ins are, typically, runaways or others who have nothing else to do, and who do not necessarily share in the same community goals as their hosts. They view requests to do the dishes or to make a contribution as abridgments of *their* freedom. In this sense, the urban commune can often be seen as a clique by those who are not permitted entry; yet this may be one of the few means such a commune has of protecting itself.

The rural commune, on the other hand, has the advantage of

isolation and of being close to nature. Often the only land which can be acquired is in out-of-the-way areas of the country in which few strangers are likely to wander by. In such areas of isolation, commune members are able to develop a special sense of themselves, a closeness with the land and with each other. While problems sometimes develop through relationships with neighboring farms or ranches this is not usually the case, especially for those communes which are in mountainous or some otherwise "uninhabitable" area. In this sense, rural communes are more compact and there is more freedom to experiment. Members can shed their clothing and make love out of doors, away from police, the clock, noisy traffic, and other forms of pollution. These units form total communities in that there is no "going to work." Work and leisure merge,[2] nothing is piecemeal. Rural communes are not half-way houses: There is no looking forward to the future—this is it.

While rural communes offer isolation and communion with nature or with what is "natural," they also suffer many disadvantages. For one thing, they may be used as a political tool in which radicals or potential radicals are syphoned off from direct confrontation with "Amerika" to "self-imposed concentration camps" where they can do little harm—leaving the rest of society to go its own way. Indeed, perhaps only a small number of Americans can ever dwell in such rural tranquility and experimentation, either because the economy, while able, is not willing to support a large essentially "leisure class," or because, if more people retreated to rural areas, the amount of isolation and privacy would decrease and the new rural areas would become the cities of the future. Perhaps this is just the point, and the communes of today are indeed the forerunners of the cities of tomorrow. Yet, neither of these issues—lack of economic support or mass migrations—appears to be an immediate problem. The political question is a central one, however, for rural communes are often means of escaping the larger society without accepting responsibility for that society. From this standpoint, rural communes come to be seen as artificial units, wherein one returns to a pastoral ideal to reclaim feelings of community and oneness while ignoring the technological civilization which is here to stay.

But rural communes are not merely summer camps; they do change people. After several months in relative isolation, commune members often speak of developing a language of their own which would be far more simplistic and germane to rural existence than their city "tongue." Values also change. The land takes on a new importance, washing dishes becomes an exhilarating experience. There is no place to rush to, and nothing to hide from—except perhaps the encroachments of urban America.

Another way of classifying communes is by function or lack of function. Most of the utopian communities of the past were built around a certain image or ideal or religious concept, and many contemporary communes are little different. The primary, functional, rural commune is that centered on specific religious tenets. While not necessarily traditional these religious groups attempt to fill the spiritual vacuum they find in contemporary American society. Many draw their religious conviction from the Bible, while other groups combine elaborate rituals of, say, the Aztecs or Buddhists with their own creative religious ideologies. There are many types of functional communes. Twin Oaks in Virginia attempts to practice the principles of behaviorist psychology laid down by B. F. Skinner in *Walden Two*. At this commune, a system of psychological reinforcement and labor credits are built into an operating community which produces looms and conditioned babies. The idea behind *Walden Two* is to weed out undesirable traits in man by conditioning them out. Yet another type of functional rural commune is that which centers around economics— the Israeli kibbutz for example. Work camps and certain progressive schools provide still other examples of types of communes which build their cooperation about a functional ideal or project.

The urban equivalent to these types of communes is represented by architectural and political communes in which groups of persons in similar professions decide to live together, using their occupations as mediums of solidarity.

Opposed to the functionally based communes are those which, at least initially, attempt to exist without function, but rather come into being because of the people themselves who will form the community. These communities typically last a short time, although they often develop into a functional commune. A nonfunctional commune would be one which emphasized a more "do your own thing" approach, and which was more flexible in its idealization, rules, and values, but which, at the same time, had a more difficult time maintaining control and accomplishing necessary tasks. On the other hand, the more functional communes suffer from a lack of flexibility, but have an easier time maintaining control, making necessary decisions, and acting on them. Again, the prime factor is the compatibility of the membership and its willingness to build a commune, its willingness to try, and to experiment. People learn as they go along; we can't read a book about communes and expect to be able automatically to like living in one. Nor can we *not* expect to change. The nonfunctional communes often hold to the philosophy that things will work out—let's not worry about what we will eat tomorrow. As such they rarely last a long time, but then, for their membership, time is not an important commodity, nor is worrying about questions of survival. After all, meadows and trees rarely concern themselves with whether or not the sun will shine in the morning—and they are still alive and well. And when they die, they die only to become the soil which future generations will thrive on.

Inside the Commune: Problems and Prospects

Most communes have certain problems in common, solutions to which are in some cases provided by the particular ideology on which the commune is based, but more often than not must come from the membership's efforts to agree on a particular answer. Perhaps the first problem which must be faced is where and how you are going to live. Most property can be acquired in any of several ways: it may be purchased, rented, leased, borrowed, or received as a gift. Several large communes have had the good fortune to acquire land or buildings through personal gifts from wealthy sympathizers; others have been able to borrow or lease their land at a nominal cost. Much rural acreage is typically not too expensive, although one must have some capital to begin with. If it is to be a communal effort, then the land will be owned cooperatively, each person putting in a certain amount of money and receiving a commensurate share of the property, or everyone putting in what they can or all that they have. Making a considerable financial contribution, while not a substitute for personal commitment, often ensures that one's interest in the effort is more than academic.

Related to the problem of getting land or a city building is the issue of how many persons are going to live on the commune. Size is an important variable in that it will have a profound effect on what type of work is done, what type of organization will be necessary, and how much money or labor is needed to sustain the commune. For smaller communes of from eight to fifteen persons, most decisions can be arrived at cooperatively without much formal organization or delegation of authority. That is, a mood is sensed, and the job gets done or it does not get done, but there are no elaborate rules to follow. For larger communes, a type of town-meeting arrangement might have to be worked out; and the problem of power and authority must be faced. However, even in the smaller communes there comes a time when "ego trips" have to be handled, and positions of power

clearly dealt with according to how the group wishes to handle decision-making. In many cases, a few simple rules will have to be set
down. At Ananda commune the following were accepted:

1. No job shall be played up as more dignified than any other.
2. No one may act in such a way as to harm another. . . .
3. Voting must be considered a privilege, not a duty. No one should vote
   unless he has formed a definite opinion on the subject under consideration.
4. No hallucinogenic drugs or alcoholic beverages may be taken by any
   member of the community, on or off community property.
5. Personal savings and movable possessions may be willed or sold to
   others. . . .
6. The community is the sole employer of all of its members. No member
   may engage another in any labor for wages except through the agency
   of the community.[3]

These rules may be held as quite mandatory, owing to the religious
nature of this particular commune. Twin Oaks commune, which is
based on the model laid down by B. F. Skinner in *Walden Two,*
numbers among its principles:

1. No use of titles.
2. No speaking negatively or discussing the personal affairs of others.
3. Members who have unorthodox views should not discuss these with
   nonmembers.
4. Seniority should not be discussed.
5. No boasting.
6. An individual's room is his own property.

While rules may be adopted, some communes have difficulty squaring
their often idealistic philosophies with what goes on in their day-to-
day lives.

Once the land is claimed in some manner, how will the rural
commune support itself? Many youth leave for communes or begin
them with the hope of living off nature, or farming. With little
grounding in agriculture, they often find this not as easy or romantic
as it first may have appeared. Most existing communes attempt, at
least at first, to combine small agricultural harvests (a vegetable garden)
with other sources of food or revenue. While some communes are
able to subsist off the savings of some of their members, others live
off welfare checks, food stamps, or government surplus. Still other

communes rely on handouts from the rest of the surrounding community or from strangers passing through. Some send a few of their members into the surrounding community to work; others get money from sympathetic parents. Foraging for food can also be done in farm country, or at local supermarkets. (Rumor has it that if meat is dropped on the floor by a butcher it must be thrown out, but before it is. . . .) Many communes are also able to sustain themselves for rather lengthy periods of time through small industry—weaving, crafts, candle making, nursery schools, and so forth.

Once begun, the main problem seems to be the working through of interpersonal conflicts, many of which arise out of who is going to do what tasks on the commune, how many people are freeloading, or direct conflicts of interest. For most commune members, college education or city life does little to help them to make their own rules or to run their own lives. The rural commune thus represents a radical change and necessitates constant re-evaluation of oneself. Many of the problems faced by communes are of a rather practical nature, though they directly involve the philosophy on the basis of which the commune was set up. Ownership is one such issue. Some communes restrict ownership to only those possessions which can be kept in one's room. Others feel everything should be shared. Housing is another example: Is everyone going to stay in one house, or in separate cabins (but eating together)? While most communes are almost puritanical in their sexual experimentation and marital relationships, others have openly broached group marriage arrangements and other innovations. Again, the ideal of flexibility is important. For example, there are usually more men than women on any given commune. This raises the problem of how sexual relationships are to be handled—restricted to couples only, a rotation, whoever wants to sleep with whom, two men and one woman, which? Many communes just flow with it. If you feel like sleeping with somebody, then you sleep with them— that is, if they are of the same inclination.

Children are often raised by the entire commune. Thus, each child will have many parents who give him far more attention than his own parents ever could. Moreover, he gains a variety of experiences from close relationships with different parents, and this allows greater flexibility in living arrangements. Yet, particularly for many of the early communes, children were left to fend for themselves, ignored by parents who were too stoned to know or care where they were.[4] Since the early fad has passed, however, there is a greater sense of responsibility among most commune members, and such incidents are relatively rare, as are communes of more than thirty persons. Communes in many ways represent new types of extended families and as such, provide a means of experimenting with alternatives to the traditional and possibly outmoded nuclear family.[5]

Health may sometimes be a problem. Many communes handle "normal" health problems, such as childbirth, on their own. Herbal or "natural" medical remedies are also experimented with, often with great success.

Communes run into problems with two types of outsiders—neighbors and visitors. While local townsfolk or farmers often befriend commune dwellers with food or other help, some are abhorred at the group living situation, alleged sexual promiscuity, nudity, and drugs. Often these charges are more rumor than fact, yet this is enough to get local people sufficiently up in arms to expel the "freaks." Many farmers, however, see the commune as a new type of frontier town, a return to fundamentals, to organically grown food, and welcome their new neighbors. As we said earlier, visitors can be a constant problem, especially at well-publicized communes.

A special problem developed in New Mexico, where Chicanos came to resent hippie commune dwellers whom they felt were playing at poverty while Chicanos starved. Moreover, they saw a direct clash in values between those of the Mexican-American and those represented by middle-class white hippies living on *their* lands. The same situation developed in the Haight-Ashbury district of San Francisco, where ghetto dwellers felt that hippies were making a mockery of the ghetto by playing at being poor when they had other options available. Similar clashes will no doubt take place between American Indians seeking a return of their lands, and middle-class white commune dwellers they find residing on them.

Many communes have "outlawed" all drugs, to prevent busts by local law-enforcement people, while some turn-on frequently. In fact, most commune members seem to have so much to do, and feel so peaceful with those they are with (particularly in the country), that they hardly think about drugs at all. It is as if drugs represent another world, a world they have long since left behind.

Commune Is a State of Mind

Some critics claim that rural communes are a return to the Bronze Age, and as such can make little contribution to the problem of American Society. Besides the contributions already mentioned, many aspects of commune life are applicable and have been employed in dealing with the problems of larger population centers. Already there are planned towns in England and in some parts of the United States (for example Columbia, Maryland). Within these units, cars are often outlawed and homes blend in with recreation and work centers. Even more extensive development can take place in urban areas as well as in the planning of new communities. Backyard fences can be knocked down and cooperative gardens developed and harvested. Streets can be torn up and the land cultivated. Such urban cooperation can extend to all areas of economic, social, and political life, rather than being limited to "after-hours" explorations. Urban communities can take the best of both worlds—the rural commune and technological development—to create a new society.

As presented here, communes are not an either/or type of solution. For some of us they will prove worthwhile enterprises; for others, they may only be interesting or even heartbreaking experiences. Moreover, there is room for a vast variety of communes and noncommunal living enterprises—the small communities described here are but one form such enterprises take. However, something more basic is at stake here, for "commune" is a state of mind. The boundaries of the world are shrinking, but within these boundaries are human beings. The *world* is our commune—not for purposes of exploitation but because all life shares something in common.

The last section of this book has dealt with many questions dealing with alternative ways of changing America. To those who are starving in a ghetto in New York City, or on a Mississippi Delta farm, talk of communal living, acid trips, and encounter groups must indeed seem frivolous. In fact, much of the rhetoric of this book pales beside the passionate outcries of social discontent or of lovers embracing in a city park. Yet (as we hope it has been made clear), the intent is neither frivolous nor pale, for it is these very outcries which must be assuaged —not on a piecemeal temporary basis, but fundamentally and, hopefully, for all time. This is not a call to ignore the poor, and those dying because of our guns in lands far away. Rather, the need is to think of altering the entire society when one thinks of feeding the poor and silencing the guns.

NOTES

[1] Much of the data on communes gathered for this chapter is from personal interviews and visits to local communes. What "data" does exist is mostly

personal recollections or pamphlets put out by more prosperous collectives. There are two magazines which deal with communes: *The Modern Utopian* and *The Green Revolution*. Other articles which deal with the subject are: "Making Communities," *Alternatives*, January, 1971; "Communal Living," *Editorial Research Reports*, vol. II, November 5, 1969; Nathan Adler, "Even the Romans Had Their Hippies," *National Observer*, January 11, 1971; *Twin Oaks Newsletter* and *Provisional Member* Booklet; William Hedgepeth and Dennis Stock, *The Alternative* (New York: The Macmillan Company, 1970); and Benjamin Zablocki, *The Joyful Community* (Baltimore: Penguin, 1971). Those persons interested in finding out more about communes by doing their own research might want to use the following guidelines developed by Robert Thamm.

1. General Information
    a. Name and location of community
    b. Type of community (educational, religious, political, psychedelic, gerontological, nudist, scientific, etc.)
    c. Size of community and type of people to which the community caters
    d. Age ranges and groupings of members
    e. Description of physical facilities (amount of land, layout of buildings, functions of buildings, etc.)
    f. Estimate of amount of capital investment to date in physical facilities
2. General Statement of Community Philosophy (common values)
3. Political Structure
    a. Distribution of power among members in making policy for the community (centralized, semi-centralized, decentralized)
    b. Description of decision or policy making structure
    c. Description of how policy is administered and enforced
    d. Degree of sanctioning (weak, moderate or strong rewards for meeting community expectations and weak, moderate or strong punishments for deviating from expectations: indication of typical kinds of rewards and punishments used in the community)
4. Economic Structure
    a. Distribution of material wealth among members (centralized, semi-centralized, decentralized)
    b. Criteria for distributing wealth (characteristics of those members who receive the most wealth; the least wealth)
    c. Description of economic structure (work roles, rules and relationships)
    d. Degree of status differences attributed to economic positions
5. Religious Structure
    a. List of basic ethical tenets

     b. Description or religious structure (roles, rules and relationships)

     c. Description of ceremonies, rituals or celebrations

6. Family Structure
   a. Subgroupings of community into family-like units
   b. Description of family structure (roles, rules and relationships)
   c. Living arrangements and conditions (who lives with whom else and under what circumstances)
   d. Child rearing practices and policies

7. Educational Structure
   a. Description of educational structure (roles, rules and relationships)
   b. Degree of formality in the learning situation and status differences between teachers and students)
   c. Criteria used for grouping and rewarding students
   d. Description of subjects in which students are encouraged and discouraged to become proficient
   e. General description of the educational process

8. Structure of Interpersonal Relationships
   a. Distribution of involvement with others (degree to which members are encouraged to become dependent upon or committed to one, a few or many other members of the community in terms of [1] child-parent relationships, [2] friendship relationships and [3] erotic or mate relationships
   b. Degree to which members seem to be concerned for the welfare of each other, have developed empathy and have a giving and sharing orientation toward each other as opposed to a selfish, competitive and defensive system of emotional exchange
   c. Views on marriage, monogamy, polygamy, jealousy, possessiveness, love and sex
   d. Degrees to which stress is placed upon self-adornment, physical attractiveness, stylish dress, material possessions, etc., in being accepted by other members of the community
   e. Types of escapes or diversions used most in the community (drugs, alcohol, television, music, art, competitive contests, gossip, scapegoating, withdrawal, projection, etc.)

9. General Structural, Attitudinal and Processional Characteristics
   a. Degree of community alienation from the society in general (extent to which the community is underground rather than open to society)
   b. Degree of toleration of deviation (extent to which alternative values and structures are allowed and encouraged within the community)
   c. Degree of general structuring (extent to which roles and rules

are highly defined, have little room for interpretation and
strongly sanctioned)
d. Degree of internal conflict, competitiveness or cooperation
e. Degree of ethnocentrism, dogmatism and authoritarianism
f. Degree of discrimination and discriminating criteria (age, sex,
race, intelligence, manual capacities, other innate traits, etc.)
g. Process and method of motivating behavior
10. Future Plans for the Community
a. Size of membership desired
b. Expansion of physical facilities
c. Objectives, goals or prospects

[2] Paul and Perceival Goodman, *Communitas* (New York: Random House, Inc.,
1960), p. 154.
[3] Kriyananda, *Cooperative Communities* (Nevada: Ananda Publications, 1968),
pp. 47–48; For other discussions of utopian communities of the past, see
Glenn Negley and J. Max Patrick, *The Quest for Utopia* (Garden City:
Doubleday & Company, Inc., 1962); Ron Roberts, *The New Communes*
(Englewood Cliffs, N. J.: Spectrum, 1971).
[4] For examples of this see Lewis Yablonsky, *The Hippie Trip* (New York:
Pegasus, 1969); Robert Hauriet, "Communing in Meadville," *Ramparts*,
November 30, 1968, p. 10.
[5] Herbert Otto, *The Family in Search of a Future* (New York: Appleton-
Century-Crofts), 1971.

18

the nexus of change:
the individual
in society

In this book we have taken an unorthodox approach, exploring social change as it can grow from individual responsibility rather than from broad institutional or societal transformations. This view conflicts with the many traditional theories of social change which argue that "society changes itself."

Three basic assumptions underlie this work: (1) the individual is responsible for his own actions; (2) the individual is responsible for the problems of the society he lives in; (3) social problems in American society are interconnected in an ecological framework. Our argument is fundamentally sociological in that the individual is viewed in a social context. On the other hand the individual, rather than the society, is viewed as the locus of social action. The book's perspective, therefore, may be construed as social–psychological.

All societies structure their members' values and roles in such a way that they reflect the particular environmental contingencies of that society. Typically, the more complex the society, the greater the number of possible values and roles individuals can be socialized into. Implicit in much sociological thought is that whatever an individual does or can expect to do is predetermined by the society he is born

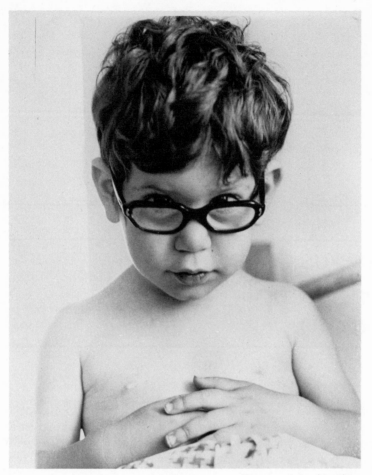

Courtesy of Cynthia Gliner

into. A ghetto dweller has greater likelihood than a middle-class sub-
urbanite to earn a low income, perceive the world as hostile, and have
a blue-collar job. Most sociological theories of social change are
deterministic; individuals are seen as dependent. They are changed
and do not, for the most part, do the changing. Individuals count only
as they join with others to form a social change movement of one
sort or another. Thus it is argued that social change occurs because of
shifts within or between societies, rather than because of changes
within or between persons.

Several types of social change theories overlap in one degree or
another.[1] Most theories of society are functional—that is, they see

society as composed of many parts which are directly dependent on and related to one another. A given society is considered to be in equilibrium if all the institutions of a society are performing adequately. Disequilibrium (and, consequently, social change) results from a change in one of the institutional areas, which then must of necessity cause a change in all other related areas. Most commonly, such change derives from factors exogamous to or outside the social system. For example, the depletion of iron ore in Canada creates a shortage of steel which can be used to make new cars. Many Americans are used to getting a new car each year because their old cars are either mechanically or "psychologically" obsolete. They are now either caught without a suitable identity, or without any available transportation. One means of restoring equilibrium would be to create a functional alternative. Instead of finding identities in new cars, they might turn to encounter groups. Or, they might try to find a new source of iron ore. If they decide to choose encounter groups, this might seriously affect the economy: Automobile workers would be laid off and the price of used cars would go up. It could also have an effect on the family structure—encounter groups may make marriages more honest, and possibly may make them less binding as "permanent" contracts on their members.

Consider another example. Suppose a war is generated in Asia because of an ostensible security threat to American society. Initially, defense industries create new engineering and munitions manufacturing jobs. Many young men are enlisted to fight in the war. Domestic problems are largely ignored because most public finances are being invested in the effort to defeat the communists. After several years, however, the war "winds down." Domestic problems long ignored make demands on a larger share of the budget. The need for munitions and engineers capable of producing them declines. There are mass layoffs at plants relying heavily on war contracts. Unemployment in this sector of the economy has a chain reaction, for many workers have less ability to purchase consumer goods. In time, other workers are laid off. People begin to question whether everyone need be employed. There are discussions about the work ethic, a guaranteed wage, the creation of problem-oriented occupations. If work can no longer provide meaningful identities, then what other institution will supply them? Can we maintain a large defense establishment without using public funds to address domestic needs? Thus an ostensibly external threat transforms the equilibrium of the social system.

Change can also occur from inside the system. Suppose that freeways become so crowded that people are forced to drive in car pools to work, or that the smog level increases so much that all automobile transportation is prohibited. In areas such as California these transportation changes would result in a relinquishment of some degree of private property, individuality, and identity. Cooperation would have to be emphasized to get people to and from work and entertainment centers. Consequently, the banning of automobiles may not be possible unless other values and attitudes also change. The environment cannot be separated from other aspects of society.

According to equilibrium theorists—most functionalists—social change will result either from the needs of outside social systems coming into conflict with one's own, or, from a more evolutionary perspective, the gradual internal growth of a society. The latter process can be seen in American society as the development of specialization through industrialization. Technology creates demands on other areas of American society (*viz.* the effects of television on leisure pursuits). It is conceivable that American society can also evolve itself *out of existence* through the creation of industrial wastes, pollution, overpopulation, and a host of other maladies.

The most stringent of all the determinist models for social change is that posed by the behaviorists, notably B. F. Skinner.[2] Skinner argues that man is a product of his environment who responds to positive and negative reinforcements which that environment supplies. Whatever action we take finds its motivational locus in our society, not within ourselves. We wish to eradicate smog because the air makes our eyes tear and our lungs choke: In behaviorist terms, the pollution in the air is "negatively reinforcing." Consequently, we will continue to try to alter the make-up of our atmosphere until we find one which is more positively reinforcing. There is no such thing as individual freedom. Man is a dependent variable. Social change takes place when we can no longer stand the situation we are in, either because our environment has made us extremely uncomfortable, or because other persons who compose part of that environment have done so.

What functional theories of social change do not tell us is, *who* is going to initiate change, and why they should do so? Functionalists have typically argued their case from an ex post facto point of view. They look at how America changed in the past, what functional alternatives were created, and how our society has been transformed. The behaviorists beg the question: How is it going to be transformed now? Who is going to change the environment so that we feel more comfortable? Neither behaviorism nor functionalism hold within their collective theories a mandate for individual participation in social change.

As such, these perspectives can only be employed in discussing past, not present and future actions. Hence, to invoke these theories in social planning is intellectually and morally dishonest.

There are far deeper reasons why functionalism and behaviorism can tell us little about social change in American society. Functionalism makes existing institutions and arrangements preeminent in social planning. It says: These institutions must be functioning adequately because we are still relatively happy—our televisions work, our schools are in operation, we get two or three weeks of vacation a year. Some groups may express discomfort, but the system is coping adequately with these problems. So why worry? To label the social system itself dysfunctional would thus be to recognize that its entire make-up must be transformed. Piecemeal problems can continue to be covered up, and functional alternatives developed, both of which make fundamental change impossible. Functionalism hopes for an equilibrium, and does everything in its power to bring such an equilibrium about. There is no moral judgment rendered, because there are no individuals involved in the social system which is constructed. Society and the institutions which compose it are anthropomorphosed; it acts as if it were human; there is little need for us to do anything. We are not part of the plan.

Behaviorism falls under the same criticism: Whatever is positively reinforcing is good, whatever is negatively reinforcing is not. But psychologists tell us there are a host of rationalizations and forms of sublimation we may use to justify what is. Comfort, it seems, is often more valuable than change, all damaging consequences of maintaining comfort notwithstanding. "Walden II" becomes a paradise because all pain has been conditioned out of its populace—but by whom? What gives them the right to decide for us? And who controls the controllers? It has always been this way, they say, so it is at least better that man should do the conditioning, than society. It is comfortable to live in suburbia, despite the war, racism, pollution, boring schools, work, spouses, houses. It is comfortable because it is safe and secure most of the time. Where are the negative reinforcements to come from which could force us to change our environment if they have already been "conditioned" out of us? Who is going to change American society?

Conflict Theories

Conflict theorists attempt to deal, in part, with many of the arguments presented above by demonstrating that conflict is inherent in any society, and that out of such conflict social change takes place. The most prominent conflict theorist is Marx, who posited that the juxtaposition of social classes within any given society develops into the dominance of one class over the other. Subsequently, each dominant class has within it the seeds of its antithesis and its own destruction. The clash between the feudal landowners and the bourgeoisie gave rise to a middle class which helped bring about the Industrial Revolution. Industrial needs created a working class, far more numerous than the bourgeoisie and capable of overthrowing it, which resulted in a dictatorship of the proletariat. Marx based his dialectic on materialism. When no one is left poor, when there is a dictatorship of the proletariat, there is no need for class conflict. It can be argued, however, that conflict can still continue in other areas, between life styles and generations, over political ideologies, and so forth. Conflict is valuable because if change is inevitable, then it is through conflict that the best alternatives are worked out.

Conflict theorists hold that one can predict social change, once the causes of a specific conflict can be ascertained. But does understanding conflict lead to acting on the basis of one's analysis? Not necessarily. We can understand a potential conflict between two generations, but this need not result in immediate social change, nor need it tell us as individuals what we must do, if anything. Conflict is neither right nor wrong, though it may be useful or destructive for a given society or social situation. If the proletariat in American society is reactionary, will it act to overthrow the middle and upper classes, and would such a revolution be "good"? In a complex society, there may be many different types of conflicts occurring at the same time. How are we to gauge our own circumstance if conflicts overlap and there is no clear-cut way of determining who is the enemy and who is the victim? Indeed, they may be one and the same. Even more important, in a society which emphasizes internal safety and security, is conflict possible? Marcuse has pointed out that it is becoming increasingly difficult to set up a dialectic in American society, for America reaches out to co-opt or discredit all such tendencies. We are encouraged to "tolerate" each other.[3] If it is impossible to put oneself in a conflict situation, to disagree with part of American society, then there is no need to act, for there is no conflict to resolve. Conflict theory again tends to reflect analyses of the past, rather than to prognosticate the future of American society. It leads us to understand general tendencies in society without demonstrating how we fit in or what we can do about them.

Part of the lack of relevance of conflict and functionalist theories is that in the effort to make them general enough to cover all situations, they do not cover any. They are so abstract as to appear irrelevant, as far away as an Asian war and the Chairman of the Board of General Motors. While functional theories demonstrate that people are related to one another through needs, there is no obligaiton or moral commitment resulting from this relationship.

The problem with attempting to apply any theory of social change is that we try to fit the situation to the theory, rather than developing specific criteria and explanations from specific circumstances. While intellectually gratifying, such theory building has done little to bring about social change in American society. How valid are theories which discuss social change, but do not discuss why such change is necessary and how it can be brought about? This is not to say that functionalism and behaviorism are invalid theories, but that they are inadequate for dealing with social change in American society.

We Are Part of the Problem and Part of the Solution

Determinist analyses of American society leave us two choices: either we must wait for our society to be transformed by others (social change agents, international forces, evolutionary development, changes in the physical environment), or we can change our society ourselves. If American society itself is the social problem, then we are part of the problem. American society cannot be transformed without us. We are by definition social change agents. If we do not act the problem will still remain, we will still be responsible for its existence, and we will have made a decision—for the status quo.

Social psychologists tell us that an individual grows by incorporating the reactions of others to his actions. Mead has divided this process into the "I" and the "Me." [4] The "I" is the individual when he initiates a given course of action—for example, a baby when it points to a ball and says "guh." The "Me" is the incorporation by the baby of his mother's reaction to his attempt at naming the round object he pointed to; it is the sum total of the past reactions of others to his actions. In a more abstract sense, we learn to anticipate the reactions of others to our actions. Yet, there is always a point in all our actions when we are the *initiator*, the "I."

Here is where social psychology merges with existentialism. Existentialists posit that the self exists, that it must create its own essence. For the social psychologist, this essence is the sum total of our experience with the world, or the reactions of others to our actions. The existentialist says we are free to choose in that there is no a *priori* essence we must assume. As such, we must take responsibility for our own actions, since there is no one else to do so. The social psychologist finds that the individual is born into a given social context, yet, he too must create his own essence, he too must initiate action, and consequently, assume responsibility for his own life. Though values and roles already exist, he must acquire them; he will not automatically become the image held out for him. At the same time, he is part of the social environment in which he finds himself; he uses its language to define the choices open to him. If he does not act to adopt the values and roles held out to him, then he acts to change them—he does not exist in isolation. He willingly chooses one or the other; in either case, he is responsible for the society in which he interacts. The possibility of such choice becomes all the more necessary in a society where the roles and values individuals are socialized into become irrelevant to their existence—in an absurd society such as America. From a functionalist perspective, we are shaped to support certain institutions within American society. Our participation is necessary for their continued existence and legitimation. In complex society, such participation is not inevitable. We can choose not to participate, and in the process alter the fabric of American society by constructing alternative institutions.

The existentialists point out that man is condemned to freedom since he must choose; there is no one, and no social system, which can do it for him. If societies exist to order an otherwise chaotic and nonsensical universe,[5] to bring meaning to an absurd world, however arbitrary, capricous, and tentative that meaning may be, then responsibility for the creation, acceptance, and transformation of the meaning of that system must always rest with the individual. If the knowledge we use to justify our everyday lives no longer works, we must find new knowledge. Societies, in the final analysis, are man-made regardless of the ongoing impact they have on their would-be creators.

If individuals are responsible for their own actions and for the societies they would transform, how can they keep from being manipulated by others who also realize their responsibility and would act in the best interests of the "greater good"? Everyone risks manipulation to one degree or another, if for no other reason than the fact that we are social animals and are heavily influenced by interactions with other people. Yet, if we are the locus for all our actions, if we assume responsibility, then the likelihood that manipulation will become disastrous is reduced. We know what our values are and why we hold them. They cannot be easily bastardized. To place ultimate responsibility for transforming society in the hands of others is to fail to assume responsibility for one's own life.

We have argued that reality-busting is possible, that we can step out of our roles and material possessions, that we can actualize ourselves. We obviously cannot easily if ever discard twenty, thirty, or forty years of socialization, of past choices and decisions which we have made. But taking our past into account, we can still choose. The process of choosing ends only with our death. At best, perhaps, we can recognize the process of socialization for what it is; we can understand how manipulation occurs. This in itself is a beginning. In stepping back and looking at ourselves we may also discover that individual actualization is a figment of the imagination. Since man is a social animal, group actualization may be all that is possible. This does not eliminate responsibility; rather, it makes social responsibility all the more necessary.

Bridging the Gap

The problem with all this is that American society works for many of us. It is not absurd to us. We do not *feel* the problem. We see no contradictions, no meaninglessness. We laugh and cry and watch television and play catch with our children and this is the way it has always been. We can point out the symptoms of decay, but the society is not yet in dissolution, and there is the nagging hope that someone may yet pull it back together. In the meantime. . . .

There is a gap between "knowledge" and social change, not the knowledge which tells us about the problems of American society, but the knowledge which leads us to do something about them. Existing theories of social change cannot bridge this gap, for they do not define this as an issue, nor do they hold any remedy for it. They largely ignore the question of individual motivation, and as such act as apologies for the status quo. As America stands today, individual change need not precede institutional change; changing one's head need not come before social action *if* others are already effectively engaged in such change, *if* institutions are in the process of making us more aware. There is little evidence that this process is taking place. If social change in American society is to occur, *we* must initiate it and accept responsibility for the society which we bring about. If we do not participate, then we must bear responsibility for the consequences.

NOTES

[1] Richard P. Appelbaum, *Theories of Social Change* (Chicago: Markham, 1970).
[2] B. F. Skinner, *Beyond Freedom and Dignity* (New York: Alfred A. Knopf, Inc., 1971).
[3] Herbert Marcuse, *One-Dimensional Man* (Boston: Beacon Press, 1968).
[4] Paul E. Pfuetze, *Self, Society, Existence* (New York: Harper & Row, Publishers, 1954).
[5] Stanford Lyman and Marvin Scott, *Toward a Sociology of the Absurd* (New York: Appleton-Century-Crofts, 1970).

topical index